The Collected Works
of
J. Krishnamurti

Volume XVI

1965–1966

The Beauty of Death

COLLECTED WORKS VOLUME 16

Photo: J. Krishnamurti, ca 1968 by Mark Edwards © Krishnamurti Foundation Trust, Ltd.

Copyright © 2012 by Krishnamurti Foundation America
P.O Box 1560, Ojai, CA 93024

Website: www.kfa.org

Printed in the United States of America

ISBN 13: 9781934989494
ISBN: 1934989495

Contents

Preface

Jiddu Krishnamurti was born in 1895 of Brahmin parents in south India. At the age of fourteen he was proclaimed the coming World Teacher by Annie Besant, then president of the Theosophical Society, an international organization that emphasized the unity of world religions. Mrs. Besant adopted the boy and took him to England, where he was educated and prepared for his coming role. In 1911 a new worldwide organization was formed with Krishnamurti as its head, solely to prepare its members for his advent as World Teacher. In 1929, after many years of questioning himself and the destiny imposed upon him, Krishnamurti disbanded this organization, saying:

Truth is a pathless land, and you cannot approach it by any path whatsoever, by any religion, by any sect. Truth, being limitless, unconditioned, unapproachable by any path whatsoever, cannot be organized; nor should any organization be forced to lead or to coerce people along any particular path. My only concern is to set men absolutely, unconditionally free.

Until the end of his life at the age of ninety, Krishnamurti traveled the world speaking as a private person. The rejection of all spiritual and psychological authority, including his own, is a fundamental theme. A major concern is the social structure and how it conditions the individual. The emphasis in his talks and writings is on the psychological barriers that prevent clarity of perception. In the mirror of relationship, each of us can come to understand the content of his own consciousness, which is common to all humanity. We can do this, not analytically, but directly in a manner Krishnamurti describes at length. In observing this content we discover within ourselves the division of the observer and what is observed. He points out that this division, which prevents direct perception, is the root of human conflict.

His central vision did not waver after 1929, but Krishnamurti strove for the rest of his life to make his language even more simple and clear. There is a development in his exposition. From year to year he used new terms and new approaches to his subject, with different nuances.

Because his subject is all-embracing, the *Collected Works* are of compelling interest. Within his talks in any one year, Krishnamurti was not able to cover the whole range of his vision, but broad applications of particular themes are found throughout these volumes. In them he lays the foundations of many of the concepts he used in later years.

The *Collected Works* contain Krishnamurti's previously published talks, discussions, answers to specific questions, and writings for the years 1933 through 1967. They are an authentic record of his teachings, taken from transcripts of verbatim shorthand reports and tape recordings.

The Krishnamurti Foundation of America, a California charitable trust, has among its purposes the publication and distribution of Krishnamurti books, videocassettes, films and tape recordings. The production of the *Collected Works* is one of these activities.

Madras, India, 1965

---- ✳ ----

First Talk in Madras

There are many issues we have to talk over together, many problems that confront us daily. And to talk things over together, certain things are obviously necessary. First, you and the speaker must be in right communication with each other, because unless there is a right relationship established through communication with each other, no problem can be rationally, sanely talked over together. So it is necessary that you as well as the speaker should be working together, thinking out the issues together. You are not merely listening to what is being said, but you are actually taking a share, partaking, in what is being discussed—which means that each of us must work together, intensely, at the same level, and at the same time. And that is the only way we can establish any kind of communication with each other.

I do not know if you have not noticed that in all relationships when both are intensely aware of the issue, when both feel vitally, strongly, at the same time, there is a communication taking place which is really a communion which goes beyond the word. But first one has to understand the word and not try to go beyond the word. It seems to me also necessary to listen so that we, both of us, are hearing not only the word but the content of the word, the meaning of the word, the significance of the word. Because

we can translate one word differently while the speaker intends that that word should be used in a particular way, or gives it a different meaning.

So the one that hears must also be aware of the interpretation given to the word, the prejudice with which he approaches a sentence, the meaning of that sentence. And also he must be naturally aware of how he reacts to what is being said. All that demands a great deal of work on your part because these talks would be utterly empty, without much meaning, if you merely listened to the speaker, agreeing or disagreeing, and then you went home with certain concepts which you can formulate for yourself, agreeing or disagreeing with them. So there is the task that lies for each one of us: it is not that the speaker does all the work and you merely listen.

And I think it is very important to understand this because we are concerned, are we not, with bringing about a radical revolution in all our relationships between man and man. Relationship is the very essence of all existence, not only outwardly but, much more, inwardly. And a radical mutation has to take place within the structure of relationship of the society in which we live—the relationship between people, between families, and so on. All life is relationship, and until we understand clearly the problem of relationship in our life, at whatever level we may try to live, fully or fragmentarily, we will always be in a state of conflict, confusion, and misery.

So what we are going to talk over together throughout these talks is how to bring about a radical mutation in our relationship economically, socially, politically, and all the rest of it, and also in our relationship with ourselves, in the relationships which we have created as an image, according to which we function. Unless there is a change in the image that each one of us has about oneself, about the society, about the various values that we have given to life, unless we look at all these problems with clarity, mere outward change brought about by communism, by socialism, by war, or by great inventions will have very little meaning. Because in ourselves the image of ourselves will persist, and according to that image we live. Unless in that image there is a mutation, unless that image is completely shattered, we cannot possibly have right relationship and therefore a way of life totally different from that which we are living now.

And to investigate into all these problems, we must realize also that you are not being persuaded to anything—a concept or a formula. Propaganda is a most dreadful thing because it is trying to influence you to think along a particular way, and we are not doing that here. What we are trying to do is to understand total existence, the totality of life, not one fragment of it. So there is no question, right from the beginning, of any authority, of any desire on your part or on the part of the speaker to be persuaded to think differently, or to discard the old and accept the new. For when you see something very clearly, which is the intention of these gatherings—to see things very clearly—that very act of seeing is action.

To see is to act. And if one does not see very clearly, naturally all action becomes confused. And we go to somebody else to tell us what to do because we cannot see for ourselves what to do, clearly, precisely, all the time, all the days of our life; we resort to another to help us to see clearly. Nobody can help another to see clearly: that must be established between the speaker and yourself. Therefore your responsibility in listening becomes very significant because you have to find out—not the method—if it is possible to change radically so that we live a totally different kind of life.

So we are going to talk over together like two friends discussing a problem, neither one trying to persuade the other to accept or to discard. And to talk over together, both must listen: and that is going to be our difficulty.

Listening is one of the most difficult things to do. We never listen. We are listening to our own thoughts, to our own ideas, to our own concepts, to the ways of how we should or should not behave. We are concerned with our own occupations, with our own problems, with our own sorrows, and we have our own answers and explanations; or we have the explanations and the sayings of another whom we respect or whom we are afraid of—which is the same thing.

The act of listening is really one of the most difficult things to do, like the act of seeing. To see something very clearly demands your complete attention—to see a tree outlined against the sunset, to see every branch of it clearly, to see the beauty of it, to feel the intensity of the light against the leaf, the shape of the branch, the shape of the trunk, to see the totality and the feeling of the beauty of the totality of that tree. To see, one must be extraordinarily alert, attentive. But if your mind is occupied, you will not be able to see that tree in all its excellence; or if your mind is interpreting, giving its biological name to it, your mind is then distracted. Therefore you are not seeing very clearly.

Similarly you will not be able to hear, listen very clearly, if your mind is not deeply interested, is not taking part in what is being said—completely, not partially. And you cannot give your total attention if you say, "I agree with this and I do not agree with that," or if you compare what is being said with what already you know, or if you translate what you hear in terms of your particular experience, your own particular knowledge, or your own particular culture.

So a man who listens has to be completely aware of what is being said, and he cannot be attentive if he is merely hearing the word and opposing it, or if he is asserting his own particular opinion. We are not discussing opinions—that is dialecticism, that has no value at all. What we are doing right through the talks is to face facts, not your fact or the speaker's fact. There are only facts—not your favorite fact or my favorite fact, to be translated according to your fancy. We are going to deal completely with facts, actually with *what is,* and from there move, from there go profoundly. But if you do not see the fact as fact, then we cannot proceed further together.

So having made that introductory talk, let us proceed with what we are supposed to talk over together. We said that there must be in ourselves and in our relationships a great change because we cannot as human beings lead the lives that we are living—in battle with ourselves. The society is you, and you are the society. The psychological structure of society has been created by each human being, and in that psychological frame each human being is caught. And until the human being breaks that psychological structure within himself, completely and totally, he is incapable of living peacefully with a great sense of reality.

So we are concerned with bringing about this mutation in ourselves as human beings—not isolated but in relationship to each other, which is society—because we must have peace. Peace and freedom are absolutely essential because nothing can grow, function fully, completely, except in peace, and there can be no peace without freedom. We have lived for many millions of years in conflict, not only inwardly but outwardly. There have been during the last five thousand five hundred years, fourteen thousand wars and more—two and a half wars every year during the recorded history of man—and we have accepted that way of living; we have accepted war as the way of life. And nothing can function or blossom in hate, in confusion, in conflict. And as human beings we have to find a different way of living—to live in this world without inward conflict. Then that inward sense of peace expresses itself in action in society.

So one has to find out for oneself whether one, as a human being living in relationship with the world, can find that peace—not an imaginary, mythical, mystical, fanciful peace—whether one can live without any kind of conflict within oneself, and whether it is possible to be totally free—not imaginarily free, not free in some mystical world, but actually be free inwardly, which will express itself outwardly in all our relationships. These two are the main issues.

We have to find out whether man—that is, you and I—can live in this world functioning differently, without any conflict at all, and therefore can bring about a social structure which is not based on violence. This country has preached nonviolence for thirty or forty years and more, and you all accepted the ideal of nonviolence and repeated the word. For many thousands of years you have been told not to kill, and overnight all that is gone—it is a fact, it is not my opinion—and strangely there have been no individuals who have said, "I will not kill," and faced the consequences. All this—that is, to live verbally, to accept ideals so easily and discard them so easily—indicates a mind that is not serious at all, a very flippant mind, not a grave mind that is concerned with world issues.

One of the major issues in the world is war, not who attacks whom or who defends, and so on. And as long as you have sovereign states, separate nationalities, separate governments with their armies, frontiers, nationalism, there must be war. Wars are inevitable as long as man is living within the frontiers of an ideology. As long as man is living within the frontiers of nationalism, or within religious frontiers, or within the frontiers of dogma—Christian or Hindu or Buddhist or Muslim dogma—there must be wars. Because these dogmas, these nationalities, these religions divide man. And you listen to what is being said, and naturally you will say, "What can I do as a human being when my country and my government call on me to fight?" and inevitably you will fight. That is part of this social, economic, political structure. But you do not solve any problem that way. As I said, there have been, for the last five thousand years and more, every year two and a half wars. So we must find a different way of living—not in heaven but on earth—a different way of behavior, a different value. And you cannot find it unless you understand this problem of peace, which is also the problem of freedom.

So our first demand is whether it is possible for each of us in all our relationships—at home, in the office, in every way of our life—to put an end to conflict. This does not mean that we retire into isolation, become a monk, or withdraw into some isolated corner of our own imagination and fancy; but it means living in this world to understand conflict. Because, as long as there is conflict of any kind, naturally our minds, our hearts, our brains cannot function to their highest capacity. They can only function fully when there is no friction, when there is clarity. And there is clarity only when the mind that is the

totality—which is the physical organism, the brain cells, and the total thing which is called the mind—is in a state of nonconflict, when it functions without any friction; only then is it possible to have peace.

And to understand that state, we must understand the everyday conflict which mounts up, the everyday battle within ourselves and with our neighbors, the conflict in the office, the conflict within the family, the conflict between man and man, the conflict between man and woman, and the psychological structure of this conflict—the 'me' of the conflict. Understanding, like seeing and listening, is again one of the most difficult things. When you say, "I understand something," you really mean, do you not, not only that you have completely grasped the whole significance of what is being said, but also that that very understanding is the action itself—it is not that you understand and then act, but understanding is action. And you cannot understand if you are merely intellectually, verbally comprehending what is being said; if you merely listen intellectually—that is, verbally—surely that is not understanding. Or if you merely feel emotionally, sentimentally, surely that also is not understanding. You understand only when your total being comprehends—that is, when you do not look at anything fragmentarily, either intellectually or emotionally, but totally.

So understanding the nature of conflict demands not the understanding of your particular conflict as an individual but the understanding of the total conflict as a human being—the total conflict, which includes nationalism, class difference, ambition, greed, envy, the desire for position, prestige, the whole sense of power, domination, fear, guilt, anxiety, in which is involved death, meditation—the whole of life. And to understand the whole of life, one must see, listen, not fragmentarily, but look at the vast map of life. One of our difficulties is, is it not, that we function fragmentarily, we function in sections, in one part—you are an engineer, an artist, a scientist, a businessman, a lawyer, a physicist, and so on—divided, fragmentary. And each fragment is in battle with the other fragment, despising it or feeling superior.

So the question then is how to look at the totality of life nonfragmentarily? Have I made myself clear? When we look at the totality of life—not as a Hindu, a Muslim, a communist, a socialist, a Catholic, a professor, or a religious man—when we see this extraordinary movement of life in which everything is included—death, sorrow, misery, confusion, the utter lack of love, and the image of pleasure that we have bred through centuries for ourselves, which dictates our values, our activities—when we see this vast thing comprehensively, totally, then our response to that totality will be entirely different. And it is this response, when we see totally the whole movement of life, that is going to bring about a revolution in ourselves. And this revolution is absolutely necessary. Human beings cannot go on as they have been, butchering each other, hating each other, dividing each other into countries, into all the petty, narrow, individualistic activities, because in that way lies more misery, more confusion, and more sorrow.

So is it possible to see the totality of life?—which is like a river moving endlessly, restless, stormy, with great beauty, moving because it has a great volume of water behind it. Can we see this life so totally? Because it is only when we see something totally that we understand it, and we cannot see it totally, completely, if there is self-centered activity which guides, shapes our action and our thoughts. It is the self-centered image which identifies itself with the family, with the nation, with ideological conclusions, with parties—political or religious. It is this center which asserts that it is seeking God, truth, and all the rest of it, and which prevents the

comprehension of the whole of life. And to understand this center, actually what it is, needs a mind that is not cluttered up with concepts, conclusions. I must know actually, not theoretically, what I am. What I think, what I feel, my ambitions, greeds, envies, the desire for success, prominence, position, prestige, my greeds, my sorrows—all that is what I am. I may think that I am God, I may think I am something else; but it is still part of thought, part of the image which projects itself through thought. So unless you understand this thing, not according to Shankara, Buddha, or anybody, unless you actually see what you are everyday—the way you talk, the way you feel, the way you react, not only consciously but unconsciously—unless you lay the foundation there, how can you go very far? However far you may go, it will only be imagination, a fantasy, a deception, and you will be a hypocrite.

You have to lay this foundation—which is to understand what you are. And you can understand what you are only by watching yourself, not trying to correct it, not trying to shape it, not trying to say this is right or this is wrong, but by seeing what is actually taking place—which does not mean you become more self-centered. On the contrary, you become self-centered if you are merely correcting what you see, translating what you see according to your likes and dislikes. But if you merely observe, there is no intensification of the center.

And to see this totality of life needs great affection. You know, we have grown so callous, and you can see why. In an overpopulated country—a country that is poor, both inwardly and outwardly, a country that has lived on ideas and not actuality, a country that has worshiped the past, with authority rooted in the past—naturally the people are indifferent to what is actually going on. If you observe yourselves, you will see how little affection you have—affection being care.

Affection means the sense of beauty, not external adornment only. But the sense of beauty can come about only when there is great gentleness, great consideration, care, which is the very essence of affection. And when that is dry, our hearts are dry, and we fill it with words, with ideas, with quotations, with what has been said; and when we are aware of this confusion, we try to resurrect the past, we worship tradition; we go back. Because we do not know how to solve the present existence with all its confusion, we say, "Let us go back, let us revert to the past, let us live according to some dead thing." That is why, when you are confronted with the present, you escape into the past or into some ideology or utopia, and your heart being empty, you fill it with words, images, formulas, and slogans. You observe yourself, and you will know all this.

So to bring about naturally, freely, this total mutation in the mind itself demands grave attention serious attention. And we do not want to attend because we are afraid of what may happen if we really thought about the actual, daily facts of our life. Because we are really afraid to examine; we would rather live blindly, suffocated, miserable, unhappy, trivial; and therefore our lives become empty and meaningless. And life being meaningless, we try to invent significance in life. Life has no significance. Life is meant to be lived, and in that very living one begins to discover the reality, the truth, the beauty of life. To discover the truth, the beauty of life, you must understand the total movement of it. And to understand the total movement of it, you have to end all this fragmentary thinking and way of life; you have to cease to be a Hindu, not only in name, but inwardly; you have to cease to be a Muslim or a Buddhist or a Catholic, with all the dogmas, because these things are dividing people, dividing your own minds, your own hearts.

And strangely, you will listen to all this, you will listen merely for an hour, and you will go home and repeat the pattern. You will repeat the pattern endlessly, and this pattern is based essentially on pleasure.

And so you have to examine your own life voluntarily, not because government influences you or somebody tells you. You have voluntarily to examine it, not condemn it, not say this is right or this is wrong, but look. And when you do look in that way, you will find that you look with eyes which are full of affection—not with condemnation, not with judgment, but with care. You look at yourself with care, and therefore you look at yourself with immense affection. And it is only when there is great affection and love that you see the total existence of life.

December 22, 1965

Second Talk in Madras

If we may, we will continue with what we were talking about the other day. We said: Man, in recorded history, has had wars beyond memory; and man has had no peace at all, both outwardly and inwardly. In some part of the world or other, there has always been a war—people killing each other in the name of nationality, and so on and so on. And we have accepted war as the way of life, both outwardly and inwardly. The inward conflict is much more complex than the outward conflict. And man has not been able to resolve this problem at all. Religions have preached peace—"don't kill"—for centuries. No religion has stopped war! And as human beings, not as individuals, we have not faced this problem, and we have to see if it cannot be resolved totally.

I think we have to differentiate between the individual and the human being. The individual is localized, a local entity with his particular customs, habits, traditions—with his narrow conditioning, geographical, religious, and so on. But man belongs to the whole world with its conditioning, with its fears, with its dogmas. So, we can see that man, whether he lives in India or in Russia or in China or in America, has not been able to solve this problem. And it is a major problem, a problem that each one of us, as human beings, has to resolve.

To resolve a problem, one must see the problem very clearly. Clarity and observation are necessary. To observe there must be clarity, light—artificial light or sunlight. Outwardly, if you would see a leaf clearly, you need light, and you must visually observe it. It is fairly easy to observe a leaf objectively, given a light—artificial or otherwise. But it becomes much more complex when you go inwardly, where one needs also clarity to observe. We may wish to observe the whole phenomenon of human beings—his sorrows, his miseries, his everlasting conflict within himself, the greed, the despairs, the frustrations, the mounting problems, not only mechanical but human. There, too, one needs clarity, which is light, to see this mechanism within the human being. And to observe, choice is not necessary. When you see something very clearly, as you do this microphone or that tree or your neighbor sitting next to you, then choice is not necessary, conflict is not necessary. What brings about conflict within and without is when we do not see clearly, when our prejudices, our nationalities, our peculiar tendencies, and so on block clarity, prevent light. And when there is light, you can observe.

Observation and light go together; otherwise, you cannot see. You cannot see that tree, the trunk, the sides, the nature of it, the curve of it, the beauty of it, and the quality of it, unless there is a great deal of light. And your observation must be attentive. You may casually look at that trunk and pass it by. But you have to look at it, to observe it in detail, carefully, with a great deal of care and affection and tenderness—only then can you observe.

Then, observation with clarity needs no choice. I think we must understand this very clearly because we are going to go into problems or issues that need a great deal of observation, a great deal of detailed perception, seeing, listening. We always deal with symptoms—like war, which is a symptom. And we think we understand the symptoms if we examine the cause or understand the cause. So between the symptom and the cause, we are everlastingly vacillating, backward and forward, not knowing how to deal with the cause; and even if we know how to deal with the cause, there are the innumerable blocks, the innumerable influences that prevent action.

So our issue then becomes very simple: to see very clearly, you need a great deal of light; and the light does not come except through observation, when you can see minutely every movement of your thought, of your feeling—and to see clearly, there must be no conflict, no choice.

Because we have to find a way of living in which war, inwardly or outwardly, is totally abolished. And it is a strange fact, a phenomenon, that in a country like this which has preached for millennia, "Don't hurt, don't kill, be gentle, be nonviolent," there has not been one individual who has stood for what he thinks is right—which is, not to kill—who has swum against the current and gone, if necessary, to prison and got shot. Please think about it, and you will see what an extraordinary thing it is, how much it reveals that not one of you said, "I won't kill"—not whisper to each other, "War is wrong; what is one to do?" but say it out and if necessary go to prison, be shot and killed! Then you will say, "What will that solve?" It solves nothing, but at least you are behaving—your conduct then is dictated by affection, by love, not by an idea. Do think about this in your spare time—why you have not stood for something which you have felt in your heart. Your scriptures, your culture, everything has said, "Be gentle, don't kill another." It indicates does it not, that we live on ideas and words! But the word or the explanation is not the fact. The fact is: there is conflict within and war without. There have been two and a half wars every year in the recorded history of man! The first woman must have cried and hoped that that would be the last war; and we are still going on with wars! Here in the South you may feel perfectly safe and say, "Let them fight it out in the North," or "Let them fight in Vietnam," "Let others weep," as long as you are safe! But this is your problem, a human problem: how to bring about a change in the human mind and heart.

As we were saying, this problem, like every other problem, with its symptoms and causes, can never be solved unless we enter into a different area, a different field altogether. You understand? Inwardly, human beings have been caught in this wheel of everlasting suffering, conflict, misery; and they have always tried to solve it in relation to the present, in relation to the social, environmental, religious conditions. They have always dealt with the symptoms or tried to discover the causes—which means resistance, and when you resist, there is still conflict.

So, the problems which every human being has—with their symptoms, with their causes—cannot be solved unless each human being moves to a different dimension altogether, to a different inquiry. And that is what we propose to do. We know there are wars. We know that as long as there are sovereign governments, politicians, geographical divisions, armies, nationalism, religious divisions—Muslim, Hindu, this or that—you are going to continue wars even though computers are coming in to tell you, "Don't do it; it is no longer profitable to kill somebody else for your country." Computers, the electronic brains, are going to dictate what you

should or should not do; and your activity is altogether different when a machine dictates!

So our problem then is: Is it possible to look and to live and to understand all these problems from a different area altogether, from a different field, from a different dimension? Please don't draw a conclusion: God, inner self, higher self, or the atma! All those words have no meaning at all! Because you have had them for thousands of years; all your scriptures have talked about them, and yet you, as a human being, are in conflict, in misery; you are at war, outwardly and inwardly. The war inward is competition, greed, envy, trying to get more. The battle is going on everlastingly within you. And you try to answer these problems, these symptoms, by trying to find out their causes and hoping by some chance to resolve those causes—the communist's way of doing it, the socialist's way of doing it, or the religious way of doing it. But the fact is that the human being has never, except perhaps for one or two, resolved the problem of conflict.

And to understand this problem we must have a different mind—not this stale, deadly mind. The mind is always active about symptoms, answering the symptoms and saying that it has resolved the problem! We need a new mind, a new mind that sees; and it can only see when there is light—which means a mind that has nowhere, consciously or unconsciously, any residue of conflict. Because it is this conflict within that brings darkness—not your intellectual capacity for observation. You are all very clever observers! You know what are the causes of war, you know what are the causes of your own inward conflict. They are very, very simple to observe intellectually. But action does not spring from the intellect. Action springs from a totally different dimension. And we have to act. We cannot go on as we are going on, with this nationalism, wars, conflict, competition, greed, envy, sorrow.

You know, all that has been going on for century upon century! The computer is going to take charge of all the drudgery of man, in the office and also politically; it is going to do all the work for human beings in the factories. And so man will have a great deal of leisure. That is a fact. You may not see it in the immediate, but it is there, coming. There is a tremendous wave, and you are going to have a choice to make: what you will do with your time.

We said "choice"—to choose between various forms of amusement, entertainment, in which is included all the religious phenomena, temples, Mass, reading scriptures. All these are forms of entertainment! Please don't laugh—what we are talking about is much too serious. You have no time to laugh when the house is burning. Only we refuse to think of what is actually taking place. And you are going to have the choice—this or that? And when choice is involved, there is always conflict. That is, when you have two ways of action, that choice merely breeds more conflict. But if you saw very clearly within yourself—as a human being belonging to the whole world, not just to one potty, little country in some little geographical division, or class division, or Brahmin, or non-Brahmin, and all the rest of it—if you saw this issue clearly, then there would be no choice. Therefore an action which is without choice does not breed conflict.

And to see very clearly, you need light. Please follow this a little; even if you do it intellectually, it is good enough because something will take root somewhere. And you cannot have clarity if you do not realize that the word, the explanation, is not the thing. The word *tree* is not the tree! And to see that fact, the word is not necessary. We point to an objective thing; you touch it, you feel it; then you see it very clearly. But inwardly, when you go deeply within, it becomes much more subtle, much more un-

tenable; you cannot get hold of it—and for that, you need much more clarity. Clarity comes when you begin to see that the word is not the thing, that the word does not produce the reaction of thought—thought being the response of memory, of experience, of knowledge, and so on.

So to observe, clarity is essential. But the inward clarity must be firsthand, not secondhand. And most of us, most human beings, have secondhand clarity, secondhand light, which is the light of tradition, the light of the scriptures, the light of the politicians, the environmental influence, the communist doctrine, and so on—which are all ideas giving light artificially; and by that light we try to live, and so there is always contradiction in us. That is, the idea is entirely different from the fact—as the word tree is not a tree; the word *good,* or *greed,* or *sorrow* is not the fact. And to observe the fact, the word which breeds thought with its associations, memories, experiences, knowledge, and so on must not bring a reaction. I will go into it, and you will see clearly.

What we are talking about is a life in which there is no conflict at all, a life on this earth—not in heaven, not in some utopia, but actual daily living in which there is not a symptom or a shadow of conflict. Because it is only when there is peace that goodness can flower, not when you are in conflict, not when you are trying to become good, not when you are idealistically pursuing the idea of being good. When there is peace, it flowers. And therefore when there is clarity, there is no choice, and therefore there is no action of will. Because what you see, you see very clearly, and there is no need for choice or will. Choice and will breed conflict. And yet we have lived on choice and will. Will means resistance, control, suppression; and suppression, control, and resistance depend on choice. And when there is no choice, there is no exertion of will.

So, is it possible to function as a human being, living in this world, without any form of conflict which comes into being when there is choice and when there is will? First of all, to understand this, one has to understand, to look into, to observe, not only the conscious mind but also the unconscious mind. We are fairly familiar with the conscious mind—the daily activities of what you do, what you say, your going to an office day after day for the next forty years, getting the mind more and more dull, heavy, stupid, bureaucratic, continuing a life of routine, a mechanical life. And that superficial consciousness, the outward consciousness, is fairly easy to observe and to understand. But we are not just the outward layers of consciousness; there is a great depth to us, and without understanding that, merely establishing a superficial tranquillity does not solve the problem. So one has to understand this whole consciousness of man, not only the superficial, but the deeper layers of it.

When we observe—without reading psychologists, the Freuds, the Jungs, and all the rest of the modern philosophers and psychologists—we know what the unconscious is: the racial residue, the experience of the race, the social conditions, the environment, the tradition, the culture—culture being political, religious, educational—which are all deeply embedded in the unconscious.

Now, can you look at it, can you observe it, if there is no light? You understand my question? To observe, you must have light, and to observe the unconscious, you must have light, clarity. How can you have clarity about something of which you do not know? You have an idea, only a concept, but not the actuality. And without understanding the unconscious, mere adjustment on the surface will not bring about freedom to live peacefully.

Please, we are not talking some deep philosophy; it is very simple. Consciousness is a word—isn't it? Now, the word is not the

thing. The word *consciousness,* if you observe, through association sets thought in action, and you say that consciousness is this or that or something else. If you are so-called religiously minded, you will say that there is a spiritual entity, and so on. If you are not, you say that it is merely the environmental product. That is all. But the word is not the thing—as the word *tree* is not the fact. So consciousness, which is the word, is not the fact. Please follow this.

So, to have clarity you have to observe the fact without the word—which means you observe without the machinery of thought in operation. And the machinery of thought is consciousness. Right? Look, sirs! The speaker says that killing is wrong. Now what has happened? He has made a statement, and you respond to that statement according to your conditioning, according to your immediate demands, according to the pressure of the other countries, and so on. So you have set the machinery of thinking going, through reaction, and therefore you are not listening to the fact, you are not seeing the fact; but your thought is reacting. Right? That is very simple. So, the word is not the thing. So the investigation of the unconscious becomes totally unnecessary, has no meaning whatsoever if the word is not the thing, and yet you are observing—then what takes place is complete attention. Then you are looking without any distraction, which is total attention. Total attention is the essence of the consciousness and beyond. That is, you are only conscious when there is friction; otherwise, there is no consciousness. That is, when you are challenged, you respond. If the response is totally adequate to the challenge, there is no conflict, there is no friction. It is only when the challenge is inadequately responded to that there is friction. It is this friction that causes, that brings into being, consciousness.

Please observe it within yourselves, and you will see that if you could find a way of avoiding death—I am taking that as an instance; we will talk about death another time—if you could find a way of overcoming death, medically, scientifically, or in some other way, then you would never be afraid of it. Therefore there is no conflict between living and dying, and therefore you will be totally unconscious of death. It is only when there is friction—which is fear—that consciousness is produced, and that consciousness says, "I am afraid to die."

So what we are talking about is a state of mind in which conflict has been totally eliminated—not through choice, not through will, not through any form of assertion or acceptance of a doctrine or commitment to a particular action which breeds in you the absence of self-identification with that issue or with that commitment, and you then think you are living peacefully, whereas you are not, as it is still the operation of resistance going on.

So, is it possible to live in this world knowing that you cannot possibly solve your problems through suppression, through acceptance, through obedience, through conformity, through imitation—which man has done for centuries? Is it possible to live a different kind of life altogether? Now, when you put that question to yourself, when you respond to that challenge, what is your answer? Obviously, the first answer—if you are at all intelligent—is that you do not know. Or you will assert that it is not possible. Or you will reply according to your tradition, according to your ideas. Therefore your response is inadequate to the challenge. You have to listen to the question: Is it possible to live in this world, not in isolation, not in a monastery, not as a monk, but as a human being, in great peace both outwardly and inwardly, especially inwardly? If we can live peacefully inwardly, then every action is peaceful, and therefore there will be no war.

So, to find out if it is possible to live without a conflict, first of all one has to understand what conflict is—not the symptom. You understand? One can show you the symptom and the cause, but the seeing of the cause or the symptom is not going to dissolve the symptom or the cause. Obviously you have to come directly into contact with it—which we never do. Let me explain.

Man has suffered; man, inwardly, has lived always in a battlefield because there is the self-centered activity—the 'me' first, and everybody else second. 'Me' first—my concern, my safety, my pleasure, my success, my position, my prestige. 'Me' first—identified with the country, with the family, with the doctrine. And we hope that through identification, we will dissolve the 'me'! We know the cause—the cause is egotism; to put it brutally, the cause is self-centered activity. We all know that. We also know what the result is, what it will produce outwardly in the world—namely, war. War is the ultimate expression of the inner conflict. There is war going on all the time, in the business world, in the political world, in the world of the religious people, between the various gurus, the various sects, the various dogmas. We know this. Intelligence tells you that this is so, but yet we do not live peacefully!

So peace cannot be brought about through the mere analysis of the cause or the symptom. So one has to enter into a different area, a different dimension.

Now to enter into a different dimension—if you will do it with me now, you will find out for yourself how to come to it. Not intellectually, not emotionally, not verbally. Because you have done all that; you have played with the intellect; your brain is as sharp as a needle, but you have not solved the problem. You cry over it if your son or husband or brother is killed; you are sentimental, emotional, but you have not solved it. So intellect, emotion, mere assertion of words, reading the Gita everlastingly, all the stupid stuff one does in the name of religion, the circus that goes on—all this has not prevented man from killing man. You kill, not with bayonets and guns only, but also with words, with gesture, when you compete with another in the office, when you are aggressive, brutal, seeking your own success—all those are wars. So, intellect, emotion, ideas—which are organized words—have never solved any of your problems; you have to find a different way of living in which there is no conflict whatsoever.

How is this to come about? Because time is disorder anyway. If you say, "I will get it tomorrow, or in the next life," all that becomes immaterial. When a man is suffering, he does not think about tomorrow or the next life; he wants an answer. And if you don't find the answer, you live on words, beliefs, dogmas—and they have no value at all; they become escapes! We know all that.

How do you enter into a life—now, not tomorrow—so that the past drops away from you completely? You know, when we are confused, we either worship the past, return to the past, or cultivate a utopia, hoping that thereby we will solve it! Economic revolutions, social revolutions, have had this idea of utopia, and they have never brought it about, either in Russia or in any other place! So words have no meaning any more, nor do ideas. Unless you put away this from your mind—the word, the idea, emotionalism, intellectualism—you will not be able to follow what we are talking about next.

So what takes place when you are not looking to the future? There is no tomorrow—except there is a tomorrow when you have to go to the office, or keep an appointment, and so on. Psychologically there is no tomorrow. I will explain to you why there is no tomorrow, intellectually, in detail. There is no tomorrow, actually, because it is an invention of thought, psychologically to give a

certainty of continuity for one's own well-being. Actually there is only the now, the present living; and you cannot live now if you are burdened with the past.

So what brings about a total mutation in the mind? You understand, sir? We have shown you the map of the human life, though not in detail. We have shown you the map, and we all say, "There must be a new mind, a new way of living." How is this to come about? Please listen to this. How is this to come about? How do you find it? Are you waiting for me to tell you? Don't laugh, be serious. Are you waiting for the speaker to tell you? If you are, then that is going to create another friction; therefore, you will not be free of friction; therefore, there will be conflict. But if you understand that neither word nor emotion nor intellect has any answer, what happens? All the doors which you have invented—socialist doors, communist doors, religious doors, psychological doors—are closed; there is no way out. When you know that, what happens to you?

Now begins the real meditation. You understand, sirs? Now begins a mind that is no longer driven by any outward or inner influence, a mind that is no longer controlled by an idea, by any pleasure, by any values which it has created for itself as a guide. All those are gone; they have all failed miserably; they have no meaning any more. So, if you are actually doing it, what has happened? You do not again say, "I will think about it tomorrow, agree or disagree"—then you and I are not in communication with each other. But if you actually understand this very clearly, what takes place? What actually takes place is light, clarity. And clarity, light, is always negative because the very description of it, as well as the imitation of the description, is the positive action that prevents light.

I hope you and I are both working together. What takes place when you listen—not to the word, not to your reactions, not to your agreement or disagreement to an opinion? When you are quiet, you learn; your mind, your whole being, is alert, aware, and you are listening. Then something happens when you see. Now in that attention, in that listening, there is clarity. That is clarity.

(It began to rain, and the talk came to an end.)

December 26, 1965

Third Talk in Madras

If we may, we will continue with what we were talking about the other day—which was, if I remember rightly, to find a different dimension, a different field, which cannot be discovered by mere intellection or sentimentality or emotionalism. Because, as we were saying, our life actually as it is now—not ideologically, or giving to life a wider, deeper significance—is a life of misery, confusion, anxiety, a sense of guilt and deep frustration; and because of the boredom, the loneliness, and the fear of our everyday life, we must obviously find a way or a state or an existence which will not be merely repetitive as it is now.

As we have also pointed out, the word or the explanation is not the actual fact. The fact is one thing, and the word—the explanation or the idea or the opinion or the philosophy about that idea, about that fact—is another. I think it is very important to understand this. Because most of us are caught in words—like *God, fear, communist, socialist.* Words—like *death, love*—are loaded with meaning. But death, love, and hate are entirely different from the words themselves or from the explanation of these words. And most of us have developed the intellect to such a degree, fortunately or unfortunately, that we are satisfied with words and explanations; and we think we understand when there are explanations or

detailed expositions. But actually what we understand are the words and the meaning of the words, but not the fact. So one has to be aware of facile explanations and words that are loaded with meaning through tradition, through usage. Because words—like *God, Christian, Catholic*—awaken certain reactions, and these reactions prevent the understanding of the fact, the understanding of what actually is. Unless one is aware of this process of reaction through words, the words become tremendously important—like the word *Hindu* or *Muslim.*

And what we are going to talk about this evening demands, I think, that one has to find a way of living one's daily life which is not contaminated by the past—the past being not only time but tradition, experience, knowledge, memory. This does not mean that we must function with a blank mind or live in a state of amnesia. But one has to understand the repetitive process or the mechanical process of existence as it is. Because most of our life is imitative. Our speech, our thoughts, the way of our life, what we do—the whole of consciousness is the result of imitation. Please don't deny it or accept it, but rather listen to find out the fact or the falseness of what is being said. Unless one understands this extraordinarily complex process of the imitative life which we do lead, freedom is not possible. And when there is no freedom, obviously there is no discovery of something totally new. Perhaps many of you have not even thought about all this. And if you are thinking for the first time about this matter of imitation, don't jump to conclusions, but rather let us together explore the issue.

Because, as we said, the responsibility of listening—if I may use that word *responsibility*—is heavy on you. The speaker may convey certain facts, point out certain facts. And to listen to the facts is extremely arduous. Because to listen to a fact, or to observe a fact, demands freedom from opinion. Obviously! If you say that it is not possible to live without imitation, you have already come to a conclusion, and therefore you cannot proceed further to question if there is not a state of mind which is totally uncontaminated by time. If you accept that, again it is not possible further to uncover, to discover for yourself the fact. So your responsibility in listening becomes important because we are working together. You are not merely listening to the speaker; we are together partaking, sharing, in this investigation so as to discover for ourselves firsthand if there is, or if there is not, the possibility of a new mind. A new mind is not merely the result of thought putting together what, it thinks, is a new mind—which merely becomes an idea, an end, which you try to imitate or practice or try to follow; but it is not a new mind.

So we have to go mutually together, sharing every step, into this whole process of imitation. And we have to find out whether it is possible for a mind which is imitative, which is the result of time—for a brain which has been cultivated, developed through centuries upon centuries, through the process of time and tradition—to discover by becoming quiet, a new mind, a new space. That is what we are going to talk about this evening.

When we use the word *imitation*, we mean, don't we, to follow, to practice, to obey, to conform to a pattern, to adjust to what we think is right, and to avoid what we think is wrong; conforming, following, adjusting, submitting, obeying authority—the authority as law, and the inner authority as one's own memory, experience, knowledge. Please, you have to listen fairly closely. Otherwise you and I will cease to communicate with each other.

You know, communication is really communion in these matters: to commune with nature, to commune with that sunset, to commune with that tree against the light of the setting sun, or to commune with each other, and, especially now, to commune with the speaker, and the speaker to commune with you. All that is only possible when you look, as at that tree and the light of the setting sun, with attention, with care, with affection. And it is not possible to commune with something if your mind is somewhere else, when you don't give your whole attention to the beauty of that light, the tree and the flower, and the intimacy of nature. But the word *communion* is not the fact, nor is the description of what communion is the fact.

There must be a sense of urgency. Because the house is burning; there is so much misery, chaos, callousness, war, indifference, butchery that is going on in the world; there is the dirt, the squalor, the poverty—all this needs solution. And one cannot be indifferent; one cannot hide behind formulas, concepts, gods, theories—they have no meaning any more, and I doubt if they ever had.

And so to commune with each other, as we are trying to do now, we must have this sense of urgency. Being urgent means an intensity—not casualness, not indifference, but a serious intention and therefore intensity. And also there must be a certain quality of affinity, a sense of affection, care. When you look at that tree, you can casually look at it, and it means nothing. But when you look at that tree and do not let thought or reactions interfere, when you look at it with an intensity which is attention, then out of that attention comes care. You are looking after that tree, not merely enjoying it; you are going to look after it, care for it, nourish it, see that it flowers, that it is not spoiled, destroyed. All that implies communion, not a mere verbal exchange of clever argumentation or dispute over opinions. All this implies seriousness. And it is only the man who is very, very serious that knows what it is to live—not the flippant people, not the people who merely enjoy their professional life.

So communion implies intensity and a sense of care which goes with it—tenderness, affection, love. That must exist between us. This does not mean that you are going to accept what the speaker says, or reject it—that is not affection. Together we are going to examine with affection, with care, with intensity.

There must be peace in the world, and there must be freedom—not political peace, not the freedom of certain democracies, but the inward freedom from anxiety, fear, despair, the incessant conflict that goes on within ourselves, the battle. Unless there is that freedom and peace, we cannot possibly flower in goodness, in beauty, in affection. The world does not want more philosophies, more organized religions, more dogmas. What it needs is a totally different mind, a mind which is not caught up in the daily fear of life. And you cannot possibly find that new mind through the old mind. You cannot possibly find the quality of that freshness if you don't understand this whole phenomenon of imitation. And we are going to go into it.

The brain, as we know, is the result of time and copying—imitation. Our education, our society, our culture—all this makes the brain conform. The difference between the mind and the brain is not so easily put into words. We use these words to see the difference, but the words are not the facts, nor are the definitions the facts. The mind is the overall thing, the totality, which observes, which exists, which has its being through the brain. So, you have to understand the nature of the brain, the memory, experience, knowledge; and that understanding also gives you the meaning, the significance, the nature of the mind. We only divide the thing for convenience. They are not two different things in different compartments, divided into fragments and tightly held together, tethered by our concepts.

Our reactions are the outcome of our process of living, which is based on acceptance, following, obedience to authority, and fear. Please watch your own reactions. You are not listening to the speaker; you are listening to the operation of your own brain as it reacts to what is being said. What we are saying is that thought, which is the response of memory—memory being experience, knowledge—is always imitative, and therefore there is no fresh thought. If there is a fresh thought, that thought can be recognized as being a new thought; and that recognition is out of the past, and therefore it is still of the old—perhaps at a higher pitch—it still belongs to the past. So thought can never be free. How can it be? Because it is tethered to memory. The electronic brain and the science of cybernetics, which produces these extraordinary machines, are based on this business of association, memory, and so on—which is how we also function! So thought is never original.

Please observe yourself. Do not accept what the speaker is saying; please observe your own thinking. If you are observing, you will see that there is nothing original. Thought is the result of a series of imitations, conformities, obedience, and acceptance—which we call knowledge—and on that the brain, the thought, the cells, and so on function. Take a very simple example—I don't like to talk in examples. When you are asked, "Where do you live?" or "What is your name?" your response is immediate; there is no time interval between the question and the answer because you are very familiar with that question, and you know your name and where you live. So the machinery of thought functions with extraordinary rapidity because you are very familiar with it. But the machinery of thought functions slowly when the question becomes a little more complicated; you need some time, you need a lag between the question and the answer. But when you do answer, it is still based on knowledge—knowledge which is the accumulation of experience, your own experience, or the experience of society or of culture, and so on.

So thought is repetitive; it is never free. And a mind that seeks to free itself through thought, through practice, through imitation, through a particular form of discipline, can never be free and therefore can never discover if there is something original. I hope I am making this statement clear. That is, the whole of consciousness—whether the conscious or the unconscious, whether you are aware of the unconscious or not—is the result of imitation. Obviously! And we function within that limited area of human consciousness—which is also the result of the animal because there is a great deal of the animal still in the human being. Within that field we function. I do not think this needs a tremendous argument or investigation; this is a simple fact.

So within that field of consciousness we try to solve our problems—the problems of war, the problems of peace, the problems of individuals and human beings, the problems of our own grief, sorrow, death, misery, confusion, the fear and the agony of existence. And therefore we never seem to solve our problems. That is, as the scientists are saying, man has lived for two million years and more. And man has always struggled; to him life has become a battlefield, not only outside but inside; he has not gone beyond sorrow, anxiety, fear. He may outwardly be not afraid of animals, snakes, and all the rest of it; but inwardly there is the terror, the torture.

Man has, through centuries, become a tortured human being. Please look at yourself. As you can look at yourself in a mirror, you can look at yourself psychologically. Then you will see what you go through—the anxieties, the fears, the ambitions, the competition, the greed, the envy, the brutality—in the life that you lead. And man has not been able to solve it. What man has done is to run away from it—run away through the worship of God, through dogma, through belief, through rituals, through ideology, through formulas, through ancestral worship, or

through anything to avoid the present agony, the present anxiety. And this has been the state of man for thousands of years. We can mesmerize ourselves by reading the Bible, the Gita, this or that, by attending talks, whether it is the interpretation of the Gita or something else—which is all so infantile! But the fact remains that each one of us, as a human being, has not been able to solve this thing. We can only solve this if we can discover a new mind which will tackle these problems and finish them.

Now, to discover the new mind, not only is it necessary for us to understand the responses of the old brain, but also it is necessary for the old brain to be quiet. The old brain must be active but quiet. You are following what I am saying? Look, sir! If you would discover for yourself firsthand—not what somebody else says—if there is a reality, if there is such a thing as God—the word *God* is not the fact—your old brain, which has been nurtured in a tradition, either anti-God or pro-God, in a culture, in an environmental influence and propaganda, through centuries of social assertion, must be quiet. Because, otherwise, it will only project its own images, its own concepts, its own values. But those values, those concepts, those beliefs are the result of what you have been told, or are the result of your reactions to what you have been told; so, unconsciously, you say, "This is my experience!"

So you have to question the very validity of experience—your own experience or the experience of anybody else; it does not matter who it is. Then by questioning, inquiring, asking, demanding, looking, listening attentively, the reactions of the old brain become quiet. But the brain is not asleep; it is very active, but it is quiet. It has come to that quietness through observation, through investigation. And to investigate, to observe, you must have light; and the light is your constant alertness.

Clarity does not come if you don't observe, if you don't listen, if you don't watch all your reactions—what you say, what you feel, what you think. When you begin to quote the Upanishads, the Bible, Shankara, Buddha— they are just words, words of somebody else— it is not a discovery for you. To find out if there is something beyond this imitative, copying reaction of the brain, the brain must understand all its reactions to the innumerable influences—from your grandmother to the present press, from the ancient teachers to the modern gurus. Everybody is influencing each other, and one has to be aware of this. And it is only through this alertness of watching, listening, that there comes clarity; and that clarity brings to the brain peace, quietness, and therefore attention.

So we are faced with the fact—not an opinion, not an idea, not a concept—that the whole of our consciousness, not just some part of it, is the result of imitation, whether it is the imitation of Shankara or Buddha or somebody else; it does not matter who it is. One has to discover the fact of imitation, which is conforming, which is based on authority, which is the outcome of fear.

Here, one has to understand the authority of law and also the authority imposed upon oneself through experience, knowledge, or pleasure. Obviously, one has to obey the law—you have to keep to the right or to the left side of the road, depending on which country you are living in; you have to pay taxes, buy stamps, and all the rest of it. The buying of stamps may help you to subscribe to the war; by paying taxes you may be supporting war! If you are a pacifist, you are lost. If you are a human being, you say, "I will not kill"—not because of some idea, not because of some concept; but because you have love in your heart, you will not kill anybody. Does it mean you will not buy a stamp? Does it mean you will not pay any tax? Surely not! Not to pay a tax, not to buy

stamps, not to travel by railway, but walk over the earth—all that does not solve the problem. What gives rise to the problem of war is nationalistic, linguistic, geographical divisions. And what starts war is religious differences—you are a Hindu, I am a Muslim; you with your dogmas and limitations, I with mine. Unless we transcend and go beyond all that, mere nonpayment of taxes, or not going by a train, is not going to solve a thing—it only means a personal fancy, exhibitionism, nothing else! You are rather uncomfortable when I say all this because you don't see the total issue. You see life in fragments, and you hope to find an answer through fragments. But through fragments there is no answer to the misery of life.

So we come to a point when you see that whatever you do inwardly is a process of imitation. Of course you have to go to an office, keep your appointments. We are not talking of the obvious time factor or the obvious activities that one has to do. But we are talking about the fact that you conform and that whatever you do inwardly—control, suppress, copy, follow—is a process of imitation, and therefore your action then becomes repetitive. Whether it is a pleasurable repetition or a nonpleasurable repetition, it is based on trying to conquer fear. I do not know if you are following all this.

So whatever you do, whatever positive action you take with regard to imitation—it is still imitation. Isn't that a fact? If you say, "I must lead a life of nonimitation," that very saying indicates you have not understood the question, the issue. If you say, "I must find a way to free myself from imitation," then, in the search to find a different way, the motive is still imitative because you want to escape from this imitation and to establish a new kind of imitation, a new habit. Sir, look! If one disciplines at all, that discipline—that is, conforming to a pattern, conforming to a norm—is based surely on the fear that you may not do the right thing, that you may not be happy, that you may not find food, that you may not find God, etc., etc. So your discipline is based on imitation, which is the result of your reaction to fear. Surely! So whatever you do with regard to imitation will still be the act of imitation! That is a fact; if you examine it, you will see it is so. Then what are you to do?

You have so far followed, even verbally, intellectually, what has been stated. If you have gone beyond the word, not intellectually, then you are faced with this issue: knowing that the whole of your life, from the moment you are born to the moment you die, is conforming, imitating, obeying, adjusting to social laws or to a particular idiosyncrasy which is your own particular character, when you are faced with that, you realize that any activity born of thought, born of an idea, born of a concept—as an idea, an ideology, a formula, a tradition, or a prompting from the past—is imitative.

Then what is one to do? I hope I have made my question clear. Our brain says, "You must act, you must do something when you are confronted with this immense, very complex problem." Your reaction, the reaction of the brain, is to do; it is to think to find a way out. Now, to find a way out, to do something about it, is what we call positive action. That is what we always do. I lack courage, and I must find a way to overcome it; and so I develop various characteristics which I call "courage to face fear." That is our operation always. When we are confronted with a problem of any kind, the instinct in reply is to do something about it, either through thought, through emotion, through action, or through some kind of activity—which is the activity of the old brain. Right? The old brain is the result of time, experience, knowledge of the past; therefore, it is imitative, and its response to a problem will inevitably be imitative.

So what is one to do? We said that the response of the old brain is imitative, and whatever it does has no answer. And that response of the past is what we call the positive activity of life—which only breeds more confusion, more conflict. So, you are confronted with this immense question—that the old brain is imitative and its responses are imitative; therefore, thought, in which is included the feeling and the emotion and all the rest of it, is imitative; and therefore through thought you cannot find a way out. The intellect is not the door through which you can escape from this problem, nor is emotion. Therefore all positive action must entirely cease—which means the old brain must be completely negative, which means the old brain must be completely quiet. You are following? The old brain can only be quiet if it has observed its activity in the light of its own perception. You are following? Look, sir! I can see that tree because there is light; otherwise, I cannot see the tree. There is that light— whether it is artificial light or the light of the sun—and I observe. Otherwise, however much I may observe, there is no seeing.

So the old brain has to be quiet, has to be negative. You understand now what we mean by the negative and the positive? That negative state and quietness can only possibly come, not through discipline, not through conformity and all that, but only through its observing the whole process of its own thinking and becoming observant. To be quiet and observant is to have light, and without light you cannot observe. So it is not a trick of sitting still, meditating, forcing—all those tricks which one has made for centuries upon centuries, calling that process meditation, are nonsense. Meditation is something entirely different—if we have time, we will discuss it some other day. When you are confronted with this immense fact, you will see that the whole of life including your atma, your soul, your God, everything, is imitative. You repeat because you have been told.

The communist is told, "There is no such stupid thing as a soul," and he repeats, "There is no such stupid thing as a soul." He repeats, and you repeat.

So the whole of life, every corner of our consciousness, is imitative, recognizable. You know, when you recognize something, it is already known; therefore, it is the past; therefore, it is still imitative, and therefore it is still within the field of the known. So, when you are confronted with this immense problem, the answer to it lies in complete quietness of the brain, which has come about naturally, through observation, in the light of its own perception. And therefore out of this clarity comes the new mind. And only then can one discover the nature and the structure of what is the original—if there is something original. Don't translate it in terms of your own particular theology or particular concept. Because one has to find something new, original, not contaminated by thought. Otherwise one is merely a repetitive machine, quoting this, following somebody else, arguing this, quarreling over words, over opinions, belonging to this sect or that society—it all becomes so utterly immature!

And we have to find a new way of living—which is not to go to sleep, or escape into monasteries or mountains, or do some immature act like that. But to find a way of living in this world, now, so that the mind is free from conflict, is possible only when the mind is free from conflict—which is essentially the conflict of imitation. Then you will find that the brain becomes extraordinarily sensitive. It is only the highly sensitive mind that is highly vulnerable, that is quiet—not a mind, not a brain that is reacting all the time according to its old pattern. It is not for you to find it; you cannot find a thing. The idea of searching for truth is utter nonsense! Because to search for something implies that you are trying to find, uncover something. How can you find, with a dull and repetitive mind, something which is not to be sought after, which is something alive, moving, which is totally new? So you cannot seek it.

I know it is one of the fashionable things or religious things to seek truth or God! You have to throw that word overboard; it has no meaning. But what has meaning is to find out if the brain can be extraordinarily sensitive, quiet, and free. Out of that freedom alone can one live peacefully in this world and create a new world, a new generation, a new people.

December 29, 1965

Fourth Talk in Madras

If we may, we will continue with what we were talking about the other day when we met here.

We were saying how greatly important it is that there should be a mutation in the mind—not mere reformation, not mere improvement, but a total change. As we pointed out, man has lived for so many centuries with sorrow, with misery, with confusion. And the human being does not seem to be able to find a way out of this. He is caught in a web of circumstances of his own making and has not been able to transform himself totally. He has been more or less civilized, which has been the function of most religions—to tame him down from the vicious animal—but there is still a great deal of the animal in most of us. And as there is so much decay, corruption—moral, spiritual, ethical, as well as aesthetical—it obviously is necessary to bring about, or rather to be aware of the factors that need, a radical change in our thinking and feeling.

And it is necessary to bring about this mutation, primarily inwardly. Though most societies, most governments are concerned with the improvement of external matters, making life a little more comfortable—having more food, more clothes, and all the rest of it—very few are concerned with bringing about this inward revolution.

This evening, we would like to talk about a change that must always be instantaneous. All mutation is instantaneous. It cannot be thought about with a structure built round the change, nor can it be carefully planned out, step by step, what man should do. We went into that, more or less, last time.

So, I would like to discuss, talk over together, this question of time. But before we go into that, I think it is necessary to examine what is learning because both of us are going to learn about time. And perhaps if we could understand what is involved in this matter of time, then we could see the implication and the intimation or the hint that is intrinsically in the question of how to bring about a change.

For most of us, to learn is to accumulate knowledge or a technique, or to commit to memory certain ideas through experience, through being taught; and that process is what we call learning. That is, to cultivate memory, and having cultivated it, having gathered enough experience, knowledge, having stored it up, from there to act: that is what we generally call learning. It is always in the past—that is, having learned, I then apply. Having accumulated, added to my information, to my knowledge, to my experience, having stored it up, from there I proceed to act—that is, having learned, from that knowledge I function.

But I think there is a vast difference between learning and having learned. The one is always in the active present, and the other is always in the past. The learning process is always going on, infinitely. But if one has learned and then adds to it what one is learning, then learning ceases. I think one has to go into this a little bit, so that both of us understand this clearly.

Learning, which is the active present, is the doing, is the acting. The doing, the acting, is in the learning. Acting is not separate from learning. I learn as I do, as I act—not having learned, I act. The two are different states altogether. This we must clearly see from the very beginning if we are to understand this question of time. That is, one learns a technique, studies it, stores it up in memory; and having stored it up, having cultivated it through experience, through study, through memory, one acts. That action is entirely different from the action which comes in the act of learning. I act as I am learning—not having experienced, I act. I hope this is clear. The two are entirely different. The one is mechanical; that is what the computers, the electronic brains, do. The computer has been given all the information necessary about a particular subject, and when a particular question with regard to that subject is put to that machine, the machine gives a prompt answer. And that is what we do. Therefore, in that, there is no freedom.

So, one begins to discover that knowledge does not give freedom. Only learning gives freedom. Because that is not mechanical, you are learning all the time; and from that learning, there is acting all the time. So, if that is very clear, we can proceed to examine this whole question of time.

We use time as a means to bring about change. We are talking about psychological time, not time by the watch. Time by the watch is necessary. Otherwise you will not be here, I will not be here; you will not be able to catch your bus and go to your office tomorrow morning, and so on. Chronological time is absolutely necessary; that brings about some order and some efficiency.

Now, is there psychological time at all? And what do we mean by time in that sense? We understand what we mean when we say, "yesterday," "today," "tomorrow"—by the watch. I have to catch a train, a bus, or an airplane in a few days, and so on; that is very simple. But when we are talking about a time which is altogether in a different dimension—which is psychological time— is there such a thing? And if there is, what is it? And we have to understand that in relation to what we mean by mutation, by this tremendous, radical revolution. If we do not understand the whole significance of time, we shall not be able to understand the implication of mutation.

Chronological time is a fact; there is no question of doubting it. But is there any other time? And if there is, what do we mean by that? To investigate that, to go into that really very deeply, you have to consider something entirely different—which is: there is a division, a separation, a fragmentation between the observer and the observed. Please, this is not an abstract subject, so don't go to sleep, don't become vague. This needs very clear thinking on your part, neither agreeing nor disagreeing. A really clear mind that wants to find out neither agrees nor disagrees; it follows, examines—not on the basis of one's prejudices, likes, and dislikes. So it needs a mind that is willing to think this out, right to the end. It is only such a mind that is a serious mind, and it is only the serious mind that is going to find the answer—not the mind that discusses philosophically the question of time.

So, what do we mean by time—if there is such a thing as time? And is it possible to put an end to time? We are used to thinking in terms of a gradual process: I will change, I will be good, I should be, I must not be, and so on. All that involves time. That is: I will, in the future, do it. The very action of "will" is time. Please look at if very carefully. The action of "should" and "should not" is time because there is an interval between *what is* and 'what should be', and to arrive at 'what should be' involves time. Chronologically there is time involved when you have to get from here to your house.

And equally, when you want to change *what is*, you think of it in terms of time—which is, I should do that. Therefore the "should" implies time—which is, after gathering experience, having learned, I act. It is not learning and acting. I will go into it. Perhaps it is not clear to you for the moment. If it does not become clear, I am sorry. One has to explain this very carefully and go into it step by step; and your mind must be equally alert and aware and follow the implications; otherwise, you will miss it.

So, the time that we know, that is psychological, involves "will"—the "should" and "should not," "I must" and "must not"—which obviously is to move from one center to another center, a distance to be covered by time. So you invent an excuse for tomorrow, and so on. Therefore, wherever there is an action of will, time is involved. And when you have time, there are other factors entering into it, other influences which modify what should be. So the cause produces the effect, and the effect then becomes the cause. Look, sirs! If I may suggest, please do not translate what you hear into your own terminology; don't translate what is being said in terms of Sanskrit or your own particular language because your language, your Sanskrit words are loaded, and therefore you will not understand directly what the speaker means. So do not interpret what is being said into your own words; just follow—even intellectually, if you will.

As we said, unless we understand this question of time, mutation becomes meaningless. Then we are only concerned with self-improvement, with becoming better, nobler, more kind, less kind, this or that—which involves time. So we see that where there is the function of knowledge as will, time is involved. And when time is involved between the actor and the action, there are other factors coming into being; therefore, the action is never complete. I intend to give up something—that is, I will do it tomorrow. What is taking place between now and tomorrow? There is an interval, a lag of time. In that space, there are other factors coming in, other pressures, other strains. Therefore 'what should be' is modified already, and so is my action. So the action is never complete. I start out to do something tomorrow, inwardly—give up, do, conform, imitate, and so on—and there are other factors, other pressures, other strains, other circumstances that come and interfere; therefore, there is always, between *what is* and 'what should be', the action which is being modified all the time, and therefore such action is never complete.

Then also, through habit, through tradition, through acquiring knowledge technologically, we are used to saying, we have got the habit of saying to ourselves, "I will do it another day, I will change gradually." So again, this idea of gradualness involves time; in that is involved the whole business of modification. So one has to find out much more deeply what time is.

We see chronological time. We see time as will in action. We also see that the mind—through laziness, through indolence—has invented time to postpone action, which is: the idea and the action. There is the idea based on organized thought, according to tradition, knowledge, information; and according to that idea, there is action—which involves gradualness. Again, that is a very, very superficial thing, and one has to go much deeper into this question. I hope I have made this, up to now, fairly clear.

We have to find out if there is time at all. Because if I can understand it, or if there is an ending to time, there is immediate action. The mind, then—the brain—is not indolent; it has not the energy to be indolent. If I know I am going to die tomorrow, I will act immediately. So I have to brush aside this superficial explanation of time. This is what we have done verbally. And if you treat this explanation as an explanation and merely as

words, then it is not a fact. Then what has taken place? Then you are merely adding this to the knowledge which you have already, and from that knowledge you are going to act, and therefore you are never free to learn.

Is there time? Because if there is no ending to time, there is no freedom, there is no end to sorrow; then life is merely one series of continuous reactions, responses, and so on. So, is there an ending to time? If the mind can discover it, understand it, then action has a totally different meaning. Right? Sir, if you are told that your house is on fire, you will not be sitting here! If you are told that there is no tomorrow, you will be horrified! There is a tomorrow chronologically, but there will be no psychological tomorrow. And if there is no tomorrow, it is a tremendous revolution inwardly. Then love, action, beauty, space, freedom—these have a totally different meaning.

So that is what we are going to discover—discover, not learn, not accumulate some information from the speaker, with which you agree or disagree. You are going to discover it, feel your way into it. And then it will set you free from time. You know, feeling which is not stimulated by thought is entirely different from the feeling brought about by a stimulus. Do listen to this a little bit. The feeling about space is entirely different from the word *space* in relation to what you think or feel or know about space. You understand, sirs, what it is to feel something, to look at something? Feel that sunset, do look at it, and also that tree, with its leaves; of the dark day, see the intensity, the extraordinary light, the beauty of that. To feel it is entirely different from the mere stimulation which that sunset gives you—there you are dependent; there you say that it is a beautiful sunset which awakens in you memories, feelings, ideas, and so on. But to come to that beauty with immense feeling which is not stimulated is entirely different.

So we are going to go into this question of time, nonverbally. To communicate, words are necessary; otherwise, you will not know what we are talking about. You and I do know, I hope, English. So words are necessary. The word is not the thing. That light—unless you feel it and see it, the mere word *light* or *beauty* has no meaning. So one has to feel one's way into what we are going into. We are inquiring into this question of time.

Time by the watch, we know, is a fact. We also know time as will, which is also a fact. We know also the gradual process when thought says, "Do it tomorrow; that is good enough"—which again is time. We know this is also a fact. Now what is time beyond this? Is there such a thing as time? To find out—not merely theoretically or intellectually or emotionally, but actually to feel your way into it—one has to go into this question of the observer and the observed. For instance, when you look at that sunset, there is the observer and the fact, the observed; there is a division between the observer and the observed. That division is time.

Now, the observer is not a permanent entity. Don't say that the observer existed first. Please let me here caution you. Look at it all as though you have never read a single sacred book—sacred books are not important anyhow. Look at it as though you are looking at it for the first time. Do not translate what Shankara or somebody else said—that there is the original observer, the original entity which is the silent watcher! You can spin a lot of words and theories, but don't do it, because then you are missing the whole point.

As you watch anything—a tree, your wife, your children, your neighbor, the stars of a night, the light on the water, the bird in the sky, anything—there is always the observer (the censor, the thinker, the experiencer, the seeker) and the thing he is observing: the observer and the observed, the thinker and the thought. So, there is always a division. It is this

division that is time. That division is the very essence of conflict. And when there is conflict, there is contradiction. There is the observer and the observed—that is a contradiction; there is a separation. And hence, where there is contradiction, there is conflict. And when there is conflict, there is always the urgency to get beyond it, to conquer it, to overcome it, to escape from it, to do something about it—and all that activity involves time.

So, as long as there is 'the observer and the observed' as two separate entities, there is always time. This does not mean that the observer identifies himself with the observed; in that process of identification, too, time is involved. If you say you believe in God—belief, not the truth—then you try to identify yourself with that. To identify yourself with that involves time. Obviously, because you have to make an effort, to struggle, to give up this, to do that, and all the rest of it. Or, you blindly identify yourself, and you end up in an asylum.

So, one sees this division within oneself. And one sees that as long as this division exists, time will inevitably continue, time can never come to an end. And is it possible for this division to cease to exist?—which is, the observer is the observed, the seeker is the sought. Don't translate it into your own terminology: the seeker is God, a spiritual entity, or whatever it is; therefore, thought says, "I am the atma or some other entity like that." If you say all this, you are deceiving yourself; you are not feeling your way into discovery; you are merely stating or asserting something which has no validity at all.

So, how is it possible—again, the "how" is not the method; we are just asking—for this division between the observer and the observed to come to an end? As long as there is this division, time will go on, and time is sorrow. And a man who will understand the end of sorrow must understand this, must find, must go beyond this duality between the thinker and the thought, the experiencer and the experienced. That is, when there is a division between the observer and the observed, there is time, and therefore there is no ending of sorrow. Then, what is one to do? You understand the question? I see, within myself, the observer is always watching, judging, censoring, accepting, rejecting, disciplining, controlling, shaping. That observer, that thinker, is the result of thought, obviously. Thought is first—not the observer, not the thinker. If there were no thinking at all, there would be no observer, no thinker; then there would only be complete, total attention.

So, how is it possible for this division between the thinker and the thought, the observer and the observed, to come to an end? Here no time must be involved. You understand? If I do certain practices in order to break down this division, time is involved; and therefore I perpetuate, continue, the division as the thinker and the thought. So, what is one to do? You put that question, not verbally, but with astonishing urgency. You are urgent only when you feel something very strongly; when you have got violent physical pain, you act; there is an intensity. There is this question of sorrow—not only individual sorrow, but the sorrow of man who has lived for so many millennia, suffering, tortured, never finding a way out. And to find a way out is an immensely urgent question. So, one must understand this question very deeply—which is to listen to it, listen to what has been said.

You know what it is to listen? To listen to that breeze among the leaves without any resistance, without interpretation, without distraction. There is no such thing as distraction when you are listening. When you listen to that breeze among the leaves, you listen with complete attention, and therefore there is no time involved at all. You are listening; you are not translating, not interpreting, not agreeing or disagreeing, not saying, "I will think about it tomorrow." You are in a state of actual listening—which means you are so concerned, if I may use that word, because you are in sorrow. So you give your whole mind, your whole body, your whole nerves, everything you have, to listen.

Now, if you have listened that way, then we can go to another problem which will help the understanding of that division, and the ending of that division between the observer and the observed. We must have order; there must be order—not only social order, but outward order, order in the room, order in the street, cleanliness. Without order you cannot function. All order is virtue; order is righteousness, and without order you cannot function efficiently. So order, both in society and also inwardly, is essential. Society and the human being are not two different entities; when there is order in the human being, there will be order externally. Because there is disorder in all of us, there is disorder outwardly. And the mere patching up of order outside, social order—and there must be social order—will not solve this inward disorder.

So, order is virtue, and virtue cannot be cultivated any more than you can cultivate humility. If you cultivate humility, you are only covering up your vanity. Humility is something that must blossom naturally. And without humility, there is no learning. So order is virtue, and virtue cannot be cultivated. Do please listen to it. When you cultivate virtue, it is no longer virtue. You cannot cultivate love—can you? You can cultivate hate, greed, envy; you can be more polite, more gentle, more kind, more generous, but that is not love. Love is something which is not of time, nor of memory. And that quality of love is compassion, in which is included tenderness, kindness, generosity, and so on. But generosity is not love; kindliness is not love. As you cannot cultivate love or humility, so you cannot possibly cultivate virtue. And yet all our habit, all our tradition, is to cultivate virtue—which is merely resisting the fact. The fact is: In spite of what you have said for centuries, you are violent. You may not hit another because you are afraid to go to jail. But you are violent because you are ambitious, greedy, envious, and when your country is attacked, you sit up and take notice, and you identify yourself with the country, and you are willing to shoot another—which is all the animal, inherent violence.

Now, to bring order in violence is to end violence, and the ending of violence must be immediate—not tomorrow. The ending of violence, which is order, does not involve time. Please understand this. If time is involved, which is will, which is postponement, which is gradualness—gradually, through ideas, through conformity, I will get rid of violence—you are not really free of violence. To be free of violence is now, not tomorrow.

So, there must be the feeling of righteousness, which comes into being without motive when you understand the nature of time. You understand, sirs? When you are good because you are going to be punished, or because you are going to be rewarded, then there is a motive; therefore, it is not goodness, it is fear. So righteousness is always without motive. And in that field of human relationship, of righteousness, time does not exist. When you love somebody, what does it mean? To love somebody, an animal, a human being, a tree, the sky, the open space—when you love something, what does it mean? It means, surely, not intellection, not the reaction of memory, but an intensity between two individuals or between two objects, an intensity at the same level and at the same time; then there is a communication—nonverbal, nonintellectual, nonsentimental. Love is not sentiment, love is not emotion, love is not devotion.

So when one understands the nature of time—what is involved in it—virtue then is order, which is immediate. When you understand this

virtue—which is order, which is immediate—then you are beginning to see that the division between the observer and the observed is nonexistent. Therefore time has come to a stop. And it is only such a mind that can know what is new.

Look, sir! We know space only because there is the object which creates the space around it. There is this microphone; because of that there is space round it. Do listen. There is space inside the house because of the four walls, and there is space outside the house, which the house as an object creates. So, when there is space which an object has created, then there is time.

Is there space without the object? You understand the question? You have to discover this. This is a challenge. Not that you must respond or not respond—you have to find out. Because one's mind is so petty, small, it is always functioning within the limits of its own self-centered activities. All those activities are within that center and round that center, in the space which the center creates within itself and round itself, as this microphone does. Therefore when there is space which an object or a thought or an image has created, that space can never give freedom because in that space, there is always time.

So time ceases only when there is space without the object, without the center, without the observer, and therefore without the object. It is only such a mind that can know what beauty is. Beauty is not a stimulant; it is not brought about, or put together, by architecture, by painting, by looking at the sunset, or by seeing a beautiful face. Beauty is something entirely different; it can only be understood when the experiencer is no longer there, and therefore experience ceases to exist. It is like love—the moment you say verbally, or feel, that you love, you cease to love. Because then love is merely a mentation; love then is merely a feeling, an emotion, in which there is jealousy, hate, envy, greed.

So, you have to understand the nature of time, not theoretically, not intellectually, but actually, inwardly. Because when you understand the nature and the structure of time, then action is immediate; therefore, there is the ending of sorrow—now, not tomorrow. And to understand time, you have also to understand space and also beauty. There is very little beauty in the world—there are a lot of decorations—and without beauty there is no love.

So one has to understand all these things, and it is only time that prevents living. If you have gone into this very deeply—not verbally but actually, as we are discussing, as we are talking—then you will see that this sense of timelessness comes into being without your asking. It comes into being because you have listened without any resistance, without any knowledge, because there was not you listening as a listener, but there was only listening. Then, when time has stopped, you will find that sorrow, conflict, and contradiction come to an end.

January 2, 1966

Fifth Talk in Madras

There was a preacher once who used to give sermons every morning to his disciples. And one morning when he got on the rostrum, a bird came and sat on the window-sill there and began to sing. And presently he flew away. So the wise man turned to his disciples and said, "The morning sermon is over," and went off. I wish we could do the same! (The singing of a bird preceded Krishnaji's talk, and so he smiled and made the above observation.)

I would like to talk over this evening something which I think is rather important. And the importance of it lies not in verbal communication but rather that each one of us can discover, examine, and understand the reality of it for ourselves. One is apt, I am afraid, to be satisfied with mere explanation, to take the word for the thing and go away with a stimulated feeling that one has gathered some knowledge, understanding, for oneself. One cannot gather understanding from another because the understanding, the truth of the matter, can be gone into, examined, and felt for oneself. And so verbal communication becomes only important to convey a certain meaning, a certain depth. But one has to examine very closely for oneself that which is being said, neither accepting nor rejecting, but closely examining. And to examine really deeply, one needs to have a certain attention. And attention seems to be one of the most difficult things because when we want to attend, we are distracted—thought interferes, and so we resist thought and the distraction. But actually there is no distraction at all. The idea that we are distracted when we want to concentrate only implies that you resist what you call distraction, but actually there is no distraction. When your thought wanders off, give your whole attention to that thought; don't call it distraction.

Because, to attend means great energy. To give one's whole attention demands total energy. Sirs, may I request you to listen, rather than take notes? Because when you take notes, you are not listening, you are not being attentive. Attention is now, not when you get home and read over the notes. This is not a lecture; the speaker is not a professor delivering a lesson. But rather, we are trying together to understand this very complex problem of living. And to understand it one needs attention, one needs the full intention to understand. And you cannot understand, listen attentively, when you are taking notes. And when you look at the sunset or the tree, or listen to that bird, it is not a distraction. It is part of this total attention. If you merely resist the noise that bird is making and feel disturbed, or if you do not want to look at that sunset because you want to give your whole attention to something that is being said, then you are merely concentrating and therefore resisting. Whereas if you listen to that bird, watch that sunset, hear the hammering across the road, and see the sunlight on the leaf, then it is a part of total attention; then it is not a distraction. To attend so completely you need energy. And that is what I am going to discuss this evening.

Energy is force. And very few of us have the energy to bring about a radical transformation in ourselves. The force, the energy, the drive, the passion, the deep intention— very few of us have it. And to gather that energy, to have that energy, in which is included this tremendous intensity, passion, drive, force, we think that certain forms of habit are necessary—a certain establishment of a behavior, morality, a certain resistance to sensation, with which we are all quite familiar. We have lived for so long, for so many generations, for so many thousands of years, yet we have not found the energy which will transform our ways of living, our ways of thinking, feeling. And I would, if I may, like to go into this question because, it seems to me, that is what we need—a different kind of energy, a passion which is not mere stimulation, which does not depend on, which is not put together by, thought.

And to come upon this energy, we have to understand inertia—understand not how to come by this energy, but understand the inertia which is so latent in all of us. I mean by inertia "without the inherent power to act"—inherent in itself. There is, as one observes within oneself, a whole area of deep inertia. I do not mean indolence, laziness, which is quite a different thing. You can be physically lazy, but you may not be inert. You may be tired, lazy, unwilling—that is entirely different. You can whip yourself into action, force yourself not to be lazy, not be indolent. You can discipline yourself to get up early, to do certain things regularly, to follow certain practices, and so on. But that is not what we are talking about. That can be easily dealt with and understood; we can come back to it a little later, if time allows.

What we are concerned with is this inertia which is so inherent in all of us, which very few of us come upon and actually do something about. We know what to do about laziness; we know what to do about a mind that is dull. You can sharpen it, polish it, freely discuss it; but that is not what we are talking about. We want to go into this question of inertia which is without the power to act, which is so inherent in all of us, deep down. This inertia is essentially the result of time. This inertia is the result of accumulation. And what is accumulated is time. One needs time not only to gather information, knowledge, experience, but also to act according to that experience, knowledge, information.

So there is this accumulative process going on, of which most of us are little conscious. Both in the unconscious as well as in the conscious, this accumulative process is going on all the time. As you are listening to me, you are gathering, you are accepting, accumulating. That very accumulation is going to result in inertia. You watch it. You will see, if you examine this a little bit closely. I learn a technique, and it takes time by the watch, by the day, by the year; and I store it up. And according to that knowledge, according to that technique, I function. But also at a deeper level this accumulative process is going on as knowledge, as tradition, as my own experience, or what I have read, and so on. There is also that accumulative process going on of which I am not conscious at all.

Please don't merely, if I may request you, listen to the words, but actually go through what is being said, actually open the door so that you will see this process going on.

Look! If you are a Hindu, you have gathered tremendous knowledge about God, about this, about that. You have accepted it for various reasons, which are obviously fear, conformity, public opinion, and so on. You have accepted it; it is there, both in the conscious as well as in the unconscious—not that there is a division between the two; it is a total movement. This accumulation is inertia, and this inertia is time. To accumulate you must have time; otherwise, you cannot gather. Please don't say, "How am I not to accumulate?" When you say, "How am I not to accumulate?" you are again accumulating inevitably. Please, this needs very careful, subtle thinking out, going into.

This inertia is without the power of inherent action. Inherent action is: not acting from what one has accumulated as knowledge, as an idea, as a tendency, as a temperament, as a capacity or a gift or a talent. Essentially a gift, a talent, knowledge, is inertia; and we strengthen this inertia through various forms of resistance. I resist any form of change, both outwardly and inwardly; I resist it through fear of insecurity and so on—one does not have to go into this in great detail.

So there is inertia through accumulation, through resistance, and through commitment to a particular course of action. Please follow this a little bit. Inertia, which is the lack of the power to act in itself, is also the result of having motives. Right? That is fairly simple. So this inertia is built, put together, through motivation, through accumulation as knowledge, as information, as tradition—outwardly as well as inwardly—as a technique, and also through commitment to a series of actions. There is the communist, the socialist, a particular type who meditates in a certain way; one is thus committed, and therefore that commitment strengthens the inertia. Though one may be terribly active outside, walk up and down the lane, pursue every reform and do all kinds of things, it is still an activity which is strengthening inertia. And inertia is built through resistances: I like, I don't like; I like you and I don't like you; this pleases me, this doesn't please me. So there is this inertia built up through conformity, through activity, and so on. You see this happening in yourself. I am not saying something fantastic. This is what is going on in all of us, all the time.

So we enlarge that field of inertia through various forms of knowledge, commitment, activity, motive, resistance. And becoming conscious of this, you say, "I must not; I will not commit myself to any action," or "I will try not to have motives," or "I will try not to resist." Please follow this. The moment you say, "I will not" or "I should," you are only strengthening the inertia. That is fairly clear. That is, the positive process is the strengthening of the inertia, as is the negative process also. So we have to realize this fact that all our life, all our activity, all our thinking, strengthens this inertia. Please follow this. You are not accepting a theory; you are not disputing an idea with your own opinion. This is a fact, a psychological fact, which you can observe if you look at yourself very deeply. If you cannot look, don't agree or disagree but examine.

So what is one to do? How is this inertia to be broken up? First, I must be conscious of it. I can't say, "I am inert"—which means nothing. You will translate it in terms of laziness, or insufficient physical activity or mental pursuit or stimulation. And that is not what we are talking about. We are talking of something at a much deeper level, which is: The whole of consciousness is inert because the whole of consciousness is based on imitation, conformity, acceptance, rejection, tradition, gathering, and acting from that gathering as knowledge, as technique, or as experience. Ten thousand years of propaganda is consciousness. A mind that realizes this extraordinary state—what is it to do?

What is a mind to do which has become aware of this inertia, and which knows, not verbally but actually, that the whole of consciousness is essentially inert? It can act within the field of its own projection, of its own concepts, of its own knowledge, of its own information, of its own tradition, of its own experience which is being gathered. The gathering, which is consciousness, is inherently inert. Right? Please, you are not accepting what is being said. If you look at it very deeply, you will see that it is so. You may invent; you may think out that there is a state of mind which is beyond being inert—God or whatever you call it. But it is still part of that consciousness. So, what is one to do? Can one do anything at all?

Now, to find out what to do and what not to do is meditation. Now I am going to go into that. First of all, that word *meditation* is very heavily loaded. Especially in this country and to the east of this country, that word brings all kinds of reactions. You begin immediately to sit more straight—I see it happening. You pay a little more attention; you react according to your tradition. Or because you have practiced—whatever it is you practice—for years, thinking about a mantra or a phrase, repeating it, and all that, at the very mention of that word, all this surges up, and you are caught in the thought. To the speaker, that is not meditation at all; it is a form of self-hypnosis, a form of worshiping a projection of your own mind, conditioned as a Hindu, as a Buddhist, or as a Christian; and you can get caught up in that marvelous vision, seeing Christ, Buddha, your own gods, and all the rest of it. But that is not meditation at all. You can sit in front of a picture everlastingly, and you will never find anything beyond the picture. You can invent.

You know, there is a story where a patriarch is sitting alone under a tree, and a disciple, a seeker, comes and sits in front of him, cross-legged, with the back straight and all the rest of it. And presently the patriarch says, "What are you doing, my friend?" The disciple says, "I am trying to reach a higher level of consciousness." And the patriarch says, "Carry on." Presently the patriarch takes up two pieces of stone and rubs them, making a noise. The disciple then says, "What are you doing, Master?" The patriarch replies, "I am rubbing these two stones to produce a mirror!" And the disciple laughs and says, "Master, you can do this for the next thousand years, you will never produce a mirror." The patriarch then says, "You can sit like that for the next million years."

So meditation is something entirely different. If you would go into it, you have naturally to abandon all your concepts of meditation, all your formulas, your practices, your disciplines, your concentration, because you are entering into a field which is something totally new. But your practices, your visions, your disciplines are all the result of accumulated activity and therefore lead essentially to deeper inertia. So, what we are concerned with is: What is a mind to do, that is aware of this inertia and how it has come about? Can it do anything? Knowing that any activity on its part is still the result of this inertia which is consciousness, how is that mind to be totally still and yet completely awake? You understand the question? That is, one sees deeply within oneself this field of inertia. And one realizes that any activity on the part of the brain—any activity, any movement in any direction—is still within the field of consciousness and therefore imitative, accumulative, and therefore strengthens the inertia. One also realizes that not to strengthen that inertia, one cannot practice, one cannot say, "I will not be inert"—which is part of the same old game. Then one sees what is necessary—a total inaction which becomes action in silence.

Now, how is the mind to be still? When I use the word *how*, it is not a method or a system. I am asking, "Is it possible for the mind, for the brain also, to be totally awakened, totally still?" The brain is the result of time, with all its accumulated knowledge, information, reactions, and conditioning. And the brain will respond much too quickly for you to control it because it has been trained for centuries to react. So the brain cells have to be quiet for the total mind to be quiet. Do you see the difficulty of the problem? Do not just say, "I will force myself, I will control my thoughts"—it becomes too silly, too immature; it has no meaning.

So, one sees that any movement in any direction, at any level of consciousness—conscious or unconscious—strengthens this quantum, this field, this area of inertia; and therefore the mind has to be totally still, and also the brain. And it is only when there is the totality of silence that there is action which is not of inertia. But if you say, "I must make my mind silent," and practice all kinds of tricks, if you take drugs, practice and do all kinds of things, then you are still building within the field of that inertia. Only when the mind—including the brain, including the body naturally—is totally still is there an action which is not of the inert. Obviously, silence is outside the field of consciousness, and that silence has not been put together by consciousness, by thought, by desire, by motive, by resistance, by practice, by any trick that one plays. You are following all this? So, that silence is something entirely different, and that silence can only come about when the brain, the mind, realizes that any movement within it is strengthening inertia.

So meditation is not tradition; it has nothing whatsoever to do with all that nonsense. I call it nonsense because any grown-up man can see the basic fact of what is involved in the ordinary, traditionally accepted meditation—which is self-hypnosis, a habit of doing something over and over again, and so the

mind becomes dull, stupid, ugly. We are not talking about that. We are talking of meditation as something entirely different, and in that meditation there is great fun, there is tremendous joy, there is a new state altogether. And that can only come about, not sought—you cannot seek it, you cannot pursue it, you cannot ask, "How am I to get it?" All that has no meaning. Meditation then is the understanding, or being aware, of the total process of consciousness, and not doing a thing about it—which means dying on the instant to the past.

Let me go into this question of death a little bit. Man has never understood death; he has worshiped it. He has lived in order to die; he has made death much more important than living. Cultures have done it, societies have done it. And people have various ways of escaping from death—reincarnation, resurrection, immortality, all kinds of things. The people who believe in reincarnation, whether factual or not—if they really believe in it, they will obviously be concerned with what kind of life they lead now, not tomorrow. If you lead a righteous life now, a tremendously full life, there is no tomorrow; and if there is a tomorrow, the field is much greater to play with. We neither believe in reincarnation nor in anything else, but we just play with those words. Because if we really believe, then every word, every thought, every deed, everything matters now. So man has never understood this extraordinary phenomenon of death. Not physical dying. I don't mean that; that obviously takes place, though scientists are trying to prolong life and are saying that perhaps human life can be prolonged indefinitely—then we can indefinitely carry on with our miseries, with our pettiness, with our unfulfilled ambitions, going to the office for the next hundred years!

And we have various ways and means of facing death—rationalizing it, escaping from it, belief, dogma, hope, and all the rest of it.

But we have never really understood it; we have never felt what it means to die. Unless we understand this phenomenon psychologically, not physiologically, we can never understand this sense of a new action born out of total silence. Do you understand? That is why one has to die to everything one knows—which is consciousness, which is the past, which is the accumulated result of time. Because it is only in death, in total death, that there is something new, that there is a total silence in which a different kind of life can be led. I am not hypnotizing you. Please listen carefully. Total death means: Can one die—not to something which one has accumulated, which is comparatively easy—so that nothing enters into that silence? You understand it?

Sir, look! There is this whole question of forgiveness. I think, to forgive is something essentially false. Listen to this until I finish. You receive a hurt, an insult. You examine it, and then say, "I forgive the man." But if you don't receive the hurt at all, there is no forgiveness. You understand? It does not mean that you have built a barrier around yourself so that nothing penetrates—which is what most people do anyhow. But it means that you have to be so alive, so sensitive, so clear, that nothing enters—nothing which needs to be stored up, to be examined and then acted upon as forgiveness or compassion or action based on an idea. You are following?

So, to die to the past implies, doesn't it, not only that the past ceases, but also that the present does not enter and accumulate and create a consciousness and inertia. I do not know if you are following all this. Sir, look! That which is tremendous light has no shadow; it is clear. Out of that clarity there is an action which is entirely different from the action which is born of confusion, accumulation, and all the rest of it. So we are talking of dying to everything known and functioning in light—going to an office and so on—functioning from that freedom from the known.

Look, sirs! Can you die to a pleasure—not argue or control or suppress, but just die to it? You like something, and without argument, without any mental process, without any talk, just die to it, just drop it. Now, when you do that, a different quality of mind has come into being. I do not know if you have done it. It is not something fantastically difficult—to give up something without any motive. When you see something very clearly, the seeing, the examination, creates the light, and the light acts—not "you decide" or "you don't decide." When you see something very clearly, there is action which is entirely different from the action which has been put together by thought.

So we are talking of a dying to the things that one has experienced, known, accumulated, so that the mind is fresh, the mind becomes young. Because it is only the very young mind that can be silent—not the dead, old mind. The scientists are saying that the child is born already conditioned and all the rest of it, but I am using the word *young* in a different sense.

So, silence, meditation, and death are very closely related. If there is no death to yesterday, silence is not possible. And silence is necessary, absolutely necessary, for an action which is not accumulative, and in which, therefore, there is no inertia being built up. Death becomes an ugly, frightful thing when you are going to lose what you have accumulated. But if there is no accumulation at all—all through life, from now on—then there is no what you call death; living then is dying, and the two are not separate.

The living which we know is a misery, confusion, turmoil, torture, effort, with an occasional, fleeting glance at beauty and love and joy. And that is the result of this consciousness which is inert, which is in itself incapable of new action. A man who would find a new life, a new way of living, must inquire, must capture this extraordinary quality of silence. And there can be silence only when there is death to the past, without argument, without motive, without saying, ''I will get a reward.'' This whole process is meditation. That gives you an extraordinary alertness of mind; there is not a spot in it where there is darkness; there are no unexamined recesses which nothing has touched—meaning that there are no recesses which you have not examined.

So, meditation is an extraordinary thing; it is a tremendous joy in itself. For, then, in that is silence, which in itself is action; silence is inherent in itself, which is action. Then life, everyday living, can be lived out of silence, not out of knowledge—except technological knowledge. And that is the only mutation that man can ever hope to come by. Otherwise, we lead an existence that has no meaning except sorrow and misery and confusion.

January 5, 1966

Sixth Talk in Madras

I believe this is the last talk for the time being.

Man has always been seeking something beyond his own conflicts, miseries, and his everyday, monotonous, lonely existence. And some people have said that there is something beyond the measure of man. We have either worshiped them or followed them, and thereby destroyed them. Or, because we ourselves are in so much misery and confusion, we cling to any hope that anyone offers—the more abstract, the more imaginative, the more satisfying and comforting, the better it is! But apparently few of us have found anything for ourselves that is original, that is really true.

That word *true* is a difficult word because each one interprets it according to his own temperament, to his own knowledge, to his own experience. And philosophers and teachers have twisted that word and given that word so many meanings—there is the mathematical truth, the abstract truth, and so on. And we try—in our confusion, in our misery, in our utter despair—to find something that is lasting, that is true, that is not put together by imagination, by the mind. And not having found it, we turn to some other authority, other teachers, books, and so on.

And this evening it would be good, if we can, to communicate with each other about something that is not communicable in words only—which does not mean we must be off, away into some fantasy, mythology, or some fancy. But if we could partake, share—which is really communication—not only by examining verbally, but by examining beyond the word, we would, if it is possible, discover, each one for oneself, something that is untouched, unspotted, original. That is the intention of the speaker for this evening.

Intention is one thing, and the actuality is something else. Because each one of us is a complex entity driven by so many pressures, twisted by so many strains, not knowing what to do, what to think, how to think, what to feel. So, it becomes extraordinarily difficult to partake together in something that needs very close examination, that needs a very healthy, sane mind—not a mind that is twisted, not a mind that is afraid and anxious. Obviously a mind that is afraid, that is confused, that is satisfied with explanation only, cannot possibly examine.

And one has to be aware from the very beginning that the word and the explanation have no meaning at all when you are really thirsty, really hungry, to find out. So, you discard explanations, whether given by any teacher, by any book, by any psychologist, or by any advocate of a new life. You discard even what the speaker says to find out clearly for yourself. And I think that is very important.

Most of us who have at all thought about life, who have lived in this murdering, brutal world—a world that is so utterly callous—probably have never asked of ourselves, or put to ourselves, questions that will bring the right answers. We may ask—and we do—"What is the purpose of life?" That is one of the favorite questions. "Is there God? Is there truth? What is the way to meditate?" and so on—these seem to me to be so utterly empty. But to put a right question needs a certain quality of mind. To put a right question demands that you be very clear in yourself of the words you use and the motive of your question. Because the motive and the word are going to dictate the answer. If you are afraid, and you put the question, "How is one to be rid of fear?" your motive is concerned only with getting rid of fear, not with understanding the whole structure of fear. If you are interested in understanding the whole structure of fear—the understanding then brings about an end to the structure of fear—then your question will be entirely different; then your examination is not based on a personal motive, on a motive of trying to overcome this or that.

So it is rather difficult to put a right question. To put a right question one must be extraordinarily mature—not in age, but inwardly. Maturity does not mean spiritual growth—there is no such thing as spiritual growth. Maturity implies, does it not, the total comprehension of existence—not one department of it, but the whole perception, the listening, the seeing, the understanding, the love, the whole quality of a total living. It is only such a mature mind that can put a right question, and that question will have the answer not outside the question but in the question itself.

So, this evening, we are going to examine. And you cannot examine if you don't pay attention. Attention is not something you cultivate; you don't say, "I will practice being attentive"—it then becomes mechanical. What is a mechanical thing can never be attentive. Even the computer, the most complex machinery, though it has a great deal of information, cannot be original. So to examine needs attention. Attention is not mechanical. You have to attend completely. When you, with all your being, attend to that sunset, without any emotion, without any sentiment, without any demand, then your mind, your brain, your body, your nerves—everything functions in complete union, and that state is attention. It cannot by any means be practiced day after day, by looking at the sunset every day at a certain time and saying, "I must put away my feelings, my sentiment, I must concentrate"—it will never take place.

So attention comes into being when there is the urgency and the immediate need to comprehend life. And you cannot comprehend this extraordinary movement of life intellectually or emotionally or sentimentally or according to a certain pattern of thinking—ideas, dogmas, systems.

To understand something you must give attention. And understanding is not a verbal statement or feeling that one has emotionally, intellectually, understood. Understanding is something immediate, and that understanding in itself is action—it is not that one understands first and then acts, or that one will attend and then act.

So, as we said, we are going to examine. And to examine you need to observe—to observe not according to your temperament, not according to your fancy, not according to your theology, not according to your culture in which you have been brought up—to see, to listen, without any prejudice, without any bias. So we are going not only to examine *what is* but also, in examining *what is*, to go beyond it.

Our life as it is, our everyday life, is a matter of relationship. Living is a relationship. To be related implies, does it not, contact, not only physically, but psychologically, emotionally, intellectually—a relationship. And there can be relationship only when there is great affection. I am not related to you, and you are not related to me, if between us there is merely an intellectual, verbal relationship; it is not a relationship. There is relationship only when there is a sense of contact, a sense of communication, a sense of communion; all that implies a great affection.

And our relationship, actually what it is, is very confused, unhappy, contradictory, and isolated—each one trying to establish for oneself, round oneself, in oneself, an enclosure which is unapproachable. You examine yourself—not what you should be, but what you are. How unapproachable you are, each one of you! Because, you have so many barriers, ideas, temperaments, experiences, miseries, concerns, preoccupations. And your daily activity is always isolating you; though you may be married and have children, you are still functioning, acting, with self-centered movement. So actually there is hardly any relationship between a father and a mother, a daughter and her husband, and so on, within the community.

Unless one establishes a right relationship, all our life will be a constant battle, individually as well as collectively. You may say that you, as a communist, as a social worker, or as a socialist, work for the community, forgetting yourself; but actually you don't forget yourself. You cannot forget yourself by identifying yourself with the greater, that is, the community! It is not an act of dissipation of the 'me', of the self. On the contrary, it is the identification of the 'me' with the greater, and therefore the battle goes on, as is so obvious in those countries where they talk a great deal about the community, about the collective. The communist is everlastingly talking about the collective, but he has identified himself with the collective. The collective then becomes the 'me'

for which he is willing to struggle and go through all kinds of torture and disciplines, because he has identified himself with the collective, as the religious person identifies himself with an idea which he calls God. And that identification is still the 'me'.

So life, as one observes, is relationship and is based on the action of that relationship—isn't it? I am related to you—wife, husband, as a part of society. My relationship with you or with my boss brings out an action which is not only profitable to me first but also to the community; and the motive of my identification with the community is profitable to me too! Please follow this—one has to understand the motive of all one's actions.

And life as it is, actually every day, is a constant battle; it is a constant misery, confusion, with occasional flashes of joy, occasional expression of deep pleasure. So unless there is a fundamental revolution, a tremendous change in our relationship, the battle will go on, and there is no solution along that way. Please do realize this. There is no way out through this battle of relationship. And yet that is what we are trying to do! We don't say, "Relationship must alter; the basis of our relationship must change." But being in conflict, we try to escape from it through various systems of philosophy, through drink, through sex, through every form of intellectual and emotional entertainment. So unless there is a radical revolution inwardly with regard to our relationship—relationship being life, relationship being "my wife," "my community," "my boss," "my relationship"—unless there is a radical mutation in relationship, do what you will—have the most noble ideas, talk, discuss infinitely about God and all the rest of it—it has no meaning whatsoever, because all that is an escape.

So the problem arises then: How am I, living in relationship, to bring about a radical change in my relationship? I cannot escape from relationship. I may mesmerize myself; I may withdraw into a monastery, run away and become a sannyasi, this and that; but I still exist as a human being in relationship. To live is to be related. So I have got to understand it and I have got to change it. I have to find out how to bring about a radical change in my relationship because, after all, that produces wars—that is what is happening in this country between the Pakistanis and the Hindus, between the Muslim and the Hindu, between the German and the Russian. So there is no way out through the temple, through the mosque, through Christian churches, through your discussing Vedanta, this, that, and the different systems. There is no way out unless you, as a human being, radically change your relationship.

Now, the problem arises: How am I to change, not abstractly, the relationship which is now based on self-centered pursuits and pleasures? That is the real question. Right?

This means really understanding desire and pleasure. Understanding, not saying, "I must suppress desire; I must get rid of pleasure"—which you have done for centuries. "You must work without desire"—I do not know what it means. "You must be desireless"—it has no meaning because we are full of desire, burning with it. It is no good suppressing desire; it is there still, bottled up, and you put a cork on it, you discipline yourself against desire. What happens? You become hard, ruthless!

And so one has to understand desire and understand pleasure. Because our inward values and judgments are based on pleasure, not on any great, tremendous principles, but just on pleasure. You want God because it gives you greater pleasure to escape from this monotonous, ugly, stupid life which is without much meaning! So, the active principle of our life is pleasure. You cannot discard pleasure. To look at that sunset, to see the leaves against that light, to see the beauty

of it, the delicacy of it—that is a tremendous sense of enjoyment; there is a great beauty in it. And because we have denied, suppressed pleasure, we have lost all sense of beauty. In our life there is no beauty; actually there is no beauty, not even good taste. Good taste can be learned, but you cannot learn beauty. And to understand beauty, you must understand pleasure.

So you have to understand pleasure: what it means, how it arises, the nature of it, the structure of it—not denying it. Don't let us fool ourselves and say, "My values are godly values. I have noble ideals." When you examine deep down into yourself, you will see your values, your ideas, your outlook, your way of acting, are all based on pleasure. So we are going to examine it, not merely verbally or intellectually. We are going actually to find out how to deal with pleasure, its right place, its wrong place, whether it is worth it or not worth it—this needs very close examination.

To understand pleasure we must go into desire. We must find out what desire is, how it comes, what gives it a duration, and whether desire can ever end. We have to understand how it comes into being, how it has its continuity, and whether it can ever come to an end—as it should. Unless we really understand this, this pretending to be without desire, struggling to be without desire, has no meaning; it destroys your mind, twists your mind, warps your being. And to understand whatever there is to understand, you need a very healthy, sane, clear mind—not a distorted mind, not a mind that is twisted, controlled, shaped, beaten out of its clarity.

So we are going to find out how desire comes into being. Please follow all this, because we are going to go into something else—don't wait to understand that! You have to begin from the beginning to understand where this examination is going to lead us. If you are not capable of examining this, you will not be capable of understanding or examining that. So don't say, "I will skip this."

You know, it is really quite simple to understand how desire comes into being. I see that beautiful sunset—there is the seeing. And seeing the beauty of it, the color of it, the delicacy of the leaves against the sky, the dark limb—it awakens in me the desire to keep on looking. That is: perception, sensation, contact, and desire. Right? It is nothing very complicated. I see a beautiful car, nicely polished, with clean lines—perception. I touch it—sensation. And then desire. I see a beautiful face, and the whole machinery of desire, lust, passion, comes out. That is simple.

The next question, which is a little more complex, is: What gives desire duration, continuity? If I could understand that, then I would know how to deal with desire. You are following? The trouble begins when desire has a continuity. Then I fight to fulfill it; then I want more of it. If I could find out the time element of desire, then I would know how to deal with it. We are going to go into it; I will show it to you.

We see how desire arises: seeing the car, the sunset, a beautiful face, a lovely ideal, the perfect man—the word denies the man. We see how desire comes into being. We are going to examine what gives desire the power, the strength, to make it last. What makes it last? It is obviously thought. I see the car, I have a great desire and I say, "I must have it." Thought, by thinking about it, gives it duration. The duration comes because of the pleasure I derive from the thought of that desire. Right? I see a beautiful house, architecturally and functionally excellent, and there is desire. Then thought comes in and says, "I wish I had it." Then I struggle. The whole problem begins. I cannot have it because I am a poor man; therefore, it gives me frustration, and I hate; and so the whole thing begins. So the moment thought

as pleasure interferes with desire, the problem arises. The moment thought which is based on pleasure interferes with desire, then the problem of conflict, frustration, battle begins.

So, if the mind can understand the whole structure of desire and the structure of thought, then it will know how to deal with desire. That is, as long as thought does not interfere with desire, desire comes to an end. You understand? Look! I see a beautiful house, and I can say that it is lovely. What is wrong with it? The house has nice proportions and is clean. But the moment thought says, "How good to have that and live in that!" the whole problem begins. So desire is not wrong, desire is never wrong; but thought interfering with it creates the problem. So instead of understanding desire and understanding thought, we try to suppress desire, control desire, or discipline desire. Right?

I hope you are all following all this, not merely listening, but working as hard as the speaker; otherwise, you are not partaking—then you are merely listening with one ear, and it is going out of the other; that is what we all do! Listening is to be attentive. And if you listen to this really, with all your heart, you will see this, and you will know then what life is—a totally different way of living.

So, we are examining the machinery of thinking. The machinery of thinking is essentially based on pleasure; it is like and dislike. And in pleasure there is always pain—obviously! I don't want pain, but I would like to have the constant continuation of pleasure. I want to discard pain. But to discard pain, I must also discard pleasure; the two cannot be divorced, they are one. So, by understanding thinking, I am going to find out if the pleasure principle can be broken. You understand?

Our thinking is based on pleasure. Though we have had a great deal of pain—not only physically but inwardly—a great deal of sorrow, a great deal of anxiety, fear, terror, despair, they are all the outcome of this demand to live and establish all values in pleasure. It does not mean that you must live without pleasure, or that you must indulge in pleasure. But in understanding this whole structure of the mind and the brain, which is based deeply on pleasure, we will know how to look at desire and not interfere with it, and therefore how to end the confusion and the sorrow which may be produced by prolonging it. Right?

Thought is mechanical. It is a very good computer! It has learned a great deal—many, many experiences, not only individual, collective, but human. It is there, in the conscious as well as in the unconscious. The total consciousness is the residue, is the machinery, of all thinking. And that thinking is based not only on imitation and conformity but always on pleasure. I conform because it gives me pleasure; I follow somebody because it gives me pleasure; I say, "He is wrong," because it gives me pleasure. When I say, "It is my country; I am willing to die for this country," it is because it gives me pleasure—which again is based on my greater pleasure of security and so on.

So thought is mechanical—it doesn't matter whose thought it is, including all your gurus, all your teachers, all your philosophers. It is the response of accumulated memory, and that memory, if you go much deeper into it, is based on this principle of pleasure. You believe in atma, the soul, or whatever you believe in—if you go down deeply, you will see it is pleasure! Because life is so uncertain—there is death, there is fear—you hope there is something much deeper than all this, and to that you give a name; this gives you immense comfort, and that comfort is pleasure. So thought, the machinery of thinking—however complex, however subtle, however original you may think it to be—is based on this principle.

So you have to understand this. And you can only understand when you are totally attentive. Now, when you listen with complete attention to what is being said, you will immediately see the truth of it or the falseness of it. There is nothing false about it because it is factual—we are dealing with facts, not with ideas which we can discuss or about which you have your opinion or somebody's opinion. These are facts, however ugly or however beautiful. And that is the way we have functioned for centuries upon centuries: we have thought, we have said to ourselves, "Thought can alter everything." Thought is based on pleasure, and will is the result of pleasure and we say, "From that we will alter everything." And when you examine, you will find that you cannot alter a thing unless you understand this pleasure principle.

So, when you understand all this, conflict ceases. You don't end conflict deliberately; conflict ceases—which does not mean you become a vegetable! But you have to understand desire, to observe it functioning daily and to watch the interference of thought, which gives desire a time element. In the examination and the understanding of these, there is inherent discipline. Sir, look! To listen to what is being said needs discipline—to listen not only verbally but inwardly, deeply, not according to some pattern. The very act of listening is discipline, surely—isn't it?

So, when the mind understands the nature of pleasure, thought, desire, that very examination brings with it discipline. Therefore there is no question of indulging, not indulging, should, should not—all that goes away. It is like some food you eat which gives you a tummy ache! If the pleasure of the tongue is greater than the tummy ache, then you go on eating, and you constantly say, "I must not eat"; you play a trick on yourself, but you go on eating. But when the pain becomes greater, then you pay attention to what you eat. But if you were attentive at the first moment when you had pain, then there would be no need to have the conflict between pleasure and pain. You are following?

So all this brings us to a certain point, which is that one must be a complete light to oneself. We are not, we rely on others. As you are listening, you are relying on the speaker to tell you what to do. But if you listen very carefully, the speaker is not telling you what to do; he is asking you to examine; he is telling you how to examine and what is implied in the examination. By examining very carefully, you are free of all dependence, and you are a light to yourself. That means you are completely alone.

We are not alone. We are lonely. You are the result of so many centuries of culture, propaganda, influence, climate, food, dress, what people have said and have not said, and so on; therefore, you are not alone. You are a result. And to be a light to yourself, you have to be alone. When you have discarded the whole psychological structure of society, of pleasure, of conflict, you are alone.

And this aloneness is not something to be dreaded, something which is painful. It is only when there is isolation, when there is loneliness, then there is pain, then there is anxiety, then there is fear. Aloneness is something entirely different because it is only the mind which is alone which is not influenceable. This means the mind has understood the principle of pleasure, and therefore nothing can touch it—nothing; no flattery, no fame, no capacity, no gift can touch it. And that aloneness is essential.

When you see the sunset attentively, you are alone—are you not? Beauty is always alone—not in the stupid, isolating sense. It is the quality of a mind that has gone beyond propaganda, beyond personal like and dislike, and that is not functioning on pleasure. A mind can perceive beauty only in aloneness. The mind has to come to that extraordinary state when it is not influenceable and there-

fore has freed itself from the environmental conditioning and the conditioning of tradition and so on. It is only such a mind that can proceed in its aloneness to examine or to observe what is silence. Because it is only in silence you can hear those screeching owls. If you are chattering with your problems and so on, you will never hear those owls. Because of silence, you hear. Because of silence, you act. And action is life.

When you understand desire, pleasure, thought, you have discarded all authority because authority of every kind—inward, outward—has led you nowhere. You have lost total faith in all authority, inwardly; therefore, you don't rely on anybody. Therefore through your examination of thought and of pleasure, you are alone. And being alone implies silence; you cannot be alone if you are not silent. And out of that silence is action. This needs further examination.

To us action is based on an idea—as an idea, a principle, a belief, a dogma. And according to that idea I act. If I can approximate that action according to my idea, I think I am a very sincere man, a very noble man! And there is always a difference between idea and action, and hence there is conflict. When there is conflict of any kind, there is no nobility, there is no clarity. You may be outwardly very saintly, lead a so-called very simple life—which means a loincloth and one meal. That is not a simple life. A simple life is much more demanding and far deeper than that. A simple life is a life in which there is no conflict.

So silence comes because there is aloneness. And that silence is beyond consciousness. Consciousness is pleasure, thought, and the machinery of all that, conscious or unconscious; in that field there can never be silence, and therefore in that field any action will always bring confusion, will always bring sorrow, will always create misery.

It is only when there is action out of this silence that sorrow ends. Unless the mind is completely free from sorrow—personal or otherwise—it lives in darkness, in fear, and in anxiety; and therefore, whatever its action, there will always be confusion, and whatever its choice, it will always bring conflict. So when one understands all that, there is silence, and where there is silence, there is action. Silence itself is action—not silence and then action. Probably this has never happened to you—to be completely silent. If you are silent, you can speak out of that silence though you have your memories, experiences, knowledge. If you had no knowledge, you would not be able to speak at all! But when there is silence, out of that silence, there is action; and that action is never complicated, never confused, never contradictory.

And when one has understood this principle of pleasure, thought, aloneness, and this emptiness of silence, when one has gone that far—not in point of time, but actually—then, because there is total attention, there is an act of silence in which there is total inaction, and this inaction is action; because it is totally inactive, there is an explosion. It is only when there is a total explosion that there is something new

taking place—new, which is not based on recognition and which is therefore not experienceable; therefore, it is not "I experience, and you come and learn from me how to experience."

So all these things come naturally, easily, when we understand this phenomenon of existence—which is relationship. Relationship is, with most of us, confusion, misery; and to bring about a tremendous, deep mutation, a radical change in it, one must understand desire, pleasure, thought, and also the nature of aloneness. Then out of that comes silence. And that silence, because it is totally inactive, acts when it is demanded to act; but as it is completely inactive and therefore without having any movement, there is an explosion. You know, scientists are saying that galaxies are formed when matter ceases to move and there is an explosion.

And it is only when there is an explosion that a new mind, a truly religious mind, comes into being. And it is only the religious mind that can solve human problems.

January 9, 1966

Bombay, India, 1966

---- ✳ ----

First Talk in Bombay

I think it is right that we should establish what we mean by "communication." We—both of us—must understand this question, because it is one of the most difficult things to communicate with another.

Most of us do not listen at all; we naturally have ideas—our own opinions, prejudices, conclusions—and these become a barrier and prevent us from listening. After all, if one is to listen, one must be attentive. And there is no attention if one is occupied with one's own thoughts, conclusions, opinions, and evaluations—then all communication ceases. This is an obvious fact, but unfortunately, though it is a fact, we rarely are aware of this fact. One has to put aside one's own thoughts, conclusions, and opinions, and listen—only then is communication possible.

Communication implies responsibility—responsibility on the part of the listener as well as on the part of the speaker. The speaker wishes to convey something, and the listener must partake, share, in what is being said. It is not a one-sided affair. Both you and the speaker must be in communication with each other; that is, the words the speaker uses must have the same meaning for you also. There must be not only a verbal communication but also an intellectual understanding of the words and also of the nature and significance of the words and the sentences. There must also be an emotional contact. You may be intellectually very aware of agreeing or disagreeing, rejecting or accepting; but that will not lead us far. Whereas if there were an intellectual awareness of what is being said, of what is implied, and also an emotional contact, then communication with each other would be possible.

Merely to listen to a talk of this kind intellectually has very little meaning. But if you could listen intellectually, emotionally, and physically—that is, if you could give your own total attention to what is being said—then communication would become an extraordinarily interesting affair. We rarely communicate anything to another directly. You have your conclusions, your experiences, your knowledge, your information, your tradition, the society, the culture in which you have been brought up; and if the speaker does not belong to the same category, the same tradition, the same culture, and if the speaker denies the whole structure of that culture, of that narrow, limited conditioning of mind, then communication between you and the speaker will be nil. So to communicate with each other, there must be not only an intellectual, rational, clear thought but also an open attention; and then only is it possible to understand very deeply what is being said—not agreeing or disagreeing but seeing the validity and the truth of what is being said. Therefore, it is responsibility on your part as well as on the part of the speaker.

We are going to share together, and sharing essentially is communication. If you merely hear what is being said and do not partake in what is being stated, then communication is not possible. Therefore, communication has significance only when both of us are in relationship, sharing the same problem and trying to find out not only the solution but also the full implications of the problem that one has. Then only, it seems to me, will "communication" and these talks have some meaning—which means really that one has to listen.

To listen, several things are required. First, one's own mind must be quiet; otherwise, it cannot listen. If your mind is chattering, opposing, agreeing or disagreeing, then you are not listening. But if you are quiet, if you are silent, and if in that silence there is attention, then there is the act of learning. And all communication is learning—not a repetition of what has been said—to a person who would understand, who would listen, who would really grapple with the many problems of life into which we are going.

One has to listen, one has to be in communion with the problem. And you cannot be in communication with the problem if you do not listen to it, if you do not learn the whole significance of that problem; and you cannot learn if there is no quietness, if there is no attention. And you have more or less to establish a relationship between the speaker and yourself: not a relationship which is based on words, on ideological conclusions, but a relationship that intends to investigate together the problem of existence—investigate together—not that you listen and the speaker investigates or explains, but both you and the speaker are going to take a journey together, a journey of exploration, a journey

of investigation, a journey to understand this extraordinary thing called life. This means an active sharing on your part, not a dull, indifferent attention, but an active sharing on the part of the listener who is taking the journey with the speaker.

One sees right throughout the world a general decline, a deterioration. Technologically there may be very tremendous advancement—electronic brains, computers, automation, going to the moon, and all the rest of the technological knowledge. There is also the so-called progress in science. And man has looked to science, to politics, to the so-called religions, to the organized beliefs, and so on to help him solve his many problems; and the problems have not been solved. Man has remained more or less as he has been for over two million years: miserable, unhappy, in conflict, in confusion, living in a state of despair, anxiety, guilt, not attaching any significance to existence, or giving significance to life according to his temperament, knowledge, despair, and so on. But man— you and I, as human beings—has not essentially changed; he is still greedy, envious, confused, miserable, at war. We all know this. A man who reads current history, the newspapers and the magazines, who listens to the radio, and so on, knows quite well what is taking place in his own city, in his own neighborhood, in his own country, and in other countries. He also knows that there is a deterioration, more or less, intellectually and so-called spiritually. Religion has no meaning any more except for old ladies and old men because they have to face death, and religion gives them some kind of hope. Religion has no meaning to a man who is active, thoughtful, rational, clear. There is a moral decline, as one can see in this country. There is a religious decline—not that there are not more swamis, yogis, and sects; that is an indication of decline because they are establishing that which is past—dead tradition that has no meaning whatsoever.

To a man who has observed the world, the misery, the wars, the endless sorrow of the human being—to him the scriptures, authority, beliefs, the rituals, the innumerable political speeches, the ideological and political commitments such as the communist, the socialist, the congress, the democrat, and the republican have no meaning any more. And it would be absurd, childish, immature, to look to those to bring about a change in the world, to bring about a good society—not a great society; a great society is not necessarily a good society.

Seeing all this, as you must, one demands naturally: Can human beings change? Can you and I change? Can you and I bring about in ourselves a mutation so profound that, as human beings, our relationship is not based on temporary, convenient, self-centered activity? Because what is most important is relationship. Unless there is a radical revolution in that relationship between two human beings, talking about God or about the scriptures, or going back to the Vedas, the Bible, and the rest of it, is sheer nonsense. It has no meaning whatsoever unless we establish right relationship between human beings.

And that will be the subject of our talk—how to bring about a fundamental revolution in our relationship so that there will be no war, so that countries are not divided by nationalities, by frontiers, by class differences, and so on. Unless we, you and I, establish such a relationship, not theoretically, not ideologically, not hypothetically, but actually, factually, there is bound to be a greater and greater decline and deterioration.

What do we mean by relationship? What does it mean to be related? First of all, are we related? Relationship means contact: to be together, to be related, to be in contact, to be in immediate contact with another human being, to know all his difficulties, his problems, his misery, his anxiety which is

your own. And in understanding yourself you understand the human being and, therefore, bring about a radical transformation in society. The "individual" has very little meaning, but the "human being" has a tremendous significance. The individual may change according to pressures, strains, circumstances; but his change will not radically affect society. But the problems of man, not as an individual but as a human being who has lived for two million years and much more, with his conflicts, with his anxieties, with his fears, with his coming face to face with death—the whole of that is the human issue. Unless we understand that—not as an individual, but as a human being—there is no possibility of bringing about a different culture, a different society.

So a radical transformation of the human being is absolutely essential. Because most of us are still animals. If you have observed animals, you will know how closely related we are! You observe the dog, a pet you know! How jealous he is! How he loves to be praised, to be petted, and so on, like human beings! So there is a very close relationship between the animal and the human being. Unless that animal in us is completely transformed, do what you will—have the most extravagant ideologies, commit yourself to any political, religious, or economic group—you are not going to solve the problem at all.

So we have to understand what relationship is first. Are we related? Is one human being related to another? We mean by relationship, don't we, to be in contact intellectually, emotionally, psychologically. Are we in such contact? Or, is there contact, relationship, between the image that you have about yourself and the image you have about another? You have an image about yourself, ideas about yourself, concepts, experiences, and so on. You have your particular idiosyncrasies, tendencies—all that has built an image about yourself. Please listen to it; observe it in yourself. Do not, as I said, merely listen to words—they have little meaning. But, in hearing the words, if the words reveal your own consciousness, your own state, then the words have meaning. If you observe, you have an image about yourself—that you are this, you are that; that you had this experience and that experience; that you are ugly or you are beautiful; that you want to be this or you want to be that. You have an image, an idea, a conclusion about yourself—that you are spiritual, that you are the atma, that you are the soul, or whatever it is. You have an image carved by the mind, or carved through your experience, through tradition, through circumstances, through strange pressures. There is that image of yourself, and the other person also has an image about himself. So these two images come into contact, and that is what we call relationship. Whether it is the most intimate relationship between a husband and wife or the image that you have created about Russia, about America, about Vietnam, about this or that, the contact between the two images is what we call relationship. Please do follow this. That is all the relationship we know.

You have an image about yourself, and you have created an image about another—whether he is an American or a Russian or a Chinese or this or that. You have an image about the Pakistani; you have an image about the Hindu, the Indian, with a line called the frontier—and you are willing to kill each other for the sake of that image. And that image is strengthened through a flag, through the national spirit, through hatred, and so on. So you are willing—please listen—to kill each other for the sake of a word, of an idea, of an image. The Chinese have an image about themselves, and they are willing to destroy anybody else for the sake of that image. There have been in the history of man, I believe, something like two and a half wars every year.

Man has not solved the problem of war. The first woman or the father must have cried out at the first battle. We are still crying. For us who are living in Bombay, far away from the frontier, war has very little meaning. But to everyone, as a human being, war is a problem, whether it is fought in Vietnam, in Russia, in Pakistan, or in India. It is a problem of relationship. This country which has talked about nonviolence, which has preached "ahimsa," "don't kill," for millennia, forgets it overnight and is willing to kill because it has an image about the other, and the other has an image about this country. And it is very strange, if you come to think of it, if you observe, that in this country which has talked about peace, nonviolence, morality, so-called spirituality, there has not been one human being who has said, "I will not fight"—not whisper among friends but shout it aloud as other people have done.

So all this shows what a terrible decline there is. Unless there is a radical revolution in our relationship, we will not have peace. And peace is absolutely necessary—not the peace of the politician, not the peace between two wars, not the peace between two quarrels, not the peace somewhere in faraway heaven, but peace here on this earth between you and me. We must have it. Because, unless you have peace, unless there is this extraordinary thing in your heart and in your mind, you cannot possibly blossom in goodness, you cannot flower in beauty, you cannot see the sky, you cannot see the beauty of the earth. If there is conflict in you, you cannot see anything. So peace, the thing that man has sought—not through some meditation, books and all that; we will come to all that later—is peace in relationship, so that two human beings can work together, think together, solve the problems together. We may stop wars because of the atom bombs or the new kind of bombs that may be developed, but that does not insure this peace.

This peace can only come about when there is in each one of us the understanding of relationship and the complete transformation in that relationship. So we must understand what this relationship means as it is, factually and not theoretically. It is the relationship of two images, and nothing else; and therefore there is no love between two images. How can I love you and you love me if you have an image about me, if you have ideas about me? If I have hurt you, if I have pushed you, if I have been ambitious, clever, and gone ahead of you, how can you love me? How can I love you if you threaten my position, my job, if you run away with my wife? If you belong to one country and I to another, if you belong to one sect—Hinduism or Buddhism or Catholicism and the rest of it—and I am a Muslim, how can we love each other? So unless there is a radical transformation in relationship, there cannot possibly be peace. By becoming a monk or a sannyasi and running away to the hills, you are not going to solve your problems. Because wherever you live, whether in a monastery or in a cave or in a mountain, you are related. You cannot possibly isolate yourself either from your own image which you have created about God, about truth, or from your own image about your own self and all the rest of it.

So to establish right relationship is to destroy the image. Do you understand what it means to destroy the image? It means to destroy the image about yourself—that you are a Hindu, that I am a Pakistani, a Muslim, a Catholic, a Jew, or a communist, and so on. You have to destroy the machinery that creates the image—the machinery that is in you and the machinery that is in the other. Otherwise you may destroy one image, and the machinery will create another image. So one has not only to find out the existence of the image—that is, to be aware of your par-

ticular image—but also to be aware of what the machinery is that creates the image.

Now let us see what that machinery is. You understand my question? That is, first one has to be conscious, to be aware, to know—not verbally, not intellectually, but actually know as a fact—the existence of this image. It is one of the most difficult things because to know the image implies a great deal. You can know, you can observe that microphone—that is a fact. You may call it by different names, but if we understand what you call by these names, then we see the fact of it. So there is no interpretation there; we both know it is a microphone. But it is a different thing to understand the image without interpretation, to see the fact of that image without the observer, because the observer is the image-maker, and the image is part of the observer. This is a very complex thing. You cannot just say, "I will destroy the image," and meditate about it, or do some kind of trick, or hypnotize yourself so that you can destroy the image—it is not possible. It requires tremendous understanding. It requires great attention and exploration, not a conclusion at any time; a man that is exploring can never come to a conclusion. And life is an immense river that is flowing, moving incessantly. Unless you follow it freely, with delight, with sensitivity, with great joy, you cannot see the full beauty, the volume, the quality of that river. So we must understand this problem.

When we use the word *understand*, we mean by that word, don't we, not intellectually. Perhaps you have understood the word *image*, how it is created by knowledge, by experience, by tradition, by the various strains and stresses in family life, work in the office, the insults—all that makes up the image. What is the machinery that makes that image? You understand? The image must be put together. The image must be maintained; otherwise, it will collapse. So you must find out for yourself how this machinery works. And when you understand the nature of the machinery and the significance of that machinery, then the image itself ceases to be—the image—not only the conscious image, the image that you have of yourself consciously and are aware of superficially, but also the image deep down, the whole of it. I hope I am making this thing clear.

One has to go into it and find out how the image comes into being and if it is possible to stop the machinery that creates it. Then only is there a relationship between human beings—it will not be between two images, which are dead entities. It is very simple. You flatter me, you respect me; and I have an image about you, through insult, through flattery. I have experience—pain, death, misery, conflict, hunger, loneliness. All that creates an image in me; I am that image. Not that I am the image, not that the image and I are different; but the 'me' is that image; the thinker is that image. It is the thinker that creates the image. Through his responses, through his reactions—physical, psychological, intellectual, and so on—the thinker, the observer, the experiencer, creates that image through memory, through thought. So the machinery is thinking, the machinery comes into existence through thought. And thought is necessary; otherwise, you cannot exist.

So, first see the problem. Thought creates the thinker. The thinker begins to create the image about himself: he is the atma, he is God, he is the soul, he is a Brahmin, he is a non-Brahmin, he is a Muslim, he is a Hindu, and the rest of it. He creates the image and he lives in it. So thinking is the beginning of this machinery. And you will say, "How can I stop thinking?" You cannot. But one can think and not create the image. One can observe that one is a communist or a Muslim. You can observe this, but why should you create an image about yourself? You only

create an image about me as a Muslim, as a communist, or whatever it is because you have an image about yourself which judges me. But if you had no image about yourself, then you would look at me, observe me, without creating the image about me. That is why this requires a great deal of attention, a great deal of observation of your own thoughts, feelings.

So one begins to see that most of our relationship is actually based on this image-formation, and having formed the image, one establishes or hopes to establish relationship between two images. And naturally there is no relationship between images. If you have an opinion about me and if I have an opinion about you, how can we have any relationship? Relationship exists only when it is free, when there is freedom from this image-formation—we will go into this during the talks that come. Only when this image is broken up and the image-formation ceases will there be the ending of conflict, the total ending of conflict. Then only will there be peace, not only inwardly, but also outwardly. It is only when you have established that peace inwardly that the mind, being free, can go very far.

You know, sir, freedom can only exist when the mind is not in conflict. Most of us are in conflict, unless we are dead. You hypnotize yourself, or identify yourself with some cause, some commitment, some philosophy, some sect, or some belief—you are so identified that you are just mesmerized, and you live in a state of sleep. Most of us are in conflict; the ending of that conflict is freedom. With conflict you cannot have freedom. You may seek, you may want it; but you can never have it.

So relationship means the ending of the machinery which puts together the image, and with the ending of that machinery, right relationship is established. Therefore there is the ending of conflict. And when there is the end of conflict, there is freedom, obviously—

actual freedom, not as an idea, but the actual state as a fact. Then in that state of freedom, the mind, which is no longer twisted, no longer tortured, which is not biased, which is not given to any fancy, any illusion, any mystical conception, or vision—that mind can go very far. Far, not in time or space, because there is no space and time when there is freedom. I am using the words *very far* in the sense that then we can discover—these are words which really have no meaning—then in that freedom there is a state of emptiness, a state of joy, a bliss which no God, no religion, no book can give you.

That is why unless this relationship is established between you and your wife, your neighbor, your society, between you and other people, you will never have peace and therefore no freedom. And as a human being, not as an individual, you can then transform society. Not the socialist, not the communist—nobody will do it. Only the man that has understood what right relationship is—only such a man can bring about a society in which a human being can live without conflict.

February 13, 1966

Second Talk in Bombay

If we may, we will continue with what we were talking about the other day. We were saying how important it is that there should be a radical revolution—a revolution not merely in the outward structure of society but also deep within the human mind and heart, a revolution that is not planned, that is not an ideological revolution or a revolution brought about by circumstances.

It is really a very complex problem because several things are involved in it. First we must examine the issue and understand as deeply and widely as possible the implications of this change. We all demand certain forms of change, outwardly, socially. We want, don't we, a society that is more capable of dealing with human affairs; politically, economically, we want more efficiency. And also deep within oneself, one realizes that superficial changes—however necessary, however good they are—somehow do not seem to answer the total demand of man.

We need something far deeper, far greater. And man has always been hunting after it, seeking it, through temples, through reforms, through various forms of social edicts and religious sanctions. One has wandered through the maze of all this. If one is aware of this situation, apparently one does not get anywhere. And invariably one falls in a kind of despair, lives with that despair and rationalizes it, and gives to that despair intellectual significance. Or one accepts traditional beliefs, going back to the past and living in that sanctuary, unthinking, blind, unquestioning, accepting, because that gives great comfort, because it pacifies an inquiring mind. And an intelligent, capable, inquiring mind rejects all this because there is no truth in the past, nor in the future. Truth is beyond the field of time; and so, going back to what has been said by the ancients—however wise, however true—has no meaning whatsoever in the present; but yet the mind clings to it because it has a certain fascination, it gives a certain hope. And most of us demand something to lean upon, something to hold on to, something created by the mind, or an image that hands have made, or a philosophy that gives us satisfaction. But when one has wandered through all this, the central problem still remains.

One sees that there must be order in society and there must be freedom in the widest sense of that word. And one also demands order within oneself. You cannot have order through compulsion—then that becomes merely a military affair. If you compel yourself, distort your mind, force it, suppress it, hoping thereby to bring about order, surely it brings about disorder. So force, compulsion, determination, a compulsive urge to bring about the change will not bring about a change at all; it brings about only greater disorder—which is obvious to anybody who has observed. We need social order, and also we need an inward order. And if we look at it deeply, the two are not different. We divide life, unfortunately, into the outer and the inner. Either we neglect the outer and concentrate on the inner or we discard the inner and accept the world as it is and make the best of it outwardly. We do not say that it is a single unitary movement, the outer and the inner. Unless there is outward order, there is no inward order. And to bring about inward order, the outward world must be understood and not treated as something illusory, not discarded as irreligious or as something a religious person will not touch. The two go together; they cannot be divorced at any time.

So, seeing this, how is one, a human being, to come upon this total revolution? And we mean by this "total revolution" not a revolution which is merely superficial, intellectual, moral, ethical, artistic, and so on; it is a total revolution, right through one's being. Because, if there is no sense of beauty and therefore no sense of love, however much one may outwardly bring about a reform in one's behavior, in one's conduct, in one's attitude and value, such conduct, value, and behavior have little meaning. So beauty and that strange word that we all call "love" cannot be manufactured, cannot be put together by force, cannot be the result of any form of outward compulsion. And that quality of beauty in its very essence is sensitivity, and a mind that is not sensitive, alert, watchful, aware, cannot respond totally.

So our question is: How can a brain as well as the mind—that is, the total human being—physiologically, neurologically, completely change? How can the human being completely change? Such a change is necessary—one sees that. And unless there is a change, there will always be war—one nation against another, one nationality against another, all that terrible brutality of war, your country against another country, the linguistic differences, the economic differences, the social differences, the moral differences and the everlasting battle, outward and inward. There must be change. Now, how is one to bring it about?

Please see the extraordinary complexity of this question, what is involved in it. Man has tried so many ways—gone away to the monasteries, renounced the world and taken *sannyas*, gone into the woods and meditated, fasted, become a celibate, has done everything that he could possibly imagine, has mesmerized himself, has forced himself, has examined, analyzed his consciousness, the conscious and the unconscious—he has done everything to bring about a radical revolution within himself. And he has been ruthless therefore in himself, not only as an individual, but as a human being—the two are entirely different. The individual is a local entity: a Parsi, a Buddhist, a Muslim, and so on. The individual is conditioned by the environment. But the human being is beyond that; he is concerned with the total man—not about his country, the linguistic differences, his little wars and quarrels, his petty little gods, and so on—he is concerned with the whole state of man, his conflict, his despair. When you see the whole, then you can understand the particular. But the particular cannot possibly understand the whole. So, for the constantly introspective individual, inquiry has no meaning at all because he is still concerned within the pattern of his own existence, conditioned by society—in which is included religion and all the rest of it. Whereas man—as a human being who has lived for two million years—has suffered, has thought, has inquired, has borne, whether in Russia, in China, in America, or here.

And man, the human being, has done everything to bring about a radical change; and yet, fundamentally, man has not changed at all. We are what we have been for two million years! The animal is very strong in us. The animal with all its greed, envy, ambition, anger, ruthlessness still exists deep down in our hearts and minds. And we have through religion, through culture, through civilization, polished the outer; we have better manners—perhaps a few of us have better manners. We know a little more. Technologically we have gone very far. We can discuss Western and Eastern philosophy, literature; we can travel all over the world. But inwardly, deep down, the roots are very firmly embedded.

Seeing all this, how is one—you as a human being and I as a human being—how are we to change? Certainly not through tears, certainly not through intellection, not through following an ideological utopia, not through external tyranny, nor through self-imposed tyranny. So one discards all this, and I hope you have also discarded all this. Do you understand? To discard one's nationality; to discard one's gods, one's traditions, one's beliefs; to discard all the things that we have been brought up to believe in—to discard all this is a very difficult thing to do. We may intellectually agree, but deep down in the unconscious there is the insistence on the importance of the past to which we cling. Now you know the problem. We have sufficiently examined it, and it is useless to go into it in greater detail.

So the question is: How is one, a human being, to bring about such a tremendous change in himself that one still remains in this world, functions technologically and is able to reason sanely, rationally, healthily? Will—that is, desire strengthened—does not bring about change because will is the result of, is based on, desire, and desire is part of pleasure. Follow this a little. I need to change as a human being. What am I to do? I can see that exercising will to control, to suppress, to have a drive—a positive assertive direction which the will does give—does not bring about this change. Because in that exercise of will, there is conflict; and wherever there is conflict, obviously there cannot be a change. A conflict cannot produce a change. If you and I are in conflict about some issue—as you are, as your country is, with another country—in that conflict there is no understanding, there is no harmony, there is no coming together. Wherever, at whatever state, at whatever level, there is conflict, there can be no change. So change cannot be brought about through conflict, and the very nature of will not only is the product of conflict but also creates conflict. Please listen. You must understand this before you proceed further.

You see, pleasure is the very principle upon which our brain functions. All our values are based on pleasure. Our concern, our motive, our principle, our morality—all this is essentially based on pleasure. All your gods, your hopes, and the whole structure of your values and evaluations are based on pleasure. Please do not deny it. We are exploring. Do not accept, but examine. If you say, "No, some of my values are tremendously noble," then examine. If you examine that which you call "noble," you will see that, essentially, behind it there is the principle of pleasure.

So the change brought about through will and pleasure is no change at all. That is, through determination, through an idea, through a conflict, change is not possible; it is merely a reformation, a movement within the same field, and therefore not a radical revolution. So one has to see that the application of will has no meaning at all when we are thinking of change. Will implies suppression, resistance, conformity, acceptance, obedience, the authority of another or of yourself. So, when you examine, you will see that if you are concerned with a radical revolution in the total existence of man, will has no place at all. But most of us, most of the human beings throughout the world have accepted will as a means of change. When you discard will—or rather, when you understand the whole structure and the nature of will, and therefore it has no importance whatever any more—then what are you faced with? Do you understand my question?

Man has used energy, which is, after all, will; that will creates conflict, which is still energy. And man has lived in conflict and has accepted that as the role of life, as the pattern of life, as the pattern of existence. That is, we accept conflict as inevitable. Man has lived for two million years in conflict, and so we have got used to that, and we say that it is inevitable—the conflict between man and wife, between man and man, between country and country, and all the rest of it. We say that conflict is inevitable, but it is still the action of energy, surely. If you had no energy, there would be no conflict at all. If you had no energy to quarrel, to wrangle, to discuss, there would be no conflict. So, how is one to find the release of energy, such that that energy does not create conflict at all? You understand? Am I making myself clear?

Look, sir! Energy is life. Whatever we do, think, or feel is part of that energy. Without energy we would be dead. And that energy is creating conflict all the time. That is how we live. Our thoughts, our feelings, our ambitions, and all that we do, breed conflict. Is it possible to release this energy, such that in the very release of it, conflict ceases?

Take a simple example. If you look at a tree, there are two ways of looking at it. Either you look at it with thought, or you look at it without thought and yet you are intensely aware of that tree. That is, when you look at a tree, what takes place? There is visual perception; then there is the naming of the tree and generalizing it, and so not actually looking at it. You try to look at that tree. When you look at that tree, you immediately say it is a mango tree, it is this or that. That very activity of naming that tree is the process of bringing about conflict. Whereas if you had not named, but actually observed, then there would be no conflict between you and that. Please do it sometime when you are quiet in your room. Look at a flower. Do it. You will discover it for yourself—first of all, how difficult it is to look at something. To look at something, you must give your total attention. And to give your total attention, there must be no verbalization because that becomes inattention. When I look at that flower and say, "It is a rose, I like it," or "I don't like it, I wish it were something else," and so on, I am inattentive. Therefore I am not looking. Whereas to look or to listen, I must be completely attentive. Listen to those crows. Either you listen inattentively or you listen with complete attention. If you listen with complete attention, there is no irritation, there is no conflict; you do not say, "I wish they would go away." It is only when you are inattentive— that is, when you want to listen to the speaker and discard that noise of the crows— that, in that state of inattention, there is conflict. This is simple, and you can work it out for yourself.

So conflict comes into existence only when there is inattention. Please listen to this. You cannot train yourself to be attentive. But you can be aware that you are inattentive. And when you are aware that you are inattentive, you are attentive. So what we are concerned with is to bring about this change without any conflict—conflict in the conscious mind or at the lower levels of consciousness, totally right through one's being. And the fundamental change cannot be brought about under any circumstances through conflict. Therefore if you see that, then will, discipline, control, subjugation, and adjustment have no meaning whatsoever. When you understand very clearly that there is no radical revolution in conformity, in obedience, in suppression, or in acceptance, then you will find out for yourself if you are really, deeply interested in this radical revolution of the human being. Then, you have to find out whether it is possible to live in this world using your brain completely, rationally, sanely and yet not have conflict at any level. I am going to go into that.

You know, there is so little beauty in our life. We have become so insensitive to nature; our minds, our hearts, and our brains have become insensitive because we are so occupied with our own problems, with our own interests and issues, and because we have accepted conflict as the way of life. And where there is conflict, there is no feeling. Conflict and love cannot go together. And yet the way of our life—in the office, in the temple, in the church, on the street—is a series of either casual or important conflicts. And if we would change all that, we must understand not only how to look at a tree, how to listen to the silence of an evening, but also how to live in a society which is so corrupt, which in its very essence is disorder.

To understand all this, we must understand the nature of our thinking. Our brain is the machinery of thought, and that thought is the result of a great many experiences. Before I go into this, please listen—not agreeing, because there is no agreement about this. I am not doing any propaganda. I

am not trying to make you change into something else. If you are observant, you yourself will bring about this change. Please listen. As you are listening to those birds, as you see of a night the beauty of the stars and the quiet tranquillity of a rich river, in the same way listen—not intellectually, not merely to words, but to the implications of the words. Very few of us are capable of listening because we have already our prejudices, our conclusions. We think we know. We are never learning.

To learn there must be listening, and when you listen there is attention. And there is attention only when there is silence. So, to learn there must be silence, attention, and observation. And that whole process is learning, not accumulating, learning as you are going, learning in doing—not having learned, doing. We are learning as we are going, as we are doing—not having learned, doing; the two things are entirely different. We are learning as we are examining, as we are observing—not that we have learned and then we observe. The two movements are entirely different.

Now what we are doing is learning in doing, because you are not being taught. There is no teacher or pupil. There is no guru. Because one has to walk by one's own light, not in the light of another. If you walk in the light of another, it leads to darkness. And it is very important to understand this—that you are learning. And to learn there must be silence. How can you learn if your mind is chattering, how can you look, how can you attend? Look at a boy who is learning in a school. If he is really interested in his subject, he is essentially quiet in himself and giving his attention; and from this attention he is learning. Even if he wants to look out of the window, that very act, to look, is part of that learning.

So what we are doing is learning. And to learn there is no teacher who teaches; all that one needs is attention, that sense of simple, quiet silence, and then one learns. Then, in that, there is no book, no teacher, no one to point out to you; the whole thing is happening.

So we are concerned with a way of life in which all conflict has ceased. We are going to learn. Not "what am I to do in order to live without conflict?" That is the most immature, childish question; and the moment you ask it, you create the man who will teach you what to do, and therefore you are caught. Whereas you have to see that learning is in doing; whether there is a mistake or no mistake—that is irrelevant.

Learning is in doing, not in being taught—except technologically; technologically, I need to be helped about the electronic brain and so on. But there is no one to teach you, and the learning has to begin. What another teaches is not truth. The follower destroys truth, as the guru does. So you have to learn, and learning is in doing—that is the beauty of learning. Therefore learning becomes a joy, a delight, not a bore, not something that you will have to do.

So to go into this question of how to live without conflict at all the levels of our being—intellectually, in our emotions, in our feelings, in our physical ways—we have to learn. Though the speaker may explore for you, you have to learn, and this means that you are exploring with him. Therefore learning is always together—which means learning is always a process of relationship. Please understand the beauty of this. You cannot learn by yourself. Learning is in doing, and the doing is in relationship—not withdrawing, examining, analyzing, and then learning. Learning is an act of relationship and relationship is life. And life is this tremendous movement of everyday existence, which is relationship. And to find a way of

living in which there is no conflict is the greatest discovery, the greatest way.

So, before we begin to examine—which we will do probably at the next meeting—the first thing to realize is that conflict, however much it is part of our life, cannot possibly produce, under any circumstances, a life of deep awareness, silence, and beauty. A man in conflict cannot possibly love. An ambitious man has no love at all. How can he? He is in conflict, he is being frustrated, he wants to fulfill, his drive is towards that. Therefore, there is no beauty, no affection, no tenderness. He may have sentimentality, emotionalism, but that is not love.

So the deep realization that conflict in any form, under any circumstances, however much one is used to it, however much one has lived in it, destroys, perverts—a mind that realizes that has learned the implication of conflict and begins to learn a way of life in which there is no conflict at all, and yet it will be tremendously alive, will not go to sleep, will not become lethargic, inactive, dull, stupid. It is the man in conflict who leads a dull, stupid, insensitive life—not the man who is free from conflict.

But to understand and to come upon this extraordinary state of mind in which there is no conflict, one has to understand the structure and the nature of conflict and see actually, objectively, the whole business of it. Then, seeing that, one can move to the next. But without seeing that you can never go beyond it. It is like a man who talks about the beauty of life, listens to music, goes to the theatre, sees the trees of an evening against the setting sun, but does not notice the filth of the street. Because he has got used to the filth of the street, the dirt, the squalor, the poverty, he is not really a man who loves beauty. To love beauty you must also be aware of the dirt, the squalor, the poverty, and the inhumanity.

February 16, 1966

Third Talk in Bombay

As we were saying the last time that we met here, learning is an important factor in life. Learning can only take place as an action, when there is silence as well as attention—in that state the mind learns. But that word *learning* generally implies, doesn't it, acquiring knowledge based on experience or study, committing certain ideas or principles or concepts to memory, and acting from that memory, from that knowledge. That is generally implied in that word learning. But we do not mean that at all. We mean something entirely different: learning as we go along, learning in doing—not "having learned and then doing."

The learning which we are talking about needs attention. And when you attend seriously, there is a quality of silence in that. If you would attend to the noise that is going on about here—the noise of the crows, the buses, the people sitting around you—if you attend to the various colors, the expressions, and so on, when you attend, in that attention, if you will observe for yourself, you will see that there is a certain state of silence. And, in that silence and attention there is a process of learning. This implies naturally a certain serious, earnest mind.

Again, we have to explain what we mean by that word *serious*. Most of us think one to be very serious when one is following a certain principle, a belief, an idea, or a formula; committing oneself to a particular course of action and pursuing it; or having an ideal and trying to live according to that ideal or principle, or according to a purpose or an objective. When a person does all these things, we consider him a serious person, an earnest person. I do not think such people are earnest. Because earnestness implies application, not according to an idea or a formula, but application to learning, to apply one's whole attention to learning—learning not only a particular subject, a particular part of life, but the whole of life, which is a vast field. If one commits oneself to a particular part of that life and devotes one's attention to that particular part, such activity obviously is not a very serious action. Whereas learning about the whole of life—that is, the whole of consciousness—means a great deal of attention. A person who takes just one part of that great field, which we call consciousness, and applies his whole mind to that particular part—I do not consider such a person at all serious. Whereas a person is serious, earnest, passionate, intense, when he tries to comprehend or learn about the whole process of consciousness, that is, the whole of life.

So what we are going to do this evening, if we may, is to learn about this particular thing called "consciousness," to learn about consciousness, obviously, you must come to it afresh. You may have read books, you may have ideas, opinions; but what you have read, your opinions, your knowledge according to somebody—all that is not *what is,* is not the fact. To understand a fact, opinions are not necessary; on the contrary, they are a hindrance. And to inquire into this consciousness, one must be free, not bound to any particular theory or knowledge.

So the first requirement of a serious human being who wants to learn is that he must be free to inquire—that means, not to be afraid; to be free to look, to observe, to criticize; to be intelligently skeptical, and not to accept opinions. We are going to inquire into something that demands all your attention, and you cannot attend if you have an opinion, an idea, a formula, or knowledge of what other people have said. As we said the other day, if you walk in the light of another, that light will lead you to darkness—it does not matter who it is that offers you light. But to walk in the light of one's own understanding—that can only come about when there is attention and silence, and that demands a great deal of seriousness.

As we were saying the other day, great changes are taking place in the world, in the scientific field, and in the field of medicine. There is the computer, there is automation; these are going to give man a great deal of leisure. That leisure has probably not come yet, but it is coming. Man is going to have great freedom and leisure to do what he will. Science also is probing into the question of prolonging life indefinitely, and bringing about children through different methods, and so on. All this is taking place, and that is going to revolutionize the whole of society. The family, the relationship between husband and wife—all that is going to be revolutionized. A great change is going on in the world at the present time, economically, socially, scientifically, and medically.

What is going to happen to man—that is, to you and to me—in this tremendous revolution that is taking place? What is the purpose of man? Why does he exist at all? When machinery, technology, and medicine are going to give great leisure, to prolong life indefinitely, why does man exist, what for? Drudgery and work are going to be taken away from him. There is already talk of giving man a certain sum of money when he is born, and letting him be free. That is coming. Everything is possible now. What is man to do? This is a very serious question. What are we as human beings going to do in this world when the whole idea of soul, reincarnation, and the continued existence of a particular individual is all gone?

So we have to learn anew about a new way of living. To find that out, one has to inquire into this state of mind, into this consciousness, whether it is possible fundamentally—at the very basis, at the very root—to change the totality of this consciousness. We mean by consciousness, don't we, the thought, the feeling, and the action, conscious or unconscious. That is what we generally mean by consciousness—the whole process of thinking. The senses that create the feeling, the formulas, the concepts, the ideas, the opinion, the belief that there is or that there is not—all that is within the field of consciousness. And that consciousness is the result of time—time as duration, as years, as a process of evolution. From the thoughtless to the most profound thinking, from the superficial feeling to the great depths of feeling—all that implies a great stretch of time, not only time by the watch, but also time psychologically, that is, inwardly. Thought is consciousness, thought is time. And this thinking process has taken centuries of experience, knowledge, pain, suffering, and all the rest of it, so that we are able to think.

There is thinking consciously or thinking unconsciously. And the unconscious, as well as the conscious, is still within consciousness, and we divide it for convenience; in fact, there is no such division. Now all that is the result of centuries of experience, knowledge, information, tradition—the tradition of the enormous past, or the tradition of a few years or a few days—the technological influence, the technological knowledge. All that is within that field of consciousness, both the conscious as well as the unconscious. Within that field we act. And within that field there is sorrow, pleasure, pain—there is the conscious sorrow, or the deep, undiscovered, brooding sorrow.

And to bring about a radical change—that must lie beyond this consciousness; that is beyond time. But any thought within this field of consciousness is still of time. Therefore we say that to bring about a change radically, we need time, we need a gradual process. Either we say we will change immediately—still within the field of consciousness—or we say there will be change in our next life or future life, which also is still within the field of consciousness. So, as long as thought is functioning within that field, thought being time, thought cannot produce a change at all. It can only bring about a modification, a continued modified activity, an adjustment. But within that field there is no possibility of radical change at all. I think this must be very clearly understood between us. Because in that field every action is the result of thought, conscious or unconscious; and that thought creates certain values, and those values are based on pleasure. All our values are based on pleasure. The moral, ethical, so-called noble values are essentially based on pleasure. And as long as we are functioning and bringing about, or trying to bring about, a change within that field through thought, there is no change at all because thought can only create conflict.

Please do not accept or disagree or deny what is being said. Examine, look at it as though you are looking at it for the first time, if you can. After all, that is the art of listening, isn't it? Most of us do not listen at all. You hear, but to listen implies attention. And to attend, every value, opinion, judgment, evaluation, interpretation must be set aside; and then only can you listen to your friend, to your wife, or to anything. So in the same way, we have to find out how to bring about in the human mind, in the human heart, a total revolution—not in terms of time, not in terms of evolution.

Thought is the whole machinery of accumulating memory through experience, through knowledge, through various forms of pressures and stresses and influences. That thought cannot under any circumstances bring about a radical revolution. Why can't it? Because that thought is essentially based on pleasure, and where there is pleasure, there is always pain. All our social, moral, and ethical values are based on pleasure. And our belief—which is a process of thinking—in God or no-God, is still the search for comfort, for security, psychologically, which is still based on pleasure. And therefore there is always conflict and effort. When there is ac-

tion in the field of consciousness, as the consciousness is of time, any action within that field is bound to breed conflict and sorrow. So to bring about a radical revolution in a human being, the radical revolution is to be outside the field of consciousness.

Man has lived for two million years or more, but he has not solved the problem of sorrow. He is always sorrow-ridden: he has sorrow as his shadow or as his companion. Sorrow of losing somebody; sorrow in not being able to fulfill his ambitions, his greed, his energy; sorrow of physical pain; sorrow of psychological anxiety; sorrow of guilt; sorrow of hope and despair—that has been the lot of man; that has been the lot of every human being. And he has always tried to solve this problem—to end sorrow within the field of consciousness—by trying to avoid it, by running away from sorrow, by suppressing it, by identifying himself with something greater than himself, by taking to drink, to women, by doing everything in order to avoid this anxiety, this pain, this despair, this immense loneliness and boredom of life—which is always within this field of consciousness, which is the result of time.

So man has always exercised thought as a means to get rid of sorrow by right effort, by right thinking, by living morally, and so on. The exercise of thought has been his guide—thought with intellect, and all the rest of it. But thought is the result of time, and time is this consciousness. Whatever you do within the field of this consciousness, sorrow can never end. Whether you go to the temple, or you take to drink, both are the same. So, if there is learning, one sees that through thought there is no possibility of a radical change, but there will be continuity of sorrow. If one sees that, then one can move in a different dimension. I am using the word *see* in the sense not intellectually, not verbally, but with a total understanding of this fact—the fact that sorrow cannot be ended through thought. This does not mean that you suppress thought. By negating thought, thought merely negates thought, but thought still remains.

To see a fact is one of the most difficult things. It is very simple to see the fact of this microphone. There it is; you and I have given a particular name to this object, and we say that we both see this microphone, whether it is a good microphone or a bad microphone. But to look at that tree becomes a little more complex. Because when you look at that tree, thought looks at that tree, not your eyes. Observe it, you will see it yourself. Look at a flower! Who is looking? Your eyes? Seeing with eyes means there is no opinion, no thought, no judgment, no naming but looking. When you say you are looking at a flower, your mind is looking; that is, thought is looking, thought is operating; so you never see the flower. The flower is an objective thing. But if you go inwardly to look at a fact—the inward fact, the true fact of something—it is almost impossible because of all your prejudices, your memories, your experiences, your pleasure, your pain—all that interferes with your observation. So sorrow cannot end at any time through thought—thought being the totality of thought and feeling; in that area of consciousness, do what you will, there is no end to sorrow. That is a fact, because man has never been free from that sorrow.

So time, thought, cannot bring about a change. And change in the most profound sense is absolutely necessary because we cannot go on as we are, with our separatist, narrow, nationalistic, and all the other stupidities we have accumulated through centuries, with our gods, with our beliefs, with our rituals, and all that sheer nonsense. Because we do not know what love means. How can we love if there is sorrow in our hearts, in our minds? How can we love if there is competition, greed, envy? We have

lived with violence, and we shall go on living with violence unless there is a radical, timeless change. So if you see the fact that time does not bring about a radical revolution, either outwardly or inwardly, then what takes place?

We need social change, a complete revolution in our relationship between man and man, which has bred this monstrous society. There is violence in our heart, in our relationship. Each person is concerned about himself and not about another. And action invariably breeds conflict; all our life, whatever we are doing, only brings confusion, misery, conflict. Again this is a fact. Whether that action is a conscious action or an unconscious action, it breeds conflict in all our being—whatever we do. Because the unconscious is much stronger than the conscious reasoning, conscious, deliberate activity. Please look into yourself deeply, not according to Freud or anybody else, but actually. And to look at yourself you must be free to look. If you say, "This is right or this is wrong; this is good or this is bad; I must do this or I must not do this," then you are not free to look, to observe, to wander in this extraordinary field of consciousness. So the unconscious is very strong. It is the racial, communal repository, and that guides much more than the conscious mind. And it has its own motives, its own drives, its own purposes. It gives intimation through dreams and all the rest of it—I am not going into it now. So, unless there is a radically fundamental revolution, the human conflict will endure forever. Though we may prolong our physical organism indefinitely, though we may have leisure through automation and electronic brains, sorrow and conflict will always exist.

So what is one to do? Do you understand my question? Is man to live forever in conflict, in sorrow, never knowing what it is to be totally free, and therefore perhaps never knowing what it is to love? When you realize that time, thought, is not the way to end sorrow, then what takes place? Realize—do you know what we mean by "realizing"? When you realize that a particular road does not lead to your home, you turn your back on that road and take another road. You do not insist on pursuing that road. If you insist on going on that road which does not lead to your home, mentally there is some imbalance; you are not sane, you are deaf, you are blind, insisting that road will lead to your home. That is exactly what we are doing. We insist that thought, time, evolution, will bring us out of this chaos, misery.

So knowing that action does inevitably breed sorrow—as it does in our life—and that inaction also breeds ugliness and all the rest of it, what is the human being to do? Or is there anything to be done? You understand my question? We have gone to temples, we have meditated, we have found new ways of prolonging life, and so on, we have done everything we can, we have applied our intelligence, we have committed ourselves to a course of action—communist, religious, or any other kind of action. And yet there is no freedom, there is no end to sorrow; there is conflict, there is constant effort. Seeing all that, a sane, rational man would say, "That is not the way, I will not pursue that way any more." It is only when you see very clearly that the road does not lead to your home that you do not go along that road. But to see that is to learn about the totality of thought and feeling, which is consciousness. That is, through thinking, through thought which creates activity of various kinds, through those activities, through those thoughts and feelings, there is no end to conflict, and therefore no end to sorrow. To see that fact, as you would see the fact of this microphone, as you would see the fact of those trees—it requires attention. And when you attend, your whole consciousness is silent; there is

no interference of thought. And that is the way to find out, to learn.

So is there a dimension beyond and above this consciousness? Don't jump to the conclusion that it is God; that is silly. A conscious mind thinking about God is still within the limitation of its own consciousness. You understand? If you think about God, your God is the creation of your thinking; and your thinking being the result of time, your God is of time; it has no meaning. Yet we believe, we want to be sane, we want to find truth—all this through the process of thinking. One can ask the question whether there is a different dimension. It is not a theoretical question but a valid question, a fundamental question, only when one has understood the nature of time. You understand?

Look, sir! The world is exploding in population. Go down the street and watch the millions—uneducated, backward, superstitious, and all the rest of it. And compassion, sympathy, says, "They will have another chance, next life; they will evolve as you evolve." We all believe in that. We do not want to think that our life has been lived in confusion, and that we would go down the gutter as so many people have done, like so many fish thrown away. We say only a few can realize this extraordinary freedom outside consciousness. So, we invent, or we hope that there is, evolution—that is, gradually man will become more and more free, more and more loving, kind, nonviolent, and all the rest of it. The moment you admit time, you admit the continuity of sorrow. If you do not have time, then what hope have you, knowing that you are old? You are so heavily conditioned that you can hardly break your habits—even the most trivial habit. We have to break our habits instantly—not tomorrow—not only the superficial habits, but the deeper habits, the ways of thinking, the ways of our beliefs, dogmas. We have to break deep-rooted habits. Therefore we say, "They cannot be broken immediately; we must have time." Therefore we say that we will do it next life or next week—which is the same thing, which is to admit time.

So from this one inevitably asks: Is there an action which is not of time—an action in this world, living in today, without all this confusion, chaos, miseries, quarrels, dirt, superstition and the ugly gods? Can I, can you, caught in time, break through the net of time? And it must be done immediately, instantly. Otherwise you have the hope of evolution, gradualness, and therefore you will gradually get rid of sorrow. And sorrow can never be got rid of, put aside, through time. So there must be an instant action, and there is an instant action which breaks this net of time. You will say, "What am I to do? Tell me what to do. What practice? What method? How am I to think, to break this tremendous burden of time?" These questions indicate that you are still thinking in terms of time. Practice implies time. Method implies time. To wait for somebody to tell you what to do implies time. And your doing it according to what has been said is within the field of time. Therefore within that field of time there is no hope; there is only despair and mounting sorrow.

So, you have to see the truth of it. Seeing the truth of it is meditation—which we will discuss another time. You can see the truth of it only when you are completely attentive with all your being. And you cannot be attentive if there is no silence. It is only in that silence—which is not to be achieved through time—and through that attention that there is the end of sorrow. Then one sees that there is a different dimension altogether—not the dimension of gods or all the stupid nonsense which man has invented out of his fear, out of his despair. There is a dimension of action which does not create conflict and contradiction and therefore effort. But the mind cannot come to it, do what it will, unless it under-

stands the whole field of consciousness, which is time. And that can be understood, not through time, not through thought, but by instant awareness, by instant perception.

Sirs, you have to be serious enough, earnest enough, to watch the whole movement of thought as consciousness, the whole movement of thought as a river that is flowing, the great weight of knowledge, tradition, hope, despair, anxiety, and the misery behind thought; and you have to watch all this completely—not as the watcher and the thing watched. The thinker is the thought; the observer is the observed. If you look at a tree, if you look at the beauty of the sky and the loveliness of a still night, you—the center—remain, and therefore you are the observer. The observer creates round himself space, and in that space he experiences that which is experienceable. That is, if you observe as an observer, then you are always creating the thing which is observed. If there is no observer as the center from which he is looking, there is only the fact.

Listen to those crows. Do listen. If you listen completely, is there a center from which you are listening? Your ears are listening. There is the noise, there is the vibration and all the rest of it, but there is no center from which you are listening. There is attention. Therefore, if you listen completely, there is no listener; there is only the fact of that noise. To listen completely you must be silent, and that silence is not something in thought, created by thought. When you listen to that crow that is making the noise before it goes to sleep, so completely that there is no listener, you will see that there is no entity that says, "I am listening."

So the thinker and the thought are one; without thought there is no thinker. And when there is no thinker and only thought, then there is an awareness of thinking without thought, and thought comes to an end. Please do not practice all this. Do not sit in posture, breathe right, hold your nose, stand on your head, or do whatever you do. It is all so infantile, so immature. This requires great maturity. Maturity means sensitivity, intelligence. And you cannot be attentive if you are not completely sensitive; your body, your nerves, your mind, your heart, every sense is completely alert, not made dull. Then, you will—not that you will find it, you will never find it—the thinker, which is you, will never find reality.

This fact has to be seen—that there is a dimension of action which does not breed conflict or sorrow. And to find it, to come upon it darkly, mysteriously, without thinking, there must be freedom right from the beginning, not at the end—freedom to investigate, to look, to observe; freedom from fear.

February 20, 1966

Fourth Talk in Bombay

We would like this evening to go into the question of fear. But before we go into it, we have to understand that the symbol is not the actuality. The word is not the fact. The word *fear* is not the actual state of fear. But most of us live by words. To us words are very important. They have a certain value in communication. But in themselves they have no great significance. But what has significance is the fact which the word represents.

So we must be very clear when we go into the question of fear and what is going to follow that, that the actual state cannot be experienced from the words, and that the word is not the thing. The word *tree*, the word *woman*, the word *man* is not the actual tree, woman, or man. And with most of us, the symbol interferes with the actual perception of the fact. The word, the symbol, evokes the fear; that is, the word stimulates fear, or the word bars the understanding of fear. We have to see not only the significance of the word but

also that the word does not interfere with the fact.

And, therefore, one of the important things, it seems to me, is to be free first of the word—like *Pakistani* or *Hindu* or *Parsi* or *communist*—because the word hides the fact; the word with all its memories, content, significance, prevents the seeing of the actuality. And also the word stimulates the actuality—like the word *death*; it immediately evokes many images, scenes, fancies, hopes, despair. But the word is not the fact. And it is important not only to understand this fact, this process—that the word is not the thing and the word does often prevent the perception of the actuality—but also to be free of the word, to observe the fact.

Because freedom is essential—to see, to observe, to hear, to feel, to think clearly, to examine. Freedom is absolutely necessary from the very beginning, not towards the end. That is, if I want to examine that tree or an idea or a feeling or a fact, I must be free to examine it; I must not be attached to my opinions, to my judgment, to my evaluations, to my prejudices, to my environmental influences. So freedom to examine is essential from the very beginning. And the word *freedom* is not the fact; the fact is entirely different. Because the moment there is freedom to examine, then the word becomes insignificant; and then you realize how difficult it is to be free to examine.

To most of us freedom is not important at all. We do not want it. We are frightened of it. We would rather depend; we would rather live in the old pattern, in a particular society, culture, environment, and not demand that the human being must be completely free. And this freedom cannot be given—obviously. You cannot buy it. You cannot read about it in books. Reading books, asking another what it is—all that is merely a symbol, an idea, a word; and through the word we cannot get at the fact. So when we are going to examine this thing of fear, we have to be very clear from the very beginning that freedom is necessary to examine—not acceptance; on the contrary, there must be "no-saying." You must say no rather than say yes, to find out. One of the major factors or causes of the decay in this country, of the deterioration that is going on, is that we accept, and that, after accepting, we live in that which we have accepted. We never say no. "No" means a revolt. You can revolt as a reaction—which does not lead anywhere. But in the fact of saying no to a dirty, foul street—in that very assertion, there is action. The action is not after saying no. The action is simultaneous with the saying.

Please follow all this carefully, because to understand fear, conscious or unconscious—which is one of the major problems of our life—there must be freedom to say no to it; there must be no attempt to find ways and means of escaping from it. We have developed through centuries a network of escapes. We are apparently incapable of facing the fact—facing the fact of war, the whole implication of it—facing any fact. Facing the fact demands action, whereas if you escape from action, if you escape from the fact, then the fact becomes the problem.

There is fear—we will go into it later, but first we must realize what it implies. There is fear. We have never come directly into contact with that fact. If we do, either we actually know that we are incapable of dealing with it or we know how to deal with it. But if you escape from the fact, the escape becomes the problem, not the fact. It is one of the most difficult things to face a fact because our minds refuse to look at anything directly. Please do observe this as an actuality in yourself, not listen merely to words.

Fear, that is, an awareness of danger, has many forms. There is no abstract fear. It is not an abstraction; it is an actuality. We know the process of how fear comes into being. Fear always exists in relationship to something. It does not exist by itself. And there is only one form of fear, which is for physical survival. If you see a snake, the whole metabolism of the organism changes, and you act—either you run away or you do something; you act. That is one thing. This physical reaction is necessary, is essential; otherwise, you will be destroyed. That is, the whole structure of the brain is based on survival, physical survival. But the human being carries over into the psyche this fact and says that he must survive psychologically. Am I making myself clear? We will go into it now.

So what we are frightened of is not the physical pain, the physical danger, but the psychological fear—what people will think, losing a job, survival after death, and so on. The whole machinery of physical survival is one thing, and it is absolutely necessary. The more sensitive, alert, watchful you are, the more acute and therefore the greater is the demand that you must physically survive. Otherwise you cannot think, feel—obviously. But psychologically that physical survival of man is denied because of our nationality, our religious differences, and class differences—which breed war, and so the physical survival is denied. Please understand. Obviously, this is a fact. So a man who would understand fear must be free of nationalism, of all religious beliefs and dogmas; otherwise, he is not capable of examining it. When a man is totally free of fear psychologically, he can then observe, look, listen, and in that clarity act.

So what we are concerned with is not the physical survival but the psychological survival. You want to be a Hindu; you are a nationalist with your frontiers, with your particular, geographical division; and you insist on it because that gives you tremendous satisfaction. And the other fellow on the other side of what you call the frontier does exactly the same thing. So physical survival is denied. He with his particular dogmas, religious beliefs, customs, habits, traditions, and you on the other side with your habits, with your particular idiosyncrasies, temperament, traditions, dogmas; so physical survival is denied through psychological insistence, demand—insisting on factors which are not facts at all.

We are going to investigate into fear, and we are understanding the nature of fear and whether it is at all possible to be totally free of that fear. Because fear darkens the mind, and you cannot think clearly; you are confused, you are almost paralyzed when this fear comes into being.

To be totally free of fear, no effort is necessary. Please understand this very clearly. In order to understand something, you have to look at it, to observe it—observe its nature, its structure, how it actually comes into being—you have actually to see. When you see something very clearly, you are obviously free. When you see something as poison, when you understand the whole nature of it, what is implied in it, obviously, at that moment you are completely free.

So effort is not necessary to be free of fear. Effort is necessary to escape from fear—to suppress it, to resist it, or to sublimate it. But the moment you understand the nature and the structure of fear, it is over. And you cannot understand it unless you come into contact with the fact directly and not through the symbol or the word.

Now, to understand fear we have to understand pleasure. Because all our values, all our relationships are based on pleasure. Please understand this. We are not condemning pleasure. We are not saying whether it is right or wrong. We are examining it. And to understand pleasure we must go into the question of desire. Because desire and pleasure are related

intimately with each other. Desire comes into being through reaction. You see a beautiful car, a woman, or a house; there is a reaction, then there is contact, and then sensation; that sensation sets desire going. You can observe this factually every day—the seeing, the contact, the sensation, then desire. And what gives strength, vitality, continuity to desire? Look! Am I making the question clear?

There is a perception of that beautiful house—the proportion, the line, the depth, the beauty of it. The seeing, the contact, the sensation, the desire; and then the thought "I must have it," or "I must have that man or woman"—whatever it is. And what gives strength to this desire? Please follow this. Any form of suppression, control, or indulgence denies freedom. But if I understand the whole structure of desire, I will not suppress it; I will then know how to deal with it, and I will deal with it. I see there is the perception of a nice house, a car, or a woman; desire arises—which is a normal, healthy reaction. To see a beautiful house is right; to see the beauty of it is essential. But what brings conflict into it, what makes it a problem? We are going to go into it.

So I have to find out what gives vitality, vigor, continuity to desire. If I could understand this, then desire has very little meaning. I can act upon it, or not act upon it; it won't bring about a problem. So I have to find out what gives it vitality, a continuity. Obviously, thought. I think about that house, I want that house, and the thought is building up the desire and giving to that desire strength, purpose. Then the conflict begins. That house is going to give me pleasure, and the pleasure is created by thought—how I shall live more comfortably, how I will be important then, and the rest of that business. Desire in itself is not right or wrong; it is a fact. But when thought interferes with that desire and gives it a continuity as pleasure, then the problem begins. One sees a beautiful woman—unless you are paralyzed, blind, you are bound to see her—and then a thought comes in, and the thought creates the various images of pleasure and then the problem.

So one has to understand the nature of thought—that is, first desire, then pleasure, and then why thought interferes at all. If I find out the relationship among these three, then desire becomes a very small affair. I can see a beautiful house, and leave it. I see a beautiful woman and not produce all the reactions. Thought has been built through time. Thought is time. If you do not think, there will be no tomorrow. And we have to think, but if that thinking is based on pleasure, on desire, then thought becomes a problem, then thinking becomes a danger.

So, is it possible to see a house, a woman, and yet not let thought interfere with it? Not deliberately—not say that thought must not interfere because it brings pain, sorrow, and all the rest of it, but actually see the fact, not the explanation; see the actual fact that when thought interferes with desire or when thought gives importance to desire, then it becomes pleasure, and where there is pleasure, there is always pain. The two, pleasure and pain are not separate; pleasure is pain. You can see that very obviously. Most of our values, concepts, ideals, relationships between man, woman, neighbor and yourself—all that is based on pleasure, and hence all our problems. We function with the principle of pleasure.

You know, there is a vast difference between pleasure and love. Consider it for a minute. All our relationships between man and woman, between ourselves and each other, is based on pleasure; and pleasure always brings pain. It is a fact. And where there is pleasure, there is no love. Love is not a process of thinking. Love is not the result of a thought, whereas pleasure is. If you understand that—not intellectually, ver-

bally reasoned out—if you see the fact that pleasure destroys love, and where there is pleasure there is no joy; if you see very clearly that you function on pleasure, that all your activity, all your thinking, all your being, including your gods, everything, is based on pleasure, which is the result of thought; if you see that it is thought which gives continuity to pleasure, which is desire; and if you see this whole structure—then where does fear come in at all?

Let us examine fear. Most of us are frightened of death. And there are other forms of fear—like darkness, what the neighbor will say, losing a job—a dozen other forms of fear. Fear is the same, though it may take different forms. Let us take one particular form of fear and go into it right through.

Most of us are afraid of death. We do not know what death means, but we are already afraid. And being afraid of this enormous fact, we try to escape from that fact. If you are a Hindu, you have your reincarnation; if you are a Christian, you have your resurrection. But you have not solved the problem of fear, or this question of death. You have escaped from it. Right? Don't deny it. Don't say, "Is there no reincarnation?" A man who is not frightened of death has neither hope nor despair. Now if you follow what is being said—not intellectually, not verbally, but actually—if you give your whole attention to it, if you give your whole attention to anything, conflict ceases; therefore, you are able to face it. That is, you are afraid of death; actually, you do not know what that experience is. You have seen death. The image of death is in your mind, and you cling to the things known—your house, your family, your name, your bank account. You hang on to all that because that is the only thing you have. And life as it is lived is a conflict, a misery, a despair, a travail, an anxiety, a constant battle; each of us knows this very well. This life of going to an office for the next forty years, the boredom, the stupidity of our life—that is all we know; and we cling desperately to our sorrows, to our miseries, to our confusion, to our pettiness. We would rather have that than something we do not know.

What we are frightened of is not the unknown but losing the known—the known being our miserable existence. Whether you are a millionaire or a poor man, our existence is a misery. Whether it is the life of a saint or the life of a sinner, it is still a misery, a conflict, a battle. To that we cling, and we say to ourselves, "next life, a future life"— what we know being carried over into the next, the future life; at least we hope so. What we know is this misery, this sorrow— hoping for the better, next. Scientists are inquiring into whether it is not possible to prolong life indefinitely through an artificial heart, kidneys, and the various implantations, through having the body frozen for a number of years and put on a shelf and revived after a number of years. Where is your soul? Do you understand my question? Is there such a thing as the soul, which will survive and continue?

Thought is the result of time—thought being memory, experience, knowledge, and all the rest of it. This thought faces the fact that it may come to an end—and it is a very disturbing fact. And so thought invents all the network of escapes from this one fact, and thereby postpones, further pushes away death to a distance. Obviously, sirs. At twenty you have another forty years to live, and then the inevitable death at the end of it. Even if you live a thousand years, there is always an end. So we have developed, through thought, a distance between the fact of death and the actuality of living—and the actuality of living is our misery, with occasional joy and pleasure. What we are afraid of is losing the known, losing our pleasures.

Now, to understand death you have to understand living—obviously. Because, without understanding what is living, how can you understand what is death?—which must be an extraordinary phenomenon, as living is. Is it possible to live differently? Because if there is a mutation in one's living, then death will have a meaning in that mutation.

So our problem then is: Can there be a change in the life which I lead now, which is despair, fear, anxiety, every form of cunning escape, which we call living? If that change is to be something which I know, then it is not a change. I hope I am making myself clear. Because it is a very complex question: Is it possible for me to change totally so that in the very act of that changing, death will take place?

Because what has continuity implies time. That is, I have lived a miserable life. I hope to change it in time, and so I say, "Give me time." And hence I would rather postpone death. Because I do not know what is going to happen, I demand that time is necessary to change, and I avoid death. But if I know how to change immediately, then I have no fear of death. Do you understand my question? If I know completely how to bring about a revolution in my life, then death has no meaning anymore as a thing of which I am afraid.

So the problem then is not death, not fear, not pleasure, but is it possible to change, to bring about a total mutation immediately, instantly? Now to find that out, one has to be free of the idea of time. That is, any effort implies time. Obviously that is simple. And is it possible to change? Take, for instance, a very small thing like smoking; is it possible to drop it instantly? If you can drop it instantly, there is no effort, there is no time, there is no conflict—there is a mutation. Now, you can only drop it instantly if you are totally attentive to the fact that you are smoking—not resisting, not indulging, but being attentive to the whole implication of smoking. And you cannot be attentive if you find reasons to continue, or to discontinue, smoking or its pain, or if you are frightened of it. You can only be free of it when you are completely attentive of every movement of your hand—going to the pocket, taking out a cigarette, putting it to your mouth, lighting a match, putting it to the cigarette, and puffing it—the whole of that habit.

When there is attention, there is no effort. Please do understand this simple thing. Once you understand it, everything becomes clear. Where there is attention, there is no effort. It is only inattention that brings about effort. It is only inattention that brings about conflict. So when you are totally attentive to your whole life—your miseries, your conflicts, your desires, your pleasures, your memories, your thoughts, your activities—when you are totally aware, then you can look at every fact as fact, not translate it in terms of pleasure or pain, nor give the fact a continuity through pleasure.

So a man who would understand death has to understand living. And living is not the thing which we call "living," which is a battleground, both inwardly and outwardly. Living is something entirely different, in which there is no fear at all. And to be rid of fear, there must be freedom from the very beginning so that you can examine it, you can look into it, you can face it. Then you will see that living is dying, because living is from moment to moment. What has continuity is despair, not living; and when there is despair, obviously, there is thought. Thus the whole vicious circle of thought is caused. The whole problem of life and death involves the bringing about of a mutation, not in some future date, but immediately, instantly; and that instant mutation takes place when you are completely attentive.

There is one thing which one has to go into, and that is the question of what love is. Most of us have different concepts, ideas, opinions—sacred love and profane love; love of the one man, and love of the many; can you love the many if you love the one? And we know love because we are jealous. To us jealousy is part of love. You love your wife, your children, the family; in that there is jealousy, envy, ambition, greed. You don't treat the family as a unit of convenience, but the family becomes strongly important, and the family then becomes antisocial. And where there is jealousy, envy, greed, ambition, competition, obviously there is no love. We also know that the word *love* is not the fact. And if there is no love in our heart, in our being, do what we will, there will always be misery, conflict.

So, how does the mind or the heart come upon the strange thing called love? Everyone talks about it—the politician, the crook, the exploiter, the priest, the guru. Everybody has that word love on his lips. But to find out what it is, is another thing. To know what it means is quite a different thing. You cannot possibly know it when there is jealousy, envy of another, when your wife looks at another, when you are seeking power, position, prestige. There is no love when a guru says he knows and you don't know, though he may talk about love, though he may preach about love. The moment anybody says, "I know and you don't know," the man who says, "I know," knows no love.

So love is not a thing easily to come by. One has to be aware most profoundly of the various characteristics, the various conflicts—just be aware, watch, listen. And there can be no love if the mind is dull. Most of our minds are dull because the mind is made dull through the kind of education that you have. To prepare yourself for a technological job, you concentrate all your energy on that one thing. What happens when you concentrate on one thing? The other parts wither—which means you are not sensitive, you are not aware of beauty.

And religions have denied beauty. Beauty is considered a sin because it stimulates your senses. Therefore you must deny it; you cannot look at a tree and see the beauty of it. The loveliness of the sky, of a river in full flow—all that is denied because through that way you might get sensual, which is again a pleasure. Therefore, for the so-called religious people, beauty is related to pleasure—they are not religious at all; they are really worldly people; they have not understood life.

To understand life, you cannot deny life. You have to understand it, you have to live it. And you cannot live it if you are not free—free from the very beginning, from the very childhood, so that you can look, watch, listen, feel. And out of this watching, listening, looking, you become gentle, tender, considerate, polite; *there* is a neighbor. Where there is considerateness, there is affection; and affection is not something of the intellect. And when you have that affection, then perhaps out of that will come love—not in time, not tomorrow.

And surely when violence ceases—not through nonviolence; violence ceases only when you are faced with the fact of violence—when the mind is quiet, when the heart has really understood deeply what living is—not this constant misery, despair, and sorrow—then out of that understanding you will know what love is. And when there is that love, then you can do what you like. And then the heaven is opened—not the heaven in some far-off, mystical world, but in this world, living here.

February 23, 1966

Fifth Talk in Bombay

The last few times that we met here, we have been talking over together several things, including how important it is that there should be a radical change in the human mind and heart. We went into the question of time, and we said that thought is the product of time, and thought cannot possibly under any circumstances bring about a revolution—thought can only bring about a modification, but not a radical revolution which is absolutely necessary. Also we talked over together the question of fear, sorrow, and death.

Now, this evening, I would like to talk over with you, if I may, a very complex question—to examine, which needs a fresh mind. It needs a mind that is willing to examine, to investigate, to discover for itself; it needs a mind that questions. And very few of us question. What you generally do is to question and try to find an answer. Surely a questioning that demands an answer has already ceased to be a question, because it is only interested in the answer and not in the question itself. What we are going to do this evening, if it is possible, is to question and not wait to find an answer.

To question anything there must be freedom. But if you question in order to find a convenient, comfortable, satisfying answer, you have stopped questioning; and one of the most difficult things in life is to question, never to accept, but always to say no—that way we begin to uncover. We must be always "no-sayers" rather than "yes-sayers." In that way we begin to discover for ourselves without asking somebody else.

We are going to talk over together a thing that is tremendously important. I am using the word *tremendously* without exaggeration; it is of great significance. Because, if one does not know how to meditate, if one does not know what is the meaning of meditation, it is like being blind. You will never see the beauty of the sky, you will never see the color, you will never see the movement of trees, the hills, the beauty of the earth. And to find out what it means to meditate—not how to meditate—demands a mind that is passionate. Very few of us are deeply passionate. We pursue pleasure and mistake pleasure for passion. Passion is not within the field of time, but pleasure is always within its field. And we need passion to question and to pursue that question to the very end. And where there is passion, you must have energy; and energy is not the product of thought or mentation. So we are going to find out together what it means to meditate.

We are always seeking some form of mystery in life; because our life is rather boring, lonely, ugly, insignificant, worthless, it has very little meaning. Going to the office every day, or laboring vainly—the whole of it is so boring, so lonely, without much meaning, that we would like to have some mystery in life, some romantic, mythical feeling. And we hope through meditation to come upon this mythical, romantic experience. A mind that is questioning is never seeking experience. Please do follow all this. Because, if you do not, you will be left empty-handed, and you will say at the end, "He never told us how to meditate." We are not concerned with how to meditate, but what is meditation is much more important. A mind that questions or asks how to meditate wants some experience. Because the world is very shallow, empty, dull, all our lives are without much meaning; so we want more and more experience, and we hope— through drugs, through various forms of meditation, self-hypnosis and so on—to have experience of deeper things.

So we have to understand the significance of experience. You need experience in skill. To be a skillful doctor, you need experience—that is, practice. A good surgeon has operated on many people and knows that his hands are very delicate. The delicacy of the hand, its precision, is the result of a great deal of experience. And as we said, we want an experience in a different dimension, at a different level; so we are all asking how to

meditate, what to do. Behind the "how" there is the pleasure which one seeks in greater experience. And so one seeks a method, a system, a practice; or one takes one of those modern drugs which give one a higher sensitivity, in which there is an experience; and that experience is always depending on the condition of one's mind, one's heart, one's culture, one's behavior, what one's beliefs are. So the experiences, the visions, the methods only bring about the response of one's own condition. And so any experience, any vision, any demand for greater excitement, greater vision, is still within the field of one's own pleasure.

So a man who is really inquiring into this question of meditation—and you must inquire—must put aside completely the method, the desire to experience. Because, if you desire an experience, you will project what you want to experience. So you must completely put aside all that, and then you can begin to inquire. But if you are inquiring in order to experience some fantastic vision of your particular little god, created by your particular little mind or by the particular culture in which you have been brought up, then you will experience that vision. But it is the result of your narrow, petty little state; it has nothing whatsoever to do with reality. So that is clear. There is no method, no system. Meditation is not prayer, nor demanding from or supplicating to some deity because you happen to be unhealthy, because you want a better job, and so on. If you have put away all that, then you can begin to inquire what is meditation. Because, as I said, if you are not capable of meditating, you do not know what it means; you will never know what beauty is—like a blind man, like a deaf man, you will never hear the breeze among the leaves, you will never see the bird on the wing, you will never see the beauty of the hill, you will never hear the lonely call of a night. So every human being must understand what meditation is.

First of all, as we said, any inquiry demands passion. You can inquire casually, or inquire with curiosity, or inquire with a motive. If you have a motive, a curiosity, or a casual passing questioning, then you will never have the passion to put the question and pursue it to the very end. And to have passion you must have energy. As we said, pleasure, enthusiasm, is not passion. Passion implies constant, persistent energy, not limited within the field of your own little mind. If you want to know something—it does not matter what it is—you must have great energy, you must go after it. And that is what we are going to do, if we can, this evening.

First, how is one to release the energy?—an energy which is not twisted, which is not the result of torture; an energy which is free; an energy which is not contained within the space of one's thought, of one's desire, of one's pleasure. And to release that energy which is not contaminated by thought requires great attention; that demands total self-knowing. Energy is wasted through conflict, both outward and inward. To gather that energy, it has been said that you must do certain things: you must be a bachelor, you must suppress, you must control, you must regiment, you must drill it. When you do all those things, you are shaping the energy or containing the energy within a formula and giving it a particular direction, depending on the motive.

So we expend our energy through conflict. When all the saints have said that you must be a bachelor to have this tremendous energy, what takes place? Observe it in yourself, and watch it. There is only suppression, control, and for the rest of your life you are in battle with yourself—your organism, your mind, your feeling. When you are looking at people, you are dulling your senses in order

to preserve this energy, to transform or to transfuse this energy. So you shut away any sense of beauty—even to look at a tree—because it cultivates the senses, makes you feel very strongly to look at a tree, to look at a woman or a man. And sex is taboo for a man who wants to find God—whatever that may mean. All this implies suppression, distortion, control, and putting a lid on yourself; and inside you are boiling. All that process is a distortion of energy.

And as sex and all that business is part of life, you have to understand it—not suppress it, not deny it, nor indulge in it. And it becomes tremendously important. When you deny it, and when you don't find release all round—intellectually, emotionally, sensitively—that is the only thing you have which gives you satisfaction, pleasure. We are not advocating indulgence. As I said, we must understand.

So you see that to be passionate demands energy, and that energy must be completely free, not distorted. A mind that is tortured with conflict obviously is not a free mind; its energy is always distorted, warped, conditioned, held. And how can such a mind inquire? Inquiry demands great vitality, force, energy. And we waste the energy in conflict: the conflict of duality—the good and the bad, this is right and that is wrong, this must be done, and the future idea, a formula with which you are acting. So you have to find out—which you are doing now—how to understand this duality and not be in conflict at any time with regard to it.

What is duality? There is duality—man and woman, black and white, morning and evening, the 'me' and 'not-me', I want to achieve great success, an end towards which I am working, and so on—in which we live. Yesterday, today, and tomorrow; hating and pursuing love; being violent and desiring to be in a state of nonviolence; action and inaction—we know what duality is, and we are caught in its corridor; thought is beaten, going back and forth between the two, creating misery for itself. So one has to understand it in order to go beyond it. You cannot go beyond it unless you understand it.

So one has to inquire how duality arises. Not that there is not duality, not that there is not the world and something far beyond the world, not that there is not brutality and love—but one has to understand the reality of this conflict in duality. Unless you understand it and are free of it, the energy which is taken up in conflict becomes distorted, perverted; and therefore you have no energy to question, to be passionate to find out how this duality arises, how we are caught in the opposites.

What makes a mind a slave to duality? Please listen. This is not a superficial question. It requires your attention. It requires your capacity to penetrate into this question. Why have you this division between the Hindu and the Muslim, the Catholic and the non-Catholic—why? Your country and another country, your God and another God, heaven and hell—why? To find out one has to inquire into the process of thinking. You know, one can very clearly analyze objectively. One can see very well what are the causes of war; it does not take a very clever, deep mind. There are many causes of war. After discovering the causes, you will not be able to have the feeling that war, hate, destroys humanity. No amount of analysis will give you that feeling. So one has not only to analyze very clearly, objectively, ruthlessly, sanely, but also one must have this feeling, because through analysis you will never come to the feeling—the feeling being "seeing something completely." And for that you must have passion.

So we are going to go together into this question of duality. Please, you are not merely listening to the words of the speaker. You are actually observing, through the words of the speaker, the facts in which you live daily.

Otherwise, as we are going to inquire deeply into this question of meditation, you won't be able to follow it. All this, from the beginning of this talk to the very end, is meditation; it is this sense of attention which has nothing whatsoever to do with concentration. Any child, any schoolboy can concentrate. But to go right through, putting aside all one's personal desires, ambitions, pleasures, and find out all about this question of duality, attention is necessary. Because, as I said, unless you do it, every form of conflict only distorts energy. It is wasted energy. Only when the mind has no wasted energy and is able to have complete energy without any effort will that energy go very far. And we are going to do that this evening, so that you will not only understand this question of duality but be, as we go into it, free of it. You can only be free of it, not through analysis, but by seeing the truth, which can only be perceived when you have the feeling. You have to see the truth that war, hate, does not answer any problem; and you cannot see the truth of it if you are merely intellectualizing about it.

So why is the mind, our being—why is it caught in this conflict of duality? That is, why does the very root of our being bring about this conflict? I can look at a woman, a car, somebody; why should I be in conflict? I can see that there is beauty and ugliness, but why the conflict? I can see the loveliness of a face, the ugly behavior of human beings; and yet why should I be caught in any conflict? We are going to go into this. To go into it we must question the very root and not the superficial branches, the symptoms.

As long as there is the thinker and the thought, there must be duality. As long as there is a seeker who is seeking, there must be duality. As long as there is an experiencer and the thing to be experienced, there must be duality. So duality exists when there is the observer and the observed. That is, as long as there is a center—the censor, the observer, the thinker, the seeker, the experiencer as the center—there must be the opposite.

So is it possible to end all seeking? Please listen to all this carefully. You have to end seeking. For the moment you seek, you have created the object towards which you are going. As long as there is an experiencer who wishes to experience, he has created the opposite which he is going to experience. As long as there is a censor, a judge, an entity that judges, evaluates, criticizes, condemns, justifies, there must be the opposite, and hence the conflict. Now can the thinker, the observer, come to an end without effort? If he makes an effort to end himself, then it is a perversion, it is a waste of energy, and to end the observer becomes a conflict, and so on.

So, is it possible to look without the observer? I hope I am making this thing clear. Is it possible for me to look at that house without the observer so that the observer is the observed, and therefore there is no conflict? I hope that, as this is being said, you are watching your own mind and your own heart, and doing it. Because if you don't do it, you will not know the next step to go further.

Can you look at something without thought?—which does not mean that you are asleep, or that you are vacant, blank. Can you look at that tree, at that flower, at that woman, or at that sky with the sunset, without the observer partaking, judging? That is, when you look at a flower, a man, a woman, or a child, are you looking at it, or are you looking at the image which you have of that flower, man, woman, or child? Please follow this. When you look at your wife, your child, your neighbor, you have images of your wife, your children, your neighbor— the memories are the images. The image which you have about your wife and the image she has about you are looking at each other. When you are looking at that flower, you are not looking visually, with your eyes, at that flower, but you are looking at that flower through the word, through the botanical meaning of that flower, through giving it a name; and therefore you are not looking.

So when you look and when there is no naming, no evaluation, but actual observation, then there is no observer at all. That is, if you can look at your ambition, or your hate, or your anger, what takes place? You justify it. Let us say, you have greed—which is another form of ambition. When you look at greed, what takes place? Either you justify it and say that the world has it, or you condemn it because you have moral concepts about greed; so you never are in contact with the fact of greed; you are always the entity that says, "I am greedy"—I and greed are two different things. But the observer himself is greed. If you can look at the fact of greed, violence, directly—not through words, formulas, concepts, images—then there is no observer, and therefore there is no duality. There is only the fact, and therefore there is never a conflict.

So, when you look at the fact, when there is the observation of that fact only, then, because there is no conflict, you have the energy to look, to observe, to act. So when one begins to see this duality with all its pain, anxiety, conflict, travail, and the whole business of it, when the observer is the observed, the duality loses its meaning, its vitality. And you must see it, not say, "How am I to see it?" We have explained what prevents the mind from seeing the fact that the observer is the observed. So, when you see, you are no longer in conflict, no longer caught in duality; therefore, there is a release of energy which is not being twisted and which is therefore free.

Then what has taken place with all this, if one has gone through all this? To realize all this, that conflict and conscious or unconscious effort pervert energy at any level, at any time—it has demanded your attention; you have been listening to yourself, watching, observing. In that process, a certain discipline has naturally come into being. To listen to all these talks—if you are listening at all—the very act of listening is an act of discipline. That discipline is not enforced, that discipline is not imitative, that discipline does not conform to a pattern through fear. You have listened because you are interested, and that very interest has created its own discipline. Therefore, the energy that has gone into the disciplining by suppression, conformity, and all the rest of it is now an energy which is highly disciplined—not through desire, not through pleasure or experience—and is highly capable.

All this—the previous talks and this talk—is an unrollment, an unfolding of the whole process of thinking, of the whole process of consciousness. Now, if you have gone that far, not verbally but actually, then you can begin to inquire into the question of space and emptiness. There must be space; otherwise, there is no freedom. A little mind has no space. A respectable, bourgeois, very carefully educated mind with all its problems and anxieties and fears and despairs—such a mind has no space within itself. So one has to go into the question of what is space.

What is space? Space is created by the object. Please listen, find out. There is this microphone, the object. And because of the object, there is space around it; and the object exists because of space. There is a house, and in the house there is a room. The room, because of the four walls, creates the space within the four walls; and there is space outside the house. There is space because there is a center within us. There is a center—the center that is the observer, the censor, the seeker, the entity that says, "I must, I must not," the entity that says, "I have been, I am that, I will be." That center

creates space round itself; otherwise, the center could not exist.

Now is there space without the center? You can only answer that question nonverbally, nonargumentatively, without an opinion that it is this or that. You can only answer it if the center is not. And if the center is and if that center creates space, in that space there is no freedom whatever; you are always a slave.

So freedom demands that you find out for yourself what space without the center is. Where there is the center, the object, it is creating the space round itself; and because it exists and because it can only exist in the space round itself, therefore it is not space at all. Therefore, as long as there is a center that is the observer, the seeker, there is no freedom; and freedom can only exist when there is complete space, not space within the boundaries of the mind.

And also we must inquire into the question of emptiness. It is an amazingly important question. Because, if there is no emptiness, no new thing can be. If there is only a continuity, which is time, then whatever the activity, whatever the action that is involved in the continuity, it cannot bring about something new. What it can do is to bring about a modified continuity. We have no time to go into this. It is only a mind that has understood space, that knows, that is aware of this emptiness; it is only such a mind that can be completely still.

Because stillness, silence are not products of thought. Silence is outside the field of consciousness. You cannot say I have experienced a state of silence. If you have experienced it, it is not silence. If you say, "I want to find out what silence is; I practice silence by not saying a word," this or that, it is not silence. But if you have understood conflict, duality, time, and this whole question of discipline, order, then you will have inquired and discovered for yourself what space is and what emptiness is—really you cannot discover it; it comes upon you, it is there. You cannot experience silence any more than you can experience space and emptiness. But this is absolutely essential. And then only is energy completely free, uncontaminated, without any direction brought about through pleasure.

Now if the mind has gone that far, which is all a part of meditation, then there is a fact which cannot be expressed through words. Because words always have a definite meaning. Every word is loaded. Take the word *love*. How loaded it is, how heavy it is! Or the word *beauty*. But the word love and the word beauty are not the fact. The fact of love is not the word. But to live in that quality of love and beauty, there must be this space, this emptiness, and this silence. And from this silence there is action—not "having learned, act." Because then every action is nonproductive of conflict. Then life, living in this world, going to an office every day, doing everything—into it there comes a joy; there is a bliss which is not pleasure; there is an ecstasy which is not the product of time. And without that, do what you will, social order and disorder, wars, conflicts will not bring about a happy human being.

What brings about bliss is the total awareness of this intense silence, and from that silence, action. Then you will know what bliss is.

February 27, 1966

Sixth Talk in Bombay

This is the last talk of this year. I think the more one observes the world's condition, the more clear it becomes that there must be a totally different kind of action. One sees in the world, including in India, the confusion, the great sorrow, the misery, the starvation, the general decline. One is aware of it, one knows it from reading newspapers, magazines, and books. But it remains on the intellectual level, because we do not seem to be able to do anything about it. Human beings are in despair; there is great sorrow in themselves, and frustration; and there is the chaos about one. The more you observe and go into it—not intellectually, not verbally, but actually discuss, observe, act, inquire, examine—the more you see how confused human beings are. They are lost. And there are those who think they are not lost because they belong to a particular group, a circle. The more they practice, the more they do certain things; the more they do social work, this or that, the more they are sure that the world is going to be changed by their particular little act.

The world is at war, and you think that by a particular prayer, a few of us—people gathered together and speaking certain words—can solve this enormous question which has remained unsolved for over five thousand years; and you keep on repeating them, though knowing that war can never be stopped that way. So each one belongs to a certain group, to a certain political party, to a religious sect, and so on, and remains in it more and more, holding on to the past, to what has been; and one is caught in it. One admits, when it is pointed out, that there is chaos, general decline, deterioration, outwardly and inwardly; and one realizes that man is lost. And without finding out why he is lost, why there is so much chaos and misery, without examining, without going into it very deeply, we answer superficially, saying that we are not following God, or we do not love; we give superficial, platitudinous answers that have no value at all.

And during these talks, if one has listened to them at all, one must have come to the question: Why this mess, why this confusion? If you inquire very deeply, you will find that man is lazy. The chaos is brought about through man's laziness, indifference, sluggishness, because he accepts. That is the easiest way to live—to accept; to adjust to the environment, to the conditions, to the culture in which he lives—just to accept. This acceptance breeds dreadful laziness. It is very important to understand that we, as human beings, are very lazy. We think we have solved the problem of living by a belief, by saying, "I believe in this or that." That belief is essentially based on fear and therefore the incapacity to solve that problem of fear—which indicates deep-rooted laziness.

Please observe yourself. You fall into a pattern of thought and action, and there you remain, as that is the easiest way—you don't have to think; you have thought a little bit about it, perhaps, but now you do not have to think. You are that; you are carried along by outward events, or by the push of your own little group. That gives you a great deal of satisfaction, and you think you are doing extraordinarily good work; and you dare not question because that is very disturbing. You dare not question your religion, your community, your belief, the social structure, nationalism, war; but you accept. Please look into yourself. You are so lazy. This chaos is due to this laziness because you have ceased to question, ceased to doubt—because you accept.

Being conscious of this terrible mess that is going on outwardly and inwardly, we expect some outward event to bring about order; or we hope that some leader, a guru, this, or that will help us out—that way we have been living centuries upon centuries, looking to somebody else to solve our problems. To follow another is the essence of indolence. Somebody comes along; he has probably thought out a little bit and had one or two visions; he can do this or that; and he tells you what to do, and you are quite satisfied. What we really want in this world is satisfaction, comfort; and we want somebody to tell us what to do—which all indicate this deep-rooted laziness; we do not want to think

out our problems, to look at them, to wipe out all the difficulties. This indolence prevents us not only from questioning, inquiring, and examining, but from dealing with a much deeper issue, which is: to find out what is action. The world is in chaos; we are in misery. All the solutions, the doctrines, the beliefs, the meditative circus that goes on in the name of meditation—none of these has solved a thing. And if we could find out for ourselves what is action, we have to act, to do something vital, energetic, forceful, to bring about a different mind, a different quality of existence.

So one has to go into the question of what is action. Not right action and wrong action, because if you approach action as right or wrong, you are already lost. People will tell you this is right action and that is wrong action, and you, already inclined to be lazy, do not want to inquire into it deeply. You accept it as right action because that person is a successful lawyer, and you follow it. So what we are going to do this evening, if we can, is to find out what is action. Please bear in mind that we are not thinking in terms of right or wrong action. There is only action—not right and wrong action; not action according to the Gita, the Bible, or the Koran; not according to the communist, the socialist, and so on. There is only action, which is living. One has to find out the way of life, how to live—not the method; if you have a method, a system, a practice, you have already encouraged this innate indolence. So one has to have a very sharp mind not to be caught in this trap of indolence which one is too willing to fall into.

Please listen to what is being said. How do you listen? When you listen, you listen to find out what the speaker is trying to say—to find out, not to oppose or agree. To find out for yourself means to listen, to inquire, to examine—not accepting, not saying, "I hope he will come to my point of view which is right.'' One has to listen, and apparently that is one of the most difficult things to do. Most of us like to talk, like to express ourselves. Because we have so many opinions, ideas, which are not our own; they are somebody else's. We have accepted a lot of slogans, platitudes; we trot them out and think we have understood life. So you are listening—not to explanation, not to your own prejudices, idiosyncrasies, not to what you know already, but listening to find out.

To find out, your mind must be fairly quiet. As we said the other day, to learn about anything, two states are essential: a quiet mind and attention. That is the only way you listen to another—it does not matter if it is to your wife, to your children, to your boss, to the crows, or to the call of a bird. There must be quietness, there must be attention; and in that state you are listening. That means you are already active; you are no longer sluggish; you have already broken away from this habit of half-listening, half-agreeing, half-being serious, and therefore never penetrating deeply. So, if you would listen, listen not only to the speaker but to the noise of the world, listen to the cry of the human heart, listen to the chaos, listen to your own misery, the uncertainty, the cry of despair. If you knew how to listen, then you would solve the problem. When you listen to your agony, if you have any—and most human beings have agony—you will find the answer, you will be out of it. But you cannot listen to it if you say, ''The answer must be according to my pleasure, according to my desire''—then you are not listening to it; you are only listening to the promptings of your own desire and pleasure.

Here, for this evening at least, please listen to find out. Because we are going into something which requires a great deal of attention, quiet inquiry, hesitant examination—not ''tell me what to do, and I will do it.'' Because everything is falling to pieces

around us, and there must be an action of a totally different kind, an action not according to anybody, not even according to the speaker. We are going to find out for ourselves what is action, how to live—because living is action. We have made our living so chaotic, so miserable, so immature.

And to find out what is action, there must be a great deal of maturity—not in terms of time, not maturing like a fruit on a tree, taking six months. If you take six months to mature, you have already sown the seeds of misery, you have already planted hate and violence, which lead to war. So you have to mature immediately, and you will if you are capable of listening and therefore learning. Learning is not an additive process. Learning and adding, which becomes knowledge, and from that knowledge acting—that is what we do. We have experiences, beliefs, thoughts; and these experiences, thoughts, ideas have become knowledge; and on that stored knowledge we act; and therefore there is no learning at all. We are just adding, adding, adding. We have added to ourselves enormous knowledge for two million years, and yet we are at war, we hate; there is never a moment of peace, tranquillity; there is no ending of sorrow. Knowledge is necessary in the field of technology, in the field of skill. But if you have knowledge, which is idea, and if from that idea you act, you have already ceased to learn. So maturity is not in terms of time and evolution, but maturity comes when there is this act of learning. It is only a mature mind that can listen, that can be very attentive and be quiet. It is the immature mind that believes, that says, ''This is right and that is wrong,'' and pursues something illogically.

So we are going to learn together about action. You are going to think, listen. We are going to do that together, because it is your life. It is not my life; it is your life, your misery, your confusion. You have to find out what is action.

What is action? To act, to do. All action is relationship. There is no isolated action. Action, as we know now, is the relationship of "doing" with "the idea." Surely, the idea and the doing of that idea—that is excellent in the field of skill and technology; but it becomes an impediment to learn about relationship. Relationship is constantly changing. Your wife or your husband is never the same. But laziness, the desire for comfort and security, says, "I know her or him, she or he is that way," and therefore you have fixed the poor woman or man. Therefore your relationship is according to an image, or according to an idea; and from that image or idea of relationship springs action. Please give your attention to this. That is all we know as action: "I believe, I have principles; this is right, that is wrong; this should be"— and we act according to that. Man is violent; that violence is shown in ambition, competition, a brutal expression of aggressiveness— which are all the responses of the animal— and in the so-called discipline, which is suppression, and all the rest of it; and from that we act. And so there is always conflict in action.

We say that action must conform to a pattern, right and wrong, according to principles, beliefs, the tradition, the environmental influence, and the culture in which one is brought up. So action, as far as we see, as far as our life is, is according to a particular image, a particular pattern, a particular formula. And that formula, that image, or that idea has not solved a thing in the world— politically, religiously, or economically—it has solved nothing. It has not solved any of our deep, human problems. And yet we keep on insisting that is the only way to act. We say, "How can we act without thinking, without having an idea, without following, day after day, a certain routine?" So we accept conflict as the way of life—conflict which is the result of our action, of our life, of our relationship, of our ideas, of our

thoughts. You cannot dispute this fact: having an idea, a principle, a belief that you are a Hindu, and so on—according to that tradition, in that framework, you live and act; and when you do that, there is bound to be conflict. The idea, the 'what should be', is different from the fact, the *what is*. That is simple. That is the way we have lived for millennia. Now, is there another way—a way of life which is action, which is relationship, but which is without conflict, which means without idea?

Listen to this. First see the problem. The word *problem*—what does it mean? It is a challenge. All challenges become problems because we do not know how to respond. Here is a problem—which is the world problem—something that is thrown at you, and you do not know any other way to respond to that problem except the old way; that is, conformity, imitativeness, repetition, establishing a habit; and from that repetitive, imitative, habitual way of life, you act. That habitual way of life is what you call "action," and that has brought about untold misery and chaos in the human mind and heart.

So that is obvious. We can proceed from that. Don't say that it is not so, afterwards. Don't pretend to yourself that it is not a fact. If you analyze it, if you go into yourself very deeply, it can be very simply put: you have a pleasure, and you want the repetition of that pleasure—sexual or any other form of pleasure—and you keep on living with that pleasure, either in memory or in thought; and that pleasure, that thought, pushes you to an action; and in that action there is conflict, there is pain, there is misery; the habit has been established, and from that habit you act.

So is there another totally different way of living, which is action? That means you have listened very carefully and attentively to the way you have lived, and you know all the implications, not just patches of it. To listen totally implies that you see, you hear, the whole of the problem, not just one or two sketches of that problem. When you listen to those crows in the sense that your mind is quiet, attentive, not interpreting, not condemning, not resisting, you are listening totally. You are listening to the total sound—not of a crow, but to the total sound. And in the same way, if you can listen to the total problem of action with which you are very familiar, if you can listen totally to the problem, to the issue, to the way you live—that is, from idea there is action—then you have the energy to listen to something else. But if you have not listened totally to the present way of action, then you have not the energy to follow what is going to come.

After all, to find out anything you must have energy, and you need a great deal of energy to inquire into something totally new. And to have that energy, you must have listened to the old pattern of life, neither condemning nor approving. You must have listened to it totally—which means you have understood it, you have understood the futility of living that way. When you have listened to the futility of it, you are already out of it. Then you have—not intellectually but deeply—felt the uselessness of living that way and have listened to it completely, totally; then you have the energy to inquire. If you have not the energy, you cannot inquire. That is, when you deny that which has brought about this misery, this conflict—which we have gone into—that denial, that very negation of it is positive action.

I am going to go into that a little bit. We said, "Is there any other action in which there is no conflict, which is not a repetitive activity, a repetitive form of pleasure?" To find that out we must go into the question: What is love? Don't get sentimental, emotional, or devotional! We are going to inquire. Love is always negative—it must be. Love is not thought. Love is never contradictory—but thought is. Thought, which is a

response of memory based on the animal instincts—that is, the machinery of thinking—is always contradictory. And when there is an action born of thought, that action which is contradictory brings conflict and misery. And in inquiring, in examining if there is any other activity which is not fraught with pain, with anxiety, with conflict, you must be in a state of negation. Do you understand? To inquire, to examine, you must be in a state of negation; otherwise, you cannot examine. You must be in a state of not-knowing; otherwise, how can you examine?

The way of life to which we are accustomed is what is called a positive way because you can feel it out, you can do it, day after day, repetitively, based on imitation, habit, following, obeying, being drilled by society or by yourself. All that is positive activity, in which there is conflict and misery. Please listen to all this. And when you deny that, the very process of denying, the very process of turning your back on it, is a state of negation because you do not know what comes next. Surely it is not complicated. Intellectually, it sounds complicated; but it is not. When you turn your back on something, you have finished with it.

Now we say that love is total negation. We don't know what it means. We don't know what love means. We know what pleasure is—pleasure, which we mistake for love. Where there is love, there is no pleasure. Pleasure is the result of thought—obviously. I look at something beautiful; thought comes in and begins to think about it; it creates an image. Please watch it in yourself. And that image gives you a great deal of pleasure over that scene, over that feeling; and thought gives to that pleasure sustenance and continuity. And in family life, that is what you call love; but, that has nothing to do whatever with love. You are only concerned with pleasure; and where there is pursuit of pleasure, there is imitative continuity in time—please listen to all this—whereas love has no continuity because love is not pleasure. And to understand what love is, to be in that state, there must be the negation of the positive. Right? Shall we go on with this?

Sirs, look! When you say you love somebody—your wife, your husband, your children—what is involved in it? Strip it of all words, of all sentiments, emotionalism, and look at it factually. What is involved in it when you say, "I love my wife, my husband, my children"? Essentially it is pleasure and security. We are not being cynical. These are facts. If you really loved your wife and your children—loved, not had the pleasure which you derive by belonging to a family, a narrow little group, sexually, and by furthering your own particular egotism—you would have a different kind of education; you would not want your son to be concerned only with technological studies; you would not help your son only to pass some stupid, little examination and get a job; but you would educate him to understand the whole process of living—not just one part, a segment, a fragment of this vast life. If you really loved your son, there would be no war; you would see to it. That means you would have no nationality, no separative religions, no castes—all that nonsense would go.

So, thought cannot under any circumstances bring about a state of love. Thought can only understand what is positive, not what is negative. That is, how can you, through thought, find out what love is? You cannot. You cannot cultivate love. You cannot say, "I practice, day after day, being generous, kind, tender, gentle, thinking about others"—that does not create love; that is still positive action by thought. So it is only when there is the absence of thinking that you can understand what it is to be negative—not through thought. Thought can only create a pattern and according to that pattern or formula act, and hence there is conflict. And to find out a

way of living in which there is no conflict at all, at any time, you must understand this love which is total negation.

Sirs, how can you love, how can there be love, when there is self-centered activity, either of righteousness or smug respectability, or of ambition, greed, envy, competition—which are all positive processes of thought? How can you love? You can't because it is impossible. You can pretend, you can use the word *love*, you can be very emotional, sentimental, you can be very loyal—but that has nothing whatsoever to do with love. To understand what it is, you have to understand this positive thing called "thinking." And so out of this negation, which is called love, there is action which is the most positive because it does not create conflict, because, after all, that is what we want in this world: to live in a world where there is no conflict, where there is actually peace, both outward and inward. You must have peace; otherwise, you are destroyed; it is only in peace that any goodness can flower; it is only in peace that you see beauty. If your mind is tortured, anxious, envious, if your mind is a battlefield, how can you see what is beautiful? Beauty is not thought. The thing that is created by thought is not beauty.

To find out an action which is not based on idea, concept, and formula, you must listen to the whole of that structure, see, understand that whole structure completely; and in the very understanding of it, you have turned away from it. Therefore, your mind then is in a state of negation, not bitterness, not cynicism, but it sees the futility of living that way; it actually sees it and ends it. When you end something, there is a beginning of the new. But we are afraid to end the old because the new we want to translate in terms of the old. You see that? If I realize that I do not really love my family—which means I am not responsible for it—then I am at liberty to chase another woman or another man, which is again the process of thinking. So thought is not the way out.

You can be very clever, erudite; but if you want to find a way of action that is totally different, that gives bliss to life, you must understand the whole machinery of thinking. And in the very understanding of what is positive—which is thought—you enter into a different dimension of action which is essentially love. That means—to inquire you must be free; otherwise, you cannot inquire, you cannot examine; and this chaos, mess in the world demands reexamination totally, not according to your terms, not according to your fancies, pleasures, idiosyncrasies, or the activities to which you have been committed. You have to think of the whole thing anew.

And the new can only be born in negation, not out of the positive assertion of what has been. And the new can only come into being when there is that total emptiness, which is real love. Then you will find out for yourself what action is in which there is no conflict at any time—and that is the rejuvenation that the mind needs. It is only when the mind has been made young through love, which is the total negation of the life of positive thought—not through sentimentality, not through devotion, not through following—that such a mind can build a new world, a new relationship. And it is only such a mind that can go beyond all limitations and enter into a totally different dimension.

And that dimension is something which no word, no thought, no experience can ever discover. It is only when you totally deny the past, which is thought, when you totally deny it every day of your life so that there is never a moment of accumulation—it is only then that you will find out for yourself a dimension which is bliss, which is not of time, which is something that lies beyond human thought.

March 2, 1966

Rome, Italy, 1966

※

First Dialogue in Rome

I think it would be a good idea if we could investigate the word *serious*. Most of us think we are quite serious. We think we are serious if we follow a certain action to which we are committed, or pursue to the end a particular idea, a particular belief, or having committed ourselves to a certain ideology, we pursue that throughout life, not deviating from it. We also think we are very serious if we have a concept, a formula of life, and carry that out throughout our existence.

Now, is that seriousness? If we have committed ourselves to a particular belief, and pursued that belief, if we have given ourselves over to a certain ideological formula, and have lived according to that formula or according to a belief, which is a concept, does all that constitute seriousness? I am just questioning it because that word has great content in it. If we could, as it were, open up that word, and investigate its significance and its structure, then perhaps we could establish a communication with each other, because what we are talking about is quite serious. We are not using words just for the words' sake, or having a reputation, to keep up that reputation. We are not saying something that we don't mean, at least the speaker is not.

And so, to establish a relationship between the speaker and yourself, we must understand the verbal meaning, the content of words, the nature of the usage of words. I think it would be worthwhile if we could investigate that word serious.

If you are going to come here to all these discussions, then either you are very serious, or you are just being entertained by a speaker who perhaps has a new set of ideas. So it seems to me that it's important to understand this word serious. I do not consider any person who is committed to a belief, a dogma, a formula, a course of action, to be serious at all. We have to establish that. To be really serious means to be free—free to investigate, to find out, to have passion to pursue. People do have passion to pursue according to a formula. A man who believes ardently pursues; he lives a life, but it is a life committed to an idea; and a life committed to an idea, to a formula, to a belief, to a concept, to a utopia, is just going round and round in circles. It is really a form of self-worship through identification with a belief.

By using that word serious we mean something entirely different. To inquire into, or examine into, the reality of life, into what is existence, we must be totally free; otherwise, we can't examine. If we are conditioned by belief as Catholics, as Protestants, or as Anglicans, for whom the recent visit of the Archbishop of Canterbury is very important, then we are not free to investigate. It seems to me that a person who is serious, who is essentially free, demands freedom. He may not be free, but he demands it; and in the very demanding of it, he becomes serious because he has no concept of what freedom is. If we have a concept of what freedom is and are committed to that concept, then we are no longer free to investigate freedom. But if we deny the whole commitment to a formula, to a concept, to a utopia, to a conditioned state or to propaganda—on that basis we may discuss. If the mind has been brainwashed through propaganda, through a certain belief, such a person is not free to inquire, and therefore he is not serious. I hope that's clear. If it is not clear, you and I will have no relationship in our talking together. We must really deny this two thousand years of propaganda, of which we are the result. Our social, economic, cultural structure is the result of propaganda, of our religious beliefs, and with that background, with that conditioned mind, it's impossible to examine, or to inquire into a different way of living.

Please let us establish that relationship with each other. It is not possible to discuss or talk over together any issue if you and I are not both at the same level of intensity. If I am factual, argumentative, and you are not serious in the sense in which I am using the word, then you and I have no contact. Can we establish that? Our talking together is not an intellectual examination of the whole process of living. If we are discussing, if we are merely talking together intellectually, then it will have very little more meaning than going to a cinema. But if we are not intellectual, if we are really serious in trying to find out a different way of living because we have come to a crisis, a tremendous crisis in consciousness—not economic, social, or religious, but deep—then these discussions

can be of great value. In the deep consciousness of man, there is a crisis because he has to face a tremendous change in the world, not only outwardly, but inwardly. The outward response depends on the inward state, naturally; and if the inward state is merely a response of a conditioned mind, then of course the crisis doesn't exist at all. If I am a dyed-in-the-wool Catholic, my response to this enormous change that's going on outwardly will be very limited. It will have no value at all.

Is it possible to find a way of life, a way of daily living, which is basically and radically free, and therefore revolutionary? There is only one revolution for me, and that is the religious revolution. The others are not revolutions at all; economic, social, political, and all the rest are not revolutions. There is only one revolution, which is the religious mind in revolt, not as a reaction, but a mind that has established a way of life in which there is no contradiction. All our lives are in contradiction, and therefore in conflict, either the conflict born of trying to conform, conflict through fulfillment, or the conflict engendered by social influence. Human beings have lived in this state of conflict as long as human history is known. Everything they touch turns into conflict, within and without. Either it's a war between people or life as a human being is a battlefield within. We all know this constant, everlasting battle, outwardly and inwardly. Conflict does produce a certain result by the use of the will, but conflict never is creative. That's a dangerous word to use; we'll go into it a little later. To live, to flower in goodness, there must be peace, not economic peace, the peace between two wars, the peace of politicians negotiating treaties, the peace which the church talks about, or what the organized religions preach, but peace that one has discovered for oneself. It is only in peace that we can flower, can grow, can be, can function. It cannot come into being when there is conflict of any kind, conscious or unconscious.

Is it possible to live a life without conflict, in the modern world with all the strain, struggles, pressures, and influences in the social structure? That is really living—the essence of a mind that is inquiring seriously. The question of whether there is God, whether there is truth, whether there is beauty can only come when this is established, when the mind is no longer in conflict.

Can we discuss this?

Question: How is one to avoid this conflict?

KRISHNAMURTI: You can't avoid conflict. You have to understand the nature of conflict. It is one of the most difficult things to understand conflict. We have tried to avoid conflict, so we take to drink, sex, church, organized religions, social activities, superficial amusements—every form of escape. We have tried to avoid this conflict, but we haven't been able to. The very avoidance is contributory to conflict.

Question: Could you say something about the terms of conflict?

KRISHNAMURTI: We'll go into that, sir. First let us see the basic necessity, the fundamental, radical necessity of freedom and peace. We don't know what it means yet. We can see, perhaps only intellectually, the necessity of a mind, a heart, the whole structure of a human being not having conflict, because then there is peace. That peace is really a form of moral behavior because a mind that is not peaceful cannot behave, cannot have right relationship; and right relationship is behavior, conduct, virtue, morals, all the rest of it.

If both of us understand the necessity of ending conflict—understand it even verbally for the moment—then we can proceed; then we can begin to investigate what conflict is, why conflict comes into being, and whether it is at all possible to end conflict by increasing, or by insisting upon, a factor which is called the will. Let's begin slowly. It's a tremendous subject; we can't brush it off in an afternoon. What is conflict, both outwardly and inwardly? We can see outwardly the wars, which are the result of nationalities, economic pressures, religious, personal prejudices. There have been religious wars right through the world. Perhaps Buddhism has not contributed to war, except recently Buddhist priests have burned themselves, but it is totally against the teaching. They are told never to touch politics, but politics is the new alcohol. It gives intoxication; that is nationalism. We can see the contributory factors of war, outwardly, outward ideologies; we don't have to go into all that.

Then there is the inward conflict, which is much more complex. Why is there conflict in us? We are examining; we are not saying that we should or should not be without conflict. We are examining it, and to examine we must be very clear in our thinking, very acute in our observation; we must be intensely aware in observing the whole nature and the significance of conflict. Why is there conflict? What do we mean by that word *struggle*? We are examining the meaning of the word, not what brings about conflict. When are we at all conscious of this word, of the fact? Only when there is pain; only when there is a contradiction; only when there is the pursuit of pleasure and it is denied. I am aware of conflict when my form of pleasure in fulfillment, in ambition, in various forms is thwarted. When pleasure of ambition is frustrated, then I am conscious of conflict, but as long as the pleasure of ambition continues without any blockage, I have no sense

of conflict at all. There is pleasure in conformity. I want to conform to society because
it pays me; it gives me profit. For security,
for a means of livelihood, to become famous,
to be recognized, to be somebody in society,
I must conform to the norm, to the pattern
set by society. As long as I am conforming to
it completely, which is a great pleasure, there is
no conflict; but there is conflict the moment
there is a distraction from that conformity.

*Comment: I am trying to read some book
on philosophy and there is a conflict or tension
between my limited understanding right now
and the understanding in the book, which I
am trying to attain.*

KRISHNAMURTI: That's quite a different
question. Why do I want to read a book?
Why should I try to understand someone,
whether it is Buddha, Christ, or a
philosopher? Why?

*Comment: I think a person is looking for
something.*

KRISHNAMURTI: What for?

*Comment: Well, for myself, I'd say the
truth.*

KRISHNAMURTI: What are we seeking, and
why should we seek? This really requires a
great deal of examination. You can't just say
it is God, truth, this or that; this requires
tremendous inquiry. Why do we seek? What
are we seeking—God, truth, happiness, a better way of life, more sex, more money, more
pleasure? You want God, and they want a
new society. Then what? You want something sublime, and they want I don't know
what. Before we say we are seeking, why are

we seeking and what are we seeking? If there
is a motive for seeking, there is no seeking.

*Comment: Maybe we are investigating to
see.*

KRISHNAMURTI: We are always seeking
with a motive. I am unhappy and I want to
be happy. I like to see the country, I love to
drive and I want a car—that's my motive. As
long as I have a motive, is there any seeking? The seeking is dictated by my motive;
therefore, the seeking is limited.

Comment: It is conditioned.

KRISHNAMURTI: It is conditioned. And is
there a seeking if there is no motive at all?

*Comment: It seems as though there is a
certain unknown which draws us toward itself.*

KRISHNAMURTI: To come upon the unknown, there must be freedom from the
known. We must go into this very slowly.
So, let's begin again. When are we conscious
of conflict? When there is physical pain, we
become conscious; we do something about it.
If there is no pain at all, we carry on, and
that's what we want—to live a life in which
there is no pain at all. Psychologically this is
a fact.

*Comment: There are times when people
do things even though there is pain.*

KRISHNAMURTI: That may be because they
are committed to a certain formula, certain
beliefs, a certain concept of life, and they
say, "This is part of it."

Comment: It may be a certain person that they are doing it for.

KRISHNAMURTI: Then why have pain?

Comment: I think it's just there.

KRISHNAMURTI: You can't accept pain as it's being there. Why should it be there? If we could go into this a little more closely, a little more slowly, step by step, perhaps we'll get at it.

Question: When we go into something in inquiry, even on a word, isn't there a search for something?

KRISHNAMURTI: Surely, sir. The word *search* came when we said "examine." What do we mean by seeking? If a man is very clear in his thinking, in his feeling, in his relationships, in his daily life, there is no conflict; why should he seek? The light in itself is sufficient. Clarity itself is sufficient. That is the basis of existence, and from there we can proceed. But without laying the foundation of right relationship, in which there is no conflict, we are seeking something outside. Right relationship means no conflict between man and man. If we try to go beyond, try to find something else without establishing that, without laying the foundation of that, we won't go any further. The search for truth, God, merely becomes an escape.

Comment: Though theoretically clarity and light are sufficient, are the foundation, in the actual order we start out in darkness.

KRISHNAMURTI: Why do we start out in darkness? Education, the social structure, the influences on our life, propaganda—oh, there are so many contributory factors to this darkness.

Question: Are they contributory factors to the darkness, or are they attempts to shed light on the darkness which was there prior to education or whatever?

KRISHNAMURTI: The past is infinite. Can one say, "Before the past there was clarity"? It comes to that, doesn't it?

Look, sir. If a man is born in India, or in Europe, he becomes a Hindu, or a Catholic, or a Protestant, whatever it is. He is conditioned by society, whether it is communist society, Indian society, or European society. He is conditioned by environment.

Comment: We are part of our environment, but it seems like we are not absolutely conditioned by it.

KRISHNAMURTI: We are conditioned. Ninety percent of us are conditioned.

Comment: Ninety-nine percent.

KRISHNAMURTI: We are conditioned.

Question: What happens to the one percent?

KRISHNAMURTI: Let's find out. To find out if there is one percent at all, you must uncondition your ninety-nine percent; otherwise you can't find out.

Comment: Just because a person is living in a certain social structure, holding certain dogmas or beliefs, there may be two ways of doing it. He may have been born into a religion or a certain society, and just continues along in that, never questioning it. . . .

KRISHNAMURTI: Yes, sir. Or? Or?

Comment: Or the person is actually choosing. . . .

KRISHNAMURTI: Ah, wait, wait! This is a famous fallacy, choosing. What makes him choose? Why should he choose at all?

Comment: I don't know. It seems like man does choose. . . .

KRISHNAMURTI: Why does he choose? Why doesn't he choose Buddhism instead of Catholicism, or communism? Why?

Comment: Some people are. . . .

KRISHNAMURTI: Your tendency, your proclivities, your inclination, your social background, religion—all that pushes you in a certain direction, and you say you are choosing. You see, sir, I question this whole way of choosing. Why should I choose? If a man is free, he has no choice. There is no question of choice. Finished. That is why I said at the beginning that to establish a serious discussion, there must be this examination of freedom and peace. Otherwise you can't proceed. If you say man can never be free, then you have blocked yourself. You have stopped yourself from further examination. If you make an ideal of freedom, again you have blocked yourself. You have not if you say, "Let us find out by denying what it is to be free." To be free is not a reaction. It implies no nationality, obviously—that is, outwardly—though you may have a passport. I have one from India, but I'm not anything, nor do I belong to any religion because organized religions are just like any other organized corporation. Through those I can't find God, or truth. I must be free first to find out. It further implies freedom from anger, jealousy, envy, ambition, competition, wanting fame, prestige—a complete denial of the

social structure in which I have been brought up. Otherwise I'm not free; otherwise, I cannot possibly have a right relationship with man. If you and I discuss this question of freedom, and you say, "Well, I stick to my particular conditioning, and let's talk about freedom," this is completely futile. It means really understanding my conditioning, not finding an excuse for it, not saying that it is right or wrong, that it is justified, that I can't escape from it, that it is inevitable, that I have chosen it. I have to examine my conditioning.

Question: Is a yogi who lives on the top of a mountain free from conditioning?

KRISHNAMURTI: No, obviously not. It is merely an escape. Sir, it is so obvious. He may live on the top of a mountain, or in a cell, but he is conditioned; his whole background is Catholic, Buddhist, Islam. He is the expression of his background, which says that you must retire into a monastery, to a hill, to find God. The other background says that you must so identify yourself with the community, with the state, that you are not an individual, that you are no longer thinking about yourself. You have the two extremes.

To come back to the question: "Is it possible to live a life in the modern world without conflict?" Conflict is an awareness of frustration, an awareness of blockage, an awareness of pain, an awareness of competition, an awareness of the importance of the pursuit of your own activities, or of being identified with an activity organized as a religion, of being identified as a communist, and so on.

I feel that man has never demanded freedom, absolute freedom. We want partial freedom—partial freedom being freedom from anything that causes pain, any psychological pain. From that I want to be free, divorced, or any of a dozen forms. The fundamental question is, if I may repeat it, whether it is possible to live without conflict, without war, outwardly, and inwardly without there being a battle with myself, my wife, my children, my society, my neighbor. If there is conflict, it distorts the mind, consciously or unconsciously; and a distorted mind, whether it is on the top of a hill or in a monastery, is still a distorted mind. It can pursue its own image, but it won't be reality.

Question: Can I live without any conflict at all? It seems something simple like getting up in the morning. Sometimes I just don't feel like getting up. Rationally I know there are certain specific things I want to do today, yet there's a certain part of me that. . . .

KRISHNAMURTI: Rebels, which is contradiction. That is, one part of me, one part of desire says, "I must go for a walk on this lovely evening," and the other part says, "What a bore walking is; I want to listen to what this chap is talking about," and I have a conflict. I may be putting it on the most absurd level, but that's what we are. Our desires are torn towards one thing, and the opposite of that.

Shall we go into the nature of conflict? Let's not particularize, but get the whole picture of conflict; then you can particularize it yourselves. What is conflict? We have accepted conflict as the way of life—conflict with a man or with a woman. There have been nearly fifteen thousand wars in the last five thousand five hundred years, two and a half wars every year. We have accepted war as the way of life. In ourselves there is this perpetual battle going on: "I must" and "I must not"; "I should" and "I should not." We live in an endless corridor of duality. Not that there is not duality. There is the woman and the man; there is darkness and light. Factually there is no contradiction, but we have created psychological contradiction. Why is there this conflict of duality?—"I must" and "I must not"; "I should" and "I should not."

Comment: Because we don't understand; we don't see.

KRISHNAMURTI: Why don't we see? Because we don't know that we are in conflict. We don't know, and we don't say, "I must find a way out of this completely." We have never said, "I must be totally free from conflict." We have accepted the bourgeois way of life, which is conflict, whether it is in Moscow, in London, in Rome, or in any other place. We have accepted it. If we don't accept it, we have much more trouble; we have infinite bother. That's why we avoid it.

Question: So how do we get out of it?

KRISHNAMURTI: First, let's see it. What brings about conflict?

Comment: Our desires.

KRISHNAMURTI: All right. Your desire. What is wrong with a desire?

Comment: We should have no desires.

KRISHNAMURTI: No, sir. If you had no desire, what would happen?

Comment: I would have peace.

KRISHNAMURTI: Does peace contradict desire?

Comment: No.

KRISHNAMURTI: Therefore you have to understand desire. You have to understand the nature of it, the meaning of it, the whole structure of it. Now, what is desire?

Comment: Something that you believe you need.

KRISHNAMURTI: No, no, before that. What is desire, not desire for something?

Comment: A craving that comes out from your body, from your brain.

KRISHNAMURTI: What does that mean, sir? Go into it. Let us go into the anatomy of desire, before the desire is, before it identifies itself, before desire is created by the object. You follow, sir, what I mean? Both in Asia and in Europe the religious people have denied desire. They say, "Desire is wrong, evil, sinful; turn your back against it." You must take that into account.

Comment: Yes.

KRISHNAMURTI: That's part of the structure. They say that unless you have tremendous control over your desires, unless you have them trained, those desires will lead you to distraction and not to reality; so you must discipline, control, suppress. That's part of the heritage.

Comment: If we don't suppress the whole thing, we. . . .

KRISHNAMURTI: Wait, wait! Don't say that yet. Go into it, sir; let's see. Before we suppress it, deny it, control it, shape it or whatever it is, let's see how desire comes into being—not the desire for the object or the object that creates the desire, but the feeling of desire itself.

Comment: I am discontented with what I have.

KRISHNAMURTI: No, no. We are not talking of discontent but of desire. I see a beautiful car. Instantly I have a desire for it. That is the immediate reaction.

Question: Is that the same for everybody? You can have five people walking by a beautiful car, and they won't all want it.

KRISHNAMURTI: It may be a beautiful woman, or you may want a beautiful house, a lovely garden. The object varies with each person. We are talking of the nature of desire itself, not the object.

Comment: I don't see how we can talk about desire if we don't talk about the person desiring.

KRISHNAMURTI: We are going to; you will see it in a minute, sir. I or you or someone sees something. There is a first seeing—the image, the car, the woman, the house—the first visual perception. It may not even be visual but may be intellectual, a very good idea. There is perception; there is perceiving; then there is the reacting.

Comment: The reaction could be any of a number of things.

KRISHNAMURTI: Oh, yes, of course. I said "reacting"; I didn't give a specific name to the reaction. Then there is the intervention of the mind, of thought, saying, "I would like to have that," or "not that." That's a form of desire, isn't it? It is very simple when you examine what desire is. Perception, contact, sensation, the identification with that, and the demand for the fulfillment of that. All religions have said, "Retire; don't look at the world, at the woman, the money, position; it's death to reality."

Comment: Many religions don't say that.

KRISHNAMURTI: Most do. Otherwise all the Catholic priests wouldn't be in that position. All the Hindus and Buddhists say, "Suppress; get away from desire."

Question: Do you not think it might be better to hold off judgment of religions, which may be historical. . . .

KRISHNAMURTI: No, sir. This is not a question of anything historical. We are discussing the fact—desire.

Comment: Judgment as to whether the desire of life to Buddhism, the Mayan Indians, or to Catholicism. . . .

KRISHNAMURTI: But, sir, this is human structure; not Catholic desire or Hindu desire, but human nature desires.

Comment: I think we have to understand whether a particular religion discourages desire or not.

KRISHNAMURTI: Let's forget religion. There is human desire. That desire has created so much mischief in the world—my desire, wanting to be prominent, wanting to be famous. Unless one understands the nature of desire, merely suppressing it or running away from it has no meaning. I see how desire arises: seeing the object, and the object strengthening desire. This is very simple.

What makes it more complex is when the desire has a continuity. I have to find out why there is continuity to desire.

Comment: I may desire to understand something, too. For instance, in reading a book about communism, I want to understand how it developed, what it stands for, what it means, what position it has in the world today.

KRISHNAMURTI: All right; all right.

Question: Shouldn't there be a desire for understanding?

KRISHNAMURTI: Yes, maybe. But we're not discussing the desire for understanding. We are trying to find out the nature of desire, not for something. We don't say the desire for understanding is right or wrong. What we are saying is that we are trying to understand desire itself, per se, not whether desire for this is right or is wrong. I see how desire comes into being. Then also I see how desire has a continuity, and there is the problem—not desire itself, but giving strength and vitality through time to desire. Now, what gives continuity to desire?

Comment: I want a thing and I have it, and then the desire grows.

KRISHNAMURTI: There is desire for it, and I make a lot of effort to get it, which means that there is a sustained desire. Now, what gives substance, nourishment, sustenance to maintain this desire?

Comment: That is the problem.

KRISHNAMURTI: I'm looking at it, sir; I'm looking at the problem.

Comment: You think that by getting that thing, something will be added to your life.

KRISHNAMURTI: All right, you get it. We're not going into the question of getting an object of enrichment or one which does not enrich. We are seeing the nature of desire itself.

Comment: The urge to grow is what keeps the desire going.

KRISHNAMURTI: The urge to grow, to keep the desire going means a continuity, a constancy.

Comment: As long as you have the urge to grow, it seems all right to have the desire.

KRISHNAMURTI: I am not saying "grow" or "not grow." You see, you are identifying already with growth, and therefore you're blocking the examination.

Comment: Well, I don't see how I can do otherwise. I am not what I was when I was ten years old.

KRISHNAMURTI: We are not discussing the importance or unimportance of desire. We are trying to find out what gives constancy to desire.

Comment: That doesn't present an answer because I'm not talking about the importance or the unimportance of desire.

KRISHNAMURTI: Please have a little patience; I'm coming to that; you will see it. I have to find out why desire has such potency in my life. It may be right or it may not be right. I have to find out. I see that. Desire arises, which is a reaction, which is a healthy, nor-

mal reaction; otherwise, I would be dead. I see a beautiful thing and I say, "By Jove, I want that." If I didn't, I'd be dead. But in the constant pursuit of it there is pain. That's my problem—there is pain as well as pleasure. I see a beautiful woman, and she is beautiful; it would be most absurd to say, "No, she's not." This is a fact. But what gives continuity to the pleasure? Obviously it is thought, thinking about it. Right, sir?

Comment: Yes.

KRISHNAMURTI: I think about it. It is no longer the direct relationship with the object, which is desire, but thought now increases that desire by thinking about it, by having images, pictures, ideas.

Comment: Yes.

Comment: You fight not to have it.

KRISHNAMURTI: All that fight not to have it, the whole business of thought gives it intensity. Thought comes in and says, "Please, you must have it; that's growth; that is important; that is not important; this is vital for your life; this is not vital for your life."
But I can look at it and have a desire, and that's the end of it, without interference of thought.

Question: It relates to God, too?

KRISHNAMURTI: I don't want to come into that yet. Let's take the simple things first. I have to understand the whole machinery of thought; not suppress desire, not say it is right or wrong, good or bad, noble or ignoble—that's all too immature. But I have to go into the question of what thinking is. If thought doesn't interfere with it, then there may be a different action altogether. I have to find out what thinking is, and if there is any need to think at all. These are the two questions I have to answer before I can say what I am going to do with the desire. Right, sir?

Comment: Yes.

KRISHNAMURTI: What is thinking? The electronic brains are thinking, thinking along the information which has been fed into them. And I think according to my experiences, knowledge, incidents, influences, pain, pleasure—the whole background of my memory, religious, economic; a Brahmin fasting. I react according to the whole of that background. My machinery is much more subtle than the electronic brain, but it works on the same principle.

Comment: I think the electronic brain is just regurgitating facts that have been fed into it.

KRISHNAMURTI: But aren't we doing the same? Wait, madame. Examine it; don't say no or yes. Let's look.

Comment: We are not thinking if we are only giving out what has been fed to us.

KRISHNAMURTI: But that's what we call thinking.

Comment: Ah, I see; that's what we call it.

KRISHNAMURTI: I'm thinking.

Comment: It may be true scientifically, but it is still working on the basis of what has been put into it.

KRISHNAMURTI: Please, let's look at it the other way. You are an Italian and I am supposed to be a Hindu. You have your background, your story, your culture, your religion, your experiences, your knowledge, your daily incidents and memories. And I have my memory, my banks of memory. From that I react; from that I respond.

Question: How does that fit in with the idea of freedom that you spoke about?

KRISHNAMURTI: It doesn't exist.

Comment: If you think it doesn't exist.

KRISHNAMURTI: It does not exist. That is one of the most difficult things until we're free. That's what I was going into. Unless I understand this machinery of thinking—the memory, the whole background of my culture, my tradition of ten thousand years as a Brahmin, this, that—how am I to be free?

Comment: I do it with my mind.

KRISHNAMURTI: No, we haven't come to it yet. First let us see the fact. Then how to be free from it, from which comes a different question—whether this is at all possible. You might say, "Well, if I'm free, what am I? I am nothing. I'm no longer an Italian, with all my culture, with all my glory, with my literature, my art. And if I'm nothing, I'm lost."

Question: Do you think it might be good, along with the examination of memory, to investigate, investigate, investigate?

KRISHNAMURTI: Who is the investigator? Is that what you're saying?

Comment: No.

KRISHNAMURTI: And what is the thing that is being investigated?

Question: What is the process of investigation?

KRISHNAMURTI: We are doing it; we are doing it.

Question: It seems that would be different from the process of memory, or even the process of judgment. See what I mean?

KRISHNAMURTI: I don't quite catch what you mean.

Comment: It's just that you mentioned before that memory is very important in thinking.

KRISHNAMURTI: With all of us it is.

Comment: It really is. It also seems that we have this power of investigation.

KRISHNAMURTI: Wait, wait! Do we investigate as long as we are tethered to the post of the past?

Comment: We have to determine that, upon determining the meaning of investigation.

KRISHNAMURTI: Sir, that's why to investigate, even the greatest scientist must have freedom in his laboratory.

Comment: Right.

KRISHNAMURTI: Otherwise he can't investigate. And also, to investigate very profoundly, he must be free from the knowledge which he has. Otherwise it stops him.

Comment: That's the way Freud found out about psychoanalysis. He threw away all conditioning.

KRISHNAMURTI: Yes, sir, but Freud probably got it from some others. That's irrelevant for the moment.

Comment: I think he throws away the past, goes beyond it, like a scientist, a chemist. He doesn't go back.

KRISHNAMURTI: No, no! This is theoretical. I don't know what the scientist does.

Comment: He throws away the past and goes beyond it.

KRISHNAMURTI: Ah, wait; wait. It comes to the same thing, sir. I cannot go beyond it if I am tethered to the past.

Comment: I don't see how one can get away from the past.

KRISHNAMURTI: We are going to find out. You see, you insist on blocking it by saying you cannot.

Comment: The only way I can see investigating is not to find out if there are any preconceived ideas but to live out of experience, using that as a starting point.

KRISHNAMURTI: Experience is not a starting point. Man has had experience for the last five thousand five hundred years about war. Kill, kill, kill in the name of God, in the name of peace, in the name of love, in the name of nations, etc., etc. There is tremendous experience stored up, but experience is not a criterion.

Comment: No, it is not a criterion, but it seems that if we are going to find out what thinking is, we must start with the experience of thinking.

KRISHNAMURTI: No, sir. Do please listen for a few minutes. Thinking is the reaction of accumulated knowledge as experience, as tradition, as the background. That's a fact. Look, sir. I ask your name and you reply immediately, don't you? There is no thinking; at least the thinking is so rapid it has become habitual.

Comment: I can refuse to give my name.

KRISHNAMURTI: Ah, ah, ah! (Laughter) We said, sir, that thinking gives intensity and continuity to desire. Thinking breeds pleasure.

Comment: Right.

KRISHNAMURTI: I see a woman, or whatever it is. It's a pleasure; I think about it. Pleasure gives sustenance and continuity to desire. So, pleasure is the basic principle of our life, whether in the name of God, in the name of killing, or whatever it is.

Comment: Right.

KRISHNAMURTI: You follow, sir? All our ethics, all our virtue, all our relationships are based on pleasure. Right?

Comment: Yes.

KRISHNAMURTI: You admit it so easily? (Laughter) Sir, to discover that is a terrific blow. It isn't just a passing word. My relationship with my wife, with my society, with my God, with my values, with my vir-tue, everything is based on that. I'm not being cynical but merely factual. Pleasure is what is driving me. Where there is pleasure there is pain. I'm caught in that; there is the conflict. Inherent in pleasure is pain. There is the origin of conflict.

Comment: One must see the fact.

KRISHNAMURTI: See the fact that where there is the pursuit of pleasure in the name of the most high or in the name of the most crooked, it is still pleasure, and therefore there is pain. There is the root of conflict. That's a fact, not how am I to get out of it.

Comment: That's the way of our life.

KRISHNAMURTI: Of course. And I say to myself, "Is there a way of living without this, without pleasure which breeds pain?" This doesn't mean that I can't look at a tree and say, "What a marvelous tree!" Unless I understand this basic principle of pleasure, in which pain is embedded, consciously or unconsciously, there is always conflict.

Question: Suppose I understand it?

KRISHNAMURTI: Then I have to pursue. Then I have to say that I see this fact—that as long as there is the pursuit of pleasure, there is pain. As long as I am eating wrong food, there is pain. The wrong food gives me pleasure; I eat it and I pay for it later. That's the way we live, wrong food and all the rest of it.

How am I to be free of it without conflict? If I deny it, there will be a conflict because I'm caught in it. If I accept it, then that's the way we all live.

Comment: We seek pleasure and we die with pain.

KRISHNAMURTI: That's our life. So, how are we to be free of conflict? That's a tremendous question. We have to go into it very deeply. All social, moral, ethical, and religious beliefs and doctrines are based on this. We may deny it, but if we tear it open, it is that. The mind sees this factually, as I factually see this microphone. It sees it as a fact, not as a theory, not as a hopeless state. It is so; it is like that. Then the question is: Is it possible to live without conflict? This does not mean that I must suppress pleasure.

Comment: I must suppress both.

KRISHNAMURTI: Ah, no! If you suppressed both, you'd be dead.

Comment: I don't say we must accept it.

KRISHNAMURTI: All of us have accepted it, and we live in conflict. If a man says, "No, I don't want to live in conflict; I must find a way out, totally, completely, both consciously and unconsciously," he has to tackle this problem. How is he to be free from conflict? This means freedom from pleasure and pain. Unless this is understood, your inquiry about truth, God, has no meaning whatsoever because God may be something tremendous, not your pet gods. Proceed; how do you go beyond it?

Comment: I believe that each individual can create for himself a concept of happiness that has nothing to do with pain and pleasure.

KRISHNAMURTI: Oh, my lady! No, madame. We said concepts were out.

Comment: The individual, each individual...

KRISHNAMURTI: No, no, no! There's no such thing as each individual.

Comment: I must think for myself.

KRISHNAMURTI: You are not an individual. You are the result of your country, your culture, your knowledge. We like to think we are individuals. There is nothing but second-hand.

March 31, 1966

Second Dialogue in Rome

We were talking, the other day when we met here, about being serious, what it implies, and how important it is. Only the very earnest and the very serious people, in the sense that we mean, live; the others do not. Considering the enormous complication of modern existence, perhaps outwardly it may be very simple, but inwardly it is very, very complex. We have accepted war both outwardly and inwardly as a way of life. We have never challenged it; we have never questioned it; and perhaps we dare not question it. If we do question it, we have no answers, and our mind is always seeking answers, is always trying to find a way out, a path, a system, a new method through which it can put aside all this confusion and find a different way of life. As we said the other day, man has lived, as far as human recorded history goes, for five thousand five hundred years with war; and that has been our life. We have looked to science, to religion, to priests, to various forms of Hindu escapism, to Zen.

If we are at all serious, we do not trust anyone. We have no faith in anyone, and quite rightly, too. We have no faith in the politician, in the priest, in any organized religion, nor in any book. That again is an obvious fact, except for very, very immature people. And as the world consists of 99.9 percent immature people, we are lost. Not that we are in any way superior, but that's a fact. We cannot look to any authority. It behooves us to find out for ourselves as human beings, not as individuals. We went into the fact the other day that the individual is a local entity—an Italian, a Hindu, a Buddhist, a Vietnamese, or an American, a localized entity—whereas a human being is a total being, a vast quantum of human experience, misery, conflicts, sorrow.

One has to look for oneself since there is no one else to tell what one should do or should not do, what one should think or not think. That becomes extremely difficult because one does not know if one is capable. One wants someone else to point out, and if one looks to someone else, one falls into the trap again—the trap of authority, of following, of books, of priests, and the whole circus of it. What is one to do? How is one to renew or rewrite or examine the whole process of living anew? That is the real issue that was discussed the other day, only I am putting it in different words. There is no guide, no philosopher, no friend, nothing to help us out of this dreadful mess. Either one comes to total despair, complete cynicism, as most so-called intellectual writers have done, invents marvelous philosophies of despair and sticks there; or putting everything aside, all these systems, philosophies, ideas, concepts, beliefs, organized propaganda as religion, if one is capable of doing it—and one has to do it to find out—one then comes to the problem, the central issue. One must find out whether it is possible, living in this world, not escaping from it to a monastery or to a hilltop, whether it is possible to live in this world as a total human being. This means a human being who is no longer at war with the world and within himself—there is no contradiction without or within. Contradiction breeds conflict. Where there is conflict in any form, conscious or unconscious, obviously there can't be affection, love, and all the rest of that. One can't perceive clearly if there is a distorted mind, and there is distortion as long as there is conflict.

We are saying that it is possible to live a life in which there is no conflict at all, at any time. This means denying war, outwardly and inwardly, as a means of life, as a means of living. In examining that the other day—I hope you don't mind my going over it a little bit—we said that there is contradiction as long as there are contradictory, opposing desires. We went into the question of how desire per se comes into being, not desire for something. We also went into the question of what gives potency, continuity, vitality to desire. We said that thought gives it constancy. I see something visually; out of that there is desire, contact, pleasure; and thought, by thinking about it, gives it nourishment and continuity. Naturally, it wouldn't think about it if it didn't give pleasure. We can observe this very easily for ourselves. I like that woman; I like that house; I like that picture or that music, and I think about it. I sustain by thought the intensity of that desire.

Please, don't accept anything that the speaker is saying, because we are not setting him up as another authority, which would be dreadful. If we observe sufficiently intelligently, we can see this phenomenon going on all the time. The conflict is between the various contradictory desires, sustained by thought, and thought maintains it as long as the desire is pleasureable; otherwise, thought wouldn't even think about it. If you have had a pain, you want to forget it very quickly; if you have had a pleasure, either of a sunset or of any other form, thought gives it movement, vitality, a propulsion, drive. Thought maintains it because there is pleasure in it.

Where there is pleasure, there is always pain, if you observe it. That's a fact. There is this basic contradiction in the structure of our thinking: pleasure and pain, the avoidance of pain and the pursuit of pleasure. Yet where there is the pursuit of pleasure, there is in it, inherently, pain. Hence the whole process of our living is contradictory, and therefore potential conflict. Again this is factual; it is not my imagination or your wish or not-wish; it is just a fact. We can see that our values, our ideals, our gods, our search are all based on this desire for the continuance of pleasure. If one goes into this sufficiently seriously and earnestly, one comes to this point.

There are contradictions which are inevitable, natural: man and woman, darkness and light, a dozen forms of contradiction from colors, and so on. Those variations and differences and that duality do not bring us pain. We accept them as inevitable. What gives us pain is the demand for the continuance of a pleasure. This doesn't mean that we must have no pleasure—we will go into that presently. First we must understand this basic principle.

How are we to put an end to conflict? As long as the principle exists there will be conflict. It is not a matter of agreement with me. We have to work at this with intense passion; otherwise, it becomes merely intellectual agreement and blah. We can see very well that as long as there is conflict, we can't think clearly, we can't look clearly, we can't observe in clarity. We may have no conflict superficially, consciously, but unconsciously there is a whirlpool, a world of contradiction. The more extreme the contradiction, the greater the tension, the greater will be the desire to escape, through football, amusement, church, or goodness knows what else. Hence there is a psychotic, unbalanced state, and I go to an analyst to be made normal and to return to conflict again; or if I am normal, to adjust myself to society, which is the very essence of contradiction. The whole psychoanalytical approach to this question seems to be utterly superficial, leading nowhere.

If we have really gone very deeply into this question, then what are we to do? If we have not gone that far—not verbally, not intellectually, but actually—there is no point in talking things over. It has no value at all. Unless we have done it, we might just as well gossip about someone, discuss the beauties of morning, talk about pictures and modern art, and carry on. We understand the problem very clearly, don't we? We see the importance of having a very clear mind. We might say that that is impossible—that the mind will always be conditioned, by communism, by the church, by society, or by propaganda; that it is bound to be conditioned, and therefore there is no escape from this conditioning. If we accept that, there is no question; there is no problem. All we have to do is to make the conditioning a little more clean, a little more palatable, a little more civilized, a little more decorated. But if we don't accept that, if we see the absurdity of it, then we must have a clear mind, and that clear mind can only come when there is no conflict, conscious or unconscious.

The problem then arises: How are we to come to this? How are we, seeing the basic issue that where there is pleasure there must be pain, that the pursuit of pleasure in any form is the breeding of pain and therefore of contradiction and conflict, how are we to come out of it? If such a proposition, such a question, such a challenge is put to us, how do we respond? We have to answer this; let's talk it over together. There is perpetual war outside between nations, for economic, social, ideological reasons; there is tyranny, oppression, dogmatism, both religious and political; there is all that on one side, and there is the battle inside, the unending battle—that's our life. Tracing it, watching the flow of all the ways of man, the ways man has lived through centuries upon centuries, one comes to this essential central issue. As human beings, what do we do? How do we answer it? How do you answer it? You understand the question, the problem? Who is to end it? Is thought to end it? Is will to end it? And who is the entity that wields the power as will to end it? If we say we will live in peace by suppressing all desire, all pleasure, then we will become dead sticks. If we say we will end it through the action of the will, determination, choice, force, that in itself is violence. Any exertion of will, which is opposition, resistance, breeds conflict. It isn't an easy problem! It isn't just a slick problem that we can answer very easily and superficially.

Question: Is the logical structure of man in a position to do this?

KRISHNAMURTI: I don't know what you mean, sir, by logical structure. Do you mean that the very brain cells have accepted the reaction through centuries of growth, development, pressure—have accepted this way of life? The brain itself—the cells have said, "There is no way out; I'll accept it." Having accepted it, yet resisting it, not wanting it, they invent ways and means to escape from it: drink, sex, multitudinous forms of escapes. Never wanting to go near this conflict, which is eating out the individual's heart and mind, he becomes a psychosomatic case. Do you understand the problem? I see the importance of living without conflict. I not only see it intellectually, but see it, not as a theory, a speculative hope, or a wish. I see it as clearly as I see that flower. That state must come into being. How am I to get it? How am I to come upon it? By exertion? By making more effort, which is the will? The very effort is a contradiction. To overcome something I have to exert, and the very exer-

tion implies a contradiction. I see will, determination, the exercise of choice as a decisive factor. I say, "I will," and thereby create resistance; the very resistance brings contradiction, and I am again back in conflict.

Look, sir; take a very simple thing. If I smoke and want to give it up, by saying "I am determined to give it up," I have already created a conflict. I want to give it up. I force myself to give it up. The very force is strengthening the conflict. Yet I must give it up. Perhaps I give it up through fear because it affects my lungs. I may give it up, but there is this constant fear. So will—and this requires tremendous comprehension, real understanding—will is not the way to peace, to the cessation of conflict. To break through that you must have such clarity. It's like a man who has taken the wrong road and insists on going on that road; that's what we have done. We know through experience, through knowledge, through information, through everything, that the road leads nowhere; yet we keep on going in the same way. If we see that will is no way out, we must abandon it, not only with regard to this, but totally.

Comment: So I go on smoking.

KRISHNAMURTI: All right, do it, but do it consciously. Know where it is going, what it is doing to you. Understand all the implications of being caught in a habit, being a slave to habit. If you want that, go to it. That's what we are doing anyhow. We know very well that one of the major factors that bring on war is nationalism; we realize the poison of that, and yet we keep on. We are Italians, Russians, Indians. And the mind saying that it wants to achieve a state of mind which has no conflict is already a factor which is going to breed conflict.

Comment: Then there is no hope.

KRISHNAMURTI: Ah, wait a bit, sir; I don't say that there is no hope.

Comment: The only weapon we have is will.

KRISHNAMURTI: Ah, no; will doesn't do anything.

Question: All right, what is the alternative?

KRISHNAMURTI: Wait, sir, wait! If you don't see that as false and give it up as false, you won't see the other. You can't say, "Well, I'll keep to this until he proves to me the other." You can't find the other unless you give this up. I mean, you can't have one foot there and one foot here.

Comment: The word alternative *is conflict.*

KRISHNAMURTI: Obviously. This is really a very, very tremendous question. We can't just banish it away in a morning. Just as a man has lived on war, competition, ambition, and greed, he also lived on will, resistance, and fighting. I must be that, and I am going to work for it. The stronger the will, the more achievement, the more success, the more revolution. That's what we live on. And if we see that will under any circumstances is not the way out, we have cleared the field, cleared the field to look somewhere else. But if we say, "Well, show me the other," we haven't cleared the field to look. We are like that man who said, "I belong to all religions because I don't know; there may be something to them all." This is really a very complex and profound thing to understand—that the action of will only produces more conflict. We can see that in-

tellectually because we can prove it statistically, but we're not dealing with statistics. Intellectually we say, "Yes, I see that," but the intellectual perception is not action. Intellect, however clever, however bright, however sound, is not going to solve this problem. We have used will as the way of conquering, the way of going beyond the conflict. The problem in that comes also: Who is the entity that exercises will? Who is the 'me', the 'I', the thinker? When we say, "I will do this," who is the 'I'? When we deny or accept will as the way of life—as most human beings do, 99.9 percent of them—we live in conflict. But if we don't accept it as the way of life, then we have to see who it is that is exercising this will. Again we have to go back to desire.

Question: So the 'I' is desire?

KRISHNAMURTI: Obviously. A bundle of desires, with its memories. Don't let us go into that for the moment.

Comment: But investigation also comes from having a will to see more clearly.

KRISHNAMURTI: Ah, wait a bit! Is that so? Look at that flower. Do you exercise will to look at that flower? Please, let's begin slowly. When do you exercise will? You want to look at that tree, or something more pleasurable, and you exercise your will to cut that out and look at this.

Comment: This is a simple phenomenon.

KRISHNAMURTI: Keep to the simple; we'll complicate it as we go along. Do you see anything when you determine to see? When you say, "I am determined to listen to what you're saying," all your energy has gone into the determination, not into the listening.

This is elementary. To see anything you must have freedom, not determination. To observe there must be no hindrance. If you are not interested in observing, don't observe. Who cares?

Comment: But to see smears of cancer cells that come from lungs as a result of smoking is something of investigation. Everyone doesn't see it, naturally. You have to go to a certain place and investigate what comes from smoking.

KRISHNAMURTI: But I have investigated, and I like smoking, and to blazes with regard to what they have investigated. I don't mind dying.

I am afraid that we are not pursuing the thing we were discussing. To observe a flower, anything, there must be freedom to look, not a determination which is sustained by a motive of pleasure, gain, or pain. I see clearly that will, conscious or unconscious, is not the way because will is really a process, a mechanism of resistance. If I resist, obviously there is no peace, no ending of conflict. This is so, outwardly. If I resist you by will, you are my enemy. I put you away. This is so clear that I don't understand the difficulty. The difficulty comes in because I don't know any other way, and without seeing the depth, the reality, the complexity involved in will, I say, "I'll hold on to that before I go to something else. It is better to have the evil that I know of, rather than to go after something that I don't know." Anyhow, I'll go into it. Will is not the way; at least for me it is not the way. Consciously or unconsciously, I will not resist. But that doesn't mean that I do not see ugliness, beauty, evil, dirt, squalor, and all the exploitation that is going on in the world. It doesn't mean that I also yield, that I say, "Well, as I have no will, I'll do anything that anyone wants me to do." On the con-trary, if what the world wants me to do is based on will, immaturity, and resistance, why should I accept? I have rejected will, which means that I have understood the entity who exercises will, which is desire and the memories of desire, memories of pleasure and of pain. That is the bundle from which will has its being.

Then what am I to do if I have no will at all? Please don't say the opposite, that you're just a leaf in the wind, driven by anyone, anything. That's not at all true, but quite the contrary. Then what happens? Now we come to really quite the most interesting part of it. I see that conflict cannot end through will. Will in itself breeds conflict. The very nature and structure of the will, to which we have become accustomed, the brain cells and all the rest of it, in their very structure breed conflict. I see very clearly that to live intensely, fully, completely, wholly, conflict is not necessary. Conflict, on the contrary, destroys. Will is gone, not verbally or theoretically, but actually—not as a hypothesis towards which I am working, which again becomes another conflict. Then what have I to do? How am I to give up without will, without fear? Smoking, sex, or anything I take as an escape gives me pleasure and becomes a habit, either pleasurable or painful. If it is painful it is easier to give it up, naturally. But a thing that gives pleasure—how am I to give it up without will, which means without time? If I say, "I'll give it up gradually," and day after day diminish the number of cigarettes I smoke, what has happened? There's a resistance all along.

Comment: You have to understand why you smoke.

KRISHNAMURTI: We understand why we smoke. First of all, it's a habit. We did it as small boys, and now it has become constant. We know why we smoke. It gives us something to do with our hands when we are with people, and we fiddle around. It's just that everyone does it, and we do it, too. We are like a lot of monkeys, with our intense restlessness. Take drink, if you don't smoke. It's the same thing with drink, with sex, with any habit. Now please, sirs, this is very interesting. To give up smoking, sex, a particular habit of thinking, a particular way of living, a particular food, may be a very small affair, or a most complex affair. We see will is not the way out, and a gradual process is not the way out. It must be done instantly, without effort. To give up something immediately, no time is involved at all. How do we do it, sirs? I don't know why we make a mystery of it. It's very simple. There's a wasp there, a pretty large one. There it is. What takes place when we see it? There is immediate action to get away from it.

Comment: There is fear.

KRISHNAMURTI: Please don't reduce it so quickly; just look at it; look at it. There is a wasp. You know that it stings, causes pain. There is an immediate reaction—to kill it, to run away from it, or to push it out. It is a physiological reaction; it is not an intellectual process. It may have been at the beginning, but now it is a physical reaction. There is instant movement, instant action. Your brain cells, your nerves, your whole being responds because there is a danger. If you don't respond, there's something wrong with your nerves, with your brain, with your whole nervous organism. You have to respond. So there is a state when you can respond immediately. When you see danger, physical danger, you respond instantly; the body responds before the mind enters. I once saw a tiger in the wilderness; there was immediate reaction, and that reaction is necessary. It is a healthy reaction, and it is instant.

I see the habit of smoking, or sex, a particular idea or a particular concept that I have. I hold on to it. It has become a habit. I don't react as I react to the wasp. This means that I don't see the danger as I see the danger of that wasp; I don't see the danger of pleasure in smoking, in a hundred things, the danger of the pleasure of being a nationalist, a Hindu. The Hindu still has its own division, which is a Brahmin. The fact that I'm a Brahmin gives tremendous pleasure. It gives me dignity, position, a sense of identification, vitality, which leads ultimately to war. I don't see the whole sequence of it. If I see the danger of it as clearly as I see the danger of the wasp, it is finished! I don't have to go to the analysts, and all the rest of the business. Why don't I see the danger of it? Why don't I see the danger of nationalism, racial differences, cultural differences, religious differences, ideological differences as communists, socialists, and the whole works? Why don't I see the danger of it, totally? When I see the danger of it totally, I've finished; I don't even have to think about it twice.

Please discuss with me; otherwise, I'll carry on. Why do I see the danger of the wasp and not the much more dangerous other things? They are much more dangerous because I and my children will be caught in wars. Everything will go up in smoke. Yet I keep on with my vested interests. Why don't I see the danger? To the wasp I'm sensitive, extremely sensitive; to the other I'm not sensitive. Why am I not? This brings another question: Am I sensitive at all? Am I sensitive all around, not just to the wasp? If I am sensitive to one danger, why am I not sensitive to other dangers? It means that I'm not sensitive.

Question: Does conditioning fit in here?

KRISHNAMURTI: Yes, sir, but first let's see that we're not sensitive. I'm not sensitive. I'm sensitive to the wasp, but not to nationalism, not to ideologies, not to anything that really matters. Why?

Comment: I'm used to it; I don't see the dangers of it.

KRISHNAMURTI: You are justifying insensitivity. First, look what has happened. I'm sensitive to the wasp, and I'm insensitive to the most dangerous things in life. I don't even pause to be aware of this fact.

Comment: We make things that are explained to us more absolute than they are.

KRISHNAMURTI: Sir, I don't want any explanations. I'm fed up with explanations. There have been, for five thousand years, umpteen explanations. I see this thing, a fact. I'm terribly sensitive, acutely so, to a wasp, and to nothing else. That means that I am indifferent to everything except immediate pain and immediate pleasure. Oh, sirs, this is so simple! Immediate pleasure and immediate pain are my chief concerns, and so I lead a very superficial life. I am content to live that way. If I saw the danger, not only of the wasp, but ideological danger, the danger of habits, what would happen to me? I'd be thrown out of society. If I'm not a nationalist, not a religious person in the accepted sense of the word, if I don't salute the flag and all that circus that goes on around us all day long, what will happen? Unconsciously I'm very sensitive to the danger of being thrown out without a job, without anyone feeling for me or looking out for me, to the dangers of being alone. So I say, "Please, let's forget it."

Only a man who is completely alone is sensitive, but not alone in the sense of isolation. As most of us are isolating ourselves all the time, we have become insensitive. The moment we see danger in everything that society has built up, obviously we will be alone. Unconsciously there is fear of what's going to happen. When we've gone through all that, then we say, "How is it possible to end pleasure or pain psychologically?" I'm not talking of physical pain; that we can end by seeing a doctor or a dentist, if it is possible. If not, we put up with pain and get on with it; we don't make a lot of hullabaloo about it so as to become a psychological problem.

How are we to end conflict without will? If we have no will, in the sense in which we are using the term—no resistance—is there conflict? Don't agree with me; that is like two children talking together. Because I have built around me resistances—my family, my husband, my God, my society, my culture, I know more and you know less, or you know more and I want to be like you. The very resistance to life is conflict. So we have to inquire what life is. All that I know is to resist life—life being this extraordinary movement. I don't know what that movement is; it's a movement, an endless current. And all that I've learned since I'm a human being, for ten thousand years, is to build walls around myself. The very building of those walls is a resistance and therefore conflict. The explanation is simple, but to see it, to break it down, to see the resistance, to be aware of the heavily guarded resistance, strengthened through centuries, that means instant action.

You have a resistance naturally because you have an image. You have an image of what you should be, or of what you are; and you have an image about life, which is the other. You have an image about me, and I have an image about you. I haven't actually because I don't make it, but you probably have an image about me. And there's the husband and the wife; they have images between them. The husband has an image about the wife, and the wife has an image about the husband. The two images have relationships, and nothing else. The human beings have no relationship, but the images have relationship, the images that have been created through resistance, through pleasure, and all the rest of it. Each of them says, "I love you; it's my family," and so on.

Comment: We don't want to look.

KRISHNAMURTI: We don't know what life is, and we have built a resistance to life. That's all we know—a resistance based on pleasure and pain. I say to myself, "By Jove, all my life I have done this; how can I drop it instantly, not gradually?" There is in the Hindu mind this whole concept of gradually evolving, and dropping it next life, or ten lives later, but life is too short. Then there is the whole Christian-world idea of original sin, with someone else to save you from it. This is the same thing put in different words.

If the picture, the map over which we have traveled, is very clear, then what is life? Not an ideological life, not a thing of saying, "Life is marvelous, lovely, beautiful, ecstatic; it should be, it should not be"—I don't know anything about all that. I do know what my life is. My world is the world of my wife, my children, my neighbor, my job; and that's all I know. With my image of my boss, the boss having an image of me; my image of my wife, and she having an image about me—we live in an imaginary world.

So, what is my life, actually, day to day, as it is, not as it should be? It's misery, conflict, ambition, and greed; wanting good opinions from others, wanting to be popular. I am an entity who is the result of ten thousand years of propaganda. That's a fact. Critics tell me how lovely a picture is and I say, "What a lovely picture that is!" They tell me that I must read a certain book, that I must see this and that. I am that. For my

pleasure, sex, vanity, position, and prestige I'm willing to suffer to maintain this horror. I'm not depicting something which is abnormal; this is our normal state. I look at my life as it is, not ideologically, not critically, not saying, "How terrible!" I see it is that. As I see the bloom of that flower, I see that my life is like that, without any equivocation. I don't want to improve it or change it, because that's my life; and no one is going to save me from it. We have gone through all those tricks, hundreds of times. Seeing that, can I drop it immediately? Can I drop the whole structure immediately? The authorities say, "Meditate; have a mind that is very peaceful; before you can tackle this, have a peaceful mind." How can I have a peaceful mind when I'm eaten up with ambition, greed, envy, fear, and all the rest of it?

As we cannot change this—and apparently we cannot—we invent gods, your God and my God, your savior and my savior, as a complete escape from the fact. I have a twisted mind and therefore my God will always be twisted, obviously. If it isn't God, it is the state, the communist state; if it isn't the state, it's social reform; if it isn't social reform, it is doing good, writing books, painting, and music. Unless we change this completely, we cannot go any further; and to go any further is merely escape. This cannot be changed eventually, slowly. It must change instantly, or not at all. This is logic, isn't it—sane, healthy logic? But logic isn't going to do a thing, so what am I to do? I have to learn something else. Having put the picture in front of myself, I say to myself, "What am I to do?" I know the picture very well. I've lived with it for fifty years, for sixty, eighty, ninety, ten thousand years; I know it very well. Now, what am I to do? First, I'm not going to escape—through music, through sex, through church, through religion, through literature, through anything—I'm not going to escape because escape creates more conflict.

Question: At this point may I ask a question?

KRISHNAMURTI: At any point, madame.

Question: If we consider ourselves free. . . .

KRISHNAMURTI: Ah, free?

Question: Or say, if we consider that we are really experiencing this, seeing the flower, seeing. . . .

KRISHNAMURTI: We can't "consider" it. Either it is a fact or. . . .

Question: But just for saying. . . .

KRISHNAMURTI: Ah, no; don't say it then; not for saying's sake.

Question: But couldn't this state exist for some people some of the time?

KRISHNAMURTI: It's like my saying that I'm happy once a year. I'm free once a year. The rest of the time I live in prison! What's the point of being free once a year? I see the picture; now I have to look. I have to find a different way of looking, thinking, feeling, living—a totally different way. I know the old way, and I won't touch it because the old way keeps me everlastingly in the same cage, running like a squirrel, up and down, up and down. I have to find a way of coming, a way of looking, a way of learning, a way of listening. I have to find a different way altogether.

First I must learn to look—look at that flower, and look at myself. I can't look at

that flower if there is any interference of thought or of feeling. If I want to look at you, if I want to understand you, I can't have prejudices about you. I can't have an image about you. In that case the image is looking at your image. You might have insulted me; you might have flattered me; you might have been jealous of me; you might have been kind—all that prevents my looking. I have to learn to look. Ah, no; it's not easy, because looking means having a fresh mind, a fresh eye, a fresh ear each time; otherwise, I can't look. I have to find out what it means to learn. I know what it means to accumulate knowledge, but that's not learning. Please, sirs, this has to be discussed. Don't listen to me all morning. Learning is one of the most extraordinarily interesting things.

Question: Can we learn through discipline?

KRISHNAMURTI: Discipline means resistance.

Comment: It's not in that way.

KRISHNAMURTI: If you have listened this morning to what is being said, the very act of listening is disciplining. You don't have to discipline yourself to listen. It is very simple. Look at that flower. If you want to look at it, you will have to look without thought, without feeling—just look. That's fairly easy, but to look that way implies discipline. You don't have to discipline yourself to look: first discipline, and then look. Then it's finished.

Question: How about after you look?

KRISHNAMURTI: When one looks, what happens? Do you look at that flower, or do you look at the image of that flower? Look at it, please. Experiment with yourself. Look at any flower. First begin with simple things. Can you look at the flower without any interpretation, without any condemnation, acceptance, or denial—just look? If you can do that, can you look at yourself? In any incident, can you look at the feeling that comes up, just looking, without accepting, without denying, without condemning, without justifying—just observing? To do that, in itself is discipline. You don't have to discipline before or after.

Question: Does that flower exist? Maybe it doesn't really exist.

KRISHNAMURTI: It exists, even though you don't look at it. Does your looking at it make it live? Leave that for the moment. You can turn your back on it. You may not see it, but it's there. We won't go into that now. That is a question that we will have to go into at another time. Please, look. Can I look at my husband without the image? Can I look at my wife without the image which I have built about her: pleasure, pain, hurts, flattery, nagging, the whole relationship of man and woman? To look I have to be free of the image; otherwise, I can't look. I don't know what my wife is, or what my husband is. I only know the image which both of us have.

Comment: That's what we invent, the image.

KRISHNAMURTI: Yes, of course.

Comment: When we look with an idea, we see only that.

KRISHNAMURTI: That's all. But if I can look at that flower without the image, I can also look at my wife, at my husband in that way. This doesn't mean that I'm cold, brutal,

hard, and all the rest of the business. I look, and then I begin to learn. Don't accept this just because I am saying it. This is most difficult to comprehend.

Comment: I think that to learn I have to use my will power.

KRISHNAMURTI: Ah, no, no! We must understand what we mean by learning. What do we mean by learning? Learning is always in the active present, not having learned or will learn. Learning can only take place in the active moment when we are learning. Having learned, we apply, we act. Having stored up knowledge, having learned, we act. That's not learning. That's what the machines are doing. The electronic brains have learned and give you information from what they have learned; therefore, they are not learning. The human mind can learn.

Comment: Maybe another word would be "experiencing."

KRISHNAMURTI: No.

Question: Identifying?

KRISHNAMURTI: No. Why do you want to translate it into another word and keep on repeating? The moment you say "experience," "identification," you have to inquire into what experience and identification mean.

Comment: Experiencing.

KRISHNAMURTI: Why should you experience? Who is the entity that is experiencing? And also, why should you identify? Why should I identify myself with my wife, with my husband, with my nation?

Question: Can you say, "I hate to do this, but I am being open to whatever the other wishes"?

KRISHNAMURTI: Please let's keep to the word *learning;* it's simpler. Unless each word is examined very carefully, it will lead us nowhere. I want to learn. What does it mean? I have to learn about life totally differently.

April 3, 1966

Third Dialogue in Rome

Discussion should be an exchange of thought, talking things over together rather than a continuous talk by a speaker. If we could talk things over together, during or after what I have to say, it might be more beneficial and bring greater clarification.

We were saying the other day that pleasure is the very root of our outlook on life, and with it invariably goes pain. Our whole structure, both outwardly and inwardly, is based on conflict. A mind in conflict is a distorted mind, and man has lived for centuries upon centuries in that way. We must obviously bring about a complete revolution, not only outwardly, but also inwardly. The inward revolution is of primary importance because from there a new society can be born, can be brought into being. We must observe and understand the whole structure of society, and therefore ourselves, quite differently. We were also talking about learning and what is meant by that word.

Perhaps we may be able to come upon it from a different point altogether. Man has not been able to free himself from fear. Not being able to understand it, he has built a network of escapes and has never been able to resolve this question of fear. Perhaps we can discuss it and go into it deeply. I can talk

about it, but the word is not the thing; the word is never the actuality; the symbol is never the fact, the reality. We must brush aside the word, though realizing its importance, and go behind the word. If we can do that, it may open a door which will help us to put an end to fear.

Most of us are afraid, and we have to learn about it, not resist it, not avoid it, not try to find formulas which will give us comfort, but actually resolve it completely and totally, consciously as well as unconsciously. To do that, we must be able to communicate with each other, and our communication naturally is verbal. Unless we talk it over and not merely listen negatively or attentively, it doesn't lead us very far.

You can see historically that man has in every way avoided this question of fear. It is fear that creates gods, religious institutions, the priests, the various ceremonies, and the whole circus of religion. Not being able to resolve or understand or go above and beyond fear, naturally man has developed a psychological and unconscious resistance. There is the enormous fear of death, which will be discussed a little later. The so-called religious people have invented marvelous theories, hopes, ideas, concepts. Those who, temperamentally or conditionally, are not at all inclined towards religion say, "This is the end of it; one life is good enough; let's go on and make the best of it"; but there is still the fear of death, and also the fear of actual living, the fear of facing life as it actually is and, having faced it, going beyond that. There are innumerable fears, from the most childish to the most complex, conscious as well as unconscious. The conscious ones you can deal with fairly well. For example, who cares about public opinion, what the public says? If you live in a big city, it doesn't very much matter. If you are living in a small village, then it does count a great deal what your neighbor thinks of you. There is the fear of not being able to fulfill, not being able to achieve what you want, not being successful. You know the various types of fear.

Mere resistance to fear is not an end to fear. Verbally, intellectually, you may be clever enough to rationalize fear and build a wall against it; yet behind that wall there is this constant gnawing of fear. Unless you are free from fear, you can't think, feel, or live properly. You are living in darkness. Religions have cultivated that fear through hell and all that business. There is the fear of the state and its tyranny. You must think of the public, the state, the dictators, the people who know what is good for you, the Big Brother and the Big Father. Is it possible to actually be totally free of fear? If you can discuss it, you can learn about it. If you say, "I can't get rid of it; what am I to do?" there is no problem. Someone will tell you what to do, but you will always be dependent on that person, and you will enter another field of fear.

We can't see very clearly as long as there is any form of fear, both the fears that have been built through thought, through imagination, through experience, through various forms of memory, and also those which come from bodily pain, of which many people are afraid, which interfere with the mind thinking and bring about psychosomatic fear. Unless we are completely free of fear, obviously we can't see anything clearly. Where there is fear, there can't be affection; there can't be sympathy; there can't be generosity; there can't be a sense of love. To be free from fear is a human necessity, as much as food, as much as shelter. Is it possible? When we put that question of the possibility, we put it not as an intellectual problem to be answered by an intellectual concept or by argument, but rather to learn about it. If we can learn about it and know the whole structure of it, then we are not afraid. We should be able to talk

this over. If I sit here talking and you listen, that doesn't lead us anywhere. We must go into it together.

Obviously the word is not the fact, but the word creates the fear. The word *revolution* creates fear. The word, if you are conditioned as a Catholic, or as a member of some other sect, has tremendous meaning; the word stimulates memory, which is associated with certain conditioning, and that reacts. When you see a snake or a wild animal, the immediate reaction is fear—which is a natural self-protective response which must be there, but need there be a psychological response to a word? The word *death* immediately awakens a whole series of associated memories, false ideas, and the fear of it. The word is not the fact, but the word creates the fear.

Comment: The awareness of our danger and therefore fear might present a certain problem.

KRISHNAMURTI: No, it is a healthy response; otherwise, you'd be killed. When you come to a precipice, and you just are not afraid or don't pay attention, you are in great danger; but that fear, the bodily fear, creates a psychological fear too. It is a very complex problem; it isn't just a matter of saying, "I have fear about something or other, and let me wipe it out." In order to understand it you must first be very clear about words; you must realize that the word is not the fact of fear, but the word engenders fear—unconsciously the whole structure is verbal. The word *culture* brings a deep response from memory—Italian culture, European culture, Hindu culture, Japanese culture, Chinese culture. It is very interesting to go into it. The unconscious is made up of memories, of experiences, traditions, propaganda, all words. You have an experience, and you react. That reaction is translated into words: "I was happy, I was unhappy, he hurt me," and those words remain. They awaken and strengthen the daily experience.

You have insulted me; it has left a mark, and that mark is strengthened, deepened by the word, by the memory associated with that feeling, which is really a word, a tradition. It is important to understand this. In certain countries in Asia, in India, among certain groups of people, tradition is immense, much stronger than here because they have lived longer; they are an old country, much more deep-rooted, with a tradition of ten thousand years and more. The word brings up memories and associations, which are all part of the unconscious, and it also brings about fear.

Take the word *cancer*. You hear the word and immediately all the ideas and the thoughts about cancer come rushing in—the pain, the agony, the suffering, and the question, "Do I have cancer?" The word is extraordinarily important to us. The word, the sentence, when organized becomes an idea based on a formula, and that holds us.

The word is not the fact; the word *microphone* is not the microphone, but the word brings fear or pleasure into being through association and remembrance. We are slaves to words and to examine anything fully, to look, we must be free of the word. If I'm a Hindu and a Brahmin, a Catholic, a Protestant, an Anglican, or a Presbyterian, to look I have to be free of that word with all its associations, and that's extraordinarily difficult. The difficulty disappears when we are passionately inquiring, examining.

The unconscious is stored-up memory; the unconscious, through a word, becomes alive. Through a smell, or through seeing a flower, you associate immediately. The storehouse, the stored-up, is the unconscious, and we make a tremendous lot of ado about it. It is really nothing at all. It is as trivial and super-ficial as the conscious mind. Both can be healthy, and both can be unhealthy.

The word brings on fear, and the word is not the fact. What is fear? What am I afraid of? Please, we're discussing. Take your own fear. It may be fear of your wife, of losing your job or your fame.

Comment: Yes, yes!

KRISHNAMURTI: Please, you must discuss with me; it's no good saying, "Yes, yes."

What is fear? Let us take a problem like death for the moment. It is a very complex problem. I am afraid of death. How does this fear arise? Obviously it arises through thought. I have seen people die. I also may die, painfully or quietly, and thinking has brought on this fear.

Comment: One of the strongest fears is the fear of the unknown.

KRISHNAMURTI: It is the unknown. I'm taking that as an example. Substitute your own fear—fear of your husband, of your wife, of your neighbor, fear of ill-health, of not being able to fulfill, fear of not loving, of not having enough love, of not having intelligence.

Comment: Surely in some cases it's justified. Take, for instance, if a man is afraid of his wife.

KRISHNAMURTI: All right; he is married and is afraid of his wife.

Comment: Or he's afraid of his boss, or afraid he may lose his job.

KRISHNAMURTI: Wait, sir; why should he be afraid? We are discussing fear, not of the job, of the boss, of the wife. Fear exists always in relation to something; it doesn't exist abstractly. I'm afraid of my boss, my wife, my neighbor, of death. It is in relation to something. I took death as an example. I'm afraid of it. Why? What brings on this fear? Obviously it is thought. Visually I have seen death, people dying. Associated with that, identified with that is the fact that I, myself, will die one of these days. Thought thinks about it; there is a thinking about it. Death is something unavoidable, and something to be pushed as far away as possible. I can't push it far away except with thought. I have a distance, so many years allotted to me. When it comes time for me to go, I'll go; but in the meantime I've kept it away. Thought—through association, through identification, through memory, through the religious or the social environment, through economic conditioning—rationalizes it, accepts it, or invents a hereafter. Can I come into contact with a fact? I'm afraid of my wife. That will be much simpler. She dominates me. I can give a dozen reasons for my fear of her. I see how fear arises. How am I to be free of it? I can ask her; I can walk out, but that doesn't solve the problem. How am I to be free of that fear? Look at it; I am afraid of my wife. She has an image about me, and I have an image about her. There is no actual relationship, except perhaps physically. Otherwise it is purely a relationship between the images. I'm not being cynical, but this is a fact, isn't it? Perhaps those of you who are married know better than I do.

Question: Will she have a picture of you being weak, and will you have a picture of her being tough?

KRISHNAMURTI: Tough and strong. You have dozen of reasons, sir, but there is no ac-

tual relationship at all. To be related means to be in contact. How can one image be related to another image? An image is an idea, a memory, a recollection, a remembrance. If I really want to be free of fear, I have to destroy my image about her, and she has to destroy her image about me. I may destroy mine, or she may destroy hers, but one-sided action doesn't bring about freedom from the relationship which awakens fear. I break my image about you, totally. I look at it, and then I understand what relationship is. I break the image completely. Then I am directly in contact with you, not with your image. But you may not have broken your image because it gives you pleasure.

Comment: That's the rub; I haven't broken my image.

KRISHNAMURTI: So you keep on, and I say, "All right; I have no image of you." I'm not afraid of you. Fear ceases only when there is direct contact. If I have no escapes at any level, I can look at the fact. I can look at the fact that I am going to die in ten years or in twenty years. I have to understand death; I can't come into contact with it physically, organically, because I'm still alive. I have plenty of energy; I'm still active, healthy. Bodily I can't die, but psychologically I can die.

This requires tremendous observation, going into, working. To die means that you have to die every day, not just twenty years from now. You die every day to everything that you know, except technologically. You die to the image of your wife; you die every day to the pleasures you have, to the pains, the memories, the experiences. Otherwise you can't come into contact with them. If you do die to them all, fear comes to an end and there is a renewal.

Question: Is all consciousness, unconscious and conscious, conditioned?

KRISHNAMURTI: It is conditioned in the sense that it is the result of the past acting through the present and creating a future—and all that within a pattern, the pattern of time. Is it possible to totally uncondition it, to be totally free of the past? This means that you must understand time.

Comment: Suppose my wife dominates me?

KRISHNAMURTI: No, no! Don't suppose. Then you're merely entering theory. You can speculate until doomsday. Man has been speculating for ages as to whether there is or is not a God.

Question: Can I end my fear of my wife?

KRISHNAMURTI: Of course you can, and not only of her. Sir, if you and I are in conflict, you have an image about me and I have an image about you. If you can, you split your image about me; you break it. You have no conflict. You're meeting me every day factually without the reaction of your memory about me. That is dying to your memories each day.

Comment: Yes, but since my wife hasn't broken her image, she still tries to dominate me.

KRISHNAMURTI: Of course. So you tell her, "Look, you can't dominate me; that game is over; I'm not afraid. If you want me to go and sweep the floor, I will, but psychologically your domination has come to an end." That's very difficult because with a woman and a man it's a relationship not only of pleasure, sexually and all the rest of it, but also for economic reasons. She keeps the house, takes care of the children and many other things. I become dependent, not only physically, but also psychologically, because I have identified myself with my family. If I break the image, the family is not important.

Comment: Then you become psychologically independent.

KRISHNAMURTI: Psychologically you're free, and therefore there is no fear. The word is the response of memory. The thought is the word. You can't think without words, without an image, without a symbol. So thought breeds fear. Like the word *communist*, or a dozen others.

Comment: Like the word earthquake.

KRISHNAMURTI: If there's an earthquake, there's an earthquake. I face it. But there is this whole mechanism. I see that there is no end to fear as long as time exists between the fact and me, as long as there is the division created by thought between the fact and the observer.

There is the fear of death. I take that as an example. I know I'll die, but thought has pushed it far away in the distance. Whether it comes tomorrow or in ten years, it's the same. Thought creates the time interval. If there is no thinking in regard to death, there is no time at all. It is a fact. That means that I have to learn, understand, observe, listen to the fact, whatever it is—the fact that I'm afraid of death, of my wife, of losing my job, of my wife not loving me, of darkness, and of all the things of which I'm afraid. I never come in contact with the fact because thought again has created this division between the observer and the observed. There is an interval of space between them. I am afraid; fear is something outside of me and I resist it. I am going to overcome it or escape from it. There is this division between the fact and the observer. The moment I say, "I am going to overcome fear," which means resist fear, I need time. Thought has created time, and thought has created fear; they are interrelated. The questions then arise: What is thought; what is time; and is it possible to look without thought? This doesn't mean that I become vague, abstract, woolly, blank, and all that silly stuff; but I look actively, passionately, fully, without thought, and therefore without the observer and the observed.

I'm afraid of being ill. I have known illness; I know all the unpleasantness of it; the memories are stored up in my unconscious. They are there. Each time I get some pain, I'm stirred by the fact, by something which I have remembered. The entity that remembers separates himself from the fact of remembrance and says, "I am going to be ill." Thought remembers the past illness; the thinker says, "By Jove, I'm going to be ill again; be careful," because he has had memories of it. He is afraid, and he keeps this battle going on because of fear. But this is all right. Let it come; I'll meet it, which means dying to the past. It's fairly easy to put away the pain, but to put away pleasure also is more difficult. I have to learn about it. It's not a case of my having learned and then I approach the fact. Then of course we would be back again in the same old position. Learning is a constant moving, a movement.

Can I observe the fear that I have, whatever it is, and come directly in contact with it, not identifying myself with it? That's another trick of thought, but actually I can only come into contact directly with the fact, any fact, as long as thought with its memories doesn't divide the observer and the observed.

Comment: Perceiving without an end to it.

KRISHNAMURTI: Yes, perceive, if you like to put it that way. You must be very careful here because the word *perceive*, if you analyze it. . . .

Comment: If you don't stop analyzing. . .

KRISHNAMURTI: You have analyzed it, but the analysis hasn't brought you to the fact. What brings you to face the fact is the act of listening. You say, "By Jove, I understand now what creates fear: thought"—which doesn't mean that you become thoughtless.

Question: Analysis uses thought and memory, doesn't it?

KRISHNAMURTI: Of course. Why should we analyze? When we are faced with physical danger, we don't analyze; we act. It is only when we do not face danger directly that we have the time to analyze, play around, get unhealthy, go to the analyst, and play all the tricks.

Comment: If you're faced with a situation, experience will help you. The memory of the previous experience being unpleasant, it may help you to avoid the next one.

KRISHNAMURTI: It may help you to avoid, but it will not help you to learn. I've had an experience about you. You've insulted me, flattered me, or whatever it is. I have that in my memory. The next time I meet you, that memory responds.

Comment: You avoid me.

KRISHNAMURTI: Wait; you might have changed.

Comment: Yes.

KRISHNAMURTI: I can't say that you have not changed. I can only say that yesterday at such and such a time you insulted me. When I meet you the next day, in that interval you may have changed completely, or you may not. But I must meet you, and I can't meet you if I have my memory of your insult. Therefore I can never say to another, "I know you." I can never say that I know the Germans, the Russians, my wife, or my husband. It's absurd. I can only say that I know a person as he was at the time the incident happened. In the interval he may have changed, and I may have changed.

Question: Instead of the example that you are using, let's take the position of a debtor and a creditor. It's not just once. If you are the debtor, each time that you encounter the creditor, he is going to remind you, and that creates unpleasantness. You know that he was a friend when he lent you the money, but circumstances change, and now every day he reminds you, which is an unpleasantness. Is the thing to do to avoid him?

KRISHNAMURTI: You can say, "Sorry, I can't pay you." The moment you say, "Avoid him," you have the beginning of fear.

Comment: Right.

KRISHNAMURTI: You don't want to have fear, at any cost.

Question: At the expense of the unpleasantness each time?

KRISHNAMURTI: At any time. If you can't pay, you have to find out why you can't pay. You'll try to pay. If you are double-crossing him, there's no end to it. The question is really whether it is possible to be free of fear, completely. Meet life as it arises, not with fear and not with all the structures which you have built within yourself, which are your image.

Comment: Then the thing to do is to forget your experiences.

KRISHNAMURTI: No, sir. Wait a minute. What is experience? I can't forget my experience of living in a certain house. If I forget, each time I go out I am lost. I don't know where I am. I can't be in a state of amnesia. I must know where I live. I must know my name. I must have my passport and my technological knowledge, but what do we mean by experience, apart from all that? What value has experience? Man has lived for over two million years, and he has battled. There have been wars, wars, wars, and he is still going on. What has it taught him? Nothing!

Comment: He has improved at it.

KRISHNAMURTI: It used to cost twenty-five cents to kill a Roman soldier; now it costs thirty thousand dollars to kill a soldier. It's too absurd. Has experience any value, psychologically?

Comment: None at all.

KRISHNAMURTI: That means that I live in a state where experience has no value at all, that I am a light to myself, completely. If I had no experience, psychologically, I would go to sleep. If you didn't push me, if you didn't kill me, if you didn't challenge me, I'd soon fall asleep psychologically. This takes place all the time. When I am completely secure psychologically, something takes place to disturb that state. To keep me awake, I depend on challenge and response, on experience. Otherwise I would soon go off to sleep, comfortably, within the wall which I have built around myself. It is very difficult to break down such a wall because that wall is built of ideas, and to break an idea is much more difficult than to break anything else. I depend on experience to keep me awake. If I see the absurdity of being awake through a drug, through an experience, through something, I have to be awake outside of experience.

Comment: I must experience without reference to memory.

KRISHNAMURTI: Wait, wait! I needn't. Why shouldn't I have memory? The electronic brains have memories, banks of memories. Through association they give responses, and we function in the same way. The memory that we have built up is a form of resistance against society, against everyone.

There is the obvious physical danger against which there must be protection; I protect myself. When I see a precipice, a bus coming towards me, or a snake, there is a normal, healthy response. If I'm not very careful, that is translated into a psychosomatic affair. What we are talking about is a psychological fear. I have to learn anew about this fear. I must come directly into contact with it and find out if there is such a thing as fear.

Suppose I have lied. I say, "All right; why should I be afraid of it? It's a fact and I know; the next time I might lie or I might not." But I don't want you to discover that I have lied. Therefore I am afraid of you. I avoid you. The fact is that there is fear, and it cannot be proved that it is possible to be totally free psychologically from any fear. I don't want to prove it to anyone. We are all so eager to prove that we are free from fear. It is possible to be free if we can go at it

with tremendous alertness, and that very alertness is a process of disciplining.

Life disciplines you—life being society. You have to get up at a certain time to go to the office. Society disciplines you brutally, makes you conform, and you accept such brutality, such discipline. There is constant imitation, constant standardization, constant forcing yourself to conform, to adjust, to comply, to obey. To see all that is discipline. To look at a flower, to actually look and not have thought between you and the flower is an intense discipline, nonconforming.

Comment: It means to look at it without naming it.

KRISHNAMURTI: Naming, thought, and all that.

Comment: It is difficult to look at a thing without naming it.

KRISHNAMURTI: Yes, sir. It is very difficult to see that flower near you and look at it without naming it.

Comment: Without knowing it is a flower.

KRISHNAMURTI: Ah, no. You see, you have already stipulated what it is. Your thought has already interfered. Sir, please try; sit near a tree and look at it. Look at the tree, without naming, without thought. Not that you're asleep, not that you become blank; you are intensely aware, but without verbalization.

Comment: Without saying to yourself, "That's a tree."

KRISHNAMURTI: Of course.

Comment: Without thinking.

KRISHNAMURTI: Yes. Then you will find out whether there is an observer and the observed. As long as there is an observer, there is the thinker.

Comment: Yes.

KRISHNAMURTI: The thinker with his thoughts, and therefore you never come into contact with the tree.

Comment: Only the observed remains.

KRISHNAMURTI: Of course. It is fairly easy with a tree, a flower, something objective. It is much more difficult to look at yourself inwardly, or to look at your wife, without all the responses. Learning implies a movement in which there is no accumulation, which becomes knowledge, and from which you act. Learn as you are moving, doing. You have to be tremendously alive, alert, to learn. What you have learned becomes an experience, but learning is not an experience; it is a movement.

That brings up the problem of what is new. Is there anything new? Man has been seeking in different ways, according to his culture and his conditioning, according to his tendency. He has given different names at different times to "God." He has done that for millions of years, believing or denying, but without knowing. If you want to find out, you can learn. You have to discover everything man has said about God. This doesn't mean that you become an atheist or a theist. You say, "This is all out; I want to find out." You must be completely free—free from fear, free from what people have said, free from knowledge. Whether you believe in God or not, it is all the same—who cares? You are conditioned one way, and the com-

munists are conditioned the other way. To both the believer and the nonbeliever, God is dead. The word has no meaning.

We were saying the other day that freedom is essential, psychological freedom, not freedom from anything. Where there is freedom there is peace. The two must exist; otherwise, there will be disorder. Unless freedom and peace exist, unless that really is a fact—not an idea, a theory, a hope, a utopia—mind cannot go any further. It can go sideways; it can go any other way, but it can't go straight.

Question: When you speak of conditioning, do you refer only to outside conditioning, or do we already have some conditioning when we are born?

KRISHNAMURTI: Obviously.

Comment: The conditioning we are given when we come into the world is a religion, a nationality, and social surroundings.

KRISHNAMURTI: Yes, and a family environment.

Comment: That comes afterwards.

KRISHNAMURTI: The authorities say that it is already there prenatally; it is already in the germ; the genes are already conditioned.

Comment: We are already partly conditioned.

KRISHNAMURTI: Partly, but whether we are conditioned from the beginning, or whether we are conditioned as we go along, the fact is that we are conditioned now.

Comment: Yes.

KRISHNAMURTI: Is it possible to be free? Otherwise, for ever and ever we are but slaves, although we can decorate the prison more and more. If we really want to be free, we have to be tremendously active about it and not just theorize. This brings in the whole problem of time. Does it take time to uncondition, or is it a matter of instant perception?

Comment: If it takes time, it is not deconditioning.

KRISHNAMURTI: If it takes time to uncondition myself, there is an interval between now and then. In that interval there are a great many incidents, accidents, strains, stresses which are going to alter the fact. It is like a man who is violent and angry trying to be nonviolent, trying to reach a lovely, utopian, nonviolent, idealistic state. He is violent, and at a distance is the nonviolence. To achieve nonviolence, he allows himself time. In the meantime he is sowing violence. We must see the violence, and not through an ideal, not through comparison.

We function in a habitual way. We have been taught to live with fear, to comply, to resist, to escape. Society has conditioned us; we have conditioned society; we have made society; we are caught in that. Unless we are tremendously aware of this fact, we keep on going round and round in circles.

April 7, 1966

Fourth Dialogue in Rome

We are not here discussing as children. We are trying to talk over together the serious problems in our lives. The last few times that we met here we said that it is absolutely necessary that there should be a radical revolution psychologically in consciousness itself. We said that as long as there is conflict of any kind—conscious or unconscious, at any level, whether we are aware of it or not—the mind, which is the totality of our being, cannot function clearly, harmoniously, cannot see without distortion what actually is. This conflict exists because man has always sought pleasure in which there is psychological security, pleasure of many different kinds—moral, ethical, spiritual, economic. Where there is pleasure there is inevitably pain, and a conflict between pleasure and pain. What gives sustenance to pleasure is desire, and desire is strengthened by thought. Intellectual argumentation, intellectual verbal exchange and theories have no value at all. All the theologians and the priests throughout the world have indulged in endless theories about God, about how to live and what to do, but that has not brought about a fundamental, radical revolution in man.

The last time we met we were talking about fear, and how man has lived for centuries upon centuries with fear, outwardly, and especially inwardly. Having this unresolved, deep-rooted fear, he has built a network of escapes—gods, priests, religions, amusements of every form—in order to escape from it. We went into whether it is possible to radically eradicate fear. If we live with fear, however trivial or however deep it may be, we always have a dual hypocritical activity in life. A mind that is afraid lives in darkness and strain. It is therefore necessary to be completely free from fear.

Question: Could we speak about clarity in observation? Could we go into it first regarding oneself in conflict with another?

KRISHNAMURTI: If we go into this question theoretically, intellectually, verbally, superficially, it will lead us nowhere. If we are merely discussing a different formula from that which we already have, again that will not lead us anywhere. We can invent innumerable formulas, concepts of what God is and what He is not. The modern theologians are trying to do this because they see that the whole concept of God has to be changed completely. They are still dealing with concepts, and a stupid concept is as good as a clever one. It is still a concept. Let us be clear about what we are discussing. This demands clarity. This demands the perception and rejection of theories, concepts, formulas, beliefs, and dogmas. That demands enormous, intelligent awareness into ourselves. Otherwise we indulge in superficial, intellectual, verbal explanations and dialectical exchange, all of which are of no value.

Ever since man has been, he has been seeking the extraordinary thing which he calls God. He has given it different names. Life is so superficial, so meaningless, so boring—earning a livelihood for forty years, breeding a lot of children, having a family; he says, "Is that all?" Caught in that routine, he has to invent something. In the most ancient Hindu thought, there was no concept of God at all. There was just direct communication with nature. God got more and more important as people got further and further away from nature, from feeling, from direct communication. That was of course utilized by clever people, who became priests, to interpret reality. The whole game of exploitation and vested interest of priests came into being. This is what has happened historically throughout the ages. To examine the question, "Is there such a thing as God?" one must be free of dogmas, beliefs, theories, and concepts; otherwise, one's conditioned thinking will determine the direction in which one is going to think and feel.

If one wants to discover what that reality is, there must be complete freedom from the conditioning which man lives in, which is propaganda. Every day, from childhood, one is told what God is, what He is not, how to find Him through the Savior, through the priest, through rituals. Unless one can really, seriously be aware of one's conditioning and throw it off, not eventually, but immediately, there is no way out. As far as one understands, there has always been this idea that God is outside and God is within. I don't personally like to use the word *God* because it is so heavily burdened. One must find out whether there is such a thing, such a truth, whether there is a reality, a something which is unimaginable, unthinkable, unconditioned.

How do we find out? That's the question, isn't it? The only instrument we have is the brain, thought. Let's talk it over together as two friends who are investigating something, not just one man talking, and you all listening. That really leads us nowhere.

Comment: There must be complete freedom from dogmas in order to reach this unimaginable thing.

KRISHNAMURTI: We must investigate what freedom is, what there is to be free from, who the seeker is and what there is to be sought. Is freedom merely a reaction? If I'm in prison, I want to be free. That's a reaction. I'm always contrasting freedom and slavery. The opposite of slavery is not freedom. If freedom is the opposite of slavery, then it still contains slavery. If freedom is a reaction, if it contains that which has been, it is not freedom at all.

Is there any other kind of freedom? Is there freedom which is not a reaction? There can be if one is aware of the process of reaction. Freedom is not from something; freedom is per se, in itself. If I am bound by certain family ties and break away from them, it is a reaction. That reaction will make me act again, will produce a new standard from which I will again try to escape.

Freedom also is not the result of time. Freedom is something immediate. I cannot say to myself, "I will be free day after tomorrow"; because if it is a gradual achievement, if freedom is at a distance, something to be achieved, there is a time interval between the present and 'what should be'. In that time interval there are all kinds of strains and pressures, and there is never complete freedom. If I am frightened, if I am caught and want to be free, the wanting to be free is an activity of the will, and therefore is not freedom.

How does this freedom which is not a reaction come about? It cannot be the result of desire, of will; it cannot be an aim which I must achieve, an ideological goal which I must pursue. When there is an awareness of this process of reaction from *what is* to 'what should be', then there is freedom.

Awareness implies observation without criticism, without evaluation, without justification, without condemnation. To be aware of that plant, those flowers, without identifying the species by name, just to observe without your information or your knowledge, which is thought, coming into it is extraordinarily difficult. The thought which observes has an image of that flower identified with the name; therefore, the image is looking. That's fairly easy because it's outside, objective. It is much more difficult to observe inwardly. If you are aware of *what is*, a desire to change the fact into 'what should be' is a denial of the fact. The moment you say, "This should be that," this is denied. If I say to a boy, "You must be like your uncle, who is so clever," I have denied the boy. When I compare the boy with someone who is very clever, I have denied the integrity of the boy.

If you are aware of *what is*, without condemning, without justifying, without any choice—just watching inwardly as it takes place—there is something else, which has

nothing to do with voluntary, spontaneous will. Because you have understood *what is,* you are free of it and there is this other thing.

That brings in a tremendous problem of what beauty is. The quality of beauty has to be understood, not intellectually but nonverbally. We only know beauty through comparison, or through the thing which has been created by, put together by man, or created by nature. We see a picture and say, "That's beautiful." We see an attractive woman or a tree and say, "How lovely!" There are certain standards, and there is the mixing up of good taste with beauty, but is there beauty without the object? Is there space without the object? That plant exists in space and creates space around it. This room has space because of the walls. The walls exist in space, outside. We only know space in relation to a center.

Comment: There is space outside and space inside the house.

KRISHNAMURTI: Yes, I took that as an example. The house exists in space; it creates space. Because of the house you know space. You can't think of space without a thinker, and you have to find out if there is a space without the object.

Again, take love. The word is heavily loaded, but we are not using it sentimentally, emotionally, or devotionally. We are using it nonsentimentally. When we say, "I love my country, my wife, my family, my God," or anything else, there is an object to be loved, whether the object is an idea or an entity. When the object moves, love becomes entangled, jealous. We want to know if there is love without the object. Neither beauty, nor space, nor love is the result of an object. This is an enormous investigation. To pursue that subject we must have order—order being freedom in which there is no envy, ambition, greed, or worship of success; otherwise, there is disorder, and a disordered mind cannot discover anything.

Order is virtue. You must be virtuous, but not virtuous according to the pattern of society because society is not virtuous. Only a mind free from conflict and therefore completely free has the energy to pursue. You must have passion; otherwise, you can't proceed. You must have energy, tremendous energy. Energy is being dissipated now in conflict, in adjustment, in imitation, in following authority. When you look at a flower, if you say, "I like, I don't like; this is a beautiful flower, this is not a beautiful flower; I wish I had it," all that is a dissipation of energy and prevents your looking.

If you merely suppress or isolate yourself as an escape, it is a form of self-delusion, self-hypnosis. This is what the monks and all the Hindus in India do. There must be no motive for order, for love. It must be involuntary, not purposeful. If I love you because you give me pleasure or money, or because I'm frightened or want security, it is no longer love.

We must next go into the question of seeking. Why do we seek at all? We seek because we are lost, we are confused, we are messy, disorderly; we have contradictory beliefs, ideas, desires; there is a whirlpool of contentious demands. We either turn to a dogma, to a belief, to a priest, or we turn to someone who says, "I know," and follow him. Human beings are dreadfully confused. Whatever takes place out of that confusion is still confused. We say, "Well, there are moments of clarity; in that clarity I act." But that action of clarity is negated, set aside, contradicted by the action of confusion. If we are confused, we should not do a thing because whatever we do out of confusion is still confusion.

When the mind is confused, it seeks something which it hopes is not confused, but the clarity it finds is the result of confusion, and that clarity is still confusion. I see that, and I don't act. This doesn't mean that I live in a vacuum, in a blank state. I see that any action born of confusion is furthering confusion. Therefore I stop, naturally, not because I want to seek and find, but because I am confused. That's a completely negative state. The action of confusion, which is to seek, appears to be positive. We like that; we feel that it is right, but to seek, to endeavor, to pursue, to make effort, to determine, to pray—all those are the result of confusion. If I'm not confused, I won't pray; I won't ask; I won't look. The denial of action is total negation of the positive.

The mind now is not seeking; the mind is not wanting more experience. A confused mind says, "I want more experience." It will have more experience, but always in terms of confusion. To find that thing which we call God, seeking must come to an end, which means complete negation of the positive or the negative of the world. The world is caught in the positive and the negative—obey, disobey, trying to be free of both, out of which comes confusion. The total negation of this is necessary so that the mind is no longer seeking, struggling, wanting. It is completely still, but not through discipline, through control, through suppression, through going into a monastery, shutting oneself in a cell and trying to be quiet. When this negation takes place, the mind is naturally quiet. It is empty, and therefore full of space; something new can take place.

What one does matters tremendously—what one thinks, what one feels, what one is. One has to put aside vanity, greed, ambition, the desire to be someone. This doesn't mean that one must leave society, but one is no longer caught psychologically in its structure.

Question: You say we should not act. Does that mean we should just sit and watch people murder someone?

KRISHNAMURTI: Ah, no; quite the contrary. Look, madame. What I am saying implies a total revolution in education, a different educational system altogether, one in which the whole field of living will not be neglected. Because we are now being trained only to be technicians, in mathematics, in engineering, we escape into all kinds of brutalities. Common murder is on the increase; violence is multiplying; the authorities don't know what to do. In America, in England, everywhere, even in the so-called marvelous society of Russia, there is violence.

One has to do something about the problem of starvation in Asia. To feed all the people, there must be no nationalities, no sovereign states, no Italian government, Indian government, American government. Science has enough creative knowledge to give food, shelter, and clothing to all the people in the world, if there were no armaments, no nationalities, no division into Christians, Hindus, Buddhists. But we don't want to think in those large terms. We say, "Someone is wronging me; I must immediately do something about that." Of course we must, but the issue is larger than that.

Comment: *I still think that murdering is bad.*

KRISHNAMURTI: So do the judges. They send murderers to prison, hang them, shoot them, or electrocute them. No matter what they do, murder still goes on.

Comment: *But they have to judge and then declare what is good and what is bad.*

KRISHNAMURTI: Good and bad in what sense?

Comment: *In terms of my personal choice.*

KRISHNAMURTI: Your personal choice is based upon your conditioning.

Question: *But if I try to free myself from conditioning?*

KRISHNAMURTI: There is a great deal of mischief, misery, ugliness, brutality in the world; there is tremendous violence. That we all know. What are we to do? We stop immediate violence, don't we? If we see someone being violent, we interfere or do something about it. But the issue of violence is much greater than that because in all of us there is violence. We want to hurt people, and there is violence when we are ambitious, competitive. We have to tackle not only the little violence which we come upon every day but also the great violence of man. There have been about fifteen thousand wars in the last five thousand five hundred years, and yet we are still going on. To stop war, we must do away with nationalities, religious divisions, the vested interests of the politicians and the military. It is a tremendous problem; we can't just join peace movements and hope peace will come; it won't. Peace is something which is both outward and inward. We cannot have peace outwardly if there is no inward peace. That means there must be no ambition, no greed, no envy.

Question: *Should we just live peacefully, and not join these peace movements?*

KRISHNAMURTI: Madame, I don't advise you. I am just saying that if you want peace in the world, you must live peacefully; and to live peacefully is one of the most difficult things. They have been preaching nonviolence in India a great deal for the last thirty years, and before that for thousands of years. The nonviolent violence has become an ideal. The fact is that we are violent.

What's the point of having an ideal? You have to change violence—not in terms of the ideal. To change it you have to face it; you have to be aware of it in your daily life, in what you do, in what you say, in what and how you think. All ideals are always a curse because they take you away from the facts, and it is only when you face the facts that you can do anything.

Question: You said there is no love when pleasure is the object. Isn't there always pleasure, even if you do achieve this?

KRISHNAMURTI: What do we mean by pleasure? There's a great deal of pleasure in owning a house, in possessions. It gives immense pleasure, and it doesn't matter if it's a house, a shirt, or a coat. To see that you have everything you want—a house, a wife, children, position, prestige, power, dominance—all that gives great pleasure outwardly and also inwardly. It gives pleasure if you are rich, if you are an important man, if you are capable, if you have fulfilled, if you can do things. Sex also gives great pleasure. We live in that cocoon. But in pleasure there is always pain.

I want to be a great man. This concept gives me pleasure because I see people going about who are called great. I wish I could be treated like they are. That idea gives me pleasure. To succeed I may have to cheat, do a dozen things; I may even have to kill people. In doing all that, I find there is pain, frustration.

Comment: Yes, but you also get pleasure in the happiness.

KRISHNAMURTI: I understand that, but what is pleasure, and what gives duration to pleasure, lends it continuity? If you simply say, "That's beautiful," it is finished, but if

you say, "I must have it," there is continuity.

Question: Why?

KRISHNAMURTI: We don't say why; we want it.

Comment: There is a pleasure in looking at people, and smiling at people.

KRISHNAMURTI: Of course. You smile at me. I like it, and I want more of it.

Comment: Yes, but you are the other person. I am talking of me.

KRISHNAMURTI: But I want more of it.

Comment: I want to give you something of myself.

KRISHNAMURTI: But I want it. You may not want to give it; you gave me a first smile, which was a delight both to you and to me. That delight I want to perpetuate. So I say, "Please do this thing. I like your smile; I must have it." And you say, "Sorry, I smiled at you as a friend, but later on it has become a nuisance." There is pain; I suffer. Through life we do many, many, many things hoping to find a continuous pleasure; and at the end we say, "What a bore it all is; there is no pleasure."

Question: Do you think everyone seeks pleasure?

KRISHNAMURTI: Don't we all seek pleasure? Don't you?

Comment: It is a pleasure to give.

KRISHNAMURTI: You give out of your goodness; you say, "By Jove, it's like the sunshine."

Comment: That's a pleasure, a great pleasure.

KRISHNAMURTI: All right, have it! But what happens to me? It has given me delight to receive it.

Comment: When a person takes pleasure in giving, it is always an egotistical thing; he only gives because he gets pleasure out of it.

KRISHNAMURTI: Of course.

Comment: I believe in generosity.

KRISHNAMURTI: If you say, "I believe in generosity, and therefore I must be generous," it is not being generous. It is just an idea. But if you are generous, that's a different thing. If you derive something from your generosity, as pleasure, then you're really not generous. It is like giving your love to your wife or your children; it's giving because you enjoy it.

All we have discussed this morning makes the mind not isolated but very sharply alone. One must be alone, not in the isolated sense of the monk, however. To be truly alone implies freedom. It's not the aloneness of self-pity and loneliness; it is a marvelous thing to see clearly that you are alone. When everyone around you shouts nationalistic slogans and waves the flag, and you think it's all nonsense, you're alone.

April 10, 1966

Fifth Dialogue in Rome

KRISHNAMURTI: What shall we talk about this evening?

Question: May we discuss the matter of emotional dependence?

KRISHNAMURTI: Shall we go into the question of emotional dependence and the conflict that arises from it, or would you like to discuss something else?

Question: May we discuss silence?

KRISHNAMURTI: I wonder why we ask questions. Someone has asked why there is conflict both in dependence and in freeing oneself from that dependence. Another has asked what silence is. I'm just asking myself why we ask any questions at all. Are we asking for some kind of easy explanation, or are we asking as a means of exploration? The latter means that there is no answer; you and I both are working together to discover the facts involved in that question. If we merely wait for an answer from someone, there is dependence; if the answer depends on another, we are caught in agreement and disagreement. We think we have worked very hard in agreeing and disagreeing, but that doesn't lead us anywhere. Perhaps the question has significance only when the questioner discovers for himself at what depth, or from what depth, the question is put.

We must be clear from the very beginning about these two questions, or any other questions. We must understand why we put them, and at what level or from what depth the questions come out. We must also realize that there is no answer. The understanding of the question itself, the solution, is in the question. It is not that you tell me, I listen, agree or disagree, and then comes the answer. In examining the question itself, we will come to some factual understanding.

If you are following all this intellectually, it has no meaning. If you say, "I agree with you; these are logical steps that you are taking bit by bit," we don't meet; we have lost each other long ago. I hope that we are taking a journey together. It's not that I'm superior and you're inferior, that I'm the authority and you're mere followers—all that would be too silly. Why do we depend on another emotionally? Since we are dependent, how are we to free ourselves from the dependence, and from the pain of freeing ourselves without hurting another?

Question: May we also discuss the issues involved in attachment and detachment?

KRISHNAMURTI: Physically we depend on the postman, on the milkman, on the supermarket. When we talk about dependence, what do we mean by that word? Is all relationship dependent? I depend on you and you depend on me emotionally—as a wife, a husband, a neighbor. Is all relationship, both intimate and superficial, dependent?

Analytically one can discover clearly why one depends. One is empty, insufficient within oneself; one does not have sufficient energy, drive, capacity, clarity; one depends upon another to satisfy that insufficiency, that lack of perception, the sense of not being able to stand by oneself morally, intellectually, emotionally, physically. One also depends because one wants to be secure. The first thing a child demands is security. Most people want security, in which is implied comfort. All these things are involved when one tries to find out why one depends emotionally, intellectually, and spiritually.

I depend on you because you give me pleasure, you give me comfort, you give me satisfaction, you give me a sense of security, a balance, a harmony, a companionship, a togetherness. We are going to examine presently whether it's real or unreal. I cling to you emotionally, physically, intellectually, or in some other way. In myself I'm isolated; I feel separate from everyone else. That separation is very painful. The demand to identify with another springs from that sense of isolation. Please don't accept what I am saying; we are examining, analyzing, going into it together.

Being isolated, we try to reach out for a companion, for friendship, for something that we can cling to. This is going on all around us, intellectually, emotionally, physically, in the deeper levels of consciousness—a constant demand to find someone, some idea, some hope, some kind of thing that will give a tremendous sense of being, a sense of identification with another or with ourselves. We do it because there is a sense of emptiness, of loneliness, of insufficiency in the ever self-centered activities. We identify with our state, with our religion, with our God, with our leader. Having hooked on to someone or to some idea, in that very process there is an uncertainty, there is a fear that the thing we are attached to may be rather pliable, insecure. We become jealous, aggressive, demanding, possessive, dominating, and the battle begins.

You want to be free, and I can't let you be free. You want to look at someone else, and instantly I'm confused, lost, jealous, anxious. This process is called relationship. To be in contact with another is relationship, but I'm not in contact with anyone because out of my fear, out of my loneliness, out of my anxiety, out of all my self-centered activities, I hold on. How can I be sure of another? Even though all marriages are made in heaven, how can I be sure of anything in life, including my own ideas, my own feelings? I can't be sure of anything, but I want to be completely grounded in my security with another.

We know all this intellectually. We can analyze this verbally for ourselves without going to an analyst. The pattern is very familiar. I see all this and yet I can't break through, I can't release, I can't let go. What's the next step?

Comment: Conflict immediately comes in. There is also the point of letting go.

KRISHNAMURTI: You can't let go. What is important is not letting go but finding out why you are dependent. If that is clear, then it's finished. Otherwise you may let one person go, but you will cling to someone else.

Question: How about a mother and her child?

KRISHNAMURTI: That's a quite different relationship, isn't it?

Comment: There is an emotional dependence of the mother on the child.

KRISHNAMURTI: The child is dependent on the mother, truly dependent, but is the mother dependent on the child? Of course she is.

Comment: She shouldn't be.

KRISHNAMURTI: It isn't a question of should be or should not be; the facts are that way. We are not approaching the problem directly if we say, "How am I to be free from dependence?"—whether we are dependent on a child or on another adult human being. We must go into the question of why we depend at all. Why do we depend, and is dependence relationship?

Comment: There should be independence if we want relationship.

KRISHNAMURTI: Is there relationship if there is dependence? I depend on you; is it a relationship?

Comment: It is not a relationship.

KRISHNAMURTI: Yet that is what we call relationship.

Comment: We call it love, too.

KRISHNAMURTI: We call it love; we call it protection; we give dozens of absurd words to it, but we have never really inquired into what relationship is. We are related because of inner uncertainty, the demand for security, the demand to be assured that we are related. It is a deeper, much more subtle dependence than the physical. If we did not depend, what would happen? We'd be lost; we'd have no anchorage; there would be no port where we could say, "Here I'm at home." I battle all day with my boss in the office, and when I go home, there at least I'm completely secure.

We have all had the experience of tremendous loneliness, where books, religion, everything is gone and we are tremendously, inwardly lonely, empty. Most of us can't face that emptiness, that loneliness, and we run away from it. Dependence is one of the things we run to, depend on, because we can't stand being alone with ourselves. We must have the radio or books or talking, incessant chatter about this and that, about art and culture. So we come to that point when we know there is this extraordinary sense of self-isolation. We may have a very good job, work furiously, write books, but inwardly there is this tremendous vacuum. We want to fill that and dependence is one of the ways.

We use dependence, amusement, church work, religions, drink, women, a dozen things to fill it up, cover it up. If we see that it is absolutely futile to try to cover it up, completely futile—not verbally, not a conviction and therefore agreement and determination—but if we see the total absurdity of it, that it is impossible to escape from it, whether through marriage, through drink, through God, through churches, through literature, through painting, through music, through husbands, through children, then we are faced with a fact. It is not a question of how to be free from dependence; that's not a fact; that's only a reaction to a fact.

Can I face this emptiness, this sense of isolation, the sense of not belonging to anything? It is something I've never faced before. I don't even know what it means because I have so carefully, so cleverly cultivated escapes from it. Though I know it is a fact, I am unwilling to face it. I know nothing can fill it, no words, no books, no literature, no art, nothing. Why don't I face the fact and see what happens?

The problem now arises of the observer and the observed. The observer says, "I am empty; I don't like it," and runs away from it. The observer says, "I am different from that emptiness." But the observer is the emptiness; it is not emptiness seen by an observer. The observer is the observed. There is a tremendous revolution in thinking, in feeling, when that takes place. It's not anger, and me separate from the anger, or me separate from jealousy, me separate from nationalism, and so on.

Question: Isn't the whole mental process, and all desire as well, image-making?

KRISHNAMURTI: Of course it's image-making. All our relationship is image-making. You have an image about me, and I have an image about you; the images have relationship, not you and I. The two images have a battle about everything. Idealists and people with utopias have images of what should be, and they try to force everyone, the whole community, to that state. One of the most difficult things is to be free of forming images. I want to go a little beyond that into the whole question of experience, the storing of memory, and the reaction of memory with regard to another with whom I have had an experience.

Can we be free of experience? Most of us crave experiences of pleasure and pain, which again is dependence. The more we demand a pleasurable experience—which is what most people want, whether it is God, sex or any of a hundred things—the more is involved this question of pain. I said at the beginning that if we are asking these questions purely intellectually, it has no value at all. If the asking is intense, it is possible to explore. We can't examine without passion, without vitality; and we can't have that vitality if it is a superficial question.

Can I face a fact without interpreting it? If I separate the fact from me, if I am lonely, I am the observer, and the loneliness is the thing observed. Then the actor comes into being, the actor being me. I can do something about it. I can replace it, cut it out, suppress it, resist it, justify it, struggle against it, run away from it, adjust myself to it, deny it or rationalize it, but if I see that anger is *me*, that loneliness is *me*—the rationalizer, the thinker, the actor—if I see that the observer is the observed, then there is no experience, then action becomes impossible in the ways I am used to as action.

When this takes place, contradiction and effort cease. If there is no contradiction, there is no effort. This doesn't mean that my mind is asleep. In the very effort to get rid of my dependence, my anger, my passion, my lust, in that very process of conflict the mind is breaking itself up. Conflict in any form, at any level, physical or psychological, breeds further conflict, and therefore the organism as well as the psyche is wearing itself out.

Action with regard to the fact of emptiness is not possible. The observer now is the observed, and action with regard to any fact doesn't exist. From that arises the negation of action. Inaction is the most tremendous action. The positive action that we know is reaction. The observer denies the fact. He denies that the fact belongs to him, and therefore he can act. When the observer is the observed, which is the fact, action becomes impossible. The mind which has previously divided itself into the observer and the observed has no division. There is no conflict between the observer and the observed. When this takes place, there is silence. Contradiction ceases. In silence there is tremendous attention.

From that silence we can ask a question: "What is creation?" Creation for most of us is doing, creating, painting, writing, expressing. An architect must express. If a woman is to fulfill, she must give birth to a child. Man is trying to fulfill, fulfill, fulfill, all the time, and is frustrated all the time. When the observer is the observed and the experiencer is the experience, then the search comes to an end. Then what is man to do? We demand experience, and we demand it because experience keeps us awake. Life is challenge and response. This challenge and response keeps us awake. There is tremendous doubt now about God. A few centuries ago that doubt didn't exist. Now everything is being questioned and we have to respond. There is outward challenge. Society is undergoing a tremendous change, and it is a challenge to man. The challenge keeps him moving, keeps him awake, driving, pushing. We depend on outward challenges, outward questions, outward urges, compulsions, incidents. If we see that, we put it away because it has no meaning any more. Then we have to keep awake, keep moving, keep active without experience,

without being driven, without being pushed. When we reject the outer, we also have to reject the inner. The outer challenge is the same as the inward challenge. It's a tide, which ebbs and flows, goes out and comes in. We may say it's absurd to be influenced by people, by churches, by society, but the tide comes in, and we depend on it to keep us awake. But if we see the movement and no longer depend on it, then we have to be extraordinarily alert and awake.

Comment: Just to see; not to reject.

KRISHNAMURTI: Yes, of course. How can I reject? The problem is arising in a different way with computers and automation taking over the world. Man is going to have much more leisure. Four days of it a week is coming. Three days a week is already here, from Friday afternoon to Monday morning. Social reform and all that will disappear because it will all be so beautifully organized. What will we do with this leisure? We may get lost in amusement, going to football games or to church, because that is what we want. But if we reject all that, if we see the absurdity of everlastingly chasing something, then we have true leisure. Then we look at things differently; the observer is the observed, and the action is inaction. That's a marvelous discovery.

To look at a tree completely, the mind must be totally silent. Have you ever observed a tree without the observer? Have you ever looked at another without memory, without the image, without the observer thinking, judging, evaluating, condemning, justifying? If you can do that, there is relationship with the person; otherwise, there is no relationship, and only your images, your words have relationship. "I love you" and "You love me" are but images speaking to each other endlessly. If right from the beginning we see that the observer is the observed, there is no effort or contradiction, and therefore no demand. Then we will know what creation is.

Comment: It is being.

KRISHNAMURTI: We should never take anything for granted. Always doubt, but don't close any door. Silence is the observer, not the observer is silent. We only know the beauty of light because it is on the building, on the leaf, or in the shadow, in the movement of leaves. It is the observer observing the light and the breeze, and the movement of the leaf, who says, "How lovely!"

Comment: But that light actually is lovely.

KRISHNAMURTI: The moment you say the light is lovely, you're lost. When the observer separates himself from the fact of loneliness or anger, then there is action. When the observer says, "I am not it," or "I am it"; when there is the light on that building, on that leaf, and the wind, the breeze, is among those leaves, and you see it and say, "How beautiful," you know beauty because of the movement of the light, because of that coloring, of that shape. But is it really beauty? The observer looking at it says it's beautiful. You see a painting; you say it's beautiful, or modern, subjective art. When you look at it, you are looking from a center, which is the observer who says that it is beautiful or ugly, in good taste or in poor taste, that a room is well proportioned, or that the movement a tree has in the breeze is lovely. You only know beauty because of an object, but is there beauty without the object? It is the same question as whether there is space without an object. If there is no space without an object, then there is never any freedom at all. If I only know I'm a prisoner because of the walls, these concrete walls, or walls that I have created around myself through resistance, if I only know space that way, in that space there can never be freedom. If there is no observer, no center from which I'm looking, then beauty has a quite different meaning. Then everything is beautiful. This isn't a concept; it is a fact.

Silence takes place in total inaction, which is positive action. Silence is emptiness. A silence in which there is the experiencer is no longer a silence. Then it's put together, and it can be un-put together. It's like love. I love you because you give me satisfaction. If love has a motive, it's no longer love. There is a center.

To come to this silence, as we have done, we have to be tremendously quiet. To see your wife, with whom you've lived for forty years, quarreled, and everything else; to look at her and see something new, there must be silence. The new is the creation of silence, not you creating silence, creating the new. That is creation.

Question: How can we have creation in an insane world?

KRISHNAMURTI: The world is not sane because we are not sane. The world is not different from me. To have real peace, not the peace between two wars, two arguments, or two battles, we must live peacefully. There must be no anger, no jealousy, no ambition, no greed, no prestige. Because we can't live peacefully, we join peaceful organizations and function completely in the field of time. The new is never in the field of time. The thing which is timeless is God, or any name you like to give to it; the name doesn't matter.

April 14, 1966

London, England, 1966

---　✳　---

First Talk in London

Before we talk about serious things, we should, it seems to me, establish the right relationship between the speaker and yourselves. I mean by that word *right* a communication. We should establish a communication between ourselves. It is important not only to understand the meaning of words but also to go behind the word, realizing that the word is not the thing. The word, the symbol, is not the actuality. We must penetrate through the word to discover for ourselves the actuality, the fact. Communication is only possible if both of us are listening not only to the meaning of the word but also to the indication, to the substance that lies behind the word.

We are going to talk about our daily existence. Unless we establish for ourselves a right way of living amidst this chaos and confusion, no matter what we seek, our intentions will be frustrated, because reality is in daily life, not something mysterious beyond the fact of daily existence. If we do not understand this whole significance of daily life, with all the conflicts, the miseries, the confusion, the extraordinary mess we are all in—unless that is clarified, any attempt to go beyond is merely an escape; and the more we escape from the actual, the more confusing, the more chaotic it becomes. What we are going to talk over together is not something beyond but rather how to understand the present, and whether we can be totally free from our sorrows, miseries, confusion, and anguish. Having cleared that up, if we can, totally, then perhaps we can begin to inquire whether there is or is not a reality which is other than an idea, a belief, a concept.

What we are going to do together is to examine our daily life. To examine we must be free to look, to perceive; to see things clearly we must be free. That is the first requirement if we are serious enough to want to examine the present state of our own being, our own conduct. This freedom is necessary in order to examine and to perceive. We must be free to listen to what is being said, and we must be free to look. Otherwise we can't see. Whatever we look at will be perverted. Whatever we listen to will have no meaning if we are not capable of listening totally, completely, wholly.

To find out, to examine, to unravel, to penetrate, there must be freedom to listen and freedom to perceive. We all want peace because we all realize that without peace there can be no flowering of goodness. There can be no movement that is not born out of confusion, that is not born out of our own misery. To have peace there must be freedom. We are going to talk over together these two things, peace and freedom. I mean by talking over together exactly what is said. You're not just going to listen to what is being said. We are going to take a journey together; we are going to partake, share, and therefore it is a work that you and I have to do together. You're not just here to listen to what is being said, agreeing or disagreeing intellectually, or agreeing with certain concepts, ideas, and formulas. That does not lead us anywhere, but if we can work together, explore together, not verbally, not intellectually, but factually, then I think that coming together like this will be worthwhile. But if we are merely concerned with definitions and formulas, with argument, then I'm afraid that we shall not get any further than where we are now.

I suggest that in all these talks, cooperation is necessary. We are not discussing ideals, what is right and what is wrong. We are not trying to find out or formulate new concepts. We are fed up with all concepts, all ideals, because they haven't altered our existence. What we are concerned with is a total revolution within consciousness, not in one particular field of consciousness, but with the totality of consciousness, where a total revolution must take place. The problem is not outward, not how to bring about a better society. The problem is a crisis in consciousness, and unless we each meet that crisis totally, not as a scientist, a religious person, a businessman, a poet or an artist, but as a total human being, we shall not bring about a radical revolution. What we are concerned about is whether it is possible to bring about a total revolution so that we can find a different way of living. That is what we are going to be concerned with.

When we use the word *freedom*, we mean by that word not a revolt, not a reaction; revolt and reaction are not freedom. Freedom from something is not freedom. Freedom from something is a reaction, and freedom has nothing to do with reaction or revolt. It is something by itself, for itself. It isn't a product of a motive, an ideal, or a concept. Unless there is freedom, we cannot have peace. I mean by that word *peace* not that state outwardly or inwardly between two blank walls, or between two uncertainties or two confusions. Peace isn't a thing that we can seek or find, any more than we can seek and find freedom. There can only be peace if we know how to live peacefully, not as individuals, but as human beings. I think there is a difference between the individual and the human being. The individual is the local entity, the Londoner, the Englishman, the German, or the Russian. He is the individual, the local entity, conditioned by his environment, but the human being is the man, the whole of man, whether he lives in England or India or somewhere else. In understanding the man, we shall understand the individual, not the other way around.

What we are concerned with is freedom and peace for human beings. If the individual merely revolts against the environment, it does not necessarily mean that he is free or that he will have peace. There can be peace only when there is a way of life which is peaceful, when man isn't divided into nationalities, into religious groups, cultivating certain formulas, concepts. It is these that destroy peace. The organized religious concepts deny peace. We observe what is taking place in the world and see that the world is divided into political, governmental, nationalistic areas. You're English; I'm a Russian or a German. Each has his particular conditioning, politically and economically. We are also divided in our beliefs, in our dogmas. You believe in a particular religious formula, and the whole of Asia believes in another set of formulas. There is conflict, and to have peace, surely there must be freedom from religious conditioning. That's first—freedom from conditioning. That is extremely difficult because we may rationally, outwardly, superficially deny certain religious concepts and formulas, but unconsciously, deeply, we are heavily conditioned. We must be free from all conditioning in order to have peace. If there is no peace, we cannot flower, both outwardly and inwardly. We'll always meet frustrations, and there will always be a reaction, a revolt.

What we are concerned with is the total revolution of man. How is this to happen? If we have ever thought about this, how do we answer this question? How can human beings have lived for two million years and more, carrying on in the same pattern inwardly? Though outwardly there have been tremendous changes, inwardly we are more or less what we have been: greedy, envious, ambitious, competitive, ruthless, cruel, self-centered, battling with each other for position and prestige. This has been going on for thousands of years, and man has suffered. Sorrow has been his lot. He's afraid of life and of death. Being afraid, he invents escapes, gods, and all the various forms of amusements. We have lived that way and we accept that as the norm of life, as the way of life. We see all this; we know all this fairly well. Seeing it all, not only outwardly but inwardly, is it possible, we ask, to change radically, completely; and if it is possible, how is that change to take place?

I am the result of the country in which I was born. The religious, social, economic, and climatic influences, the food and the clothes, all have influenced and shaped the mind. One has lived with anxiety, with fear, with despair, with many frustrations. One is almost on the verge of a neurotic state, if one is not already there. One sees no significance in living at all. One sees the boredom of it, the uselessness, the individual death, the endless sorrow, the conflict within and without. Seeing all this, is it possible to change completely?

If we say it is not possible, as man has said, then there is no way out. The moment we say it is not possible, we have blocked ourselves. To find out if it is possible, one has to examine, and to examine there must be freedom—freedom to perceive the actual fact, not an idea, but the actual fact of fear, and that is very difficult to see. The word *fear* is not fear. One must understand and be free of the word in order to face the fact of fear.

Similarly, is it possible to change so completely that our way of living, our way of looking at life is entirely different? It's a totally different dimension. That's what we are going to find out. And if it is possible to change, how is this change to take place? First of all, we must understand what it means to look, to perceive, to see. To see anything clearly, the thought, the word, the idea must not interfere. When we look at a tree or a flower, perceive it, we can look at it with botanical knowledge about the tree. In that case we are not actually looking at the tree. We are looking through words, through knowledge, through experience, and our experience keeps us from looking directly. I do not know if you have ever experimented, if you have ever looked at a tree directly, free from the word, from the image which that word has created, without any sense of judgment or evaluation. You cannot actually look otherwise, and that look isn't a blank state. On the contrary, it is tremendously attentive.

To observe, to see, is the first thing—to see what we actually are, not what we think we ought to be or should be; to see our greed, envy, ambition, anxiety, fear, actually as it is, without any interpretation, without any judgment. In that state of observation there is no effort involved at all. This we have to understand clearly, because we are conditioned to make effort. Everything we do is an effort, a struggle. If I want to change myself—if for instance I want to stop smoking—I have to struggle, force myself, determine, and at the end perhaps I may be able to give it up, but all my energy has gone into the battle. Is it not possible to give up something without effort? Smoking is a very trivial affair. To give up pleasure in all its forms, because pleasure always produces pain, is a tremendously complex problem which we will go into during one of these talks. What we are concerned with now is, is it possible to give up, to do things without effort? Because peace means that, doesn't it really? A peace that is achieved through battle within is no longer peace. It's exhaustion, and peace cannot possibly come about through effort. It comes only when there is understanding. That word is a rather difficult word. Understanding does not mean intellectual understanding. When we say we understand something, we generally mean an intellectual, conceptual grasp. Understanding can only take place when there is total attention. Total attention is only possible when we give ourselves completely. The mind, the body, the nerves, the whole being—all are tremendously attentive. Then only is there understanding.

We have to understand our lives as human beings. For us life is a chaotic contradiction. We're not describing sentimentally, emotionally, in any way except actually. We are confused, miserable, anxious, frightened, in despair. There is always this haunting fear and sorrow. That's our life, and inevitably there is death at the end of it all. That's all we know. We can imagine, we can have many ideals, formulas, and escapes from all this, but the more we escape, the more the contradiction, the deeper the conflict.

Can we look at our life as it is actually, not as it should be? Ideals are utterly futile. They have no meaning whatsoever. It's like the people who believe in nonviolence. Actually they're violent. That's a fact. Human beings are violent. Their words, their gestures, their acts, and their feelings show that they are violent. They have cultivated the

ideal of not being violent, which is to have peace, nonviolence. There is the fact, and 'what should be'. Between *what is* and what is desirable, between the fact and the idea—the utopia, the 'what should be'—there is that time interval. In the pursuit of 'what should be', we see that violence is being sown all the time. It is deception; it is a hypocritical way of looking at life. There is no need surely to have any ideal at all if we know how to look at a fact and be free of it. Because we don't know how to look at facts and be free of them, we think that by having an ideal we shall solve the fact. Actually the ideal, the 'what should be', the utopia, is an escape from reality. Now that we know how to look at violence, perhaps a different kind of action can take place. Let us go into it a little.

I am violent and I see that any form of escape from that reality, from the fact that I am violent, any escape—through drink, through ideals—diminishes my energy to look at the fact. I need energy to look, to be completely attentive. That again is a simple fact. If you will look at anything, you must have great energy. If you are half attentive because you have ideals you should not have, then you are dissipating energy and are therefore incapable of looking. Looking is a process which needs all your attention. You can only look if there is no sense of an idealistic pursuit or a desire to change *what is*.

The desire to change *what is* arises only when the fact is unpleasant. When the fact is pleasurable, we don't want to change it. What we are concerned with is the pursuit of pleasure and the denial of pain. Our chief concern is pleasure, not violence or nonviolence, goodness, or anything else. We want pleasure, and to achieve and to gain that pleasure, we will do anything. As long as we are looking at the fact with an intention to change it, we are incapable of changing it because our chief concern is to change it in terms of pleasure, however noble that pleasure may be. We should see this very clearly because our values—moral, ethical, and religious—are all based on pleasure. This is an actual fact, not an imaginary fact, as we will find if we look at ourselves very deeply and look at all the values that we have set up. Where there is the pleasure principle, there must be pain. We look in order to change violence to a pleasure in which there will be greater pleasure, so we are incapable of changing the fact that we are violent. We look at life in terms of pleasure.

Human beings are violent, deeply, for various reasons. One central reason is that their activity is the perpetuation of the 'me', the self. Self-centered activity is one of the reasons for violence. Again, to bring about a radical revolution I must understand the whole principle of pleasure. I love my gods; it gives me tremendous satisfaction. You love your gods, your formulas, your nationality, your flag. So do I. All that is based on pleasure. I may call it by different names, but it doesn't matter. That is the fact. And is it possible to look at violence without trying to change it in terms of pleasure, just to observe the fact that I am violent?

One must understand what it means to look and to listen. To listen is one of the most difficult things to do because what one hears, one interprets; one either agrees or disagrees. The mind, the brain is incessantly active in listening, either refuting what is said or accepting it, denying it or following it. To really listen implies complete quietness; otherwise, one can't listen. What usually takes place is that we are not listening to what is being said, or to a bird, or the breeze among the leaves. We actually are not listening. We have already translated in terms of words, images, and we look at things with these images and words and experiences— with knowledge. After all, to listen to your friend, to listen to your wife or husband is one of the most difficult things to do because

you have an image about your friend, about your wife, and she has an image about you. The relationship is between these two images, and these images are talking to each other—the images being memories, experiences, all the hurts, and all that. There is not an actual listening. To listen one must be free of the image.

In the same way, to see there must be no interference of the image. Then we can look at violence; then we can find out whether the word is creating the feeling, or the feeling of violence is independent of the word, because the word is not the thing. Though the brain is active, it is in a state of negation in looking because there is no longer the image that is looking. Each of us has an image of himself and of another. You're not actually looking at me. You're looking at the image you have about me, as you have an image about your wife or your husband, your children, and your country. We have relationships between these images, what we call relationships. When we want to listen or to look, the images interfere. The images of hurt, of what has been said, the memories, the accumulated experiences—these interfere and therefore there is no looking at all and no actual relationship between two people. There can only be a relationship between people when there is no image.

When you can look without an image about violence, what is the state of the mind or the brain that is looking? If you have no image about your wife or she about you, no image whatsoever, what is the state of your mind and her mind, your brain and her brain; what is taking place? You have no image as an Englishman, as a Christian or as a Hindu, or as a husband, a wife. There is no image at all. To be free of that image, you have to investigate very deeply into the whole question of forming images, and if you have gone into it, examined scrupulously, carefully, then your brain is not blank; it's not in a state of dullness. On the contrary, it's tremendously active, but that very activity is not the activity of the image-former.

With that attention you can look. To look at a tree or a flower or a bird is fairly simple, but to look inwardly in the same way at our violence, our pleasures, our pains is another matter. We can look and listen only when the mind, when the brain is completely quiet; otherwise, we can't see. Change is only possible, a total revolution is only possible when there is this attention that looks, an attention in which there is no longer the image-forming process of pleasure or the values of pleasure. That's what it means to be free. Freedom surely means the capacity to look, to observe, because the very seeing is the doing.

We see the whole implication of violence, both historically and actually. We know what it means. There have been, I am told, fifteen thousand wars in the last five thousand five hundred years, two and a half wars every year. We may not have them here, but in the world they are going on. In spite of religions, in spite of all the goodness, we have accepted war as the way of life. Man has accepted the violence as the way of life. The politicians, the religious people, all talk about peace. We cannot have peace if we do not live peacefully. To live peacefully there must be no violence. That requires tremendous inquiry and examination. A change, a radical revolution in consciousness is only possible when we can observe, see, listen, and know that every observation and all seeing is acting. Is it possible to end violence in ourselves immediately, instantly, not in terms of time? We are so conditioned that we say to ourselves, "I will gradually get rid of violence." We are used to gradualness and evolution, but is it possible to end violence instantly within ourselves? I say it is possible to end violence instantly when we can observe the fact completely, with total attention, in which there is no image of any kind. It's like

a person who is aware of an abyss, a danger; unless he is neurotic, unbalanced, he will move away from the danger, and that action is immediate. To see the danger, to actually see it, is to be free from images. Then we can look with complete quietness, complete silence. Then we will see that the fact has undergone a total mutation.

A revolution in the whole psyche of man cannot be brought about through will—will being desire, determination, a planned way of life which will lead to peace. It is only possible when the brain can be quiet and yet active to observe without creating images according to its experience, knowledge, and pleasure. Peace is essential because only in peace can one flower in goodness and beauty. That is only possible when one can listen to the whole of existence with all its turmoil, misery, confusion, and agony—just listening to it without any desire to change it. The very act of listening is the acting that will bring about a revolution.

April 26, 1966

Second Talk in London

Perhaps after I have talked a little, you might like to ask questions to clarify the things that we have talked about, if that suits you.

We were saying the other day, when we met in the other hall, that it is very important from every point of view that one should live in peace and in freedom. To live in peace one must lead a peaceful life, and that demands a great deal of energy because we are conditioned not to be peaceful. We are aggressive, dominating, competitive, brutal. Our way of life is not at all peaceful because essentially all our activity is self-centered and therefore breeds conflict. Very few of us insist on being free. We're inclined to revolt, go against something or other. When one is in revolt, it sets up other reactions in which one is caught, and one is constantly, if one observes, in conflict within oneself and without. We're never free; we never insist on freedom in ourselves, and so we are always caught in every kind of problem, in various types of contradictions.

Again, to be free one must have immense energy. Freedom and peace are not merely intellectual concepts or ideals to be achieved, to be striven after. To pursue, to strive after something also demands a certain type of energy, a certain discipline, control, imitation, but the freedom of which we are talking comes not through any decision or any volition or determination. It comes about, I think, when there is clarification in ourselves, when we are very clear. As most of us are confused, in contradiction, our activities springing from that confusion are bound to be more confusing, more contradictory, unclear. I think that is fairly simple to understand. If I am confused, the things I do, whatever thoughts, whatever feelings I have, are all bound to be confused. There is no part of me which is not confused. The idea that there are some moments when I am very clear is really quite fallacious. I am confused right through, if I observe, if I go into it. And out of that confusion, any thought, any action, any feeling is bound to lead to further confusion. I think we must clearly see and understand that, because we think there is some part of ourselves that is seeing things very clearly. If that part does see clearly, then the other part contradicts that which is clear. I may do something in clarity at moments, but on the other hand, at other moments I'm not clear.

There is a contradiction between the clarity which I think I have sometimes and the lack of clarity when I am confused. In that, there is contradiction. Really there is no clarity. We are confused. And it's very difficult to admit that to oneself. We like to pretend that there are moments of clarity, but there aren't.

So it becomes very important to inquire then what it is to be serious. Please, this is a very informal talk. We will discuss afterwards, talk together about things. This is not a talk where you listen and I just talk. Let us share the thing together and go into it easily, naturally, so that we begin to understand the various problems of our lives.

I was considering what it is to be serious. Most of us feel we are fairly serious, but we never question what the state of the mind is that is *really* serious, not serious *about* something. If we are serious about something, that leads to various other forms of miseries. It is like a man who takes drink seriously or who is serious about an idea, an activity, an action, serious about a commitment and pursuing that commitment to the very end. We consider people serious who have a concept, an idea, or an ideal and pursue it logically, brutally, ruthlessly, or with a certain sense of sympathy. We consider a man serious who does this, but is he? Is a person serious who pursues a course of action which he has formulated or reasoned out or accepted because he is so conditioned, and who lives according to that pattern? To me such a person is not serious at all because he has never considered, it seems to me, what it is to be serious, what the state of the mind is that is serious—not serious *about* something. If we could first go into that a little, then we could go back and reconsider peace and freedom at a different level.

We are asking what the state of the mind is that is really serious. What we generally consider a person to be who is serious is a human being serious about something fragmentarily. His mind works in fragments. He's very serious about painting; he feels very strongly about painting, art, music, or whatever it is. He is not aware of the other part of his mind; it is not even considered. His social activities, his daily responses, and so on are not important because he is completely committed to a certain fragment of existence. He may be an artist, a scientist, a poet, or a writer, but as long as the mind is working fragmentarily and is committed to that fragment, politically or religiously, surely such fragmentary activity is not an indication of seriousness, because it contradicts the other part of existence.

A serious person is one, it seems to me, who does not function in fragments, or whose mind does not think in fragments. Is it possible to be totally attentive to the whole existence of life, not just fragments, parts, but to the totality of it? If one is so serious, then there is no contradiction. It is the person who is not serious who lives in contradiction. Is that very clear? Please don't agree or disagree. Just examine what is being said and feel for yourself, be aware of this fragmentary action and not consider as serious that which is not; find out what a mind is that is really serious, which doesn't function in fragments but considers the whole. Surely such a mind is a serious mind, one that is aware of the whole total process of life.

Question: May I ask you something?

KRISHNAMURTI: Yes, please.

Comment: I recognize from my own observation the accuracy of what you say. One of the things that keeps me from being serious is this inability to bear the whole.

KRISHNAMURTI: The lady says the difficulty is the inability to bear the whole. Let me go on a little, if you don't mind. Let me talk a little bit more before you begin to ask questions and talk things over together. I am afraid it is not a question of bearing anything. There is no burden in seeing something totally. Either you see it or you don't see it. When you see it, then it is not a burden. It is only when you don't see it, when you're confused about the whole question of seriousness and all the rest of it that it becomes a terrible burden. Let me go on talking a little, and we'll come together upon this.

We are talking about seriousness because we must somehow eliminate contradiction in ourselves, for that is the source of conflict. A mind in conflict is incapable of perception, of seeing. It's a distorted mind, and when the contradiction becomes more and more acute, it leads to various forms of imbalance, psychotic states, and so on and on and on. Is it possible for a mind, for a person, in daily life, to live without contradiction and therefore without conflict? To find that out we must inquire into what a serious mind is. Perhaps if we can understand that, we will then not function in fragments but from a totally different state in which there is no contradiction at all.

Please, before you ask me, just consider what is being said, not how to achieve it, not how to arrive at it. That is all too immature.

It is essential for a man to live in peace. This means that he must lead a peaceful life. The word *lead* implies the whole, not just one part. Is this possible for a mind, for a brain, which has been trained, educated, conditioned for centuries upon centuries to live and accept a way of life in which there is conflict? The brain cells themselves are used to it. Our outlook on life is nonpeaceful. Our whole social, moral, ethical, religious structure is nonpeaceful. This psychological structure which man has created through so-called evolution for centuries is part of us. We are that. It is no answer merely to run away from that structure into a monastery or into a mental hospital, or to escape through drugs, or to say, "Well, I am against this war, but I'll fight another war. I'm against the war in

Vietnam, but if my country is attacked, I'm all for it.''

So we have accepted war, which is the extreme form of our daily life, as the way of life. Religious talk about peace and all that kind of stuff is really just idle talk; it has no meaning.

We have accepted it. Our way of life is war, not peace, because we are competitive. Our brains respond to this conditioning which is conflict, battle, struggle. Is it possible to change this whole structure of which we are part, of which the brain itself is a part? Is it possible to end it? Can thought, which has created a way of life in which there is conflict, can that very thought, which is the result of centuries of thinking of violence, end it? Can thought end a way of life which is brutal? Our intellect, our brain, our thoughts have made a way of life which in its essence is nonpeaceful, violent, and all that. Thought cannot end it. Thought has created this; therefore, thought cannot end it. It can create other patterns opposite to it, but it still has the seeds of violence in it because thought produces a way of life which is based on its own pleasure.

Thought cannot create a way of life in which there is peace. I do not know if you see that. If thought says, "I must be peaceful; I must find a way of life in which activity is peaceful, nonviolent,'' then thought only creates resistance to violence, and resistance is a contradiction. Therefore we are back again in the same muddle as before. Thought as will, thought which says, "I must; I determine to live a peaceful life,'' thought which has created a way of life which is not peaceful can only also create a way of life which it considers peaceful, but which is not peaceful. I think this is really an extraordinarily subtle problem. It isn't just saying, "I live a peaceful life.'' That is what has been done in all the monasteries and by people who have renounced the world, but they don't live peaceful lives; they are boiling in themselves.

It is quite simple, but I'll go into it. Thought has created this way of life which is our daily life. Thought can say to itself, "I'll create a different way of life, which will be peaceful,'' because thought has found that the way of life which we live, which is our normal state, is unpleasant, painful, destructive. Therefore thought, in reaction to that, creates a way of life in which it thinks it will live peacefully. But when one observes a way of life which thought has created to be peaceful, it is really in essence a resistance to violence. And therefore that way of life is also a contradiction.

One must see that very clearly, not argumentatively, not agreeing with words or intellectually seeing. If one understands it intellectually, verbally, that doesn't mean anything. But if one sees that thought cannot possibly create a way of life which is peaceful, which means no contradiction and therefore no conflict, then one asks oneself, "What is the origin of thinking?" Unless one discovers that, one can't help thought from creating a new or a different way of life. Is what I am saying reasonably clear? The origin of thinking, how it begins, must be discovered.

This demands tremendous seriousness, not fragmentary seriousness, but real seriousness. You can't play with this. You can't intellectually say, "Yes, that's very good,'' or disagree or agree and add some more or take away a little. That doesn't help in this. One must be tremendously attentive and serious when putting this question and wanting to find out. Because if one uncovers the origin of thinking, if that can be discovered, then thinking has its own place, has its importance at a certain level, and that thinking will not interfere at that deeper level.

Let me put it differently. I don't live a peaceful life. As a human being I don't know what it means. All that I know is a way of life which is war, within and without. And I also see that a mind that lives in peace is an extraordinary mind. It's full of energy. There is no dissipation of energy at any level, and only a mind that lives in peace completely right through, consciously, can function. Its action is beauty, love, virtue, because in that there is no measure of comparing with resistance.

It is essential to be peaceful. Man has talked about peace since he began. The churches, everybody has said that we must have peace, and so has everyone else. The politician talks about it, unfortunately. To him peace is merely that interval between two catastrophes, two wars, two elections, or whatever it is.

Unless the mind discovers—if it can discover—the source of thought, it will be caught again in a way of life which will ultimately lead it to conflict, to a way of life which is violence. The source must be discovered. As long as there is the observer and the observed there is a contradiction, a distance, a time interval, a gap between them, and thought must exist. Please don't take notes. This is not a lecture with you taking notes and later thinking about it at home and discussing it with somebody. We are doing it together.

As long as there is an observer and the observed, the time interval between them, the distance, the space, the division is the origin of thinking. Only when the observer is the observed, and therefore no observer at all, is there no thinking.

Objectively I see a tree which in the springtime hasn't yet put out its leaves, naked to the skies and making a delicate pattern against the blue sky. I see it, I the observer, and there is that tree—the observer and the observed. The tree is not I. The tree is something outside. I think about that tree, how lovely it is, how beautiful, how dark,

black against the naked sky; and the observer has memories of that tree, its species, its name, the memory which has been accumulated factually about the tree. The observer is the memory, is the knower who knows, and from that knowing, from memory, experience, knowledge, he looks at the tree. The observer then is thinking. As long as there is the observer and the observed, there is thought in action; that is the way it is.

Take another example. There is the wife and the husband. A tree is fairly easy to look at, but it becomes much more complex here when the wife and the husband look at each other. There is always the observer and the observed. The observer who has lived with that person recalls the pleasures, sensuous and otherwise, the companionship, the hurts, the flatteries, the comforts, the background of that relationship. Each one has an image about the other. From that image, that memory, those experiences, those pleasures, thought springs. Relationship then is between the two images. This again is very clear, and so one sees that as long as there is the observer and the observed, thought must function. There is the source of action—thought. As long as there is any division, any separation, there must be the beginning of thought, which doesn't mean that thought identifies itself with the object in order to think—on the contrary, it's only identifying itself with the object in order to pacify thinking, but still thinking goes on in the relationship.

The origin of thinking has been discovered, but when the thinker, the experiencer, the observer, is the observed, the experience, the thought, then in that state there is no thinking at all. That is the way of life in which there is peace. If you are serious, not fragmentarily at odd moments when it suits you, when it gives you comfort, when it gives you pleasure, but to find a way of life that is peaceful, in which there is no contradiction—therefore no conflict and no effort at all—you must inquire into this whole process of thinking and the origin of thinking. This does not mean that you must not use thought. Of course you must use thought, but thought, when it is used without understanding the origin of thinking and the ending of thinking, creates more conflict, more confusion, as it is doing now. But when once there is this clarification which comes about when the observer is the observed, then thinking has lost its immense importance. Peace is not an end in itself. Peace is not something to be striven after as an ideal, not something to get so that one can live peacefully. It comes naturally, without any effort, without any struggle, when thought has understood itself. This does not mean that thought puts an end to thinking, which of course would be too immature, too childish. But when one understands this whole process of thinking, then one will naturally come to something that may be called peaceful, but that word is not the fact. That's only the basis of it. We're just laying the foundations because without the right foundation, thought, the mind, cannot function at a different dimension altogether. Now we can talk about it.

Comment: Once one has obtained at-one-ment with the Almighty, then one is, as it were, in a pool of sunlight, surrounded by the barriers which God has created and put there so that one can enjoy being at the center of unconscious surrender to a perfect state, and one with the Almighty.

KRISHNAMURTI: I'm sorry, sir. I'm afraid we are not talking of the same thing, if you don't mind my saying so. There is no attainment, there is no identification of one's self with what is called the Almighty. This process is still thinking. Look, sir, man has done everything possible through these two million years and more to live peacefully be-

cause he sees that life is so brutal, so devastating, with war after war. People are now being destroyed in Vietnam. Millions have been killed in the name of religion, in the name of love, in the name of God, in the name of the Almighty. Do you follow? Man has done everything to find out, and he apparently hasn't succeeded. Some vague person might have, but it's not true of you and me, and therefore they are not at all important to us. What is important is our life, our daily existence, and we have to resolve this—not eventually, not in ten years, five years, but actually now, immediately—because if we don't, we are sowing the seeds of violence, which our children will reap. And if we say, "God is the supreme entity"—I don't—we know nothing about all that. All we know is this brutal life, this life of despair, anxiety, misery, sorrow. If we don't end it, not speculatively, not idealistically, but actually end it, then we live and create future wars.

Question: I would like to take up this question of the origin of thought. I have read your book, The First and Last Freedom, *and I have discovered that my life is brought about by myself. All the anxieties, the wars that I fight daily—I've brought them all about. But I've reached the stage in which I can't get hold, by listening to you this morning, of this origin of thought. I am a man constantly worried with business, with problems, all sorts of things. I want to be free of them all, so I read your books. I will be back in my business next week, worrying about all these problems that come and go, and so on and so on. This is Day One for me. Whither do I go with this origin of thought? How do I become free of it so I can know of this peace of which you talk? For I know that I don't live in peace. How can this come about for me?*

KRISHNAMURTI: That's what I've been saying, sir. I have explained, sir. Please let us be clear. This is not a confessional. We're not confessing our difficulties to each other. We are trying to understand the whole problem, not individual localized conflicts and problems confessed publicly. We have lived this way of life in business, at home, and that's the way of our life. If we want to live differently, we don't know what that means; we actually don't know what it means to live peacefully. We can't create a picture of it, an image of it. We can't paint a picture and follow that picture. We don't know it, and we can't pursue what we don't know. We only know this: in business, at home, everything we touch is a way of life in which there is conflict. That's all we know. We refuse to look at anything else because that's deception; it is an escape, it wastes energy. We have energy to tackle this problem. So we refuse to escape from this, from *what is*. To give full attention—therefore complete energy—to this, we mustn't look to someone or to something else; we have no time. We must completely give our whole bodies, minds, everything we have, to understand this. And I say that to understand it, one must understand this question of the observer and the observed. Please, sir, it's very clear; it's very simple to put into words, but to go inwardly into it you need a very disciplined mind, not a mind that has been disciplined—that is a dead mind—but to go into it, the very act of examining is discipline. What we are trying to do is to find out why there is this contradiction, conflict, in all that exists in our life. And I say that as long as thought is dominating, as long as thought has not been understood—how it begins its activity—you will always live in conflict, whether you do business or not.

Is it possible to do business, to live a family life, to look at a tree, without conflict? It is only possible when the observer is the observed. This requires tremendous un-

derstanding, sir. It isn't how you achieve it. You can't achieve it. You have to live it. You have to go into it. When you see a tree—you've never seen a tree because what you have done is that you have the image of the tree, and that image looks at the tree. When you look at a flower, when you look at a woman or a man, you have the image, which is the process of thinking. Can you look at the tree, at the woman, at the child, at your boss in the office, without the observer? This is very important, please, for then, when you go to the office, you can function there without the observer, and you will find out that you will love what you are doing.

Question: How can one go into it? What is the discipline?

KRISHNAMURTI: Just a minute! I am using the word *discipline* not in the sense of imitation, conformity, suppression, adjustment, forcing oneself. That is not what I consider discipline. That is just fear. That is just an acquisitive curiosity, an acquisitive pleasure. The mind, in looking at a tree, is looking at the tree with the image it has about that tree. To discover that image—whether about a tree, a person, your boss, your wife, your husband—to discover that image is disciplining. The origin of the word means really, doesn't it, "to learn." To be a disciple to something is to learn. You cannot learn if you are disciplined, but learning implies discipline. Learning is discipline. So I am going to learn—as learning. And to learn about this I have to find out what the answer is, why this observer is constantly interfering, constantly projecting his images, his concepts, his judgments, his valuations, his background. Why? Because the observer is the background. The observer is the knowledge, the conditioned entity, not simply a Britisher or an Indian or whatever it is. You are conditioned, and that conditioning is the observer who looks at that tree or that flower or that woman or that country or that flag. To discover this conditioning, this background which is the observer, to understand it, to learn about it, is the very act of learning, is the disciplining, because you have no energy to look if the image interferes.

Question: What should we do to eliminate this conditioning?

KRISHNAMURTI: Please, the word *might* or *should* implies conditional thinking. Either you see the thing or you don't see it. This isn't just a morning's talk where we spend an hour or so and then at the end of it go back to our daily lives. This is the whole of life. This is every moment of life.

Question: Is there subjective thinking which comes from the observer, and then objective thinking which is just thinking?

KRISHNAMURTI: No, no! There is no subjective thinking and objective thinking; there is only thinking.

Question: You talked of the whole total process of life. Now what exactly do you mean by that? I think we would be helped with the task here if you could give everyone an idea of what you learned in the East about the Masters and the wonderful people who are there on the other side of the world. Hasn't that something to do with the whole process?

KRISHNAMURTI: No, madame. Look, let's begin again. We must surely approach life with a great deal of skepticism. Nobody has faith in anything anymore.

Comment: Nonsense!

KRISHNAMURTI: You say it's nonsense—all right. Any thinking man who wants to discover something original, not secondhand, not something that's been handed down to him, must face life with a great deal of skepticism, which does not mean that he merely lives with skepticism. He examines; he doesn't accept or deny. If one wants to find out if there is reality, God, which man has asserted for centuries, merely following what others have said has no meaning at all. Both Catholic and Protestant churches have said that there is, and people who believe in that are conditioned like the people in Russia or in China who don't believe any of this nonsense because they are conditioned that way. Have you ever talked with anyone who really is a communist, who says, "What piffle are you talking about? There is only physical existence; beyond that there is nothing more. Don't become an old-fashioned woman, without thinking. That is silly." To find out you must be free of both the believer and the nonbeliever, mustn't you? You can't say, "Well, I'll accept this because it's more pleasurable, it's more comforting," and deny the rest. One must be free of this conditioning. Then one can proceed. But without being free from this background of one's conditioning, how can one examine? How can one find out for oneself? Before you say yes or no, before you say that what I am talking about is nonsense, you have to be free of your own conditioning and find out whether it is possible to be free, whether the brain which has been trained, on which propaganda has been poured for two thousand years or more can loosen itself and think, look at itself, without its own conditioning. That is the first thing. After laying the foundation of that, which means virtue, conduct, behavior, no competition, then you can ask, then you can meditate to find out. Meditation is something not at one level, but meditation is right from the beginning.

Question: Are we always to think only good thoughts?

KRISHNAMURTI: No, sir, no, sir, I don't mean good thought and bad thought, destructive thought and creative thought. We're talking about thought.

Question: Will you give us an example?

KRISHNAMURTI: Look, sir. When you love something, then you love. Is love thought?

Comment: I think so, yes.

KRISHNAMURTI: Can love be cultivated through thought? Then is it love, or is it the product of thought, which is not love?

Comment: I suppose one leads to the other.

KRISHNAMURTI: Sir, do consider. I am not saying that you should agree or disagree. Just consider what is being said. That is, is love thought? When I say, "I love you," is it thought that is saying it?

Comment: If you think about it, yes.

KRISHNAMURTI: Ah, if you think about love, is it love? Sir, do consider it, please. There is merely intellect. It is only the word. The intellect says, "I love you," and it is not love.

Question: Is it experience, love for somebody or something?

KRISHNAMURTI: Oh, no. If love is the result of experience, which is knowledge, which is all the rest of it, is it love? Sir, look at it. You love. Not you, sir; I am not talking personally. One loves. If one loves, is there a contradiction in that love?

Comment: Yes, in a sense.

KRISHNAMURTI: Can love go with jealousy and hate?

Comment: I suppose so.

KRISHNAMURTI: Not "suppose," sir.

Question: There is this question of energy. Actually one is bursting with energy, with the energy of action. The energy is such that immediately you want to stop it. This is an actual, physical discipline. When you talk of conflicts, are you actually talking about a physical state?

KRISHNAMURTI: No, sir, I am afraid we are not meeting each other. Look, sir, to go to the office daily requires energy. To do anything requires energy, physical energy, and that physical energy creates misery through its aggressive pursuits and brings about psychological conflicts. We are talking of this energy which outwardly creates psychological conflicts. These conflicts produce different forms of escapes, contradictions, a background of security from which I am unwilling to move. We are talking of releasing energy totally, where energy doesn't create mischief. That energy which we now expend is creating a great deal of mischief and misery. As long as that energy is not completely focused rightly, there is bound to be mischief, and that's what we have been talking about.

Comment: Last night suddenly there was a sudden impact, an energy of being.

KRISHNAMURTI: I understand, sir. Now the question is this, "Can I, as thought, recognize something as being true?" I'm just asking. Go into it a little bit; don't answer me, sir. I say that is true. That state is love. That state of peace, of freedom, I recognize. The recognizing process implies, does it not, that I have already experienced it; otherwise, I can't recognize it. Therefore it is not true recognition. It is nothing new. It has already been known. So, is truth all that state of reality which is not recognizable? When you love someone, if you do, at that moment you see that you love. The moment you put it into words, the expression has already gone.

Question: Is it possible to teach children not to name, since naming is a barrier?

KRISHNAMURTI: I would put it differently. You have to learn naming; you have to know that's a tree, that's an ant, that is this, that is that. But what is much more important, it seems to me, is not naming but the awakening of intelligence. Intelligence means to be sensitive, physically, emotionally, mentally, neurologically, with every sense. The highest form of sensitivity is intelligence. When there is that intelligence, you know where naming is interference, where it is destructive. But if you begin at the other end, with what is implied in naming or not naming, you're only making it rather confusing. The question then is, in this modern world with all the nationalities and prejudices, with what is going on in this country and in other countries, is it possible to help a child to be sensitive? You can't help another or bring about sensitivity in another if you are not yourself sensitive. You can discuss it, talk it over. In that very process you yourself are becoming sensitive.

It isn't that you are teaching him to be sensitive; both are learning to be sensitive, all around, not fragmentarily—sensitive as an artist, sensitive to business, as a human being. Then, if you are sensitive right through, that very sensitivity is intelligence.

April 30, 1966

Third Talk in London

In the two preceding talks we discussed the necessity for peace and freedom, whether it is at all possible to live in this world with these two imperative necessities, and what the state of mind must be in order to come to this, living in a world based on violence, acquisitiveness, and greed. We discussed whether, in this world, a human being functioning normally could have peace at all. If I may, this evening I would like to talk about something with which man has lived for many centuries—sorrow—and whether it is at all possible, not only consciously, but also at the deeper levels of one's consciousness, to be entirely free from this thing. Like fear, sorrow in any form dulls the mind, cripples the human heart, makes one insensitive. Living in this world, carrying on with our daily work, is it at all possible for there to be an ending to sorrow?

To really understand a matter of this kind we must, it seems to me, communicate with each other, and communication becomes exceedingly difficult when the word becomes the major factor. For most of us the word, the symbol, has extraordinary importance. Intellectually we can understand most things, most of our difficulties and problems, because we are fairly cunning, we are fairly well educated either to rationalize our problems or to run away from them. Most intellectual or fairly intelligent people can do that. But if we would go into deeper matters, we must, mustn't we, know what real communication is, what it is to commune together about a thing like sorrow. To communicate, to commune together about this, we must be intense at the same time and at the same level. Otherwise communion is not possible. We must explore this question together, and to explore there must not only be freedom to examine, to investigate, but also there must be this relationship between the speaker and the listener, a relationship in which one can not only commune with words but also go beyond the word, realizing that the word is not the thing. The symbol is never the fact, the truth. And most of us get caught in the symbol, the name, the word. But I think the word, the symbol, loses its grip if both of us are intent to explore, to uncover this question of sorrow.

I do not know if you have noticed that communication is only possible when both of us are vigorous, when both of us are intent on understanding this question. If there is no intensity of a vigorous examination, then we will slip into intellectual arguments, into saying that we understand intellectually but that we can't actually grasp what is being talked about. Then communication ceases completely.

To communicate with each other about a matter of this kind, which is a very difficult and complex question, both must be listening. Listening is an art, and most of us do not really listen at all. We listen to our own opinions, judgments, evaluations, and we hardly have time to listen to another. In any listening, which is really also examining, there must be attention, not concentration—an attention that comes easily when we give our minds, our hearts, our nerves, our ears, everything to understand something that is a complex and important part in our lives.

Let us go into this question nonintellectually because intellect alone doesn't solve a thing. This doesn't mean that we mustn't use reason, but we can't live by the intellect alone; we can't live in one part, in one fragment of our being and cut out the rest, which most of us try to do and therefore live in constant conflict and turmoil. To understand this thing we must listen, not only to the speaker, but also to the whole problem. The problem is very complex, and to listen and examine we cannot have opinions. We can't say, "I know and you don't know," and stick to our opinions, judgments, and evaluations. A man who says he knows does not know and therefore is incapable of listening.

To go into this question, there must be not only the act of listening but also the act of perception, of seeing. Really listening is seeing. To see something very clearly, to see a flower, a tree, or one's own problems very clearly, one must look negatively. A negative look implies looking at something without the distortion of prejudice, of opinion, of an experience, of what you already know, all of which keep you from looking.

This question of sorrow, with which man has lived for centuries upon centuries, has not been solved. We have escaped from it; we have invented various theories, dogmas, and the theologians have offered clever cunning reasons—original sin, and so on and so on and so on. But the fact remains that we haven't solved it. There is no end to sorrow. To understand it we must come to it afresh, not saying that it is impossible to solve it, to end it, not saying, "Tell me how to end it. What method, what system shall I use? What should I do; what should I not do?" We have played that game for centuries. We have gone to the priests, to the gods, to drink, to sex, to every form of escape. We have cunningly developed a network of escapes, and we are not beyond it. It needs a fresh mind, a new mind to look at this problem. To look at it there must be freedom from conclusions, concepts, what should be, should not be. We must look at the fact and not at what we think the fact should be. If we wish the fact to be different, then we are escaping from the fact.

We must have a fresh look, a fresh mind to investigate, and we are going to do it together this evening. We know what sorrow is. Everyone in different ways has experienced it. There is the sorrow of frustration, the sorrow of being loved, of not being loved, the sorrow of not achieving, the sorrow of loneliness, emptiness, sorrow for a wasted and useless life, a life that is utterly boring, a mechanical life of going to the office every day of our life for forty years, and at the end, dying. There is the sorrow of incapacity, of not being able to think or see clearly. There is the despair, the anxiety of the everlasting search, never coming upon anything true or original, anything which thought has not put together, and there is the sorrow of death, with its complete sense of isolation. We know various forms of sorrow, either intensely or superficially, consciously or unconsciously. Superficially we may be mechanical, trying to forget, run away, but unconsciously the sorrow is there, gnawing, darkening, making one's mind dull, heavy. We know it. And always, of course, there is old age, ill-health, and so on. I don't need to go on; we all know sufficiently what is meant by the word *sorrow*.

Is it possible to end it, not in some distant future, not, as some in the Orient believe, through a perpetual, endless evolution and ultimate realization, a ceaseless travail at the end of which is freedom from sorrow? That is just another form of escape and the more society makes progress, the more it becomes superficial, seeking enjoyment and pleasure, and burying this thing deeply within. But it is still there.

If one is at all serious, the mind has a full intent of resolving the problem, not by a casual investigation, but by pursuing to the very end with vigor, with intensity, to find

out if it is possible to end this sorrow, which creates such chaos in the world.

Is it possible to understand this question, to ask oneself and see whether it is possible to end it? One has to inquire into the question of time, not only time by the watch, by the day, by yesterday, today, and tomorrow, but also psychological time, the time that man has built within himself, in which he is caught—a time that was yesterday, the time of today and tomorrow, the time of the past with all its content of the past, the present, and the future.

Time is like a river flowing endlessly, but man has broken it up into three parts: the past, the present, and the future. The past is heavily burdened, and the future he does not know. Giving significance to life, a life that has no meaning, no purpose, no beauty, he says, "Let me live in the present." He invents a philosophy of the present. But to live in the present, man must understand the past and the future. It's a movement; you can't take this river and say, "I live just there." It's like a river that is flowing, and in this stream of time man is caught. Unless there is an end to time, there is no ending to sorrow.

We are obviously the result of the past; we are conditioned by time, by society, by the culture in which we live—Christian, communist, Hindu, Muslim, Buddhist, or whatever you will. We are caught in it, and our brains and their reactions are educated to function in the flow of time, to accept it and go with it. We are always thinking of the past, the past looking at the present, and the present creating the future. The "now" is the result of yesterday, and the "tomorrow," if there is a tomorrow, is the result of today. We all know this intellectually, and we haven't been able to find a solution. We are caught in this stream as we are caught in the stream of fear, in the stream of sorrow. We are caught in the stream of time—I was, I am, I will be. I was violent yesterday, and I will not be violent tomorrow. We are always functioning in time. If we observe our own minds, we discover this—discover it, not accept it. There is a difference, I think, between acceptance and discovery. When we discover something for ourselves, it is much more vital, it has validity; there is energy in that discovery. But if we merely accept, then all the intensity, the vigor, the examination, the vitality that is necessary, all these are destroyed. Most of us are yes-sayers and not no-sayers. We accept; we obey the tradition, what has been. We are caught, and to solve this question of sorrow we must look at time differently, time being obviously thought. Thought is the result of time. The brain cells are the result of thousands of years of cultivation, of experience. The brain is still that of the animal, with certain modifications, and we accept that as the way of life, as we accept war, violence, brutality as the way of life. Having accepted it, we move away from it to find something different. We do not want to change radically because that demands energy, examination, clarity. We want life to continue as we have known it, and we want to find something other than the actual fact, and escape from *what is.*

Every human being is caught in time. I am not talking about time by the watch, chronological time which does influence thought, but of time at a different level, time as a movement of the infinite past, moving through the present to some future. As long as I am caught in that, there is no end to sorrow. I say to myself, "I'll be happy tomorrow; I'll escape from my present misery, my deep inner psychological disturbance which brings about sorrow. I'll gradually get over it, forget it, rationalize it, escape from it or invent some future hope." But to end suffering I must understand time. Time must come to an end because thought has created sorrow; thought is time, thought has said, "I'm lonely; I'm incapable of functioning; I'm not loved; my ambition, my capacity is not fulfilling itself. I must have time to do this, and time to achieve, to become, to change." So thought, which is the result of time, and which is time, looks to something which will help it to dissolve this sorrow. If I look at myself, I will see that this is what I have done whenever any sorrow has arisen. Thought immediately comes into operation. After all, sorrow is a challenge, a challenge to which there is inadequate response and therefore, out of that sorrow, there is a feeling of disturbance, of anxiety, of fear. I lose my job. I see someone famous, rich, prosperous. I have nothing, and someone else has everything—beauty, culture, intelligence. Thought by comparing, adjusting, accepting, or denying, breeds this thing.

Thought cannot solve the problem of sorrow. Please don't accept what is being said, or deny it. We must see the fact, and when we see the fact very clearly there is neither acceptance nor denial. It is so. It is not a question of how to end thinking, or where thought must function and where it must not function. When we understand very clearly the whole movement of thought, how it operates, what is involved, the machinery of thinking, the origin of thinking and of thought, then we begin to see that the problem of time is whether time as thought can come to an end. Otherwise there is no ending of sorrow. We'll go on for another two million years or more, accepting, escaping, living a disturbed, insecure, uncertain life.

Can time come to a stop? First we must see that the mind, the brain, the whole way of thinking, all function in time and are time. We must be aware that time is a movement, a flow which we have divided into yesterday, today, and tomorrow. We must see this movement as a whole and give complete attention to it. Attention implies a complete cessation of effort, attending to the question, to what is being said, not accepting but giving complete attention, effortlessly. We can't attend by determination. If we say, "I will attend," our energy is gone in trying to be attentive. To attend does not imply concentration because concentration is exclusion. If we try to concentrate we are excluding, building barriers, resistance, forcing ourselves to concentrate, whereas in attention there is no division—the intellect, the nerves, and everything else functioning at the highest level. In that attention there is no observer.

If you give your attention to something, to a flower, to a tree, and observe attentively, completely, there is no division into the observer and the observed. If you have ever looked at a flower, completely, attentively, without naming the flower, without like and dislike, just observing completely with all your being, in that attention there is no observer and therefore no time. The observer is the result of time. It is this observer who says, "I like" and "I dislike," "It gives me pleasure," and "It does not give me pleasure," "This is worthwhile; this is not worthwhile," "I must hold on to the pleasures I have, though they bring about more pain, more anxiety, more sorrow." Pleasure invariably breeds sorrow and pain. The very nature of the observer is the censor who is always choosing pleasure. He looks at everything from that point of view, and therefore he is not attentive.

It is necessary to be attentive to this flow of time, not saying, "I will keep this, this part of time which has given me pleasure, which has given me satisfaction, this remembrance of something which has delighted me." There must be a total attention, in which there is no sentiment at all, no emotion. For most of us sorrow is self-pity, and self-pity is an utter waste of time in an emotional orgy. It has no value at all. What has value is the fact, not the self-pity which arises from the discovery that we cannot or can, should or should not. Self-pity breeds emotional anxiety, sentiment, and all the rest. When there is a death of someone whom we like, in it is always this poison of self-pity. That self-pity takes many forms, the deep consideration for the one who is dead, and so on and on and on. But where there is sorrow, there is no love. Where there is jealousy, there is no love. Where man is ambitious, competitive, seeking self-advancement, trying to attain, such a person obviously has no love. We all know this intellectually, yet we pursue the way of life that breeds sorrow.

To be attentive implies to be aware of the division of time into the past, the present, and the future, the "I have been; I must not; I will do." If we are completely aware of this whole process of time, we will see that time has come to an end altogether. Try it! To do it, actually, not theoretically, to see the fact of it, we must also know the past. We make a lot of ado about the unconscious. I don't know why. Probably it's a matter of fashion. The unconscious is as trivial as the conscious. It's as petty as the conscious mind. The unconscious is the result of time, of many thousands of yesterdays, the residue of the past, the tradition, racial inheritance, the family, the name. The conscious is also the result of the past, how we have been educated, what our job is, how we think, what we feel, how we look at things. The whole of consciousness is conditioned, and to merely investigate the unconscious endlessly seems to me to be a game that's not worth playing, unless we are neurotic, or unbalanced. In that case it might perhaps help, and probably does, but that only leads to an acceptance of the present society. If one looks at the whole structure of consciousness, it's fairly simple. It is conditioned; it has frontiers, boundaries, in which it has functioned for centuries, like the brain cells. It has been developed, trained to have reactions, modified, polished, as has the animal.

To understand all this we must give attention. When we are listening attentively, completely, to what is being said, there is no listener. When we look at something completely, there is no entity or the censor who is looking. The censor, the observer, comes into being the moment the thinking process is set going.

When this feeling of sorrow arises, give complete attention to it, neither escaping nor justifying nor trying to find a reason. We all know why we suffer. We suffer because we can't get a job or our son has gone crazy, has become a modern entity, or we have no capacity whereas someone else has. We all know the reasons, but to end sorrow is only possible when we look at this whole process of time, which is thinking. When we attend so completely we will see that there is no thinking at all, and therefore there is no time.

When someone whom we love or like does something or dies, we respond to it, after the shock is over, according to the reactions of our loneliness, of self-pity, of wanting more time to do this or that, with regrets as to what might have been and what might not have been. All that is a dissipation of attention. When the shock is over, if we attend completely and do not move away in any direction, then we will find that there is an ending to sorrow, not in some distant future, but immediately. It is only a mind that is not clouded by sorrow that knows what it is to love. Only such a mind can meditate. Meditation is not something to be achieved, something that you practice, learn, but it is this attention, attending to everything from the most little thing to the deepest thing. When you do that, you will find out for yourselves that there is a silence which is not of time, which is not of thought. When you can come upon something not put together by thought, you will find that it is something which is not of time at all.

May 3, 1966

Fourth Talk in London

Most of our lives are rather drab, uninteresting, monotonous, and mechanical. That being so, we are always seeking something more mysterious, something that will give perfume, a significance, a meaning to our lives. We take up new religions, new Sanskrit phrases, or Tibetan words; we join schools of meditation or go to concerts, read a lot of books and fill ourselves with a great deal of information about which we can chatter endlessly. If that doesn't satisfy us, we turn to these modern drugs which expand the mind, give hallucinations and various forms of vision which apparently have a tremendous meaning.

This is happening all over the world, taking drugs, LSD and so on, that give one great sensitivity and precipitate one into various states of visions and hallucinations. It seems to me it is really more important to find out for oneself as a human being, and therefore related to the whole of mankind, if there is something more than what thought puts together. Thought can create a most mysterious, fascinating, and unimaginable world. Thought can do this very well, very easily, and one can escape into it most beautifully, imagining that one is living in a world of spiritual whatever it is. But it would be worthwhile to find out if there is anything beyond the structure of mystery, of something hidden, which thought has so carefully built through the ages.

I do not know if you have ever looked into the question of meditation or tried it. One of the most important things in life is not how to meditate, or what kind of visions one will have if one meditates, but rather to find out what happens actually, not theoretically or speculatively, when thought comes to an end. Thought is based on the expanding demand of greater pleasure. Can the mind easily, without effort, understand the nature of thinking and therefore of pleasure, and discover or come upon something which may be the real source of all existence? If I may, I would like to talk over this thing with you, and perhaps we could go into it rather seriously.

Humility is rather an ugly word. It has been greatly misused. But I think the word really has great depth to it, because one can only have humility when there is nothing of the past, and therefore the mind is in a state of constantly learning without accumulating. It is only such a mind, it seems to me, that is actually in a state of humility. Then it can learn. Humility is not a thing to be cultivated any more than love. It is only the vain person, the man of pride and conceit, who cultivates the cloak of humility. But if one is to learn, there must be this sense of humility, a mind that doesn't know, that isn't always acquiring, climbing, reaching, attaining. Humility can only exist when the past, which is thought with all its structure, comes to an end. The mind must be highly sensitive, active, vigorous. Only those qualities can make the mind clear.

This morning let us try to learn something about meditation, not the word, not what you already know, what you have already read and what you may have already practiced, because no method, no system, no practice is really meditation. In the East they have many schools, many ways of meditation, many teachers who teach you meditation in a few days or in a week or in a month, and they help you to practice how to be aware, how to become sensitive, how to sit, how to breathe and do all kinds of things in order to quiet the mind so that you may have extraordinary visions. Nonsense! Let us explore together this morning. It is really not exploration. What is necessary, it seems to me, is a mind that is capable of listening and not doing anything, because the moment you do something, the moment you say, "I must, I must not, I must pursue, I must seek, I must find, I

must attain," thought begins to operate, and thought can do absolutely nothing except technologically.

In a certain area of one's existence, thought is essential; there it must function with clarity, with reason, with sanity, with vigor, with precision. But in the other field, when thought tries to enter and discover if there is something, thought brings about confusion, brings about various forms of self-deception, illusions, visions, hypocritical states. Not that there is a division between these two fields, the field in which the validity of thinking has its place and the other dimension in which thought has no place at all. These two are not separate, but to find out the nature of thinking and perhaps to end thought, you must go into the question of pleasure. Please, we're doing it together. You're not just listening to me, to the speaker, and trying to understand what he's talking about. He's talking about nothing very serious, because the word is not the thing. The idea is not the reality. The word, the symbol, is not the actual, and you must understand the nature of pleasure; otherwise, thought plays tricks upon you, creates deceptions, brings about projected visions which have no reality at all.

If we would understand what real meditation is, we must understand pleasure, and it's extremely subtle. All of us have this urge for deeper, wider, stronger pleasures. The sensory pleasures are obvious. It is not necessary to go into them; everyone knows about them. But there are deeper pleasures, pleasures to which thought has given a continuity, a vitality, a drive; and if one observes, most of our moral values, virtues, are essentially the work of thought and therefore are pleasure. The people who talk about seeking God are really seeking the continuation of everlasting pleasure, which they call whatever it is. That's what most of us want—deep abiding pleasure which can never die, which can never be corrupted, which has its own vitality. The mind, thought, is always pursuing it, consciously or unconsciously. We want a little more, something other than drinking and sex. We take drugs because our life is so drab, so meaningless, such a stupid affair, with its monotony, loneliness, and boredom. We seek pleasure in different forms, as part of our nature. Like the animal, we are always avoiding danger and seeking pleasure.

If I may make a suggestion, as we are talking about this, please be aware of your own values, thoughts, life, existence, so that you yourself will discover the importance or unimportance of pleasure. If you do not understand this basic thing, entering into a field which is completely denuded of all pleasure, and therefore a field of extraordinary bliss, cannot possibly be understood. I am not trying to persuade you, to convert you to another system, another thought, another idea. You must understand pleasure, not only the sensory pleasures which are obvious, but also the pleasures which thought creates, sustains, and to which it gives nourishment, the nourishment that comes through memory of something which has happened and has given pleasure. Thought goes back over and over and over again to a happy incident, a pleasurable sensation, a thing remembered that has given great delight. Thought reverts to it and builds a structure of expanding and strengthening pleasure. From that background, conscious or unconscious, thought then operates, judges, evaluates, looks, and acts.

Thought is the outcome of desire. There are sensory desires, such as the desire for food, but the moment thought says, "That tastes very nice; I must have more of it," the strengthening of desire has begun. Our whole life is made up of desire, the pleasure that is derived from putting that desire into action, and the sustaining of pleasure by thinking about the action which has given pleasure. If

we do not understand this but talk about meditation, posture, breathing, drugs, and practice, it seems to me it is infantile, immature.

We must be aware of the nature of pleasure and what gives it strength and vitality, which again is thought. It's really very, very simple if one understands it. We see a woman, a car, a child, a house, a picture, or we listen to music. Seeing, feeling, censoring that picture, that building, that woman, thought thinks about it and gives to that pleasure strength and continuity. When we understand this, we see at the same time that where there is pursuit of pleasure, there is always the shadow of pain, the avoidance, the resistance. Thought creates resistance around itself so that it will have no pain at all. Thought lives in this artificial pleasure because of something that it has had or wants to have. If thought says, "I understand this very well, and I must act to get beyond it," the beyond becomes another form of pleasure created by thought. Thought has built a psychological structure of pleasure. Seeing the nature of it, seeing that there is pain in it, thought says, "I must do something else. I must act differently. I must behave differently. I mustn't think about pleasure. I must resist pleasure. I must do this and that." The very action which thought creates about pleasure is still pleasure. Thought cannot do anything about it.

If I may make a suggestion, just listen. I'm not trying to hypnotize you. That would be too obvious and too simple. Just listen, because if you are capable of listening and seeing the truth of what is being said, then thought will not act. If you are in that state of listening, the fact, the truth, will act. If a seed is planted in the earth and has vitality, it will grow. In the same way, the act of listening is the soil. The act of listening is only possible when there is attention, and attention does not exist if there is interpretation, evaluation, condemnation, or judgment of that to which you are listening. If you listen completely, attentively, without any observer who is the thinker, then that very act of listening will put away what is false, and you will listen only to what is true.

The act of listening is the field. In that field every kind of seed is sown, and only the seed that has vitality, energy, strength, will come up, will flourish. That's what we are doing now. We're actually listening, neither accepting nor disagreeing nor judging. We're actually listening so completely that the very act of listening destroys what is false and lets the seed of truth take root. If we listen to the whole structure of pleasure on which our thought, our lives, our beings are based, and do anything about it—which we are all wanting to do, which we think is the most positive act—that brings about greater confusion, greater conflict and therefore more sorrow, more pain; but if we listen in this completely negative state, which is the most positive state, then the seed which has life will grow without our doing anything about it.

If thought does anything about pleasure, about desire, this is still the act of desire and the act of pleasure. Thought cannot do a thing about it, which doesn't mean that thought has not its place, its validity; but we are talking of an action that is not a pleasure and therefore an action in which there is no contradiction, no conflict, and no pain.

If there is this act of listening, an understanding of the nature of pleasure and of pain, and a realization by thought that any movement it makes in any direction, above or below, is still the search for pleasure, then thought naturally comes to an end. Unless thought comes to an end, not artificially, not through compulsion, discipline, practice, all of which are still the result of thought, thought itself can never discover anything new. Thought is the outcome of the past, the outcome of innumerable experiences of pleasure and pain. Thought as the thinker seeking something new can only recognize that which it has known, and therefore it is not new. The brain has grown through millions of years to its present state, all its cells conditioned to react to pleasure and pain. Thought cannot make the brain still because the brain is the result of time, and thought also is a result of time. No matter how hard thought tries, it is impossible for it to make the brain cells quiet.

The question then is: Can the brain that has been so conditioned, so deeply held in this principle of pain and pleasure, can that brain be quiet; can that brain actually be sensitive, alert, active, but be quiet? Thought can only react in terms of pleasure and pain. Unless that brain is completely still—not asleep, not vague, not resisting, but completely quiet—thought must operate. Through centuries upon centuries we have developed the animal instincts, the cortex, the brain, which are essentially the response of the past. Any reaction of that past, that background, is thinking, in terms of pleasure and pain. Therefore when thought says, "I am seeking God," what it is seeking is pleasure. All this idea of seeking, seeking, seeking is so absurd. Truth cannot be found by searching. Searching means thought, inquiry, taking its petty, little, bourgeois mind into vast fields of something which it doesn't know.

When we listen, thinking actually stops, which doesn't mean that the mind goes to sleep. On the contrary, it has listened actively, intensely, vigorously, without the thinker, and is so tremendously active that naturally there is no seeking. It can only be so energetic, so vigorous, when it is silent. Can this brain and the mind, can the totality of this consciousness be completely still? If it is not, thought is in operation, and thought is always seeking its own pleasure and therefore always inviting sorrow and pain. A mind that is pursuing pleasure and therefore inviting sorrow obviously cannot find what is real. It can invent, it can speculate, it can theorize, as theologians are doing all over the world, but that has no validity at all. Understanding humility, perceiving the structure of pleasure, which is desire, recognizing the psychological structure in which man is caught, which is society, and discovering whether the brain cells can be quiet and yet active—all this is meditation.

Meditation isn't something apart from daily existence. One can't be ambitious, ruthless, vulgar, crude, awful, insensitive, acquisitive, and at the same time talk about God, truth, love, meditation. That would be hypocritical nonsense. Obviously one has to be free from the psychological structure of which society is a part, of which we are a part. If the mind is not free from this psychological conditioning, which includes religions, economic states, class differences, and all the despair and agony of the competitive world, one cannot meditate. One can play around. Meditation, in the sense in which we are using the word, is a most dangerous thing. Meditation that one practices is a most tame thing. Learning to concentrate about some idea is not meditation at all, but to be aware of the total process of existence, without choice, to be so completely attentive to this, makes the mind tremendously active and revolutionary, not a domesticated animal, conforming to the pattern of society, whatever society it is, whether it is communist or capitalist.

When the mind is really very quiet, naturally, effortlessly, then the observer, the thinker ceases to be. Then relationship between man and man becomes entirely different. The relationship then is not a memory which has been collected, an image meeting another image, another memory; it is actual relationship. If we go into it then, if we have gone so far, moved deeply in that direction,

we will find out what beauty is, because we don't now know. We only know beauty in comparison, in something that has been put together by man, a beautiful building, a beautiful face, beautiful music, or this or that. True beauty implies something which is not the result of thought, and without that sense of beauty there is naturally no love. We can go on indefinitely with this because there are no frontiers of consciousness there. All consciousness is limited for us now. We are conditioned as Englishmen, Catholics, Protestants, Anglicans, Buddhists, Hindus, Moslems, communists, socialists, or whatever our background may be. All consciousness is limited, and any action of consciousness trying to go beyond itself is merely further expanding the consciousness within, pushing the borders a little further, but there is still a limitation. Probably the people who take drugs unconsciously know all this and try to go beyond, but they cannot.

Meditation is something extraordinary if it goes on, not at odd moments, but timelessly, if you are aware when you get into the bus, or the car, or when you are talking to someone; aware of what you are doing, feeling, thinking; aware of how thought operates according to pleasure and pain, not condemning any activity of thought, but just listening to the noise of thought. Out of that you really have an extraordinary mind that is tremendously alive. Being quiet, being silent, a new thing can take place. The newness is not recognizable. This sublime thing, whatever name you give it doesn't matter, is not something that is put together by thought, and therefore it is the whole of creation.

Question: Could you say something about the highly sensitive mind which is in danger of becoming self-centered and highly nervous? That has been my experience.

KRISHNAMURTI: Isn't there a danger, the questioner asks, in the mind when the whole human organism becomes highly sensitive; isn't there a danger of nervous tension? Why should we have tension at all? Doesn't tension exist only when there is resistance? There are noises going on here: a dog is barking, the buses are going by, and there is a child crying. When you resist, tension is built up. This actually takes place. If you don't build any resistance but let the noise go through, listen to it quietly, without resistance, not saying that it's good or bad, not saying, "I wish that dog wouldn't make that noise; that bus is terrible," but just listening—then, since there is no resistance, there is no strain, no effort. I think one of the problems of modern life is living in boxed-up houses called flats, where there is no space, no beauty, but constant strain. If you are vulnerable to it all—I'm using the word *vulnerable* in the sense of to receive, to let everything come—then I don't see how you can have nervous breakdowns or nervous tension.

Comment: There is something in me that is frightened to do or follow or think of or be aware of what you are saying. I'm frightened.

KRISHNAMURTI: That's it. I think that's fairly clear, isn't it? What is being said is quite revolutionary. It's very dangerous to do it because you may have to alter the whole structure of your life. Intellectually you say, "Yes, I understand every word you're saying." Unconsciously you know the danger of it, so you get nervous, apprehensive, frightened because you want to lead a very secure, comfortable, easygoing life, to live in a secluded, safe isolation. What is being talked about might destroy all that. It will! You will no longer be a Christian or an Englishman or an Indian or this or that. You'll belong to no group, no sect. You'll

have to be tremendously alone—alone not in the sense of isolation.

Anything that is alone is always beautiful. A lonely tree on a field is a most beautiful thing to look at. We are frightened to be alone, and before we are alone we are frightened of being lonely. We are lonely human beings. All our activities lead to this loneliness, which is isolation. Though we may be married, have children, have jobs, belong to groups and sects, deeply inwardly there is this isolation going on, this fear of loneliness, of being lonely, of not being related. We run to various forms of amusement, including the Mass, the church, worship, anything to get away from that loneliness. We can't understand it without understanding the self-centered activity of our lives which breeds this loneliness; but when we have understood it, gone through it, gone beyond it, then we come to that sense of being completely alone, uncontaminated, untouched by society. If we're not alone, we can't go any further.

Question: Would you say that the struggle for power is always corrupting?

KRISHNAMURTI: Politically, religiously, the separation between sovereign states on the one hand, and on the other the individual's search for power, position, prestige—all that is obviously corrupting. The man in power has reached that position through corruption, and from that position he may preach goodness, love, sanctity, and all the rest of that nonsense. The saints do it; the politicians do it; the godly people do it. They all want power. As was said at the beginning of this talk, humility is something that can't come through thought. It comes into being when there is death to the past, when we're always entering life, every day, without the past.

Question: How can we exercise discipline without creating conflict?

KRISHNAMURTI: The word *discipline* means to learn. Learning is always the active present. To learn in itself is discipline. It is not necessary to practice a discipline. You are listening to what is being said. If you are attentive, if you are listening actively in the present, that very act of listening creates tremendous discipline. You don't have to discipline yourself. This disciplining which we all do like soldiers is a terrible thing because then in that discipline is involved conformity, imitation, adjustment, fear, obedience to a pattern, and therefore it becomes mechanical, like a soldier. You have seen them drilling. It doesn't take much brains for that. To obey, to follow any pattern destroys, inevitably creates conflict. But if you want to understand this whole structure of discipline, to understand it is discipline in itself. You don't have to exercise discipline. For most of us discipline means resistance, and therefore effort, conflict, and all the rest of it follow. But if you are aware, if you are aware while getting into the bus, aware of what is taking place in the bus, watching, that very act of being aware in itself is discipline. It means being awake.

Comment: It's very difficult to listen to thoughts which suggest unpleasant or frightening things, without thinking about them and arguing about them.

KRISHNAMURTI: It's difficult to listen to one's own thoughts, but how do you find out if you don't listen?

Comment: Sir, what you are really telling us is to cultivate a private state of mind. I stress the word private. *But the point is that you do have to live in the material world.*

Surely the active world can destroy our private state of mind.

KRISHNAMURTI: Sir, I am not talking of the private mind at all. Our minds are the result of the totality of the human mind. We are the result of the society in which we live. This society has been created by each one of us. So the many is the 'me' and the 'me' is the many. There is no division between me and the many. I am the result of all that. However, I think we should differentiate between the individual and the human being. The individual is the localized entity, the Englishman, the Indian, the American, and so on, localized, conditioned by the locality, the culture, the climate, the food, the clothes. The human being is conditioned on a much larger scale. He belongs to the whole world. Our sufferings, anxieties, and fears are the same as in India, as those of an Indian who goes through terrible states, just like everyone else all over the world. If we understand that, then the private cultivation of one's own mind also disappears. We are concerned with the total structure of the human mind, not our minds, our little backyards. That's nothing. Our little backyards are as filthy as any other backyard, or as clean as any other little backyard.

Question: How can we remember to be awake?

KRISHNAMURTI: Let me finish answering the previous question. My action then is not outside the world but in the world, all the time I'm here. What I'm doing as a human being, going to the office, living with my family, I'm aware of, not as a private individual, but as a human being. When I'm aware of that as a human being, surely I'm affecting the whole of the human mind. It is because we function as localized entities that we are destroying ourselves. Sir, at the present time India is going through a terrible period of starvation and hardships. The question is not an Indian question; it is a human question. The politicians won't see that. They want to keep their localities intact, with their sovereign states, their power, their position, their prestige. They won't solve the problem that way. It is a human problem; it is a world problem. We have to deal with it as a whole world, not Indians or communists or Americans or Englishmen giving food or not giving food. Action as a human being is entirely different from the action of a localized entity. The localized entity creates more harm, creates misery, as does the human being who is still caught in the human or the animalistic struggle. Only the human being who has understood this whole structure, its anxieties and its agonies, can bring about a totally different kind of action.

Question: Sir, isn't action necessary in opposition to what we call the power principle? Only action can improve this.

KRISHNAMURTI: It would be stupid to be against action, but I must find out what is meant by action. What does it mean to act, to do? This is a very complex question. To act means action in the present, but that action in the present is not possible if it is based on an idea. If I act as a Hindu or as a Christian, my action is based on something which thought has built in order to protect itself. It is conditioned action. Such action is destructive, whether it is in the office or in the home. Action which is always in the present and therefore free of the past comes only when I'm learning, as I'm learning. Therefore action is an act of learning. It is not a matter of having learned and then acting. There's a vast difference between the two.

Question: Most of us can learn a state of mind which is very different from that which is usual in the world today, but the people who have reached positions of power and authority are still in the grip of the past. What can those of us do who can't act but can only think correctly? What can we do?

KRISHNAMURTI: We can't do anything about the men in power. They have achieved that and we know how they have got there. What can we do? We can't do anything. You say we can talk about peace, against the vested interests of sovereign governments, of armies, of the airplane manufacturers, the whole structure, but what can we do—not buy stamps, not pay taxes? If we don't they will put us in prison, and we can't send letters. Will that solve the problem? Obviously not. But for a human being to be free from nationality and the poison of all that is a much greater action. The other produces wars, economic wars, brutality, and misery, the whole of man's existence. But a human mind, realizing all that, frees itself from nationality, sex, groups, ceases to identify itself with this or that class and is no longer a localized individual, and therefore no longer a human being conditioned by human struggles and miseries. The action which comes out of it is the only beneficial action.

Question: You think it is important that we should be aware of our existence while getting on and off a bus and things like that, but how can we remember to be aware?

KRISHNAMURTI: How can we remember all the time to be aware? I'm afraid we can't. That's why we should not try to remember. Heavens, if I try to remember to be aware, then I'm practicing awareness! Then awareness is something to be attained, something that will gradually become mechanical and therefore lose its vitality, its freshness. If I am aware at one moment, I'm completely aware, and the next moment I may not be aware; I may be unaware. All right. I will be unaware. If I'm attentive, I am at that moment completely attentive. The next moment I may be inattentive. Then I know I am inattentive. But in that state of inattention I do not breed action which will bring about misery. My concern is not how to be attentive all the time, which is again another form of pleasure and greed and all the rest of the ugliness. My concern is just to be attentive. When you have to be, you are attentive. Sir, it's like this. A drum is empty always, and when the skin is rightly taut it gives right noise, right sound. Attention is like that.

May 7, 1966

Fifth Talk in London

This is the last talk. There is no end to talking, to arguments, to explanations, but explanations, arguments, and talking do not lead to direct action because for that to take place, we need to change radically and fundamentally. That needs no argument. No convincing, no formula, no being influenced by another will make us change fundamentally, in the deep sense of that word. We do need to change, but not according to any particular idea or formula or concept, because when we have ideas about action, action ceases. Between action and idea there is a time interval, a lag, and in that time interval there is either resistance, conformity, or imitation of that idea or that formula and trying to put it into action. That's what most of us are doing all the time. We know we have to change, not only outwardly but deeply, psychologically.

The outward changes are many. They are forcing us to conform to a certain pattern of activity, but to meet the challenge of everyday life, there must be a deep revolution. Most of us have an idea, a concept of what we should

be or what we ought to be, but we never change fundamentally. Ideas, concepts of what one should be do not make us change at all. We only change when it is absolutely necessary, and we never see directly the necessity for this change. When we do want to change, there is a great deal of conflict and resistance, and we waste a great deal of energy in resisting, in creating a barrier.

Mere acquisition of knowledge, mere listening to a lot of ideas, to a great many talks, does not bring about wisdom. What brings wisdom is self-observation, examination of ourselves. To examine we must be free, free from the censor, the entity that is always evaluating, judging, condemning, approximating. Then only can we look, examine. There is action only when, from that observation, without creating the idea, there is direct action. Man apparently has lived for over two million years, and there have been fifteen thousand wars in recorded human history, two and a half wars every year. We are always in conflict with each other, both outwardly and inwardly. Our lives are a battlefield, and we don't seem to be able to solve our problems at all. We either postpone them, avoid them, or try to find a solution to them according to our concepts, ideas, prejudices, conclusions. We can go on living this way for another two million years, superficially having probably a little more food, clothing, and shelter, but inwardly we will always be at war within ourselves and with our neighbors, with other people. That has been the pattern of our lives.

To bring about a good society, human beings have to change. You and I must find the energy, the impetus, the vitality to bring about this radical transformation of the mind, and that is not possible if we do not have enough energy. We need a great deal of energy to bring about a change within ourselves, but we waste our energy through conflict, through resistance, through conformity, through acceptance, through obedience. It is a waste of energy when we are trying to conform to a pattern. To conserve energy we must be aware of ourselves, how we dissipate energy. This is an age-long problem because most human beings are indolent. They would rather accept, obey, and follow. If we become aware of this indolence, this deep-rooted laziness, and try to quicken the mind and the heart, the intensity of it again becomes a conflict, which is also a waste of energy.

Our problem, one of the many that we have, is how to conserve this energy, the energy that is necessary for an explosion to take place in consciousness—an explosion that is not contrived, that is not put together by thought, but an explosion that occurs naturally when there is this energy that is not wasted. Conflict in any form, at any level, at any depth of our being is a waste of energy. We all know that, but we have accepted conflict as the way of life. To understand the nature and the structure of conflict, we must go into the question of contradiction. Most of the life that we lead every day is the source of conflict. If we observe our own existence, our own life, we see how much conflict we have: what we are and what we should be, the contradictory desires, the contradictory pleasures, the various influences, pressures and strains, the resistance created by our urges, by our appetites. We accept conflict as part of our existence. Why do we live in conflict, and is it at all possible, living in this modern world, leading the life that we do, is it possible to live without conflict? This means to live a life without contradiction.

After asking a question of that kind either we are waiting for an answer, an explanation, or each one of us is aware of the nature of our contradictions and conflict. By awareness I mean to observe, to examine without any judgment, without any choice, to see our lives, our everyday lives, which are in conflict—just to be aware of them. Then we will begin to understand the structure of contradiction. Most of us know we live in contradiction, and we suppress one and follow the other, the opposite, or we disregard the whole contradictory being and live superficially, escaping; but when we become conscious of it, the tension becomes much greater because we do not know how to solve this conflict, this battle that is going on within each one of us, within every human being. Not being able to solve it, not being able to unravel it, the tension becomes much greater and hence neuroses and psychotic states. But if we become choicelessly aware of this contradictory nature of our being, just looking at it without wanting to solve the conflict, without taking sides about the conflict, just observing, then we discover that conflict will always exist as long as the observer, the censor, is different from the thing he looks at. I think this is the root of conflict. If we could only understand this, not philosophically, not through explanations or agreement, but by actually looking at it!

Take for instance this sense of loneliness, this sense of isolation that we each feel. When we become conscious of it, we run away, to churches, to museums; we listen to music, to the radio; we take to drink and dozens of other things. The tension becomes much greater. There is this fact that we are terribly lonely, isolated, having no relationship with anything. Not being able to understand it, not being able to face it, come directly into contact with it, we escape from it. And the escape naturally, obviously, is a waste of energy because the fact is still there.

In becoming aware of it, you discover that there is an observer who is looking at that loneliness. The loneliness is something different from the observer. As you are listening, if I may suggest, please don't merely follow intellectually what is being said. It will have no value at all, but if you become aware of your own loneliness, which most of us know, then you will see that you are looking at it, that the thing you look at is different from the observer. The loneliness is not you. The observer is different from the observed, and therefore makes an effort to overcome it, to escape from it, asks questions about what to do, what not to do, how to resolve it. The actual fact is that the observer is the observed, and as long as there is this division between the observer and the observed, there must be conflict.

Take another effort that we make. There are contradictory desires, each desire pulling in a different direction. There is a constant battle going on. If we are at all aware, serious, we know what is taking place within our own consciousness. The observer decides which desire shall dominate, which desire shall be pursued, or, not being conscious, he pursues one, and so engenders conflict.

Again, there is conflict as long as we do not understand pleasure. We are talking about pleasure, not a puritanical resistance to pleasure or the avoidance of pleasure or how to resolve pleasure or how to overcome pleasure. If we try to overcome desire, pleasure, any actual fact, then we create conflict, a resistance against it. But when we begin to understand the structure of pleasure, how our minds, our brains, our desires work with regard to pleasure, then we begin to discover that wherever there is pleasure, there is pain. When we understand that, not intellectually, not verbally, but actually, when we actually realize that fact, then there is not the avoidance of pleasure but the actual state of what takes place when we understand the nature and the structure of pleasure. We are talking about the necessity of gathering all energy to bring about a radical revolution in consciousness itself, because we must have a new mind; we must look at life totally differently. To bring about this explosion we must find out how we waste our energies. Conflict is a waste of energy. Resistance to

or the acceptance of pleasure is also a waste of energy.

What is pleasure, actually? There is an observation of something, a sensation through that observation, through that seeing, through that touching. Then desire arises and thought gives continuity, vitality, strength to that desire, as pleasure. We can observe this for ourselves. We see a beautiful woman, man, car, house, dress, or whatever it is. There is perception, sensation, desire, and the pleasure of ownership. Before the pleasure, thought begins to say how nice it would be to get it. This is what actually takes place. On that all our moral, ethical values are based. Thought intensifies desire as pleasure and the avoidance of pain. Thought, as the thinker watching, creates a contradiction and hence conflict.

One must be aware of all this, not as an idea that one must be aware of in order to get over the conflict, for then it's just another thought seeking another form of pleasure and there is more conflict; but if one is aware of this whole structure of pleasure, then one can look at beauty or ugliness, enjoying without thought, giving strength to that which has been perceived, but not creating a conflict. This requires a great deal of attention, a great deal of inquiry, examination. Nobody can teach us this. Really, actually, there is no such thing as the teacher and the taught; there is only learning, learning about oneself.

You find as you begin to learn about yourself—not analytically, not as an examination, layer after layer, of yourself as you are, which again will take a lot of time—that becoming aware of the totality of your being, whatever you actually are, is possible only when you understand that all consciousness is limited, conditioned. When you are aware of that, when you are totally attentive to that conditioning, then analysis becomes quite useless. I do not know if you have noticed for yourself that without analyzing, you can discover for yourself immediately the truth of your own mind, your own thoughts, your own feelings. You can see immediately. But that again requires sensitivity, not knowledge, not discipline. To be sensitive, not in any particular direction, as an artist, but to be sensitive totally, to be aware of everything around you, of the colors, of the trees, of the birds, of your own thoughts, of your own feelings—that makes the mind extraordinarily alert, sharp, clear. Then you can face the problems of existence. A problem exists only when you give root to an issue. But if you can understand the problem instantly, then the problem ceases. When there is an adequate response to the challenge, to any challenge, the problem is not. It is only when we are not capable of responding adequately to the challenge that there is a problem.

Look at the problem of fear—the problem, not how to get rid of it, not what to do. For most of us fear is constant. Either we are aware of it or there are unconscious fears, deep-rooted, with which we never come in direct contact. We have ideas, images about fear, but we are never actually in contact with the fact. However much one may be intimately related with a person, which we call relationship, what actually takes place is a relationship between the images the two people have about each other. That's what we call relationship: one image making contact with another image. In the same way, we never come into contact with actual fear. Fear is an indication of danger. When we come to a physical danger like a serpent or a precipice, there is instant action. There is no conclusion; there is no thinking about it. The body immediately reacts. But there are psychological dangers of which we are not aware, and therefore there is no immediate action.

We have many fears, and one of the major fears is the fear of death. If we are alive to life, we are aware of this extraordinary thing called death. We don't know how to meet it because we are afraid. To meet what is called death, one has first of all to be free of fear. It is this constant fear of the unknown, or rather this constant fear of letting the known go, the things that we know, our experiences, our memories, our family, our knowledge, our activity. That is what we are afraid of, not actually of death. We know that there is death. We take comfort in reincarnation, in resurrection, in various forms of beliefs, or by rationalizing the whole thing and trying to say, "Well, it is inevitable; I've had a miserable life," or "It has been a jolly good time, and let's get on with it." But if we would actually understand this question of death, which is really an extraordinary thing, we not only have to understand what living is, but we must also understand what fear is, because when we understand what living is, then we find that living and dying are very close together; they're not two different things. We cannot live if we are afraid, if we are in constant battle, if we are trying to fulfill, and being frustrated, discover in ourselves enormous loneliness and insufficiency.

That's our life, and we want to fulfill, to achieve, to become. Thought enters and avoids death, pushes it far away, holding on to things it knows. We do not know what living is. This thing that we call living is a miserable existence, a frightful mess, a battle with occasional flashes of joy, of great pleasures, but most of our life is such a shallow, drab affair that we don't know what living is. But if we were to die to all the things that thought has created within ourselves, to die actually, to die to our pleasures, to our memories, to our actual fears, then there would be different kinds of living. That living is never far from death, but to come to all this we must have passion; we must have tremendous intensity, energy, to learn about ourselves, to learn about death, to learn about fear, because the moment we begin to learn about it, fear ceases. We cannot learn if we do not know how to observe. After all, to learn about death, you understand, is really quite extraordinary, because there is actual physical death. The organism comes to an end, through old age, infirmity, some disease. Then it is too late. The mind then is not capable of quick perception because we have allowed ourselves to be so heavily conditioned. When we are ill, diseased, when the brain cells have become weary, then we cannot learn, then unfortunately we live in beliefs, hopes, and there is no way out that way. But if we become aware of our lives, the way we live, our thoughts, our feelings, the pleasures that we pursue constantly, then in that understanding, the things that we hold on to so deeply fall away. Then one dies every day. Otherwise there is nothing new.

After all, that is the religious mind, not the beliefs, the dogmas, the rituals, the sects, the propaganda that has been going on for two thousand or ten thousand years, which is not religion at all. We are slaves to propaganda, either of the businessman or of the priest. Religion is something entirely different. To find out what is truth, to find out if there is something which man has called his God, the unknown, we must die to the known because otherwise we can't come upon this strange thing that man has been seeking for thousands and thousands of years. He has invented, thought has put together, a concept of what God is or is not. He believes or disbelieves according to his conditioning. The communist, the real communist, doesn't believe. To him there is only the state. Probably eventually he will deify Lenin or someone else. There are also those who are conditioned to believe. Both are the same, the believer and the non-believer. To find out

if there is something beyond that which thought has put together, we must deny everything; we must deny dogma, belief, our hopes and fears. That's not really very difficult to do either because when we want to learn, we set aside all the absurd things that man has created out of his fear.

When there is the actual ending of thought as pleasure, dying to thought, then there is something entirely different, a different dimension, a dimension which cannot probably be explained, put into words. It has nothing to do with belief and dogma and fear. It is not a word. That word cannot be made into flesh, and to come upon it the experiencer, the observer, the censor must cease to be. That's why we said at the beginning that one must understand conflict and that there will be conflict as long as there is the observer and the observed; that's the root of conflict. When I say, "I must be different," or "I am afraid," the "I" thinks it is separate from the fear itself. Actually, it is not. The fear is the "I"; the two are inseparable. When the observer is the observed, when the thinker, the origin of thought, comes to an end, then you will find that fear in any form has also come to an end.

In that there is a concentration of energy. This energy explodes and there is the new, the new which is not recognizable. When we recognize something, it is not new. It is an experience which we have already had. Therefore it is not new. The extraordinary experiences and visions of all the saints and all the religious people are projections of the old, of their conditioned minds. The Christian sees his Christ because he has been conditioned by the society in which he lives as he has been growing up.

As long as there is an experiencer and the thing that he is going to experience, in that state there is no reality but conflict. Only when the experiencer ceases is there that thing which man has been seeking. In one's own life one is always seeking—seeking happiness, seeking God, seeking truth. One can't find it through searching but only when searching ceases, only when one is a light to oneself. To be a light to oneself, there must be a burning passion, intensity. It isn't something domesticated. Out of all this turmoil, misery, confusion, and despair comes that revolution, that inward mutation. It is only a new mind that can come upon that thing which is called God or truth or whatever name one likes to give it. But the known cannot know the unknown, and we are the result of the known. Whatever the known, which is thought, does will push the un-

known further away. It is only when thought has understood itself and has become quiet that there is an understanding of this whole process of thought, pleasure, and fear. This is meditation. It is not a practice, a discipline, a conformity which makes the mind quiet. What makes the mind really silent is the understanding of itself, its thoughts, its desires, its contradictions, its pleasures, its attachments, its loneliness, its despair, its brutality, and its violence. Out of that understanding comes silence, and it is only a silent mind that can perceive, can see actually *what is*.

May 10, 1966

Paris, France, 1966

---- ✳ ----

First Talk in Paris

Though one must distrust similarities, there is not much difference between the Orient and the Occident, the people who live in Asia and those who live in the West. Though they may have different philosophies, different beliefs, different customs, habits, and manners from the West, they are human beings like the rest of the world—suffering, with innumerable problems, anxious, fearful, often in great despair over disease, old age, and death. These problems exist throughout the world. Their beliefs, their gods are not different from the gods and beliefs of this country or of other countries in the West. These beliefs have not solved any of our human problems fundamentally, deeply, radically. They have brought about a certain culture, good manners, a superficial acceptance of certain relationships, but deeply, radically, man has not changed very much in the last two million years or so. Man throughout these ages apparently has struggled, has swum against the current of life, always in battle, in conflict, striving, groping, searching, asking, demanding, praying, looking to someone else to solve his human problems.

This has been going on century upon century, and apparently we have not solved our problems. We still suffer; we still are groping, searching, asking, demanding that some-

one tell us what we should do, what we should not do, how we should think and what not to think, exchanging one belief for another, one outlook, one idiotic ideology for another. We all know this; we've all been through the varieties of beliefs. Though we react, change our positions in the same field of life, somehow we remain fundamentally what we are. Perhaps there is a little change here and there. There are little modifications, different sects, different groups, and different outlooks, but inwardly there is the same fearful struggle, anxiety, despair.

Perhaps we can approach these problems differently. There must be—and I think there is—a different approach to our whole existence, a different way of living without this battle, without this fear, without these gods that have really lost their meaning altogether, and without these ideologies, whether communist or religious, which have little meaning anymore. Probably they never had much meaning. They helped to civilize man, make him a little more gentle, a little more friendly, but basically man has not been tamed or changed fundamentally. We are still brutal, at war with one another, both outwardly and inwardly. There have been fifteen thousand wars in the last five thousand five hundred years—two and a half wars every year. Mankind has been venomous, hating, competing, striving for position, prestige, power, and domination. This we all know, and this we accept as the way of life—war, fear, conflict, a superficial existence. That's what we have accepted.

It seems to me that there may be a different way of living, and this is what we are going to talk about during these five gatherings: how to bring about a revolution, not outwardly but inwardly, because the crisis is in consciousness; it is not economic or social. We are always responding to outward challenge, trying to answer it superficially. We must actually respond adequately to this inward crisis which has been mounting, building up through the ages. The intellectual, clever, cunning philosophies, theologies, and the various escapes of religions through dogmas cannot possibly answer these problems. The more one is serious, the more one becomes aware of these problems. I mean by ''serious'' those who are capable, who are actually facing the issues and resolving them, not postponing, not escaping, not trying to answer them intellectually, verbally, or emotionally. Life is only for the serious, and not for those who merely enjoy themselves, answering superficially, escaping from the deep crisis within.

Having stated the problem more or less, though we can go into it much more deeply, and perhaps we shall, what is the way out? The more clearly we state the problem, the clearer the answer becomes. I'm not at all sure we are very clear what the problem is, what the issue is. We try to answer according to our temperaments, education, the conditioning in the society in which we have been brought up. We try to answer the issue in fragments. If we are very intellectual we try to answer intellectually, try to live by the intellect. If we're at all emotional, sentimental, sloppy, or if we're artists, we try to answer it in that way; we try to look at everything in an emotional, sentimental way. We look at this whole problem of existence fragmentarily, in pieces, in divisions. We don't seem to be able to look at it totally, as a whole life, and a fragmentary answer is no answer at all. We can't answer these many problems according to our temperaments, according to our concepts, ideologies. The issue is much greater than the individual response.

The individual is the local entity; he's the Frenchman, the Englishman, the Indian, and so on; he's a localized entity. But the human being, though he may live in a local country, is a human being of the world. One must also be clear on this whole question, the difference between the individual and the human being. If one can understand the human being, then the individual has a place, or no place at all. But merely cultivating the back garden of one's own individuality, keeping order, cleanliness in the back yard of individuality has very little meaning in relation to the whole of human existence. Perhaps in understanding the human being one can comprehend the place of the individual, but the individual understanding cannot possibly comprehend the total human being. The problem becomes much more clear if one can look at it nonfragmentarily, look at it not as a scientist, as an artist, as a philosopher, as a theologian, and so on, but as a human being who has to live in this world, not escape from it, but look at this issue—if it is possible—as a whole.

As stated earlier, we live a life of conflict, always searching, seeking, asking, hoping; never ending our sorrows, never putting an end to violence both inwardly and outwardly. We have been playing this game for centuries upon centuries. Religions have taught man that he must struggle, make a tremendous effort, strive, battle between the good and the evil, pursue the righteous and avoid the unrighteous. Our life as we know it, actually, not theoretically, is a series of conflicts, contradictions, tensions of opposing desires, and we don't seem to be able to get out of this net. Is there a different approach altogether to this whole issue?

I think there is. I don't know how you are listening to what is being said. Are you merely listening, hearing a series of words, ideas, concepts, agreeing or disagreeing with them, arguing silently with the speaker, or are you through the act of listening becoming aware of the actual state of your own life as a human being? If you are merely intellectually responding to what is being said, then you merely try to identify yourself with the problem; therefore, you are different from the problem. I think this should be gone into a little.

There is this question of anxiety. Let's take that for the moment. In our lives there is a sense of despair because of the futility, the boredom of life, our repetitive, mechanical existence, and there is anxiety. Intellectually we can see that we are anxious, and we separate ourselves from that anxiety. The observer then is different from the thing observed. We say, "I am anxious," "I" being different from anxiety. The thinker, the observer, is different from that which he observes or thinks about. There is a division between the observer, the thinker, and the thought, the thing observed. We have to find out how we listen. If we listen as observers, as thinkers, there is something we are thinking about or observing. It is different if we listen with attention. Attention is not intellectual or emotional; attention is not directive. If we say, "I will be attentive," then it's merely an act of will, which again separates. But if we listen with attention, if we attend, there is neither the activity of the fragmentary intellect nor sentimental activity; there is a complete attention which is neither intellect, emotion, nor purely physical. Attention is physical, emotional, and intellectual; it's a total activity. There the nerves, the highly sensitive cells of the brain are all tremendously awakened, attentive. In that state of attention we can listen. Whatever is false is put aside; it has no value at all. Whatever is true remains and flowers in that attention.

I hope you are doing it as we are talking together. That's what I meant when I said that you should not merely agree or disagree with the speaker, or try to interpret what he is talking about. You will find as you listen during these five talks that he is not giving you any ideas, any formulas, any concepts. But if you are attentive, totally attentive, a relationship will be established between the speaker and the listener. Then we'll examine, partake of the thing that we are talking about together; then you are not the listener; then we are taking the journey together. This is entirely different from being concentrated; a person who is concentrated is self-centered; attention is not.

What we are talking about is the ending of this everlasting conflict. We are trying to find out if it is at all possible, living in this world, to live entirely without conflict. To find out if that is possible, we must give attention. There is no attention if you say, "I agree," or if you say, "So far I go and no further; this pleases me, this doesn't; I am a writer, and I want to interpret all this in a certain way." If we can give attention, it becomes extremely worthwhile, if we could so listen. Then we establish a communion between us. In that communion there is neither the teacher nor the taught, which again is too immature. There is no follower and no one who says, "Do this; do that." As human beings we have been through all that for centuries upon centuries. We've had saviors, Masters, gods, beliefs, religions by the dozen, and they have not solved our problems. We are as unhappy as ever, miserable, confused, suffering, and our lives have become very petty, small. We may be awfully clever, talk about everything cleverly, but inwardly there's a turmoil, an endless loneliness, a deepening, wider confusion and a sorrow that seems to have no end at all.

Having stated the problem, with which most of us are quite familiar, is there a different approach? The old approach obviously is not the way out. Of that one must be absolutely clear so that one turns one's back on it completely. The old way of the religions, with their beliefs, dogmas, saviors, Masters, priests, archbishops, and all the rest of it, whether it is Catholic, Protestant, Hindu, or Buddhist—all that one must put aside entirely because one understands that such a way doesn't give man any freedom. Freedom is something entirely different from revolt. The whole world at the present time is in revolt, especially the young, but that's not freedom. Freedom is something entirely different; freedom is not from something. If it is from something, it's a revolt. If I revolt against the religion to which I belong, out of that reaction I join another religion because it gives me, I think, greater freedom, something more exciting, a new set of words, a new set of phrases, a new set of dogmas and ideologies, but this reaction is incapable of examining. Only a mind that is in freedom, not in reaction, can examine—not only the human mind as it is but also the whole psychological structure of the social order of which one is a part, questioning, doubting, being skeptical. To question, to ask, to find out—all these demand a great deal of freedom, not a great deal of reaction. Where there is freedom there is passion, there is an intensity which is entirely different from the intensity and the passion of reaction. The passion, the intensity, the vitality, the vigor that freedom brings about cannot end, whereas the enthusiasm, the interest, the vitality of reaction can undergo a change and be modified.

To find out if there is a different way—a different way of living, not a different way of doing or acting, but of living which is acting—one must naturally turn one's back upon those things to which one has become a slave. I think that is the first thing one has to

do because otherwise one cannot examine, one cannot look. How can a mind that is so heavily conditioned through two thousand years of propaganda or ten thousand years of tradition, how can such a mind observe? It can only observe according to its conditioning, according to its ambitions, according to its craving for fulfillment. Such examination has no vitality, nothing; it cannot discover anything new. Even in the scientific field, though one may have a great deal of knowledge, to discover anything new the known must be temporarily set aside; otherwise, one can't discover anything new. It is obvious that if one is to see the new clearly, the past, the known, knowledge must come to an end.

We are asking ourselves, you and I, if there is an altogether different approach in which there is no conflict, no contradiction. Where there is contradiction there is effort, and where there is effort there is conflict—conflict being either resistance or acceptance. Resistance is sheltering oneself behind ideas, hopes, fears; acceptance becomes imitation. We are always swimming against the current; that's our life. Is it possible to move, to live, to be, to function in such a way that there is no current against which we must battle? The more there is conflict, the more there is tension. From that tension there is every form of neurosis and every psychotic state. A human being in tension may have a certain capacity, and that capacity through that tension may be expressed in writing, in music, in ten different ways.

I am trying to convey, or rather to communicate, nonverbally; though one must use words, yet one knows that the word is not the fact, the thing. Instead of always approaching reality through discipline, conflict, acceptance, denial, the things that man has practiced for centuries upon centuries to find out something, is it possible to explode and in that very explosion to have a new state of mind come into being? Can the old mind, which still has in it the animal, the old mind which is seeking comfort, security, which is afraid, anxious, lonely, painfully aware of its own limitations—can that old mind come to an end immediately and a new mind operate? Is the problem stated clearly?

Let me put it in a different way. Thought has created these problems. Thought has said, "I must find God, I must have security; this is my country, this is not your country; you are a German, I'm a Frenchman, you are a Russian, you are a communist; you're this, that; my God, your God; I'm a writer, you're not a writer; you're inferior, I'm superior; you're spiritual, I'm not spiritual." Thought has built the social structure in which we are, of which we are. Thought is responsible for this whole confusion. Thought has created it, and if thought says, "I must change all this in order to be different," it will create a structure perhaps dissimilar in some respects, but similar because it's still the action of thought. Thought has divided the world into nationalities, into religious groups; thought has bred fear. Thought has said, "I'm much more important than you"; thought has said, "I must love my neighbor." Thought has created this hierarchy of priests, saviors, gods, concepts, formulas; and if thought says, "This is wrong; I'll create a new set of activities, a new set of beliefs, a new set of structures," they will be similar, though somewhat dissimilar. They are still the result of thought.

Thought has built a communist world, and thought is now making it different, bringing about a difference in communism, which is becoming bourgeois, not so revolutionary. Thought is making it more soft, more gentle. It's still thought that is creating and destroying.

To find anything totally different, you must not only understand the origin of thought, the beginning of thought, but also whether it is possible for thought to come to

an end so that a new process can begin. This is an extraordinarily important question. You can't agree or disagree; you don't know; you probably have not even thought about it, and so you can't say you understand or you don't understand. You may say, "Yes, I understand in the sense that I can follow verbally, intellectually, what you are talking about," but this is entirely different from actually understanding the fact. Thought has created wars by dividing men into Frenchmen, Germans, Italians, Indians, Russians. Thought has divided the world into fields, into areas of belief, with their saviors, with their gods, and each one has its God! People have fought against each other. All this thought has bred, and thought says, "I see this; it is a fact; now I will create a different world." It has tried to do this in the communist world. Every revolution tries to do this, but it eventually comes back to the same circle.

Thought has created philosophies, formulas according to which we try to live. Thought has created a psychological structure of pleasure, established certain values based on pleasure. This doesn't mean that I am against pleasure, but we have to investigate the whole structure of pleasure. Thought cannot create a new world. This doesn't mean that sentiment will create a new world; on the contrary, it won't. We must find a different energy which is not the energy brought about by thought, a different energy which will function at a different dimension. Its very activities in its functioning are in this world, not in a world of escape, in a monastery, on top of the Himalayas, in some cave, in some absurd business. That's what we are going to find out. I am quite sure that there is a different way of living, but it is not a world in which thought functions. We must go into the origin of thinking, the beginning of thinking, and find out what thinking means, what its structure is, its mechanism.

When the mind, the total entity understands, gives complete attention to understanding the structure of thought, then we begin to have a different kind of energy. This has nothing whatever to do with self-fulfillment, with seeking, with wanting; all that disappears. Our concern will be to understand together. It's not just you listening and the speaker putting out certain words. Together we are going to find out the origin of thinking.

I don't know if you have noticed how thought strengthens pleasure. The more you think about something which you have considered pleasurable, the more vitality, energy, volatile strength it has. When thought fights a habit—whatever the habit, good or bad, it doesn't matter—the energy that is derived by thinking is entirely different from the energy which understands the whole structure of thought.

We are going to discover together for ourselves. It is not a case of someone telling us; then it becomes too immature. We are going to discover together the origin of thinking, whether it is possible for thought to end when it is necessary, and for thought to function with accuracy, with precision, with reason, with clarity, when it is also necessary. Now we overflow from the known to the unknown, and therefore we get confused. Where thought has to function vigorously, unemotionally, as in a technological job, there is no emotional reaction. You're trained as a technician, and there you function precisely. That precision doesn't enter into a field where you have understood the whole origin of thinking. It brings confusion in there. Thought can function fully and completely, with reason and health, without any neurotic states, where it is necessary; but there is a field in which thought doesn't function at all; in that field a revolution can take place; the new can take place. That's what we are going to uncover for ourselves as we go along.

Comment: I think there is one sort of energy which is given to everyone during sleep, and this is without thought, ordinary thought.

KRISHNAMURTI: The gentleman says we are given a certain form of energy in which thought doesn't function at all. This is one of the most difficult things. Who has given it? What is energy, sir? Wait; let's begin again. When we talk about energy, what do we mean by that? There is physical energy which we derive through food, and all the rest of it. There is energy derived through emotional states—the more sentimental, emotional. There is intellectual energy. Generally these three energies and their divisions are in contradiction to each other, and these contradictions create another form of energy. All this we can easily find out for ourselves through ordinary psychological observation.

I am ambitious; I want to fulfill; I want to reach the top; I want recognition by the world, whatever the world is. I want fame, and that engenders tremendous energy. I become ruthless. There's the energy of violence, and becoming aware of that violence I create an ideology of non-violence. The struggle between the fact of violence and the idiocy of the ideology of nonviolence creates a conflict. Every energy creates its opposite energy, and in that we are caught. I love you and I'm jealous; I'm attached. I become possessive, dominating, and that gives me tremendous energy. When you turn against me I turn it into hate; that's also another energy. We're not talking of this kind of energy at all, the energy brought about by thought. Thought may be exercised consciously or unconsciously. With most of us it's an unconscious response. The unconscious response comes from a word which awakens a whole series of memories, associations, like the word *God*, which awakens tremendous responses for both the believer and the nonbeliever.

We must be very clear what we mean by the energy which is created by conflict. Look at the energy a businessman uses to go every morning for forty years to the office, to battle, whether it's in Russia or here. Think of the energy he has! That energy is brought about by social conditioning, through ambition, through the desire for success, for pleasure, for acquisitiveness, for new cars, for houses, for more, more, more. Until that psychotic energy comes to an end, the other energy cannot come into being. The two cannot be put together. The ambition of the man who worships success, position, prestige, of the man who wants to express himself—all this is ambition in different forms—has its own energy, but this energy cannot possibly understand what love is. How can a man who is ambitious, whether in the name of God, in the name of society or in the name of his own personal fulfillment, how can such a man understand love? How can he love? The two are impossible.

One must be very clear not to mix the two kinds of energy; the two cannot be mixed. When the energy of conflict ceases, then perhaps we will understand a different kind of energy. It is that energy and no other that is going to solve our human problems, no other energy.

May 15, 1966

Second Talk in Paris

Perhaps after I have talked a little you might like to ask questions concerning what we have talked about.

I think it must be the concern of every human being, whether he lives in the Orient or in the Occident, to resolve radically the human misery, the confusion, and the strife in which we are caught. Every other issue becomes secondary—books, music, painting, the various things that we do with deliberation or because we have some kind of talent—all these seem to me to be secondary issues which will be answered rightly if we can understand and resolve the human confusion, the travail in which we are caught, the useless waste of energy, which breeds so much sorrow. Only then can we really find out—when we are free from this confusion and misery. It is only then that we can ask if there is something beyond the human mind, beyond thought, if there is something sublime, something unknowable. But such inquiry becomes utterly meaningless, without any significance at all, if we haven't resolved fear, the agony of uncertainty, the despair in which most human beings are held.

Inquiry from a confused mind, from a mind that is in great trouble, from a human heart that is agonizing, from such a field any inquiry after truth—asking oneself if there is or if there is not God, if there is something that is really beyond time—is utterly useless, a waste of energy. A confused mind, though it may appear very clever, write books, do all kinds of things, when it is seeking anything beyond itself, will still be confused, and what it discovers will be the result of confusion. It won't be something that is born out of clarity; it will be the outcome of confusion, misery, strife, despair. The first thing one has to realize is that the confusion that exists with most people cannot be resolved by escaping from it or trying to clear it up. Whatever a confused mind does is confused. I think we don't realize that. Anything it does, whether it paints, sings, or writes poems, will still be the outcome of its own confusion, and this confusion, as we were saying the last time we met here, is the result of our thinking.

I hope you are not listening to me, to the speaker, merely verbally, intellectually, because there will be no end to words, to books, to explanations. A clever mind can invent dozens of explanations, bring forth a philosophy, a system, but those do not answer or face the real issue. I hope you are not listening verbally or intellectually but observing, which is also listening, observing an actual fact, actually *what is*, not 'what should be'. Can you face actually the everyday conflict, the everyday misery, loneliness, despair that is in your heart, in your mind? Can you listen that way, not listening to a theory, to an explanation, to someone who has perhaps a little more or a little less, but actually listen to your own conditioning, your own travail, your own anxiety? There is a difference between your own awareness of your own state and what happens when someone points it out to you. No one needs to point out to you that you are hungry. You know it very well, and you do something about it, or not, as the case may be. But if you are told of the problem, of the issue, and you look at it, agreeing or disagreeing, then it is not your problem, it is not the issue that you are facing actually. What we are trying to do is not only to point out the fact of which you may be unconscious, but in the very statement to have you, yourself, discover the fact. Then it is yours, your problem; then you have to do something about it, not talk everlastingly.

If you will listen, not only to what is being said, but actually listen to find out the fact for yourself, the actuality, the *what is*, then together we shall be able to resolve it. But if the speaker is merely giving an explanation, a series of words to point out the fact, then it's not your fact, and then the relationship between the listener and the speaker has no value at all.

Human problems, not technical problems, not how to go to the moon, write a book, or learn a language, but human problems, the problem of our confusion, the problem of our utter lack of affection, the sense of loneliness, the contradictions, the everlasting urge

to fulfill and with it the endless frustrations—these are our problems, and these problems are all created by thought. We have built a society, a structure, a psychological state of the society which is the result of our greed, envy, comparison, competition, ambition, desire for power, position, prestige, fame. All that has been built by thought, and we are the result of that thought, caught in the structure, in the psychological structure of society of which we are part. Again that's obvious; we are not different from society. Society is you and I, the society which we have created through thought, conscious or unconscious, which we accept or revolt against, but it is still within the framework of a particular society. Thought through centuries has built up this society, with its gods, its teachers, its religions, its nationalities, all the terrible mess that we live in. Thought cannot free itself from what it has built. If it does, or if it thinks it does, it will still be a reaction, a modified continuity of what has been.

Thought to us is tremendously important—thought being the word, thought being the idea, thought being the past, the present, and the future, thought creating the idiotic ideologies which we so easily accept. Whether the ideologies are noble or ignoble is irrelevant. Man lives by thought, as some animals do, and we see the confusion, the misery we are in and exercise thought to bring about a change, through determination, through time, through the assertion of will, saying, "I am this, and I must be that." What the future will be has been created by thought, the ideology, the ideal, the example. Though we want to change—and every intelligent human being does want to bring about a change in the world and in himself—we use the instrument of thought to bring about a modification, and we think thought will resolve all these problems, don't we? Aren't you listening with your thought functioning? Of course, obviously! And we don't see clearly that thought cannot possibly create a new world, bring about a total revolution in human consciousness. What are we to do? Thought has created this confusion, and thought, we hope, will bring about clarity. We are quite sure that thought will bring it—clever, cunning, ideological thought, thought that is selfish or thought that is unselfish, thought that is not functioning egocentrically, thought that has dedicated itself to social reform, to revolution, to new sets of ideas, to utopias.

If we catch the significance of it, if we realize even verbally or intellectually that thought cannot bring about a radical change, and that radical revolution in the human consciousness is essential, we see that it is idiotic to go on the way we are going, struggling day after day with ourselves, in misery, in confusion, waiting for death and sorrow. We have looked to thought to resolve this, and thought has not resolved it. If we understand this even verbally, then what are we to do?

If we ask that question we are asking it to be told what to do—please listen carefully—and therefore responding through thought to find out. Isn't that true? We have stated the problem clearly and are waiting to find an answer. What is waiting? Who is the entity that is waiting to find an answer? It is still thought! Then thought wants to find out whether what you say is true or false, agreeing or disagreeing, going back to its conditioning, then saying, "How am I to live in this world if I don't think?" We are not saying we must not think. That would be too immature a statement.

You know the problem. Then when you ask, "What am I to do next?" you have to find out who is asking the question. Please, this is very serious; it's not just an afternoon amusement. If you're not serious, then it's of no value, but if you are at all serious and want to go into this tremendously earnestly, you have to find out who is asking this ques-

tion. Is it still the function of thought? Then we can go into the question of the origin of thinking.

We are not saying that thought must stop; thought has a definite function. Without thought we couldn't go to the office, we wouldn't know where we live, we wouldn't be able to function at all. But if we would bring about a radical revolution in the whole of consciousness, in the very structure of thinking, we must realize that thought, having built this society, with all its mess, cannot possibly resolve it. The communists have broken through revolution, through thought. They have rejected one ideology and accepted another, but they are coming back to the same issue.

Thought is essentially bourgeois. Thought, whether it thinks of the future or of the present, functions always from the past, from its memories, from its conditioning, from its knowledge. Thought is the very essence of security, and that is what the most bourgeois mind wants—security, security at every level! To bring about a total change of the human consciousness, thought must function at one level and must not function at another level. Thought must function naturally, normally at one level, the everyday level—physically, technologically—with knowledge, but must not overflow into another field where thought has no reality at all. If I had no thought I wouldn't be able to speak. But a radical change within myself as a human being cannot be brought about through an idea, through thought, because thought can only function in relation to conflict. Thought can only breed conflict.

Having stated all that, if you are at all serious, and I hope some of you are, you must ask yourself what the origin, the beginning of all thinking is. You must be quite sure of that, not agreeing with the speaker. That's why it matters tremendously how you listen, not to the speaker only, but to your own state of mind—which is also listening. I do not know if you have ever asked this question of yourself, and if you do ask the question seriously, at what level are you asking it? Are you asking the question at the verbal, intellectual level and waiting for someone to tell you what the origin of thinking is? If you are, the answer will always be superficial. Or are you asking the question without expecting an answer? You know, it's like seeing something very clearly. When you see something very clearly, there's no answer; there it is.

It matters greatly how you ask the question. It's like a man asking if there is God. If you are really serious, you are neither a believer nor a nonbeliever. If you believe that there is God, then you will discover what you believe. And if you do not believe, you cease to investigate. To investigate, you must put the question with all your energy, with your mind, with your heart, with your nerves, with your whole capacity, with your complete attention and not expect an answer, because the answer—if you do answer it—will be in terms of thought. I do not know if you see the complexity of the problem itself. You've asked the question, and a mind that has asked this question is not waiting for an answer, not expecting an answer, for who is going to answer it? The speaker may be able to explain it, to point it out—and we are going to go into it presently—but it is you who have asked the question, and therefore your mind is tremendously active, not in terms of receiving an answer, not in terms of trying to find out. When you have asked the question, then you're completely aware and sensitive.

In that state of attention, awareness, sensitivity, whatever is said, true or false, that state of awareness will know, but it is not intuition. Don't let's fool ourselves with words. It's not your higher self and all that non-

sense. It's the mind that has asked the question and therefore has become tremendously sensitive. In that field whatever is false comes to an end; whatever is true flourishes. You can find that out for yourself; it's very simple. It's important how you ask this question, really tremendously important, because it depends upon the state of mind that has put this question whether such a mind can find the truth or the falseness of what is going to be said. It is not according to your temperament, your conditioning, or your particular idiosyncrasies.

What is the origin of thinking? This is a most complex question, and it requires a very subtle, unafraid mind to determine it. The moment one actually discovers the origin of thinking, thought has its place; then thought will not overflow into the other field, into the other dimension where thought has no place at all. Only in that dimension can a radical change take place. Only in that dimension is a new thing born which is not the product of thought.

Let's go into it. Please listen and not take notes. Don't bother about notes because you are investigating into yourself; you are observing yourself. When you are observing yourself you have no time to take notes; you're there, attentive.

One can see very simply that all thinking is a reaction to the past—the past being memory, knowledge, experience. All thinking is the result of the past. The past—which is time, yesterday and that yesterday stretching out indefinitely into the past—is what is considered time: time as the past, time as the present, time as the future. Time has been divided into these three parts, and time is like a river, flowing. We have divided it into these fragments, and in these fragments thought is caught.

Please, you are not agreeing with me; you're watching it; you're watching it in yourself. I'm not giving a new idea, a new ideology for you to accept and practice or to which you can say, "No, this is right; this is wrong." We're just seeing *what is*. Thought has its origin in pleasure. We're not condemning or extolling pleasure; we're just watching it. We're not trying to become puritanical, saying that you must not have pleasure, which would be absurd. We'll go into that. Love is not pleasure. If it is, then it becomes thought, a picture, an image. I've had pleasure, sexually; or visually, of the sunset, of a beautiful face, of a building, of a picture. I've listened to music; that memory is there and thought thinks about it. Thinking about it, it derives greater pleasure, creating the image, the picture, sensuous or idealistic. What we think of is always pleasurable, not painful. We want to avoid pain, put it aside. Anything that is painful we put away, but it is there! Anything which gives to the nerves, to the brain, to our physical and psychological entity a feeling of pleasure, such as sex, we think about. The more we think, the more pleasure we derive from it.

Thought—please listen carefully—thought thinks about something. Thought divides itself into the observer, the feeler, the experiencer, and the thing to be experienced. Thought, having divided itself into the observer and the thing observed, obviously brings about a conflict. Then thought says, "I must get over the conflict," and invents disciplines, resistances, various forms of cunning escapes. We see that the origin of thinking is pleasure. All our activities, all our values, moral, ethical, and religious are based on pleasure. As long as there is this dual existence which thought has created, as the observer who is going to derive pleasure from the observed, as long as thought is functioning that way, there will always be conflict, and therefore no radical revolution at all.

Is this fairly clear? No, not my explanation! Someone can probably give you a better explanation; we're not concerned with explanations. We're concerned with seeing *what is*, the fact. I've had a beautiful experience of a sunset yesterday in the country, the trees against the sun, the loveliness of shadow, the depth, the beauty, from which I have derived tremendous pleasure. Thought thinks about it; I must go back there tomorrow, or keep the memory. I keep it because my life is so shoddy, so dull, so boring, so routine that I'm caught in that beauty which I saw yesterday. I've listened to a sound, to music, to a poem; I've looked at a painting. I think about it. I'm caught in it, and I want more of it. I see a beautiful face. I want to live with it. Again thought is functioning with pleasure. There is the observer, the thinker, and there is the thought, which is pleasure. The thinker has been built on the basis of pleasure: "I want this and I don't want that." "This is good," which means essentially that there is pleasure! As long as this division between the observer and the observed exists, there can be no radical mutation of consciousness.

Is it possible to observe without the thinker? I look at everything with an image, with a symbol, with memory, with knowledge. I look at my friend, at my wife, at my neighbor, at the boss, with the image which thought has built. I look at my wife with the image I have about her, and she looks at me with the image she has about me. The relationship is between these two images. This is a fact. It's not an invention on my part; it's a fact! Thought has built these symbols, images, ideas. Can I look, at first, at a tree, at a flower, at the sky, at the cloud, without an image? The image of the tree is the word I have learned which gives a certain name to the tree, tells its species and recalls its beauty. Can I look at the tree, at that cloud, at that flower, without thought, without the image? That's fairly easy to do, if you have done it. But can I look, without the image, at a human being with whom I am intimate, whom I consider as wife, husband, child? If I can't, there is no real relationship. The only relationship is between the images that we both have. So, can I look at life—the clouds, the stars, the trees, the river, the bird on the wing, my wife, my child, my neighbor, this whole earth—can I look at it all without the image? Though you have insulted me, though you have hurt me, though you have said nasty things about me or praised me, can I look at you without the image or the memory of what you have done and said to me?

Do see the importance of this, because it's only a mind that has retained the memories of hurt, of insult, that is ready to forgive, if it is at all inclined that way. A mind that is not storing up its insults, the flatteries that it receives, has nothing to forgive or not forgive; therefore, there is no conflict. Thought has created these images, both inwardly and outwardly. Can the images come to an end, and thought look at everything in life afresh? If you can do this, you will find that without your conscious, deliberate effort to change, change has taken place, a radical change! Most people are ambitious; they want to be somebody: authors, painters, businessmen, or politicians. Priests want to become archbishops. Thought has created this society and sees the advantage of becoming powerful, dominant, an important person, which happens only through ambition. Thought has created the image through observation of the man in power and wants the pleasure of owning a big house, having a picture appear in the papers, and all the rest of it.

Can one live in this world without ambition, without the image of pleasure, which thought has created? Can one function technologically, outwardly, without this poison of ambition? It can be done, but it is possible only when we understand the origin of thinking and understand actually, factually, the unreality of the division between the observer and the observed. Then we can proceed because then

virtue has a totally different meaning. It is not the moral virtue of an ugly, corrupt society, but virtue which is order. Virtue, like humility, is not something to be cultivated by thought. Thought is not virtuous; it is bourgeois, petty, and thought cannot possibly understand either love or virtue or humility.

Comment: We had a reaction to your use of the word bourgeois. *For us the word is the opposite of "anti-bourgeois." According to the communists it is the prototype of one who is in error, and we are in the right. That reaction was an example that we were not truly listening to the meaning but only to the words. It emphasizes the fact that we need to listen with all our being to what you say.*

KRISHNAMURTI: Let us talk it over together.

Comment: I cannot come to the realization that thought cannot resolve my confusion unless there is a radical change.

KRISHNAMURTI: It's very easy to say, "Well, one sees that thought doesn't solve the problem." That's very easy, but actually, does it? That's why it is very important to understand what we mean by "understanding," what we mean by "seeing something very clearly." Because if you see something very clearly, it's finished! But one has to be tremendously careful that one is not deceiving oneself. You're not deceiving yourself when you're in front of a precipice. There you understand the immense danger and you act; there is action. Without action there is no understanding. If you understand or you see very clearly, the very clarity is action. You do not see and then act. If you see and then act, what has actually taken place is that you see the idea, you understand the idea, and then you act according to that idea.

Comment: Yes, but if I am aware that I cannot act by thought, or I see my reaction to something, and I am aware that even in seeing that, I believe. . . .

KRISHNAMURTI: Is there belief, madame? It is not a belief.

Comment: No, but even if I feel that I react in such a fashion, I am aware that I cannot react in any other way, and that changes nothing.

KRISHNAMURTI: Exactly, right!

Comment: Even in believing that, even in feeling that, I feel myself incapable. I feel that perhaps I do not see clearly enough. Yet that does not seem immediately to make a change.

KRISHNAMURTI: Look, nationalism is a poison. You may not agree, but it is so for me! I see what nationalism has done throughout the world. It has divided people and brought on wars. One of the reasons for war is nationalism, and it is a poison. People know it. When you divide the world into French, Russian, American, Hindu, and so on, that division breeds conflict and it's poison. You see it, you understand it; but in your hearts, due to your conditioning, you are still French, English, or whatever it is. The moment you see, understand, that nationalism is poison, at that moment the whole thing drops.

Comment: It drops but it continues afterwards.

KRISHNAMURTI: Do we do that with regard to a precipice? We are conscious of the precipice, and we never go near it. It's only when we are not clear about patriotism,

nationalism, and all the rest that we play with it. When we see something poisonous like a snake, or a dangerous animal, like a bus coming at full speed, we don't step in the way; we move away from it. But we don't see, and we don't see because we are afraid that we may have to change. What prevents us is this fear, conscious or unconscious, of losing the things we have decided have real value and security. As long as that fear exists we may talk about seeing, understanding, how to act, and all the rest of it, but there is no possibility of immediate action, which is really instant mutation because you see the truth of it.

Question: How can we see instantly?

KRISHNAMURTI: How do you see the danger of the precipice?

Comment: It is not my thought.

KRISHNAMURTI: No, madame. What has told you? Listen; this is very important. Go into it, please. What has told you that the precipice, a snake, the bus running at full speed, is dangerous? Have your newspapers told you? Have your political leaders told you? Your priests? Who has told you?

Comment: Instinct.

KRISHNAMURTI: What is instinct?

Comment: Reality.

KRISHNAMURTI: Madame, don't translate "instinct" as reality. Instinct is what has been nurtured carefully through centuries by thought. You have seen a friend killed by a bus and you say, "By Jove, how dangerous it is!" You've seen it. You have actually experienced the fact of a precipice, how dangerous it is. When you meet a tiger, not in Paris, but in India, you know the tremendous danger of an animal like that. Why don't you know nationalism equally? I'm taking that as an example, for it is also poisonous. Why is it poisonous? Because it has brought war after war. One of the reasons for war is nationalism. War is deadly! People have been killed, your neighbors, your friends, your people, your own kin, and yet you go on with it. Why?

Comment: We have been told that it is necessary.

KRISHNAMURTI: You have been told. That means you are being influenced by propaganda. You accept because belonging to a nation gives you a great pleasure.

Comment: Not necessarily.

KRISHNAMURTI: Of course, not necessarily. Everything is not necessarily.

Question: Your statement about nationalism has meaning only in the countries that are not threatened by enemies. How would a country like India that has so much danger from China and communist. . . .

KRISHNAMURTI: There is the reply! An Indian is talking about India. Yes, sir. Frenchmen and Germans have talked about their countries. This has been talked about for ten thousand years, each country defending itself against the other. Historically it will go on because that's how we are brought up, conditioned. People accept it; they love the flags and all the rest of it; they are willing to kill and be killed. But we are talking not about India or France or Russia but about people, human

beings who are serious, who are confronted with these problems.

Question: When one looks without thought, as you have explained, without preconceived ideas, but with a fresh mind, suppose that one is like that in one's contacts with human beings. . . .

KRISHNAMURTI: There is no "suppose," madame. It does not exist.

Question: You may have come to this state of mind, this state of being, of consciousness, freshness, and awareness, but what about the other person?

KRISHNAMURTI: The lady says, "One may be free; one can observe without the image, but what about the other person who still keeps his image and is looking at me, being related to me through the image? I've dropped my image, about India, about America, dropped all my images, and someone else hasn't; my wife hasn't. What's my relationship with her?"

What's my relationship? Actually it is what the gentleman pointed out. India is attacked; we must defend. My wife says, "You don't love me anymore." No, don't laugh, sirs. Please do listen to all this. So what am I to do? Should I bring back my image because I want to conform to society, because I might lose my job, because I mightn't be popular?

Question: Does attention arise from thought or from energy?

KRISHNAMURTI: Thought and energy are the same. Energy is the same, only it is used in the wrong direction, and when it is used wrongly, all the mischief is brought into being. Is it possible to have, not various energies, but total energy that is not the result of resistance, conflict, and all the rest of it?

May 19, 1966

Third Talk in Paris

The other day we were talking about the necessity for a radical change, not at some future date, but on the instant. We discussed the fact that thought in different ways, crudely and very subtly, has created the psychological structure in which human beings are caught, both outwardly and inwardly. Thought has created this confusion, this misery, this conflict, and thought cannot possibly, under any circumstances, bring about a different structure because thought will always remain the same. We also discussed the origin of thinking. Perhaps we can go into it a little more deeply today.

The problem is: What action or inaction is necessary for a radical mutation to take place? For most of us action is fragmentary; we act as scientists, writers, businessmen, or family people, as social reformers, politicians, in so many different ways. We act according to our conditioning; if conditioned as a Hindu, a Christian, a Muslim, a communist, and so on, our whole outlook, our activity, though modified by tendency and temperament, continue to function, act according to the background out of which we have come. The background, the conditioning is not different from the 'me' and 'you'; we are the background. We are the result of our conditioning. We are conditioned entities and we function, act within the limited field of our conditioning. I think that's fairly obvious for most of us who are a little bit aware of what we are doing. We hope to bring about a change within ourselves, which we see is necessary, by an act of thought, an act under pressure, necessity, or a demand. Such action

always has a motive behind it. We function in the fragmentary field in which we live. Life for us is an action. It is not action and life. The two are not separate, but we act, we live, we have our being, we do everything in fragments. Within that fragmentary field by an act of volition, which is determination, will, desire, a compulsive urge, we try to bring about a change.

Please, we are talking quite informally; we are talking over together the problems that confront each one of us, not only the outward problems, but also the psychological, deep, conscious, and unconscious problems that each one has, that each one is caught up in. You're not listening to the speaker to find out what your problems are, because if you're trying to be informed as to what your problems are, then you are totally unaware of your problems. You depend on another to tell you what your problems are; therefore, it becomes superficial, authoritarian, and unnecessary. Whereas if you can be intelligently aware of your own problem, of conscious as well as unconscious issues, then your problem is extraordinarily acute; it cannot be postponed. You cannot possibly escape from it; it is there. You may try to cover it up, you may try to run away from it, rationalize it, go to an analyst or to a confessional, do all the innumerable things that you do in order to try to solve the particular issue, but all that is action—not only the action that has produced the problem, but also all the activities in which you indulge in order to escape from the problem. The intellectual activity that tries to rationalize the problem or tries to find an answer to the problem is also activity. Or you say to yourself, "I must understand it; what is the answer; what is the way out?" That's also action, either emotional, intellectual, or purely neurological. Being conditioned, you respond or act according to the fragmentary response of this total conditioning.

The problem is this: I know I am conditioned, as a Hindu or whatever it is. I'm aware that this conditioning is very deep-rooted, deep-seated, and whatever I do as action is a response to this conditioning. I also see the immense importance of a complete change of consciousness, of the way of thinking or not thinking, a complete revolution in my relationship to the world, to another human being. I have an image about myself—as each one has—and that image has been carefully built up, nurtured by thought, by influence, by experience, by knowledge. I am also aware that any response of that image will invariably be fragmentary, and therefore all my actions will always be limited, each action being contradictory to another kind of action. We are going to discuss this, if you wish, after we've talked a little.

I say to myself, "What am I to do?" There must be some action which will break up this conditioning, this response of the image which thought has built up. Of course all belief in God, in dogma—whether it is communist dogma, socialist dogma, or religious dogma—has no value at all because we are much more mature, beyond all that. After having put the question as to whether I can do anything at all, and after having seen that all action—all action—is the response of my conditioning, of my image, the image which I have about myself, and it can never bring about freedom from conflict and misery, then what am I to do? I have to find out if there is an action which is not the response of my image or of my conditioning.

As far as I know, all my action springs from the field of the known. When I say, "I will be something in the future, tomorrow," the something is already known; thought has projected what I will be tomorrow. All desire, motive, urge for a change is always within the field of the known, which means there is no change at all as long as I function

in that way. Am I making myself clear on this point? Clarity is in seeing the problem, not in understanding verbally what a speaker is saying. To see anything clearly, I must have clarity. The problem must be very clear, not only verbally, intellectually, emotionally, but it must be absolutely clear in every way. Clarity isn't something to be achieved. When the problem is acute and there is no answer to that problem in the way to which I am accustomed, which is thought, then I have clarity. I see that all my action is within the field of the known, whether it is the action of tomorrow, the action of today, or of the next moment. It's always within that field, and whatever action there may be within the field of the known, there is no radical revolution in there. The new cannot take place within the field of the known. I see that very clearly. Action will not bring about a change; only inaction will do it.

We have tried the various doors and avenues of thought to bring about a mutation in the mind, in consciousness itself. We all do that, if we are at all aware, through discipline, control, subjugation, obedience, following someone, believing in something, having faith in a priest, in a god, in a tyrannical government, or in an ideology. We have tried all those ways, which we call positive action, to try to end this misery, this confusion, this anxiety. After trying them all we are invariably where we began. They have all been a waste of time. When we realize that any action within the field of the known cannot possibly bring about a transformation in consciousness, or of consciousness, then there is only one thing left—total inaction. This doesn't mean that we become lazy, that we don't lead normal lives, that we go off into some fanciful dream, and so on. This requires tremendous attention to the futility of action in the field of the known. When the mind sees that very clearly, then action of a different kind takes place, which is total inaction in terms of the positive action of doing something within the field of the known.

Take the question of fear. Most people are afraid, both physically and inwardly. Fear exists only in relationship to something. I am afraid of illness, of physical pain. I've had it and I'm afraid of it. I'm afraid of public opinion. I'm afraid of losing a job. I'm afraid of not arriving, achieving, not being able to fulfill. I'm afraid of darkness, afraid of my own stupidity, afraid of my own pettiness. We have so many different fears, and we try to solve these fears in fragments. We don't seem to be able to go beyond that. If we think we have understood one particular fear, and have resolved it, another fear comes up. When we are aware that we are afraid, we try to run away from it, try to find an answer, try to find out what to do, or try to suppress it.

We have, as human beings, cunningly developed a network of escapes: God, amusement, drink, sex, anything. All escapes are the same, whether it is in the name of God or drink! If we are to live as human beings, we have to solve the problem. If we live in fear, conscious or unconscious, it's like living in darkness, with tremendous inward conflict and resistance. The greater the fear, the greater the tension, the greater the neuroticism, the greater is the urge to escape. If we do not escape, then we ask ourselves, "How are we to solve it?" We seek ways and means of solving it, but always within the field of the known. We do something about it, and this action bred by thought is action within the field of experience, knowledge, the known, and therefore there is no answer. That's what we do, and we die with fear. We live throughout our lives with fear and die with fear. Now can a human being totally eradicate fear? Can we do anything, or nothing? The nothing does not mean that we accept fear, rationalize it, and live

with it; that's not the inaction of which we are talking.

We have done everything we can with regard to fear. We have analyzed it, gone into it, tried to face it, come into direct contact with it, resisted it, done everything possible, and the thing remains. Is it possible to be aware of it totally, not merely intellectually, emotionally, but completely aware of it, and yet not act in the sense of doing something about it? We must come into contact with fear, but we don't. The word *fear*—whatever has caused that fear—the word itself keeps us from being in contact with the fact.

The word *love* is loaded, heavy with tradition, with human experience, with verbal explanations as to what it should be and what it must not be, with its division into divine love, secular love, and all the rest. To really understand that thing, the word is not important, and the word, because it is not important, does not give meaning to the feeling. In the same way, the word fear causes fear, the word being thought. So to be in contact with that thing which we call fear, the word, which is thought, must not interfere. To be in contact deeply with that fact, the observer is not different from the thing observed. Fear is not different from me; I am fear. It doesn't mean that I identify myself with fear, but that fear is me. When I'm aware of all this, there is total inaction which is the most positive action, and there is freedom from fear, total freedom.

Let's take another issue. We are all afraid of death, the old and the young. We either rationalize it, accept it as inevitable, put up with it, or forget it—but it is there. Or we create beliefs to escape from that fact—reincarnation, resurrection, and all the rest of it. Again, thought fears that it will come to an end, which is death. Not only the organism, but also the whole psychological structure which thought has created is coming to an end, unfulfilled, wanting to live a few more years to do this or that, to correct what has been and have it become what should be.

Consciously and unconsciously we know it's the end of thinking, or the end of what we think thinking is, the end of the 'me', although the 'me' invents various structures of hope. We die through illness, through old age, through accident, or deliberately put an end to our lives because they are so futile, boring, with the utter boredom of routine. We see no meaning, no significance at all to life. Really, if you observe it very carefully, there's hardly any significance in our living. We carry on day after day with the routine, with the boredom, with the repetition of pleasure, pain, and all the rest of insensitive, meaningless existence. When we realize that, we try to give significance to life; we invent a significance—God, noble work, I must fulfill, I'm a writer and I must do this, I must do that—the endless activity of the monkey which is the 'me'.

We are afraid to die. To end the fear of death we must come into contact with death, not with the image which thought has created about death, but we must actually feel the state. Otherwise there is no end to fear because the word *death* creates fear, and we don't even want to talk about it. Being healthy, normal, with the capacity to reason clearly, to think objectively, to observe, is it possible for us to come into contact with the fact, totally? The organism, through usage, through disease, will eventually die. If we are healthy, we want to find out what death means. It's not a morbid desire because perhaps by dying we shall understand living. Living, as it is now, is torture, endless turmoil, a contradiction, and therefore there is conflict, misery, and confusion. The everyday going to the office, the repetition of pleasure with its pains, the anxiety, the groping, the uncertainty—that's what we call living. We have become accustomed to that kind of living. We accept it; we grow old with it and die.

To find out what living is as well as to find out what dying is, one must come into contact with death, that is, one must end every day everything one has known. One must end the image that one has built up about oneself, about one's family, about one's relationship, the image that one has built through pleasure, through one's relationship to society, everything. That is what is going to take place when death occurs. Then we shall know what it means to die and also what it means to live because then we shall die to every misery, every conflict, every form of struggle. It's only in dying that there is something new. There's nothing new if time continues. There's only the new when time comes to an end, time being duration. Time as we know it is yesterday, today, and tomorrow. In that flow of time we are caught, and we try to solve our problems within that current, within that flow of time.

One can only solve the problem when time has come to an end as yesterday, today, and tomorrow. One must die to memory, to hurts, to all the images one has built through thought about oneself, about others, or about the world. Then one comes directly into contact with reality, which is living as well as dying, and in that reality there is no fear. That reality can only take place in total inaction, the inaction when thought has understood its own place and has no existence in a different dimension.

Question: If the grass no longer wants to grow, there is no more grass. What remains?

KRISHNAMURTI: Where is the grass, if the grass doesn't want to grow? Does the grass not want to grow? Do you know about it? Have you seen grass saying it doesn't want to grow? Please don't talk in similes when you are dealing with facts.

Comment: But I want to put an end. . . .

KRISHNAMURTI: Ah you want! You have not understood the talk at all, madame, if you say, "I want to put an end." Who is the 'you' that is putting an end? You haven't really understood this. We are discussing something which needs your attention, not your agreement or disagreement. We are looking at life most rigorously, objectively, clearly—not according to your sentiment, your fancy, what you like or don't like. It's what we like and don't like that has created this misery. All that we are saying is this: How do we end fear? That's one of our great problems because if a human being can't end ·it, he lives in darkness everlastingly, not everlastingly in the Christian sense, but in the ordinary sense; one life is good enough. For me, as a human being, there must be a way out, and not by creating a hope in some future. Can I as a human being end fear, totally; not little bits of it? Probably you've never put this question to yourself, and probably you've not put the question because you don't know how to get out of it. But if you did put that question most seriously, with the intention of finding out, not how to end it, but with the intention of finding out the nature and the structure of fear, the moment you have found out, fear itself comes to an end; you don't have to do anything about it.

Comment: If a man has fear he lives in total darkness, but all the motive force in the field of the known, as you have said, springs out of fear. If I work because I have fear that I will be hungry, I'm fighting all the tensions in the field of the known which spring from fear, and if there is no fear there is no action in the field of the known.

KRISHNAMURTI: Yes, sir. Are you implying that the moment when you know that all action is the result of fear in the field of the known, you will not earn a livelihood?

Comment: No, I mean that all action in the field of the known comes from the sense of fear.

KRISHNAMURTI: And then what, sir? What is the question?

Comment: If we try to get out of fear, if we try to live without fear, then there is no more action in the field of the known.

KRISHNAMURTI: That's what I said.

Comment: Yes, and then what happens is. . . .

KRISHNAMURTI: Wait, sir, wait! You don't know what happens then. Be careful, sir; don't speculate. This is not a speculative discussion, an immature schoolboy discussion or a theological discussion. What happens after, if? Such speculation is futile; it has no meaning. All the religious people have speculated; all the theologians, all the communists speculate, but the fact remains that we are afraid; the fact is that we function within the field of the known, and that breeds a continuous fear. Now, can it end—not, what happens after? One finds that out.

Comment: But if there is no fear there is no living, sir.

KRISHNAMURTI: Oh, that's quite a different thing, sir. You say that if there is no fear there is no motive for living. If there is no fear there is no love. Of course.

Comment: The greatest fear is death, and therefore, fear being the significance of life, the greatest significance of life is death.

KRISHNAMURTI: So you say, sir, that there is no living without fear; without fear one will not earn a livelihood; without fear there is no love. Without fear all existence ceases. This is what most people say. When they say, "I love you," in that love there is jealousy, there is anger; in that love there is ambition, success, domination. We all know that. Surely that's not love. To find out what love is, domination, fear, jealousy, envy, ambition all have to cease. Then you will find out, but you can't speculate about it. You can't say, "Well, if I'm not angry, I shan't live; if I'm afraid, I won't go to the office." If fear is driving you to go to the office, you are not efficient; you are not capable, and therefore you don't love the thing that you're doing. Because you don't love, all the other desires of amusement, of escape are born.

Comment: With fear as the motive force one goes to the office.

KRISHNAMURTI: Does one, sir? You say one does. Does one go with the motive? Does the motive of fear drive one to the office?

Comment: But there is one more thing, sir—hope.

KRISHNAMURTI: Yes, sir.

Question: The primary force is fear; the secondary force is hope. The primary force is that if I don't work I will be hungry; I will not be able to clothe myself. The secondary force is the hope that I may be able to achieve something. And to me, it seems that death is the greatest fear in life. It gives a significance to life; it tries to give some hope

after death, as you have already said about resurrection and things like that, and then tries to give some beauty to life. So that all actions in the field of the known spring primarily from fear and secondly from hope. Could I say that, sir?

KRISHNAMURTI: What you say is so, sir, but what of it? I mean, can one live everlastingly in fear? What's the point of it? Doesn't one want to resolve it?

Comment: The point of living is dying.

KRISHNAMURTI: No, sir. That has been said and achieved by so many people; clever people have written about all this. They have said that life has no meaning, and therefore we must give life a significance. Death has no meaning, and therefore it must have another significance. This is what man has done throughout the centuries, sir. We are saying quite the contrary—that one cannot find the fullness of life, the depth of life if there is fear, and to end fear is also to understand death.

Question: How can one put oneself voluntarily in contact with the state of death?

KRISHNAMURTI: You can't put yourself in contact with death. You put the question wrongly. Look, you are afraid of death, and as long as you are afraid of anything, there is no contact with that thing.

Comment: Yes, but once the contact is made, fear vanishes.

KRISHNAMURTI: Wait, madame; don't speculate.

Comment: I don't speculate; I talk from experience.

KRISHNAMURTI: Wait, wait, wait! If there is no fear of death, if there is no fear of my wife or my husband, of my neighbor, of the state, then I am in contact. I know it is not an image with which I am in contact, but I am actually in contact. Is it possible for the mind to be totally free of fear, not partly, but totally? That requires tremendous understanding, meditation; not just to say, "Well, I've had the experience of moments when I'm not afraid." Can I understand this extraordinary structure of fear? Can the whole of me, consciously and unconsciously, be aware of it? It's not for you to tell me or for me to tell you how to do it. See the extraordinary complexity of it! Notice how the word prevents the actual coming into contact with it, how the image that you have created about death, about your wife, your husband, your state, prevents you from coming in contact with the fact of your wife, the state, what another says, and so on. Can you, consciously or unconsciously, be aware of the total process?

Question: In order to understand your fear you have to face that and analyze it first, don't you?

KRISHNAMURTI: You have to face fear?

Comment: Face the cause of it.

KRISHNAMURTI: Now wait a minute. The lady says, "To be aware of fear you must come into contact with it; to come into contact with it you must be aware of the cause of fear." Wait, just listen to it all. How will you know the cause of fear? Through analysis? By examination? And when you have discovered the cause of fear, does fear end? It generally doesn't. I know I'm afraid of death, and I know why I'm afraid of death.

Comment: I think if you face it, it does.

KRISHNAMURTI: I'm coming to that, madame. Understanding the cause of fear does not end fear. Is there contact with fear? This again is really a very complex question. Do look at it a little; take a little time. There is fear, and I say I must look to the cause of it, and I examine, analyze. Time has gone on. It has taken time to examine, to find out. In that time interval other factors have come into being. Madame, if you really understand this one question, you will probably be able to answer all your own questions.

Look, take something specific; human beings are violent and they have used the ideal of nonviolence to get away from their violence. They have invented the idiocy of nonviolence, when they are violent. It is an idiocy; it's a neurotic invention. I'll show you why. I am violent, and I have an idea that I must be nonviolent. There is an interval between what I am, violent, and what I should be. The interval is time—gradually I will come to nonviolence. But in the meantime I'm being violent; I'm sowing the seeds of violence. I'm sowing the seeds of the poison of violence all the time. To end violence, the ideal of nonviolence is unnecessary. All that I have to do is to face violence, to say that I am violent, not hoping to achieve nonviolence, which is a waste of energy. So now I am violent. I know, and each one knows to what depth he is violent. Now, can I understand it? To understand, first of all I must understand the whole nature of violence, what it means to be violent. Anger, self-fulfillment, ambition, wanting to be a great success, competition, the whole human psychological structure—all these are based on violence, with occasional flashes of kindliness and gentleness.

To end this structure, is time necessary; that is, how am I to end time? What are the causes that have brought it about, which prevent me from being totally aware of the fact? When I'm totally aware of the fact, time doesn't enter into it at all, and therefore there's an ending of it. To end fear it is totally unnecessary to investigate the cause, to find out what the cause is. We know instantly what the cause of fear is, unless we are neurotic. When we are aware of it and come into contact with it directly, the observer is the observed. There is no difference between the observer and the thing observed. When fear is observed without the observer, there is action, but not the action of the observer acting upon fear.

Comment: In professional life we are forced to act in such a way that we become inactive in your sense. If we do as you say, we become unable to function in professional life.

KRISHNAMURTI: No, sir. The gentleman says that in professional life all action is within the field of the known. Of course! It must be! Otherwise you couldn't act as a doctor, as a scientist, as a professional. That's simple. But when that field of action enters into the psychological field and tries to solve human problems, then no problem can be solved. Sir, to remain a technician, without the psyche using that technology, that knowledge for its own purposes, you might write a book; but if you say, consciously or unconsciously, "I'm writing a book because it gives me power, position, prestige," then it becomes a poison, then you cease to be a writer; you want fame. It is all very simple when once you understand all this.

May 22, 1966

Fourth Talk in Paris

I think it would be very good if we could find out what we are seeking and why we are seeking. What is it that we are all after? What is it all about? What does each one of us deeply crave—asking, seeking, demanding? If we can find out what it is that we are seeking and why we are seeking, then perhaps we can go into this question of search, into this question of seeking. Man, apparently, has always sought something beyond himself, something beyond his daily routine, boredom, despair, and anxiety—something that will be completely satisfying, that will give a certain deep, abiding significance to his rather superficial, chaotic, miserable life. We seek something beyond us because we lead very superficial lives, lives that have very little meaning, lives that are mechanical, routine. We demand something mysterious, a quality of otherness. We are everlastingly seeking, through books, through following someone, establishing ideologies, beliefs, dogmas, in the hope of reaching, attaining, gaining something that is not put together by thought, that has some deep meaning in life. Because we are superficial, shallow, insufficient in ourselves we stretch our hands, our minds beyond the limitations of our own thinking, or we seek to escape from this wide and deep loneliness, this sense of solitude, this sense of isolation. We want to escape from ourselves because we see that we are so small, so petty that there is very little meaning to life. We know what we are, so why bother about it? Why be tragic or dramatic or anything about it? It is a shallow affair anyhow. Let us see if we can't leave this self-centered activity and isolation and escape into something which cannot be measured in terms of time.

I think that is what most of us are, if we look deeply into ourselves. If we are religious, addicted to some kind of sect, or if we have some particular pet idiosyncrasy that gives a particularly satisfying experience, we want to extend that experience, widen it, deepen it, make it more real. Most of us are always seeking, either to escape from the daily routine and boredom or to escape from the insufficiency of emptiness, from a sense of isolation, or we want something more, something we do not have that will make our lives rich, full, sufficient. If we examine our own behavior, our own thinking, I think we will find that we are all wanting something. The more mysterious it is, the more it has a quality of otherness, something that is extraordinarily mysterious and occult, hidden, the more we pursue it. We want some authority to guide us to that untrodden realm, so we very easily accept authority and follow either blindly or rationally, giving various explanations as to why we follow. We remain constantly seeking, demanding wider and deeper experiences because the experiences we know are not very significant. We know they are sensuous, pleasurable, rather empty and shallow, so we eagerly listen to anyone who will offer something beyond all this. We are willing to accept their words, their direction, their statements. We are always following; we are always the yes-sayers, those who say yes to everything; we are not no-sayers.

I would like this evening, if I may, to talk about this urge in man to seek something beyond himself, as he tries to identify himself with that something through various methods, systems, dogmas, beliefs; various systems of meditation, trying to capture—at least in words—that which cannot be captured by thought. Let us talk over together this question of seeking, why we seek, why we demand a variety of experiences and ultimately an experience that will quench our thirst, that will put an end to our own miserable, shallow existence.

To really go into it we must first find out what we mean by experience, and why we ask for greater experiences. The latest drug is LSD, of which you have probably heard, and which perhaps—although I hope not—some of you have taken. There is this tremendous urge for greater experience, for something that will lighten, give breadth and depth to our life, and that drug is sweeping all over the world. In ancient India they used to have it, only under a different name. It surely is the result of a demand for more intense life, a greater sensitivity, and in that sensitivity you see things differently.

Let us talk over together this demand, this longing for something, for some experience which will enrich our days with beauty, with love, with clarity. Surely experience is always recognizable. When we experience something, a pleasure, something we think is original, that experience is recognizable. We recognize it. We say, ''That was a marvelous experience; this happened and that happened.'' We saw things more clearly. It was an experience that gave us a tremendous sense of joy, vitality. An experience is always something we can recognize. When we can recognize it, it is already known, and therefore it is not something new.

I recognize someone because I met him last year or yesterday. The image of that person has remained in the memory, conscious or unconscious, and when I meet that person again, that memory responds. Similarly, when I have an experience of any kind, trivial or what is called ''sublime''—and there are no sublime experiences at all because all experiences, whether petty or grand, are in the picture of thought as memory—I want to recognize it. My mind through words describes it, has sensations about it, so it is always something from the known to the known. Otherwise I won't call it experience. It's like a very sensitive person taking one of these drugs which obviously will heighten sensitivity. He sees or experiences or has a vision of something which he is able to recognize because it is already established in his mind; otherwise, he could not recognize it and would never call it an ''experience.''

Please investigate what is being said; don't just casually listen because we are going to go into something a little later which demands the understanding of experience. We are going to talk about meditation, which is one of the most extraordinary things, if one knows what it is to have a meditative mind. It's like a man who is blind and does not see color, a man with a dull mind. If we don't know what it is to meditate, we lead a very narrow, limited life, however clever, however erudite we may be, whatever books or paintings we may produce. We remain within a very small circle of knowledge, and knowledge is always limited. To understand this question of meditation, we must go into the question of experience, and also we must inquire why we seek and what we are seeking.

Deeply our life is a confusion, a mess, a misery, an agony. The more sensitive we are, the more the despair, the anxiety, the guilt feeling, and naturally we want to escape from it because we haven't found an answer; we don't know how to get out of this confusion. We want to go to some other realm, to another dimension. We escape through music, through art, through literature, but it is just an escape; it has no reality in comparison with what we are seeking. All escapes are similar, whether through the door of a church, through God or a savior, through the door of drink or of various drugs. We must not only understand what and why we are seeking, but we must also understand this demand for deep, abiding experience, because it is only the mind that does not seek at all, that does not demand any experience in any form, that can enter into a realm, into a dimension that is totally new. That is what we are going into this evening, I hope.

Our lives are shallow, insufficient in themselves, and we want something else, a greater, deeper experience. Also, we are astonishingly isolated. All our activity, all

our thinking, all our behavior leads to this isolation, this loneliness, and we want to escape from it. Without understanding this isolation—not intellectually, not verbally or rationally, but by coming directly into contact with what we are actually seeking, coming into contact with this sense of loneliness—without resolving that, totally, all meditation, all search, all so-called spiritual, religious activities have no meaning whatsoever because they are all escapes from what we are. It is like a shallow, dull, petty little mind thinking about God. If there is such a thing, the mind and its God will still remain petty.

The question arises whether it is possible for a mind so heavily conditioned, so caught up in the daily travail and conflict of life, to be so wide and deeply awake that there is no seeking, no searching for experience. When one is awake, when one has light in oneself, there is no seeking. One does not want any more experiences. It's only the man in darkness who is always searching for light. Is it possible to be so intensely awake, so highly sensitive, physically, intellectually, in every way, that there is not a dull spot in the mind? Then only is there no seeking; then only is there no urge for more experience.

Is it possible? Most of us live on sensations, sensuous sensations, and thought gives pleasure to them. By thinking about those sensations we derive great pleasure, and where there is pleasure there is pain. We must understand this process, how thought breeds time, pleasure, and pain; how thought, having created it all, tries to escape from it; and how the very escape breeds conflict. I am in sorrow, and I would like to be happy. I would like to end sorrow. Thought has created sorrow, and thought hopes to find an end to sorrow. In that dual state thought creates conflict for itself.

Most of us are faced with this sense of isolation and loneliness, a sense of void.

Though one may have a family group or whatever it is, one knows this sense, this deep anxiety about nothing. Can one be free of it; can one really go beyond it—not escaping from it, not trying to fill that isolation, that loneliness, that emptiness with knowledge, with experience, with all kinds of words? You all know the things that one does to fill this void in oneself. Can one go beyond it? To understand and be free of anything, one must come into contact with it. As we were saying the other day, one has an image about death, and that image, created by thought, brings fear of death. In the same way one has an image of this emptiness, of this loneliness, and that image prevents a direct contact with the fact of loneliness.

If you would look at a flower, look at it. You can only look at it if there is no image of that flower in your mind, if you don't name it, if thought is not operating when you are looking at the flower—thought as knowledge of the species or the color of that flower. Then you are directly, immediately in contact with that thing. When there is such contact, there is no observer. The observer is the image-maker who prevents coming into direct contact with a fact, with a flower, with death, or with that thing which we call loneliness.

Please, actually go through with what is being said. Listen so that you see the thing directly, are directly in contact. If you are in contact with anything—with your wife, with your children, with the sky, with the clouds, with any fact—the moment thought interferes with it you lose contact. Thought springs from memory. Memory is the image, and from there you look, and therefore there is a separation between the observer and the observed.

You have to understand this very deeply. It is this separation of the observer from the observed that makes the observer want more experience, more sensations, and so he is everlastingly pursuing, seeking. It has to be completely and totally understood that as long as there is an observer—the one that is seeking experience, the censor, the entity that evaluates, judges, condemns—there is no immediate contact with *what is*. When you have pain, physical pain, there is direct perception; there is not the observer who is feeling the pain; there is only pain. Because there is no observer there is immediate action. There is not the idea and then action, but there is only action when there is pain because there is a direct physical contact. The pain is you; there is pain! As long as this is not completely understood, realized, explored, and felt deeply, as long as it is not wholly grasped—not intellectually, not verbally—that the observer is the observed, all life becomes conflict, a contradiction between opposing desires, the 'what should be' and the *what is*. You can do this only if you are aware of whether you are looking at it as an observer when you look at a flower or a cloud or anything. If the entity is observing through his knowledge, there is no contact with the object.

A mind that is in conflict of any kind, at any level, whether it is in the office or in the home, conscious or unconscious, is a tortured mind; whatever it sees is distorted. Please do understand this very simple truth or fact: that whatever it sees must be distorted as long as there is conflict—conflict of ambition, fear, the agony of separation, and all the rest of it. A mind in conflict is a distorted mind. This conflict can only end when the observer ceases to be, when there is only the observed. Then virtue, that is, behavior has a quite different meaning. Virtue is order, not the virtue of social order, for society is disorderly. However much it may implant the idea of morality in the mind, society is immoral because it engenders conflict; it creates human beings who are ambitious, greedy, envious, seeking power, position, prestige. Without this order deeply within oneself, thought will create disorder which it will call virtue.

Order is not a matter of time; it isn't "I will be orderly, virtuous, day after tomorrow." Either we are or we are not. In the interval between *what is* and what we think should be, disorder comes into being, disorder being conflict. Out of conflict there can be no virtue, no morality. I say to myself, "I am angry; I will get over it; I'll practice patience, love, and all the rest of it." That is, I'll gradually come to that state where I'm not angry. That process, the idea of gradual achievement, breeds not only conflict but also this disorderly, anxious, destructive existence. Time as a process of realizing is always disorderly. Of course it takes time to acquire knowledge, to go to the moon, to learn a new language, but when we use time as a means to overcome some peculiar tendency of our own, then such usage of time, which is really using thinking to bring about a change, brings with it not only conflict but also a deep sense of indolence.

When you see something dangerous, you act immediately! There is no time interval; the idea is not separate from the action; action is the idea. A mind that is virtuous in this sense in which the speaker is using that word, without laying the foundation, does not perceive through effort but through direct perception. When you see the fact nonverbally there is immediate action. A man who is vain and proud may try to cultivate humility, but humility cannot be cultivated, any more than you can cultivate love. If he faces that fact of pride nonverbally, actually comes into contact with it—and this is only possible when there is not a separate observer who says, "I am proud," but the observer is the observed—then there is a direct contact with the fact. To come into contact with the fact, energy is needed, and that energy comes into being when the observer is nonexistent.

Having done this, you can begin to understand what meditation is because the understanding of the observer and the observed is part of meditation. Unfortunately the East has supplied various systems of meditation; they think they are experts at this. There are the various schools of meditation which have certain practices, breathing in certain ways, sitting in certain positions. They say, "Practice, practice, try, struggle, dominate, control; eventually you will get somewhere." Obviously you will get somewhere, but it will not be worth getting. What you will get is the projection of your own thinking, which has no validity whatsoever.

It is a very complex question. One has to completely deny authority in any form, whether external authority or the authority of one's own experience and knowledge. One needs a very subtle, quick mind, a mind that can reason, that is healthy, not neurotic. All neuroses take place when there is self-centered activity, when there is this observer wanting to express himself in various activities, because he creates conflict in himself. All this is part of meditation. It demands awareness to observe *what is* without interpretation, to look without judgment, without choice, and therefore to act, not in terms of ideas, but to act as one does when one sees a precipice, a danger—immediate action! That immediate action, when one observes, when one perceives, in which no time is involved, brings about virtue, order.

Have you ever seen a monkey at close quarters? There are plenty of them in India. If you have seen one, you have noticed how restless it is, scratching itself, chattering, in endless movement. So is our mind. It is a chattering mind, a mind that is vagrant, that wanders all over the place, chattering like a monkey. One realizes that and says, "I must control it," and one begins to concentrate. One doesn't realize that the entity that is concentrating, the entity that demands control or exerts domination is still the entity that is like the monkey.

The observer is the observed! Therefore, concentration—please listen—concentration leads merely to isolation, exclusion. Any schoolboy knows how to concentrate, or any man interested in something can concentrate. He puts on blinkers, creates a wall around himself, and observes, acts. Such concentration, being exclusion, creates conflict; but there is an awareness which is not concentration, in which one can concentrate without exclusion. Awareness is something really quite simple, so simple that you don't even think about it. As you enter a hall like this, you are aware of the color, the shape of the pillars, the dimensions of the room, and so on and so on and so on. You are aware, and then you begin to distinguish, criticize, give a name to the various colors. Such verbal differentiation is called distraction, but there is no distraction at all, ever. There is only distraction when you try to concentrate on something; then everything else is a distraction. But there is no such thing as distraction when you are aware of everything that is going on. If you are aware, there is no distraction at all. From this awareness comes attention. When you give your whole attention, your nerves, body, mind, heart, everything is attentive! You are attentive when there is danger. In that attention, if you observe it, the mind is extraordinarily quiet. It is only in silence that you can perceive anything; it is only in silence that there is perception, seeing.

If you look at that microphone attentively, look at it totally, your mind is very quiet; it doesn't need concentrating, exclusion, an effort. This silence of the mind is necessary. It is not something to be achieved, not something put together by thought, for such silence is sterile, dead. A man through prayer can achieve a certain quality of silence; through repetition of words you can bring about a quietness of the mind, but this is so

immature. It's not silence at all, the mind has drugged itself; but where there is attention, there is silence.

It is the function of the brain to receive and react. The brain is always active; the cells are conditioned through centuries of certain patterns of behavior. When one is conditioned as a Christian and one hears the word *Christian*, the brain cells react to that word very quickly, instantly. Is it possible for the brain cells themselves—which have been so highly trained to react instantly according to their pattern of behavior, thought, and all the rest of it—is it possible for those brain cells to function without agitation, without all the turmoil that ordinarily goes on when one hears a word like *death?*

Silence is not merely a quality, a verbal quality, a verbal statement to be realized, but the silence of a mind that has understood the whole process of what we have talked about this evening. Then there is a silence from which all action takes place when one has gone into it very deeply and has done it actually, not theoretically, has responded immediately to the fact of what one is. It is only this silence that can see something totally new, something in which thought has no place whatsoever, because thought is the response of the old. Thought always functions within the field of the known. Only a silent mind, one which is actually completely empty of the known, can perceive whatever is new. It perceives, not as the observer perceiving something outside of itself; there is only perception. Only such a mind can come upon something that has no word, that has no measure in terms of time. Right, sirs!

It is very easy to ask a question, but it is more difficult to ask a right question. In the very asking of the right question, you have the answer. So, it is very important to find out how to put the right question. This doesn't mean that I am trying to stop you from asking questions. To put the right question you need tremendous awareness, attention, but if you were to ask yourselves the right question, out of that attention the answer is there. You don't have to ask anybody. You don't have to follow anybody! So I hope you'll ask the right questions.

Comment: Attention is transformed, is greater at the moment when the observer becomes the observed. . . .

KRISHNAMURTI: Oh, no! The observer doesn't become the observed.

Comment: He observes it in himself.

KRISHNAMURTI: No, sir. Look, sir. There is the observer who says, "I'm frightened, I'm greedy, I'm envious, I'm anxious, I'm guilty." The feeling and the observer are two different states. This is fairly simple, isn't it? The entity who says he is frightened, the observer who says, "I'm frightened"—to him fear is different from the observer. There it is. You can observe, see it for yourself. At the actual moment of great pain you don't say anything. You are the pain! There's not you and the pain. Then later on, a few seconds or a few minutes later comes the thinker who says, "By Jove, I must do something about it." Now, the entity, the observer, is not different from the fear. The fear is the observer. It doesn't mean that the observer becomes the fear or identifies himself with the fear; there is only fear! If you are so aware that the observer is not, but only fear, then you will see that fear is not something to be got rid of or conquered. When the observer is not, fear is not.

Question: If there is no observer, who is aware?

KRISHNAMURTI: Look at the flower. There are no flowers here! Look at the speaker, which you have been doing all evening. Look at the speaker without the observer. Can you look; can you see the speaker who is sitting on the platform, without the observer with his thoughts, with his imagination, with the images he has built about the speaker? Can you? Don't say no or yes. Can you look at your wife or your husband without the image of the husband or of the wife, which is the observer?

Question: Can we not integrate the two?

KRISHNAMURTI: Oh, no! It is not a question of integration. Please don't bring in words. It is not integration. That's a dreadful word.

Comment: One can observe the speaker but the instant the thing is within, it is a different matter.

KRISHNAMURTI: It is fairly easy to observe, see the speaker, or the flower; it is something outside. But to look at fear, at our own petty little demands for self-expression is something else. If you observe, the question then is, who is aware of what is observed? Isn't that it? I'm not talking of identity. What does "identify" mean? I identify myself with my family, with my wife, with my country, with the book I'm writing, or with the picture I am painting. I identify with something. I am different, and I identify with something which is not me, or I identify myself with myself, which is the image of myself. The word implies a dual state. The question is this, sir: If there is no observer—no, the difficulty is that the moment you say, "If there is no observer," the "if" maintains that it is not an actual fact; it's a condition. If I am healthy; but I am not; I am ill. Wait!

Comment: The word in itself is an idea.

KRISHNAMURTI: No, no! It is not an idea! We are trying to avoid phrases, words that have a content of the future and are therefore unreal. What the fact is, *what is,* not 'what should be' is what interests us. When you put the question, "If there is no observer, who is it that observes?" you are putting the wrong question. You should never put the question "If there is no observer." A very healthy man doesn't ask what he will do if he is healthy; he is healthy. He doesn't even know that he is healthy. It's only the ill person, the person who is in conflict that demands, that is seeking, asking, wanting. He is always unhealthy. He can put that "if" question: What will happen if I achieve freedom? But it is a wrong question. You will find out what will happen when you're free, but to put the question while you are still a prisoner has no meaning. In the same way, to put the question, "Who is the observer? What is aware when there is no observer?"—it has no meaning. It becomes intellectual, verbal, theoretical.

Question: If you are in the state of mind where you are completely attentive, does it mean coming into reality?

KRISHNAMURTI: I am sorry; such questions have no meaning. Forgive me. Be in that state and find out! That has much more validity, much more vitality and energy than saying, "If this happens, what will happen?" That's a dissipation of energy and therefore a wrong question. That doesn't mean that I want to choke off your questions.

Question: Is there such a thing as memory of awareness?

KRISHNAMURTI: No, sir; you are aware or you are not. Don't complicate a thing that is so very simple. That's one of our peculiarities; we want to complicate things because our minds are so cunning. We want to play with things; we don't see things simply, and to see the fact, the truth of *what is,* the mind must be extraordinarily simple, uncluttered. Because after all, this simplicity is innocence, and innocence is not a memory. It isn't that you were innocent and you're going to come back to it. Only a mind that is aware, very simply, very quietly, without effort, without determination, without direction—only such a mind is innocent; only such a mind can perceive what is real.

May 26, 1966

Fifth Talk in Paris

This is the last talk. If I may, I would like to talk over with you this morning a rather complex problem, and I hope you will have the patience and the interest to go into it with me. Naturally one has to go into such a problem verbally, with words, with explanations, but the word and the explanation are not the thing; they never are. The symbol is never the reality, but apparently we get lost in symbols, in conclusions, and take them for reality and are easily satisfied by these conclusions and symbols. If we are going to inquire, to examine into something that needs a great deal of penetration, we must be extraordinarily sensitive to words, avoiding every form of conclusion, deduction. That word *intuition,* which is often used, we must avoid totally.

I would like to talk over this morning what we mean by living. I know many of us put that question when we are in great trouble, when we have no special meaning for living and there is despair, a sense of deep, inviolable frustration. Then we put that question with a motive, and when we have a motive the question is already answered. The answer would be, naturally, according to our motive, what we want it to be, what we want the living to be. To inquire into this very complex and rather subtle question, we must examine without motive whatever happens, whatever the truth of the examination may be. Examination ceases the moment there is a motive because the motive projects the answer in terms of our own experience, conclusions, conditioning. To examine this question, which is really quite interesting and needs a great deal of penetration, we must be free from all sense of motive.

That is going to be most difficult for most of us because we generally ask questions for a purpose. We only want to find out, either out of curiosity, which of course has very little meaning, or we want to find out because we are deeply troubled. We are in confusion, agony, deep suffering, and out of this suffering, agony, and despair we put the question. When we do put such a question, if we ever do, we want an answer in terms of our own suffering; we want an answer which will resolve our particular suffering. So, we cheat ourselves, and we cannot find what we mean by living.

To find out what the reality of it is, the real significance, the real meaning, the depth, the beauty, the fullness of it, we must inquire into several things. First, we must inquire what freedom is; then we must find out the nature of time and also what is meant by space. It seems to me that if we don't understand these, we shall never find out for ourselves as human beings, not as local individuals, but as total human beings, what it means to live, what is meant by living. Living surely is always in the active present; the very word *living* means now. It does not mean living in the past or in the future, but in the present. To understand what that living in the present means, we must inquire into the past. We can't just say, "Well, I will live in the present." It means nothing to say, "The present is the only important thing," or to give to the present an extraordinary meaning intellectually, hypothetically, and if one is in

despair to give to the present a philosophy born out of this despair. To understand the present, the living present, one must go into the question of time.

Time is a duration, a movement. It is always flowing from the past through the present to the future. The past is the knowledge, the experience, the conclusion, the tradition, the racial inheritance, and so on. That past, flowing through the present, not only conditions the present, but also brings about the future. What I was is modified in the present—as I am, and what I will be tomorrow. This whole process of yesterday, today, and tomorrow—the conditioning of yesterday, which is modified in the present, taking shape tomorrow—all that is consciousness, surely. All that is within the realm of the known; the known is time, both factually and psychologically. Factually, by the watch, chronologically, the arrangement for today was made yesterday, and tomorrow will be chronologically what I make it today. That's what we are doing all the time.

Psychologically it's much more complex. The whole psyche is made of time, is of time. The whole process of thinking is the result of the past, is the result of the known, as experience, knowledge, conclusions. All that is in the flow of time, and the whole of time is conditioned by consciousness. That consciousness is: I was, I am, I shall be—modified, enlarged, extended, limited. The whole of that is consciousness, what we are, both the conscious and the unconscious. We seem to give a great deal of significance to the unconscious, but the unconscious is the past. It is as trivial as the present of a mind which is conditioned by a dozen yesterdays, or a thousand yesterdays. Both the conscious and the unconscious are very trivial. I don't see why such an enormous fuss is made over the unconscious, why there is this constant inquiry, analysis, trying to understand it. The unconscious is the residue of time—time being yesterday with all its traditions, knowledge, influence, conditioning, propaganda, racial inheritance, family influence. Time is a movement which this consciousness has created and in which it is caught, caught in what was yesterday. That yesterday, modified in the present, which will be tomorrow, is the whole process of thinking.

Please, this is not a matter of acceptance or agreement. If we examine it closely for ourselves, it is fairly obvious. We can go into it more in detail, verbally, intellectually, but the fact remains that all consciousness is conditioned, and conditioning is within the field of time. And so we ask ourselves, "Is there an end to time?" If we are always functioning within this field of time, as yesterday, today, and tomorrow, if all activity is modified by the past in the present and so has a continuity tomorrow, there is no freedom in this process; we will always be slaves to yesterday, to today, and to what will be tomorrow. There is no freedom in that. We are caught in it because we live in this division of time as yesterday, today, and tomorrow; that's our life; that's what we call living.

Is it possible, not theoretically, not hypothetically or in a theological sense—is it possible to be free of time? We'll answer that question, not verbally, but as we begin to examine the other part, which is: Is it possible for a mind which has been conditioned for centuries upon centuries to free itself? It cannot be done by thought because thought is the result of time, and thought cannot free consciousness which is limited. There must be a different action altogether, which is not born out of will, the will being again yesterday, today, and tomorrow—I was, I am, I will be. Is it possible to find out, not theoretically but actually, if time has a stop? If it has not, there is no end to sorrow; there is no freedom for man, and if there is no freedom for man, then he has no space at all.

We only know space visually, the distance from here to our house, the distance from this place to London, or to Mars, to the moon; space between, physical space. A man caught in a small space in a flat, living there for thirty years day in and day out, wants space, physical space. He goes out into the country, takes a holiday far away where there are open spaces, where he can see the limitless sky, the vast sea, deep forests, shadows, and the movement of wind and bird and river. Physically he demands space. Living in a city or town, always walking on pavements and seeing the opposite window and chimney, he wants physical space, but he never wants psychological space. There he is satisfied to be a prisoner. He is caught; he is in the prison of his own ideas, conclusions, beliefs, dogmas; he is caught in the prison of his own self-centered activity as fulfillment and frustration; he is caught in the prison of his own talent.

He lives psychologically, inwardly, inside the skin, being always caught in a prison in which there is no space at all. Having no space, being a prisoner, he begins to think about freedom. It's like a prisoner held within four walls, wanting freedom; it's like a blind man trying to see color. Without having psychological space, not being free psychologically, he has no space at all, and therefore he is always a prisoner. There is surely space between two notes, and that's why one listens to music. There is an interval between two thoughts, which is space, and there is space for most of us because of the object. The object creates space around itself. This microphone has created a space around itself, and it exists in the space of the four walls. Because he exists, the thinker, the 'me', the doer, creates psychological space around himself. His space is self-conceived, self-formulated, and therefore limited. He is never free.

Is this too difficult, or too abstract? Unless one goes into the question rather deeply within oneself—which is part of meditation—there is no freedom at all. There is a center in each human being; that center creates a space around itself, as these four walls create a space within them. This hall, because of the walls, has created a space in which we exist, we sit, we talk. The center, which is the 'me', has created a space around itself, and in that space, which is consciousness, it lives, functions, operates, changes, and therefore it is never free.

It is deeply worthwhile to go into this question because freedom can only exist where there is space, space not created by an object. If the space is created by the 'me', as the thinker, it is still creating walls around itself, in which it thinks it is free. Whatever it may do within that space created by the center, there is no freedom. It's like a man condemned to live in a prison. He can alter the decorations, make himself a little more comfortable, paint the walls, do all kinds of things to make life more convenient, but within those physical walls he is never free.

Psychologically we have created walls around ourselves—walls of resistance, walls of hope, fear, greed, envy, ambition, desire for position, power, prestige. They are created by the thinker. The thinker has created the space around himself in which he lives, and therefore he is never free. Beauty is not only the thing that you see; that's a very small part. Beauty is not the result of thought, is not put together by thought. Like love, thought has no place where affection is. Where there is jealousy, envy, greed, ambition, and pride, love is not. We all know that. But, to find out what it means to love, there must surely be freedom from all travail, all jealousy, all envy. Then we will know.

In the same way, to be free implies no psychological walls created by the center. Freedom means space. Freedom also implies an end to time, not abstractly but actually. Freedom means to live completely today because we have understood the whole structure, the nature, the meaning of the past. The past is the conscious as well as the unconscious. We have understood the whole of that. Because of that understanding there is the active present, which is living. Can this actually happen in our daily life? Can I go to the office without having psychological time, without being a prisoner to greed, envy, and ambition? If I cannot, then I am a slave forever.

The routine, the boredom, the utter meaninglessness of spending one's life in a beastly little office or in a factory turning out cars or buttons or whatever it is for the rest of one's life is a dreadful phenomenon. Though automation and the science of cybernetics will improve man's condition, one will still have to live his life of routine, which has no meaning. Because it has no meaning one tries to escape into all kinds of amusements, including the church. But if one is aware of this total process of living and sees the significance of time as thought, time comes to an end. This comes about not by volition, not by demand or because one wants it, but because one sees the whole meaning of time. One becomes aware of this consciousness, not as an observer, but by being aware, by being totally attentive.

As we were saying the other day, when there is total attention, when you attend completely to something, that is, when you give your body, your mind, your heart, everything that you have, completely—in which there is no resistance, no thought, but complete attention—then you will find that there is no observer at all. Only in the state of inattention does the observer come into being. Inattention breeds the observer. But to be aware of inattention and to be attentive are two different states.

I'm afraid one can't go into it much more in detail. Perhaps this is not the occasion, but if man wants to be free—and he has to be free to find out, to live—time must have a stop; there must be space, not space between the observer and the observed, but space in which there is no observer at all.

If you've ever looked at a flower, what takes place? First you name the flower. You say it belongs to a certain species. Then you say, "I like it" or "I don't like it," "How beautiful; I wish I had it," and so on. Thought, past knowledge, interferes with seeing. What you are seeing is not the flower but the conclusions, the likes and dislikes which you have. Can you look at the flower without the observer? That means to look without the knowledge, the pleasure, the naming, and so on. Then when you look you will see that there is no observer who is looking; then you are directly in communion with that flower.

It's fairly easy to do that outwardly, but to do it inwardly, with your wife, with your children, with your neighbors, with your boss, and all the rest of society—to look, not with the previous insults, information, flattery, but simply to look—then only can there be attention. When there is total attention there is silence. Then you can listen completely to anything, to the song of a bird, to what another says. In that silence you can listen to what is being said, to your own thoughts, demands, fears. You must listen completely, silently. And it's only in that silence that you can listen. When you do listen totally, that which you are afraid of ceases to be.

Living surely does not mean all the turmoil, the ache, and the burden of yesterday, but it means that one has seen the full significance of yesterday. That, one can perceive instantly. One can see the whole of it at a glance, the triviality of all the past. When one is totally aware of the past, then only is there freedom to live in the present. From there one can move, one can enter into a totally different dimension, but that becomes a theory, an idea, if one is not free because it is only in freedom that there is something new. Freedom demands energy, and only when there is an explosion of energy is there something new, which is beyond time.

Question: What part does evolution of the person play, and what part comes back to nature?

KRISHNAMURTI: By evolution we mean to become, to grow, to evolve, to attain—like the seed becomes the tree. Is there evolution? Is there free will to choose, to evolve, to become? Sir, what is the 'you' that is going to become? You will become the Master, the great teacher, the man who knows a tremendous lot, who has a better position in a few years time, more cars, better houses, better clothes, more knowledge. You will become more virtuous, more noble. You who are caught in this little misery of your life will gradually grow out of it and attain bliss or heaven or whatever it is. That's what we are all brought up on; we are fed on that. If you make tremendous endeavors you'll eventually reach something which you call bliss, God, or whatever that is.

You need time, many days, many months—in the Orient they say many lives—to attain the unattainable. Is that so? You mean to say that you want to live in this misery, sorrow, day after day, and gradually get rid of that suffering—in ten years time? If you have a violent toothache, will you say the same thing, "I will gradually get rid of it"—or is there an end to sorrow on the instant, not in time, not in terms of duration? And what is it that continues? If you say, "Well, in ten years time or even tomorrow I will be happy; I will be something different from what I am today,'' what are you today? A set of ideas, memories, words, experiences, the result of propaganda, social influence, economic conditions, climate, clothes, food—you are the result of all that, a bundle of memories. That, you want to perpetuate, and eventually you will grow into some beautiful God, or butterfly.

I'm afraid in that way there is no end to sorrow. Evolution has not made man any more bright, intelligent, free. There have been in recorded human history for the past five thousand five hundred years nearly fifteen thousand wars, two and a half wars every year, and we still carry on with that game. There may be more and better communication, more leisure, better bathrooms, better cars, better clothes, better food, but is there any other progress? Surely, there must be an end to time for something new to take place. That which has continuity is never creative. It is only when time ends that creation takes place, and a mind that depends on yesterday, today, and tomorrow as a means of achieving something lives in utter, hopeless despair.

Comment: I have not quite understood what you mean by inward space.

KRISHNAMURTI: Let's keep it very simple. We live in small flats more and more because it's convenient, and because space is very limited in cities with their factories and their centers of amusement, whether it's the amusement of the cinema or of the church. We want a little more space physically, but we don't want space inwardly. We are closed in by our concepts, by our opinions, by our judgments, by our knowledge, by our capacities. We are held tight and are never free. Freedom means space, both outwardly and inwardly. Outwardly we can go to the moon, into a garden, into the park, into the bois, but inwardly there is no bois. We escape into imagination and talk about God and

all kinds of imaginary things, but actually we have built a wall around ourselves through our self-centered activity. We live in misery, conflict, anxiety, guilt. How can such a center, which has bred all this, be free without space, which means to end all that? It cannot be ended gradually through time, through the evolutionary process. It must be ended immediately, as you act when you see a physical danger; there is instant action. But we do not see the immense danger of sorrow, of our petty little minds struggling to find something which is beyond time.

Question: If this radical change which you have been talking about for such a long time is so simple, how is it that nobody seems to get it?

KRISHNAMURTI: The questioner says, "You've talked a jolly long time, for many years. Is there anyone who is free?" How can anyone answer that question? It is not whether your neighbor is free, but whether you are free as a human being. It is not how to improve society, which is corrupt. You are a part of society; society is not different from you. You are that; you and I have made that. Can a human being—you, I, or another—be free? That freedom is not a matter of time. I think one of the greatest sorrows man has is to think that through time he will become something different. Time only breeds disorder. I wish you could see this simple fact. Look sir, they've preached nonviolence in India for many, many decades because the preachers, the talkers, the doers, the do-gooders realized that violence must stop. Therefore they had the idiocy of an ideology which is called nonviolence, and the ideal is over there. The actual fact is violence, which is here. The ideology has no value at all; what has value is the fact of violence. But if you have the ideology, then in the meantime you're sowing the seed of violence, and that's very pleasant for many people. But if you have no ideology at all, but only facts, you have the fact that man is violent, brutal. Is it possible to end it, not gradually, but immediately? I think it is possible only when you are totally aware of the fact that you are violent, without any excuse, without any explanation, but totally attentive to that fact. To be attentive you need tremendous energy, and one of the dissipations of energy is to think you can dissolve violence gradually.

Question: Is attention the result of self-discipline in the present?

KRISHNAMURTI: That very question implies time. The root of the word *discipline* means "to learn." The very act of learning leads to discipline; the very act of learning is discipline, not that you discipline yourself in order to learn, but learning is discipline. To learn, I must listen. I cannot listen if I'm frightened, if I'm anxious, if I want to get a job out of that learning. The doing is the learning, and the learning is discipline. Sir, if you have listened this morning, that very listening has brought about discipline. For most of us discipline means conformity to or following a pattern, control, suppression, imitation, obedience; all that implies conflict. As a soldier is disciplined to function automatically, we also want to function without deep awareness and just do things mechanically. But learning is doing. While doing, acting, you are learning, and that in itself brings its own discipline.

Comment: In order to learn, one must be very much present and out of time.

KRISHNAMURTI: All right. Learning is beyond time. Unless one does it, one indulges in theories. Please don't give explanations, but do it. Volumes have been written about all this, endless theories have been advanced, but the doer who sees it and acts is far beyond all the words, all the volumes, all the theories, and all the gods.

Question: This state of complete attention, this total concentration of energy, is it permanent?

KRISHNAMURTI: No, madame. How eager we are to have everything permanent! We want permanent relationships, don't we, a permanent wife, a permanent husband, a permanent relationship with regard to ideas, action, everything. It must be permanent, which is mechanical—all the time being certain. Is there anything permanent in life, your ideas, your relationships, anything? Perhaps your house is permanent; even that may not be; there are earthquakes. Is there anything psychologically permanent, including your gods, your beliefs, your amusements? Surely, there is nothing permanent, and yet the mind demands permanency, security, because it's frightened to live in a state of uncertainty. To live in such a state requires a great deal of balance, understanding; otherwise, one becomes neurotic. Only when the mind is not caught in the desire for permanency is it free, because there is nothing on God's earth, or inwardly, that is permanent. Even your soul is not permanent; it's an invention of the priests.

May 29, 1966

Saanen, Switzerland, 1966

────────────────── ✳ ──────────────────

First Talk in Saanen

As there are going to be ten talks and seven discussions, I think we ought to go into many things rather carefully and hesitatingly so that we all understand what we are talking about. Don't be impatient. In one talk we cannot cover the whole ground of life. If you are hearing it for the first time and you want everything answered in the first talk, I'm afraid that is quite impossible. What we can do together is to inquire whether it is at all possible, living in this modern world with all its complex problems, with its travail and misery, with the confusion that exists both within and without—whether it is at all possible for a human being, living in this world, functioning so-called normally, to free himself from the many problems that exist not only around him but also in him. We can inquire whether it is possible to be totally free and thereby perhaps enter into a different dimension of existence altogether.

It seems to me that it is worthwhile and necessary to go into this question, and that requires enormous patience. That demands a great deal of examination and investigation, not from the particular point of view of one's own idiosyncrasies, tendencies, nationality, and dogma, but rather we must inquire into the whole human problem. If we could only understand man as a whole—the man that is living in India, Russia, America, China, or here! Perhaps when we understand the whole of man, we can begin to understand the particular man, which is you and me. To understand such an immense problem—and it is a great and very complex problem—we must understand what it is that we each want as human beings, what we are all seeking, what we are all trying to do. I think that if we could put to ourselves the question of what it is that we are seeking, what it is that we want to experience, how deeply we want to be really peaceful and how profoundly in our being we want to be free, then perhaps we would be able to inquire intelligently. Most of us do want to experience something. Our lives are narrow, rather petty, limited, rather bourgeois, if I may use that word without any derogatory meaning.

We all know that, and we want to go beyond and experience something that is much more vital, that has great significance, that will solve all our problems. I think that is what man throughout the world is seeking. He calls it by different names: religious experience, a heightened sensitivity, great capacity to comprehend the total existence of man, to be free from all this incessant conflict, to find something that is more than the thing put together by thought. Most of us are rather fed up with analysis, examination, inquiry, probing, asking, questioning, doubting. Most intelligent people have been through all that. They have read so much. They know all the answers to almost every question intellectually, but knowledge doesn't seem to satisfy all the questions which the mind puts. It finds an answer for itself which doesn't seem to satisfy completely or to answer the problem totally. The mind is always seeking, seeking to find out what death means, what love means, what right relationship is, how to be free from this constant conflict within and without, how to be free of wars, how to have peace, what freedom means. We are always asking, asking, asking, and in the very asking, in that very questioning, we want someone to reply, someone in authority, someone who knows, someone who has a deep understanding of life. We look to others, and thereby we depend on and are caught in the opinions of the very clever ones, of the ancient teachers, or of the very latest erudite scholars.

We are concerned with opinions, and opinions are not the truth. Discussing opinions has very little meaning. It only leads to dialectical, clever, intellectual argumentation. To find out for oneself as a total human being, it is very important how we put the question, with what purpose we put the question, what the motive is behind that question, because the motive generally answers the question. If you have a purpose in putting a question, that very purpose dictates the answer. Your questioning is already answered, and therefore your questioning has no value whatsoever because you have a motive, a purpose, an intention, a direction towards which you want to go, and you put that question in order to find out if it is right or wrong. A man who puts a question with a motive is really a most shallow person because his answer is already dictated, conditioned by his motive, his purpose, his direction. Can you question without a purpose, without seeking? That is the real issue, and it is very interesting to go into that. Our lives are troubled; we are miserable, confused; we

are in sorrow; there are these incessant wars which threaten security; there are these ideologies, theories, dogmas, beliefs, fears, and all the things that we are heir to. We want all these questions answered. It is a normal, healthy demand to ask ourselves if it is possible to be free of them all, but as we said just now, to put a question with a motive has very little meaning.

Can we put a question and leave it, not try to find an answer, not try to find a solution to our problems? There is a solution, a total solution, a complete answer to all our problems, whether the problem is death, love, the cessation of wars, or all the antagonisms and prejudices of races and classes, all the absurdities of the mind. There is an answer, but it is very important to put the question rightly, and that we apparently find very difficult to do. We are so eager to find an answer, a solution, because we are concerned with the immediacy of existence—what will happen now. Impatience dictates the answer. The answer is invariably comforting, gratifying, and we think we have found the answer.

Please, let us be very clear from the first of these talks that you are not merely listening to the speaker. The speaker has no value whatsoever, nor what he says. What has value is how you understand yourself in listening to what he says. He is like a mirror in which you see yourself reflected. Your consciousness, your daily activity, your unconscious demands, pursuits, and fears are exposed. When you so listen, then you begin to discover for yourself not the ideas, the conclusions, the assertions of the speaker, but rather you see for yourself what is true and what is false. The moment you understand for yourself as a total human being what is true, then your whole problem is resolved; but if you are merely listening to the speaker intellectually, arguing with him, concerned with one opinion, your own opinion, and your own knowledge, or the conclusions which you have acquired from some other person, you are everlastingly comparing what the speaker says with what another has said. You remain in the world of words, in the world of opinions, conclusions, and these have very little value. I hope that you will listen, but not with the memory of what you already know; and this is very difficult to do. You listen to something, and your mind immediately reacts with its knowledge, its conclusions, its opinions, its past memories. It listens, inquiring for a future understanding. Just observe yourself, how you are listening, and you will see that this is what is taking place. Either you are listening with a conclusion, with knowledge, with certain memories, experiences, or you want an answer, and you are impatient. You want to know what it is all about, what life is all about, the extraordinary complexity of life. You are not actually listening at all. You can only listen when the mind is quiet, when the mind doesn't react immediately, when there is an interval between your reaction and what is being said. Then in that interval there is a quietness, there is a silence in which alone there is a comprehension which is not intellectual understanding. If there is a gap between what is said and your own reaction to what is said, in that interval, whether you prolong it indefinitely, for a long period or for a few seconds—in that interval, if you observe, there comes clarity. It is the interval which is the new brain. The immediate reaction is the old brain, and the old brain functions in its own traditional, accepted, reactionary, animalistic sense. When there is an abeyance of that, when the reaction is suspended, when there is an interval, then you will find that the new brain acts, and it is only the new brain that can understand, not the old brain.

I think it is important to understand the operation, the functioning, the activity of the old brain. When the new brain operates, the old brain cannot possibly understand the new brain. It is only when the old brain, which is our conditioned brain, our animalistic brain, the brain that has been cultivated through centuries of time, which is everlastingly seeking its own security, its own comfort—it is only when that old brain is quiet that you will see that there is a different kind of movement altogether, and it is this movement which is going to bring clarity. It is this movement which is clarity itself. To understand, you must understand the old brain, be aware of it, know all its movements, its activities, its demands, its pursuits, and that is why meditation is very important. I do not mean the absurd, systematized cultivation of a certain habit of thought, and the rest of it; that's all too immature and childish. By meditation I mean to understand the operations of the old brain, to watch it, to know how it reacts, what its responses are, its tendencies, its demands, its aggressive pursuits—to know the whole of that, the unconscious as well as the conscious part of it. When you know it, when there is an awareness of it, without controlling it, without directing it, without saying, "This is good, this is bad; I'll keep this, I won't keep that,"—when you see the total movement of the old mind, when you see it totally, then it becomes quiet.

Then you have to go into the question of what seeing is, what observation is, what perception is. I wonder how you see things. Do you see them with your eyes, with your mind? Obviously you see things with your eyes, but you see with the mind much more quickly than with the eye. You see the world much more quickly than the eye can ever perceive. You see with memory, with knowledge, and when you so see things, that is, with the mind, you are seeing what has been, not what actually is.

Please, as I said, do the thing that we are listening to, do it actually as we are listening—that is, see how our minds look, with all our knowledge of the past, with all our miseries, anxieties, guilt, despair, hope, and all the rest which we have accumulated, which is the past. With all that we look, and so when we look at the old mind, we are looking at it still with the knowledge of the old mind; therefore, we are not looking at it at all. To look at anything, and it does not matter what it is—your own mind when it is operating, a tree, the movement of the river, the clouds chasing across the valley—to really look, the past must be quiet. In order to look, all knowledge of your own intentions, your worries, your personal problems, and so on must be absolutely set aside, which really means that there must be freedom to look, freedom to look at the complex time-consuming brain, which is the past, freedom to observe all its reactions and really let it come out. Then you can observe.

We cannot observe if we have defenses, if we have resistance, and most of us have very carefully cultivated these self-defensive mechanisms which prevent our looking. We are Christians, Hindus, atheists, communists, or goodness knows what else—we are all these things and through them, through the activity of the old mind, we look at life, and we never look at the old mind with freedom. It is only in freedom that the old mind responds, shows itself. If I am defending myself, in order to find it out I must be free to look, and it is only in freedom that we can look, can understand. It is only in freedom that the old responds naturally and then we can understand it. It seems to me that we never ask, we never demand to be completely free. We demand conditional freedom, freedom from some immediate pain, anxiety, or problem, but such immediate demand for freedom is not freedom. Freedom implies total freedom. It is only in that freedom that we can discover, as the great scientists do. Only when they are completely free in their laboratories or wherever they work can they

discover something totally new. Outside that they are just like any other human beings.

The demand for freedom and the insistence on freedom will reveal naturally and easily the various conditionings and bondages and defenses which man has carefully built up through time. In that revelation of the past one begins to be free, actually free from the past, both the conscious and the unconscious.

Question: How is one to explore the unconscious?

KRISHNAMURTI: First, what is the unconscious? Many people have written about it with various prejudices, biases, conclusions; but if you discard all of those, discard altogether what others have said—and I hope you will—then you can begin to inquire for yourselves what it actually is. Then you are not dependent on what others say. What is the unconscious? Are you waiting for me to tell you, or are you inquiring? How do you inquire? You can only inquire when you are passionately interested. If you really want to know, not casually, intellectually, or with curiosity, if you really want to know passionately, deeply for yourself what this unconscious is, then what happens? What happens when you are tremendously keen on finding out for yourself as a total human being, rejecting all that anyone has said about it? Then what happens? Your mind becomes very sharp; your mind becomes extraordinary active; your mind is looking, not asking but observing, watching. There is a difference between asking and looking. If you are asking, you want to find an answer, and that answer will depend upon your conditioning, your tendencies, your hopes, your fears. But if you are observing, there is no demand, no asking; you are watching. I hope you see the difference between the two: questioning and observing. Now you are observing, which means that you are completely alive, active, not looking to someone to tell you what it is, and therefore you are not afraid to discover. You are not repeating what someone else has said. What is it that you discover?

Question: How am I to understand the unconscious?

KRISHNAMURTI: Aren't we talking of two different things? You are using the word *understand* in the sense of observe, get to know, become acquainted with, see all its contents, how it operates, how it functions, how it is boiling, the whole of it. I say: Are you discovering for yourself what the unconscious is, or are you looking at it with the knowledge of what others have said about it? Now watch it! Please look at it carefully. If you are looking at it with the knowledge of what others have said about it, it is already part of the unconscious, is it not?

Question: How do we explain to children what happens after death?

KRISHNAMURTI: Madame, we are discussing something entirely different, aren't we? We will go into that question of death and all the rest of it at another time.

Comment: I thought you had finished.

KRISHNAMURTI: Ah, no, no! How can we finish this question in two minutes? You understand what I said just now? If I look at the unconscious with the knowledge of what others have said about it, I am already functioning in the past; I am not looking; and what has been said about it has become the unconscious. I discover that my unconscious is all that has been said about death, God, communism, how I should behave, the race, the racial inheritance, the whole of the past—that is the unconscious. I have discovered it! I don't repeat it; therefore, what I have discovered has vitality.

Question: If we are all that background, the past, who is the observer who is looking at the past? How do we separate the past and the entity who says, "I am looking at it"?

KRISHNAMURTI: Who is the entity, the observer that is looking at the past? Who is the entity, the thought, the being, whatever you call it who says, "I am looking at the unconscious"?

There is a separation between the observer and the observed. Is that so? Is not the observer the observed? Therefore there is no separation at all! Go slowly into this. If you could understand this one thing, it would be the most extraordinary phenomenon that could take place. Do you understand the question? There is the unconscious as well as the conscious, and I say that I must know all about it; I must know the content and also the state of consciousness when there is no content—which is a step further, which we will go into if we have time.

I am looking at it. I say: The observer says that the unconscious is the past; the unconscious is the race into which I was born—the tradition, not only the tradition of society, but of the family, the name, the residue of the whole Indian culture, the residue of all of humanity with all its problems, anxieties, guilt, and so on. I am all that, and that is the unconscious, which is the result of time, of many thousands of yesterdays, and there is the 'me' who is observing it. Now, who is the observer? Again, find out for yourself; discover who the observer is! Don't wait for me to tell you!

Comment: The observer is the looker.

KRISHNAMURTI: But who is the looker? The observer is the observed. Wait, wait! Madame, this is very important. The observer is the observed. There is no difference, which means that the observer is the observed. Then, what can the observer do about the unconscious?

Comment: Nothing!

KRISHNAMURTI: No, madame, this is really a very important question. You cannot just throw it off and say, "Nothing." If I am the result of the past and I am the past, I cannot do anything about the unconscious. Do you see what it means? If I cannot do anything about it, I am free of it! Ah, no, no, madame; don't agree so quickly; this requires tremendous attention. If I cannot do anything whatsoever, at whatever level it is, about suffering—physical as well as psychological suffering—if I cannot do anything about it because the observer is the observed, then I am totally free of it. It is only when I feel that I can do something about it that I am caught in it.

Question: What happens when I cannot do anything about it? Is not the past the present? The mind is caught in that, and what can it do?

KRISHNAMURTI: The present is the past, modified. But it is still the past, which is going to create the future, the tomorrow. The past, through the present, is the future. The future is the modified past. We have divided the past into the present and the future, so the past is a perpetual movement, modified, but it is always the past that is functioning. So there is no present! The past is always operating, though we may call it the present and try to live in the present, try to push away the past or the future and say, "The present is the only existence that matters";

yet it is still the past, which we divide as the present and the future. Now, what happens, the questioner asks, when I realize that the past is me, the observer who is examining the past, when I realize that the observer is the past? What takes place? Who is going to tell you? The speaker? If I were to tell you what takes place, it would be just another conclusion which becomes part of the unconscious. You will function according to what has been said and not discover anything for yourself. All that you are doing when you are waiting for the speaker to tell you is merely accumulating. That accumulation gets modified as the present and the future, and you are perpetually living in the current of time. But when you realize that the observer, the thinker, is the past, and therefore there is no division between the observer and the observed, then all activity on the part of the observer ceases, doesn't it? That is what we don't realize.

Comment: But time is an illusion.

KRISHNAMURTI: Ah, no, no! Time is not an illusion. How can you say time is an illusion! You are going to lunch; you have a house, you are going back home; you are going to get on a train, and that journey is going to take five hours or an hour. That is time. It is not an illusion. You cannot translate it as an illusion. It is a fact that the unconscious is the past and the observer says, "I have to empty the past; I have to do something about it; I have to resist it; I have to cleanse it; I have to remove certain neurotic conditions," and so on and so on. So he, the observer, the actor, looks on it as something different from himself, but when you look at it very closely the actor, the observer, is the unconscious, is the past.

Question: How is one to empty the past?

KRISHNAMURTI: You cannot. You empty the past totally when there is no observer. It is the observer who is creating the past; it is the observer who says, "I must do something about it in terms of time." This is most important. It is very important to understand, when you look at a tree, that there is the tree and there is also you, the observer, looking at it. You who are looking at it have knowledge about that tree. You know what species, what color, what shape, what kind it is; whether it is good. You have knowledge of it, so you are looking at it as an observer who is full of knowledge about it, as you look at your wife or husband with the knowledge of the past, with all the hurts and all the pleasures. You are always looking with both the observer and the thing observed present—two different states. You never look at a tree. You are always looking with the knowledge of the tree. This is very simple. To look at another—wife, husband, friend—demands that you look with a fresh mind; otherwise, you cannot see. If you look with the past, with pleasure, with pain, with anxiety, with what he or she has said to you, that remains; and with all that, through all that, you look. That is the observer. If you can look at a tree or a flower or another human being without the observer, a totally different action takes place.

July 10, 1966

Second Talk in Saanen

Shall we continue with what we were talking about the day before yesterday? We were saying in different words the importance of a total revolution in the mind. We are used to changes in patches, fragmentary changes, and these changes take place either under compulsion, as a means of defense, or for a purpose, a moral, ethical purpose. We all recognize that there must be a fundamental, radical, total revolution of the mind. Man has lived for so long in conflict, within himself and without, in misery, functioning within the borders of his egotism, wars, deception, dishonesty, cruelty—with those things we are quite familiar. Those who are at all serious see the importance of a change, of a mind that can grapple with all these problems and yet live in this world, not withdrawing from it into a monastic life, yet living totally differently. I think we all see that.

One also sees that there are fragmentary changes through the act of will. I want to change. I exercise a great deal of will, effort, and try by perseverance, constancy, and pursuit to bring about a modification, but there is no total change. There is this extraordinary battle going on within oneself, which expresses itself in outward conduct, outward relationship. If one is at all serious, how is one to bring about a complete change in the mind? I'm sure one must have asked this question dozens of times. What is one to do? One knows that one lacks sensitivity, affection, a great, deep quality of genuine affection which is not tinged with any self-interest or self-pity. One knows that one functions within the borders of the ego, the everlasting, self-centered activity. Knowing all this, what is one to do? How is one to break through this boundary of self-defense so that one is absolutely free from conflict, from misery, from sorrow, from all the travail of human existence?

That is what we are going to discuss—whether it is at all possible to live on the instant so completely that time doesn't exist, not to change by slow degrees, not to be free in some future time, or in some future life if there is one, not to think that I will be something tomorrow. How is this to happen?

People have tried different ways, forcing themselves not to think at all because they see that thought is the origin of all mischief. They have tried drugs, of various degrees, that will heighten their sensitivity, that will give a different quality to their actions. They have tried drugs that will drive away all fear so that there is no defense, so that they are completely open, so that there is not the thought of 'me' at all. They have tried so many ways, identifying themselves with an idea which they call God, or with the state, or with some future existence. They put up with constant miseries, sorrows, and anxieties. We all know this; we have tried various forms of this kind. Perhaps it may have a little effect temporarily, for a day or two. But it soon wears off and we are back again, perhaps a little heightened, but back again to the daily routine, to the daily, dull, insensitive existence, putting up with our misery, defending, quarreling, eking out our life until death comes. Again, we know this. We ask ourselves if it is at all possible to totally shed, put away, eschew this sort of existence so that we have a totally different mind, a totally different existence, so that there is no division between nature and ourselves, between another and ourselves, so that there is a heightened, deepened quality and meaning to life. I think that is what most of us are seeking. We may not be able to articulate it, put it into words, but deep down that's what most of us want, not personal happiness. That has very little meaning, but what does have meaning is a life that has tremendous significance in itself, a life in which there is no conflict at all, where there is a total absence of time. Is it possible?

One can ask that question intellectually, verbally, theoretically, but such a question obviously leads to a theoretical answer, to a possibility, which is conjectural, conceptual, but not factual. But if one asks seriously, with full intent and passion, because one sees the futility of the way one lives, if one really asks it, then what is the answer? What is one to do or not do? I think it is very important to ask this question for oneself, not accept the question put by the speaker, because a

question put by the other has very little, superficial value. But if one asks it oneself, in all earnestness and therefore with intensity, then one has a relationship with the speaker and one's mind is willing to examine, to penetrate deeply, without any motive, without any purpose or direction, but with an urgency that must be answered, an urgency that puts away all time, all knowledge and really penetrates to find out if it is at all possible to break through the boundaries of self-centered activity.

We were talking about this the day before yesterday, about the observer and the observed. We were saying that the observer is the observed, that the whole of consciousness, which is the mind, thinking, feeling, acting, ideation—all the turmoil, confusion, and misery in which we live—the whole of that is within the observer and the observed. Please listen, if I may suggest, not to the speaker, but to the fact of your own mind when it hears the statement that all consciousness is divided between the observer and the observed. There is the experiencer demanding experiences, whether of pleasure or the putting away of pain, demanding more and more, accumulating knowledge, pain, suffering, and there is the thinker, the observer, the experiencer, separate from the observed, from the experienced.

There is the one who says, "I am angry." The "I" is different from the anger. There is violence and the entity who experiences the violence. When one says, "I am jealous," jealousy is something different from the entity that feels jealous. When one looks at a tree, or at one's wife or husband, at another person, there is the observer, seeing the other. The tree is different from the observer. The whole of one's consciousness and existence is divided between the observer, the experiencer, the thinker, and the thought, the experienced, the observed. There is a strong feeling of sex, or of violence. I am different from that feeling; I must do something about it; I must act. What am I to do? I must, and I must not. What should I do and what should I not do? There is this endless division, and the whole of that is our consciousness. Any change within that consciousness is no change at all because the observer always remains separate from the observed. Unless one understands this, one cannot proceed further.

When I say, "I am aggressive; I must not be aggressive," or "I indulge in aggressiveness," in that there is the 'me', who is aggressive; aggressiveness is something different from me. I must fulfill; fulfillment is different from the entity that is trying to fulfill. There is always this division, and within this field we are trying to change. We are trying to say that we must not be violent; we must become nonviolent; we must not be aggressive; we must be less aggressive; we must not fulfill. All this is going on within the field, and within this field there is no possibility of radical change.

If there is to be a total revolution in the mind, the observer must cease, totally, because the observer is the observed. When you are angry, the anger is not different from the observer. The observer is anger. When you say you are a Frenchman, a German, a Hindu, a communist, or whatever it is, the idea is the 'you'. The 'you' is not different from the idea. If there is to be a total revolution—and there must be a total revolution—you can't carry on as you are, in endless battle, outward and inward, in confusion, misery, with a sense of guilt, a sense of failure, a sense of loneliness. There is no quality of affection or love. Love and affection are surrounded, hedged about with jealousy, anxiety, fear. There is a total change only when the observer is the observed, and the observer cannot do a thing about what he observes.

Shall we discuss that for the moment? Afterwards I'll continue talking.

Question: Sir, am I the tree?

KRISHNAMURTI: Obviously you are not the tree. You are a complex entity, with your nationality, your tendencies, your ambitions, your fears, your frustrations, but you are not the tree. If you try to identify yourself with the tree, you are still not the tree. You can never be the tree. But if you as the observer cease and only look at the tree without all your conditioning, there is a quite different relationship between you and the tree.

Look, sir. Most of us are violent, aggressive. It is the remnant of the animal in us. How are we to be free of the violence and the aggressiveness? Obviously we cannot be free merely by saying that we must not be violent. That doesn't lead us anywhere because we have merely stated intellectually that we must not be; we are in a constant state of conflict, struggling not to be violent. The very struggle not to be violent is violence. We are not disciplined; we are not orderly, deeply within ourselves; and we discipline ourselves from morning till night. At least many ugly so-called saints do. All saints are ugly. They have forced themselves constantly to discipline, to conform to a pattern, to a pattern which they have established for themselves, or which has been established by another, and they try to beat the record. They are trying all the time, disciplining themselves, and that very act of conformity, discipline, forcing, is violence, from which they are trying to escape. They are not free from violence.

How am I, a human being with the relics of the animal, violent, aggressive, brutal, defending—how am I to be totally free from all violence? If I make an effort not to be violent, I am still violent. If I make any kind of effort to be nonviolent, the very effort to be nonviolent is part of violence. Then what am I to do? I must first see that the entity making effort to be nonviolent is in itself violence. Therefore the entity can do nothing.

This is rather subtle and difficult to understand. Perhaps I understand it verbally, intellectually, but to understand it factually is something entirely different.

I realize that the whole of me is violence, not part of me, but the whole content of me, because I have been trained to make effort, to overcome, to defend, to be aggressive. The whole content of me is violence. The whole of me is violence. What can I do? Any movement towards nonviolence is still violence. Any movement on the part of the observer to be nonviolent is still part of violence because the observer is the observed. If this is really clear, that the observer is the observed, then all action on the part of the observer ceases, and when the activity on the part of the observer ceases, there is a totally different activity.

Comment: One cannot stop the activity.

KRISHNAMURTI: Sir, please do listen to this. We'll take time. We'll go into it slowly; don't be impatient. You look at a tree. What actually takes place? There are vibrations from the sight of it as the eyes look at the tree, and immediately the knowledge of that tree comes into being. You say, "That's a pine; I like it," or "I don't like it; it gives me hay fever, and I must get away from it." You look at that tree with all the background, with all your knowledge, with all your thoughts. You can't stop the thoughts, the knowledge, all the things that arise as a reaction when you look at the tree. What are you looking at? You are not looking at the tree, but at the background which is looking at the tree. Now, don't bother about the tree, but observe the background. How do you look at the background? Do you condemn it? Do you say, "It is preventing me from looking at the tree, and therefore I must stop it; I must break through"? How do you look at it? Do you look at it as someone outside the

background? Do you look at it as the observer and the observed, or do you look only at the background, without the observer? And if there is no observer, is there a background?

The tree has no importance whatsoever. What has importance is how you look, what your background is, and how you look at your background. Therefore self-knowledge is of the highest importance. Without knowing all the reactions, all the background, the consciousness, the demands, the fears, the whole of that which makes up the 'you', without knowing that, it is absolutely useless to try to look at the tree without the observer. What you are anxious about is to see the tree, to try to identify yourself with the tree and to feel something most extraordinary. If you want to feel something most extraordinary, then you should take LSD, lysergic acid. It gives you a heightened sensitivity for the time being, and then there is no division between you and the tree. Not that you are the tree, but there is no division, no time, no interval; there is a tremendous feeling that the whole of the universe is you, and you are not separate from the universe. Not that I have taken LSD!

You must understand the nature of yourself, your tendencies, your idiosyncrasies, your prejudices, the structure of your relationship with another, the anatomy of fear in which you are caught, the urge to fulfill, the urge to be someone with all its frustrations, the pursuit of pleasure, sexually and in so many other different directions. If the mind is not aware of all that, of the conscious as well as the unconscious, then the interval between nature and yourself can never be transcended.

It is very important to find out how you look at yourself and who the entity is that looks. Is the observer that looks at himself different from the thing he observes? Obviously not! The thinker who looks or the center, the evaluator, the judge who looks at himself is manufactured, put together by thought, and therefore is the result of thinking. There is no difference between the thinker and the thought; they are one. When you realize that, totally, not partially, then all the content of the unconscious comes out, easily, because there is no defense, no condemnation, no judgment. It is a movement in which all the background flows and moves, finishes. When anything is in constant movement, there is no resting place, and therefore there is no residue.

That is the real problem for any intelligent, serious man. Seeing the world, seeing humanity, the 'me', and the necessity of a total, radical revolution, how is it possible to bring it about? It can only be brought about when the observer no longer makes an effort to change, because he himself is part of what he tries to change. Therefore all action on the part of the observer ceases totally, and in this total inaction there is a quite different action. There is nothing mysterious or mystical about all this. It is a simple fact. I begin not at the extreme end of the problem, which is the cessation of the observer; I begin with simple things. Can I look at a flower by the wayside or in my room without all the thoughts arising, the thought that says, "It is a rose; I like the smell of it, the perfume," and so on and on and on? Can I just observe without the observer? If you have not done this, do it, at the lowest, most simple level. It isn't really the lowest level; if you know how to do that, you have done everything. Then you can look at yourself without the observer; then you can look without the observer at your wife, at your husband, at all the demands of society, at your boss in the office. You will see that your relationships undergo a total change because there is no defense, no fear.

It is one of the easiest things in life to listen to someone telling you something, to accumulate knowledge, reading books on psychology, on the latest scientific discoveries. You accumulate all that, store it up, and try to utilize it in your daily life, which means that you are trying to conform, to imitate what has been, the past. You are always living in the past. The past is your existence. The existentialists come along and tell you, "You must live in the present." What does it mean, the present? Have you ever tried to live in the present, to deny the past, deny the future, and live completely in the present? How can you deny the past? You cannot scrub it away! The past is of time: your memories, your experiences, your conditioning, your tendencies, your urges, your animalistic instincts, intuitions, demands, pursuits—all that is the past. The whole of the consciousness is the past, the whole of it. And to say, "I will deny all that and try to live in the present" has no meaning; but if you understand the process of time, which is the past, all the conditioning, all the background which flows through the present and forms the future—if you understand this whole movement of time, then when there is no observer as one who says, "I must be" or "I must not be," then only is it possible to live not in the past, not in the future, not in the "now." Then you are living in a totally different dimension which has no relationship to time.

If you listen as most of you have listened to the speaker for forty years or more, you are still caught in the web of time. If you were to listen to your own processes, to your own thinking, to your own ideas, to your motives, to your fears, and understood them totally, not fragmentarily, then you and the speaker could proceed at a level that is not always this petty, little affair.

Question: All my life is a mechanical process. Is not the seeing of that also a part of consciousness?

KRISHNAMURTI: Of course it is, when there is the observer.

Question: What is the relationship of the brain which accumulates daily facts and the new brain?

KRISHNAMURTI: How will I find this out? I need the daily facts; I need to have technological knowledge; I need to have memory to go to my house; I need the memory which recognizes my wife, my husband, my house, my job. What relationship is all that to something which is not mere knowledge, mere accumulation of the past? What relationship has that which is made up of time, which is the result of time, to something which is not of time? There is no relationship. How can there be? How can a routine, mechanical process have a relationship with something which is not mechanical or routine at all? There must be a mechanical functioning and at the same time a totally different functioning which is not of time.

Let us go into this. It requires an understanding of time. The time process is mechanical: yesterday, today, tomorrow; what I was, what I am, what I shall be. Accumulation, memory, identification, the various quarrels, the desire to fulfill—all that is a mechanical process, a time process. That must go on if I am to live in this world at all and function normally. I only know that; I only function in that; I do not know the other which is a dimension in which time is not. People have talked about it; people have said they have experienced it; they have described it; they have done all kinds of things about that and have tried to bring that into this. There must be an understanding of the whole process of time, time by the psyche as well as by the watch. I must understand time psychologically as well as time by the watch.

Let me put it differently. Reality cannot be earned. One cannot say, "I will do this," or "I will do that," or "I will try to observe the observer and perhaps experience something." That state cannot be gained, earned, bought.

All that one has to do is to observe the activity of oneself, become aware of one's own activity without any choice, see it actually as it is.

Question: Is progress in this direction possible without suffering?

KRISHNAMURTI: Sir, in this direction there is no progress at all. We cannot progress towards it. Progress means gradual growth, gradually growing day after day, suffering painfully and eventually achieving something beyond thought. That is how we have been trained; that is how we have functioned, but towards that there is no progress. Either it is, or it is not.

Sirs, will you please consider until we meet again one simple fact? Observe yourself without criticizing, without condemning, without defending. Just observe what is taking place. Just listen to that train going by without irritation, without feeling that it is interfering, that it is a nuisance, and so on. Just listen; watch all the activities of your life, the way you talk, the way you eat, the way you walk. Don't correct the walk; don't correct the way you eat. Just watch, so that by that watching you become astonishingly sensitive. This requires great sensitivity and therefore great intelligence, not conclusions, not experience. To be intelligent you need tremendous sensitivity. There can be sensitivity only when the body is also sensitive—the way you observe, see, hear. Out of that minute observation, without any choice, without any evaluation, justification, comparison, condemnation, you will see that your body becomes extraordinarily alert, sensitive. The whole of your brain, the whole of your mind, the whole of your entity becomes sensitive. Then you can proceed to inquire, but merely to inquire theoretically what is or what is not is of very little importance.

July 12, 1966

Third Talk in Saanen

I think we should be clear that we are not playing an intellectual game. What we are talking about is a very serious affair. I mean by that word *serious* the intention to go through to the very end of what we are talking about. Most of us lead rather superficial lives, lives of immediate concern, immediate pleasures, and immediate profits. When these are satisfied, we look further afield. We begin to investigate, inquire, search out something much more satisfying. I do not consider such a mind a serious mind. A serious mind is concerned not only with the immediacy of all the demands of life but also with the resolution of all human problems, not at some future date, but immediately. It does not allow time to distract; it does not allow any influence to push aside the mind that wants to investigate and live completely and totally. I am afraid that most of us, though we take so much trouble to come here, are not too serious. We are not serious because, first, we do not know what to do, how to set about to resolve the many pressures, strains, problems, and anxieties of life. We are uncertain. Also we are not serious because deep down there is fear. No one can make us certain; no one can give us assurance of a right direction because unfortunately there is no direction. It is like a river that is constantly on the move, passing over rocks, going over precipices, always in motion. The moment we demand to be assured, to be certain, that very demand breeds fear.

If we have gone into it sufficiently to know all this, we want to be assured. We want some authority who has gone a little deeper into the matter to tell us what to do and show us on the map the roads, the bridges, the waterfalls, and where the dangers lie. We think that we do not have the intelligence or the capacity to really find out for ourselves, to uncover, not only the conscious problems but also the unconscious, deep down issues that torture our lives. We are always looking to someone, wanting to improve, wanting to find out the right thing to do. That very desire breeds authority. You and I do not know, and therefore we are willing to follow someone who knows, who can direct, who can guide. Authority, which is bred from uncertainty, breeds further fear. In this vicious circle we are caught. We don't know what to do; we look to someone, and that very look engenders fear. In this way of life we live. A priest, a dogma, or a belief gives us a certain assurance. Therefore we look to certain authorities—the authority of an idea, of a person, of a dogma, or of an organization. In that very process fear is engendered. Is it possible for us to understand the whole process of existence without looking to another, no matter who it is, including the speaker? Is it possible for each one of us as human beings not to look to anyone, to any book, to any philosophy, to any guru, to any teacher, and discover for ourselves as we go along? I say that it is possible. That is the only way to live; otherwise, we will always be followers, afraid, neurotic, uncertain, unclear.

How is one first to be clear? How is one to see and to act so that there is no confusion, and action doesn't breed further misery, further conflict, further darkness? Is it possible for each one of us to look at ourselves and at our problems so clearly that there is no shadow of a doubt cast over the problem, and therefore the problem is resolved totally? If one can do that, then one can go into the question of fear; but one must first understand the demand that each one has, the demand to be certain, to be assured, to be encouraged, to be patted on the back and be told, "You are doing very well; that is the right path; follow it." Is it possible? It is only possible if each human being is totally free and doesn't depend on anyone because he sees the problem very clearly. Problems will always arise, a problem being a challenge and a response. Life is always challenging, and when the response to the challenge is inadequate, not complete, in that inadequate response problems arise. A problem implies something thrown at one, some issue with which one is suddenly faced. If one cannot reply to that challenge totally, completely, with all one's being, with one's nerves, one's brain, one's mind, one's heart, then out of that inadequate, insufficient response a problem arises. All our lives we are trained and educated not to respond totally. We respond fragmentarily. Occasionally when we are not thinking, we respond so easily and naturally that no problem exists. But for most of us problems arise all the time. Can we see what the challenge is and reply to it easily, effortlessly, totally, so that no issue arises from it, whether it be with regard to health, relationship, intellectual problems, or anything else?

First, let us consider whether it is possible for each human being to respond so freely, without any defense, so completely, without any motive that no problem tortures the mind. We are going to go into that because if we can do it, then the heavens are opened. Then—there are no words for it! Then we are not tortured, distorted human beings. Why is it that we do not respond completely, totally? We have asked the question, "Why?" Are you searching for an explanation, for the causes, or without asking why or looking for explanations, are you completely with the question? Here is a question: Why is it that I as a human being do not respond to every challenge in life so completely that there is no friction? I am with the challenge all the time; there is no defense; there is no running away from it. Why? When I ask myself that question, the instinctive response is to find the cause. I say to myself, "I have been educated wrongly; I have too many pressures, too many responsibilities; I have so many worries; I'm so conditioned; all my back-

ground prevents my responding completely." Whatever the challenge is, whether it is an unconscious challenge or a conscious challenge, a challenge of which I am not aware or a challenge of which I am aware, I have explanations; I know the causes. Then I say, "How am I going to get rid of those causes in order to response totally?" What have I done? In trying to understand the causes that prevent me from responding totally to the challenge, in trying to rid myself of them, I have already stopped acting completely to the challenge. There is the challenge, whatever it may be. I know I cannot respond to it totally, and I am investigating why. This lack of response to the challenge immediately creates another problem. If there is any interval of time between the challenge and the response, that interval creates a problem. Whether I am investigating the cause or trying to resolve the cause, that interval has already created a problem.

Comment: If I get rid of the cause, the problem will disappear.

KRISHNAMURTI: If you merely try to rid yourself of all the causes that keep you from responding to the challenge immediately and adequately, you are not facing the challenge completely. You have allowed an interval of time in which you are examining the cause and trying to get rid of the cause. So the challenge goes by, and there is a new challenge. Challenges are not going to wait for you, for your convenience. Your examination or analysis of the inadequacy is unnecessary, has no importance. What is important is that you respond immediately, whether rightly or wrongly, and that immediate response will show you where you are wrong.

Let us realize that life is a movement, an enormous river, with tremendous force, energy, drive, moving, moving, moving. I, the 'me', the human being, am part of that movement.

I, as a human being, have been conditioned, as a Hindu, a Catholic, a communist, what you will. I respond to every movement of life according to my conditioning. My conditioning is so small, petty, narrow, shallow, stupid, and from that conditioning I respond. My response will always be inadequate; therefore, I'll always have problems. I realize that. So I say, "By Jove, I must get rid of my conditioning; I must free myself from all my conscious inhibitions, the traditions, the weight of the past." While I am doing that—analyzing, dissecting, examining—challenges are pouring in on me. I am creating problems because I am not responding. While I am looking to free myself from conditioning, I am creating problems because challenges are always taking place, and I am not responding to them. I see this; I understand completely the waste, the futility of this useless examination.

I am no longer wasting my energy, my thought, my emotion, by saying, "How am I to get rid of it; how stupid to have these conditionings; what am I to do?" All the thoughts which go into this examination become such utter waste of energy. I see that. Therefore I have tremendous energy, and whatever the challenge is, I meet it. I learn as I meet the challenge, not from the background of my conditioning, but I learn as I go along. What has taken place? I am no longer concerned with my conditioning. I am no longer wasting my energy saying, "This is right, this is wrong; this is good, this is bad; this I must keep, this I must put away." Instead of wasting my energy on all that, now I have my total energy to meet the challenge. It is a waste of energy to examine my background, to condemn it, or to encourage it. Now I have the energy which has been previously wasted on examination, on analysis. I have that energy, and with it I meet the challenge. That energy is going to learn to see the depth of the challenge, of challenge as it arises. That energy is always

new. As it meets the challenge, it is not creating a background and therefore creating a new problem. Have you got it? The challenge is being met with clarity because I have the energy to meet it, energy that is no longer afraid of not being able to meet it. That energy now is no longer being dissipated. That energy is freeing the mind from its conditioning, whether it is nationalistic conditioning, communist conditioning, ideological conditioning, or the conditioning of the family, the name. It is breaking through all that. A mind that can meet a challenge with total energy is not creating a problem. It is only a mind that is responding to a challenge with a background, with its conditioning, which is always inadequate, that creates a problem.

If that is very clear, not intellectually but actually, if we do this completely, with all our being, with our total attention, then we can go a little further. Why are we dependent on any challenge? Most of us are asleep; we have taken shelter, refuge, in our ideologies. We have defenses. We want to be safe, secure. We want to be safe in our religions, in our beliefs, in our dogmas, in our relationships, in our activities, and this breeds gradual, sleepy, mechanical conditioning. A challenge comes to wake us up. The importance of the challenge is that it does wake us up, but when we wake up we respond from a background and therefore create more problems. Being unable to solve the problems, we go back to sleep again. Again a problem, a challenge comes; we wake up momentarily but are again put to sleep. This is the way we live. If we see this whole process of meeting the challenge completely, with complete attention, then the question arises: Need there be any challenge at all? Is there any challenge at all? A man who is completely awake has no need for challenge; he has no problems; he meets every challenge anew. A mind that is completely awake has no problems and therefore doesn't depend on challenge to keep itself awake. That can only be understood when we have met the problem, the challenge, with complete energy, not from our background. A mind that has no challenge is completely free, and from that freedom it can go further. We won't go into that because it demands a completely different state of mind.

It is only an inadequate response to a challenge that breeds fear. There is the fear of death; the fear of losing a job; the fear of loneliness; the fear of being nobody; the fear and the frustration of trying to be somebody, becoming famous, through various means; and the fear of not being famous. Such fears breed neurosis, a neurotic state of mind. When there is fear, there is no affection, there is no love, there is no communication. When there is fear, there is a greater defense. When there is fear, the mind invents all the gods, the ceremonies, the rituals, the divisions of people: European, American, Chinese, Hindu. Then the fear begins to invent a peace, a coming together of all the nations. It is fear that is dictating. Fear cannot possibly resolve all these problems. Is it possible not to have fear? We are not discussing this or talking about it at the intellectual level. It has no meaning whatsoever if we consider it as an idea. We can't live on ideas. We can't live on a fragmentary thing called the intellect, on emotion, which again is another fragment, or on sentiment. We are not inquiring intellectually into the ways of fear. We are trying to find it and put an end to it, completely, whether it is with regard to death, with regard to your wife running away from you, your husband neglecting you, or anything else.

Is it possible to be free from fear, not only consciously, but deep down in the unconscious, deep down in our hearts so that there isn't a shadow of fear at any time? If we have no fear, then the gods which the mind

has invented, the utopias, the priests, all the doctrines, theologies, and beliefs—all the idiotic, childish nonsense disappears. Is it possible to be free from fear, not at some future date, not by cultivating resistance to fear—which is another form of fear—not by inventing some theory or belief to hide the fear? Fear cannot be undone through analysis. It is a waste of time when we are dealing with fear. When I am afraid, and the shock of fear comes into being, if I say, "Well, I'll go and find out how to get rid of it," I have not solved the problem. By going to an analyst, examining our dreams, or doing any of the enormously complex things that man has invented to get rid of fear, we have not been able to get rid of it. Now we are asking ourselves if it is possible to be free of fear without all this stuff.

This is a challenge, a challenge to each one of us. It is very important to find out for yourselves how you are responding to it. If you say that you can't get rid of it or don't know how to get rid of it, you have already created a problem. If you say, "Tell us how to get rid of it," then you depend on the speaker, and fear is further encouraged. Or if you say that you had a fear once and got rid of it, but you don't know how, then the memory of that freedom remains in your mind, and with that memory you try to resolve the present fear. How do you meet this challenge of fear, not when you go home, not tomorrow, but now? You are afraid; each one of you has fear, conscious or unconscious. If it is unconscious, revive it, bring it out into the open and expose it. When you have exposed it, how do you meet it? It is really quite difficult to answer that question—how you meet the fear that has been exposed, if you really want to expose it to yourself.

Most of us do not want to expose it because we are so scared, so frightened that we do not know what to do with it. We are so used to running away from it through words, through so many networks of escape that we have, that most of us are probably incapable of exposing the fears that we have, not to someone else, but to ourselves. When we have exposed it to ourselves, it has already become very simple. At least we know that we are afraid. There is no escape from it. If we are afraid of death and do not try to escape from it through theories, beliefs, the idea of reincarnation, hope of any kind, through any of the dozens of ways by which the mind tries to escape from the actual fact, then we know that we are afraid. We have no escape. That becomes a simple fact. It is only when we escape that the complexity begins. I am afraid of my wife, my husband; I have defenses—those defenses are pleasure and all the rest which we will go into at another time. I have avoided the fact. I have never said, "Look, I am afraid of my husband, my wife." When I realize that, it becomes an extraordinary fact, a simple fact. I do not know how to deal with it, but it is there.

Can you expose these fears to yourselves—old age, ill-health, the innumerable fears that you have? You probably cannot expose all of them—you can if you have the intention—but at least you can expose one, the nearest and the dearest fear, and you are with it. How do you deal with it? How do you come into contact with it? What do you do with it? First of all, can you look at it without any turning away from it, without trying to avoid it, to overcome it, to condemn it, but just look at it? You know what the avoidance of a fact is, what it means to avoid a fact. You know how cunning the mind is when it is avoiding a fact. Either it is justifying it, saying, "How can I live in this world if I am not afraid," condemning it, or trying to escape from it. The very word *fear* creates the fear, gives depth to the fear.

Most of you know what it is to be lonely, to find yourselves suddenly cut off from everything, from every relationship, from every contact—complete isolation. I am sure you have all felt this. You may be in the midst of your family or you may be traveling in a bus or in the tube, the underground railway, and suddenly feel completely lonely. That breeds fear. I am going to go through that, examine it, intellectually first, and then see what happens. I am lonely; I do not like the feeling of it; it is a terrible feeling because I do not know what to do with it. It has suddenly come upon me; I am caught in it; I run away from it. I begin to talk, to look at a newspaper; I turn on the radio, go to church, amuse myself in ten different ways. This escape from it creates conflict. The fact is there and I am running away from it, and the flight from it is the fear—the flight from it. There is no fear when I look at it! It is only when I move away from it that there is fear, and I am used to that.

I do not know what it means to look at this emptiness, this loneliness. All I have known all my life is to run away from anything which I do not like, whether it is someone whom I don't like or some idea, some purpose, some thought. I push it away, run away, build a defense. That is all I know. Now I say to myself, "I won't do that because it does not solve anything; the thing is still there; it is like a wound, festering; it is no good putting a covering over it; I must heal it, understand it, go through with it, finish with it." It is not determination to say that I won't escape, because if I say that I won't escape it is a resistance against escape, and that breeds another conflict. If I don't do anything of that sort, then I can look at that emptiness, that loneliness. I am not condemning it; I am not justifying it; it is there, like the rain that is falling on the tent. Whether I like it or not, it is there. It is a fact. Then I can look at it, but how I look at it is the most important thing, not how to escape from it. That we all know; that is too infantile; that has been done for thousands and thousands of years;

that I brush aside because it has no value at all, because I am a serious person and I want to go through with it. I want to understand it and go beyond it. I am not a trivial person, a frivolous person. It is only the frivolous, not the serious person that runs away and thereby creates more and more problems. What is important now is how I look at it. If I know how to look at it, I have resolved it.

How do I look at it? First I see it as something outside of myself. That is what we all do; we see it as something away from the 'me', an object outside of the 'me'. The 'me' is different, and there it is, this loneliness, this isolation. When I look at it that way, the observer then tries to do something about it, tries to condemn it, tries to alter it, tries to overcome it, tries to identify himself with it. Please follow this; it is very simple if you know about it. Be very simple, because life is a tremendously complex problem, tremendously complex, and we can only understand it if we are very, very, very simple, but not childish. If we are very simple, taking facts as they are, then we can go with it, beyond it, and above it; we can transcend it and we are out of it. The observer says, "I am afraid." He is outside of it and therefore he begins to operate on it, consciously or unconsciously. But is the observer different from the thing observed? Please follow this carefully. If the observer were different, he would not be able to recognize it. I must be familiar with you in order to recognize you. Then I can say, "You are so and so," but if I do not know you, I have no contact, no relationship; I don't know you.

The observer knows, recognizes this feeling of emptiness, loneliness, and because he recognizes it, he is part of it. The observer who recognizes it as fear already knows what fear is; otherwise, he could not recognize it. Therefore the observer is that emptiness, that loneliness. Then what can the observer do, who observes, who is that emptiness, that

loneliness? Please do not answer intellectually. Up to now he has been active in doing something about it, but suddenly he realizes that that loneliness is himself. What can he do? Obviously he cannot do anything. Total inaction takes place because he cannot do anything, and out of that total inaction the thing that was is not, which is the most positive action. The positive action has been escape from *what is*. The *what is* is the observer, the seer. The observer can do nothing about it because it is himself.

I do not think we see the beauty of this, the beauty of total inaction with respect to *what is*, the beauty of the total action which comes into being when there is total inaction. For most of us beauty is something outside. An object is beautiful—the mountain, the tree, the house, a face, the river, the sky of a night, the moon with the stars. This appreciation of the object as beauty or not beauty is what is called positive action. To me that is not beauty at all. It is only a very small part, on the periphery. Beauty is this total inaction, and out of the total inaction there is an action which is tremendously positive, but not in the sense of the positive and the negative. That beauty does not depend on any outward object. Only a mind that knows total inaction can see what freedom is and therefore is free.

Question: From childhood there has been a certain sense of fear, a certain sense of enclosure, a stifling feeling that has remained with me from the beginning, and somehow I cannot come out of it. What am I to do?

KRISHNAMURTI: First of all, sir, don't analyze. That is a thing we have done sufficiently, and it is a waste of time. You know why you are afraid. If you do not analyze, question, ask, then you have energy, as I was explaining just now. Then you are full of energy to meet this thing as it arises. The thing that has been there so long, from childhood, is still there, and it will arise when you go out of the tent, or when you are walking in your house. Meet it! Meet it as though you were meeting it for the first time. You will not be able to meet it as for the first time if you are all the time analyzing, looking, and saying, "Why this?" or "Why that?" Only out of innocence can you solve problems, and innocence is a mind that is meeting everything anew.

July 14, 1966

Fourth Talk in Saanen

During the last three talks we have been considering the importance and the urgency of radical revolution in the mind. Such a revolution cannot be the outcome of a planned, systematized intention because any revolution that follows a certain plan, a certain philosophy, a certain idea or ideology, ceases to be a revolution. It merely conforms to a pattern, however ideological, however noble. Human beings have lived for over two million years in a constant state of battle, within themselves and without, in conflict. Life is a battlefield—it actually is—both in the business world and in the intimate world of the family. Any society that is to be created anew, afresh, must surely put an end to this conflict. Otherwise both society and the individual, the human being, will be held in the prison of their own conflicts, miseries, and competition. That is what is actually taking place, both in the recorded history of human beings and at the present time. We don't seem to be able to break through this cage, this prison. Perhaps there are one or two exceptions, but those exceptions do not matter at all. What is important is whether we, as human beings, can really bring about a tremendous change within ourselves so that we are different human beings and lead a different kind of life, without a moment of conflict.

When we ask that question seriously of ourselves, we generally do not know what to do. The psychological structure of society is so strong, so oppressive, so demanding, that as human beings who are part of that society—the human being is not different from society—when we ask ourselves whether it is at all possible, we either become rather cynical, saying that it is impossible, or we escape through imagination into some mythical world which has no reality; or we think that little by little, gradually, slowly, we can change our hearts and minds by constant effort, brutalizing our minds and our hearts. This is what is going on throughout the world, both in the East and in the West. If we don't do any of these things, then we worship the state, or just live as best we can in a world that has utterly no meaning, that is a complete mess, without any significance. That is what most of us are actually doing, although we may pretend to be serious. Our main intention is to find in the midst of this misery, chaos, and confusion some kind of pleasure that is really satisfactory.

We don't seem to learn at all. That word *learning* has great significance. There are two kinds of learning. For most of us learning means the accumulation of knowledge, of experience, of technology, of a skill, of a language. There is also psychological learning, learning through experience, either the immediate experiences of life, which leave a certain residue, a storehouse of knowledge, or the psychological residue of tradition, of the race, of society. There are these two kinds of learning how to meet life: psychological and physiological; outward skill and inward skill. There is really no line of demarcation between the two; they overlap. We are not considering for the moment the skill that we learn through practice, the technological knowledge that we acquire through study. What we are concerned about is the psychological learning which we have acquired through the centuries or inherited as tradition, as knowledge, as experience. This we call learning, but I question whether it is learning at all. I am not talking about learning a skill, a language, a technique, but I am asking whether the mind ever learns psychologically. It has learned, and with what it has learned it meets the challenge of life. It is always translating life or the new challenge according to what it has learned. That is what we are doing. Is that learning? Doesn't learning imply something new, something that I don't know and am learning? If I am merely adding to what I already know, it is no longer learning. It is an additive process, with which I meet life. Let's be clear about this because what we are going to discuss presently may be rather confusing if we do not understand this. Learning surely implies a fresh mind; that is learn*ing*—not having learned, and from what it has learned it now functions, acts. A mind that is learning is always acting, not from what it has already acquired, but it is learning in the very acting.

As we said the other day, life is a movement, an immense river, of great depth, beauty, with extraordinary speed. As I move along with it as a human being, I am learning. I cease to learn when I am merely functioning with what I know already. In that case I never meet life anew; I always meet life with what I already know. That's clear. I have to learn a different way of living, in which there is no conflict, no battle, no wars outwardly or inwardly. There have been so many wars, brutalizing wars, wars that have no meaning. No war has any meaning; there is no righteous war or wrong war. All wars are unrighteous. We have to learn, and apparently we are incapable of learning. Though this present older generation has faced two catastrophic wars, it doesn't seem to learn. We continue to live psychologically in a society in which there is competition, greed, envy, and the worship of success,

which are all indications of conflict, of battle. As a human being I have to learn a different way of living altogether if I am at all serious. If I want to find a way of life which is totally peaceful, I have to learn all about it as though I had never lived before. It is only when the mind is at peace that we can learn, can see, can discover. A mind in conflict cannot possibly see very clearly; whatever it sees is distorted, perverted. Peace is absolutely necessary, not only inwardly, but outwardly. First of all, we don't want peace; we don't demand peace. If we did, we would have no nationalities, no sovereign governments, no armies, but as human beings we have vested interests, and we do not want peace at all. All we want is a satisfying comfort within this field of agony. We want to carve out a little peace, a little corner somewhere within our own mind and heart, and then live in it, in that decomposing, rotten, little ego.

If we really demand peace, both inwardly and outwardly, we not only have to have tremendous psychological revolution, but also we have to learn anew how to live. No one is going to teach us, no philosopher, no teacher, no guru, no psychologist, certainly not the army leaders or the politicians. We have to learn anew about everything—how to live without conflict. To understand conflict and to understand peace, we have to go into the question of pleasure because without understanding pleasure and its opposite, pain, we cannot have peace or live a life in which there is no conflict. We are not saying that we should not have pleasure or that we should lead a puritanical life. Man has tried all those systems, disciplined himself, killed all his desires, pleasures, tortured himself, denying every sensual pleasure, and yet he has not resolved the conflict; he has not resolved the psychological torture. If we would really seriously understand the nature of conflict and the ending of conflict, which is peace, we must go—not intellectually, but actually, factually—into this question of pleasure, which is desire. We cannot be at peace with another or with ourselves if there is no love, if there is no affection. Desire is not love; desire leads to pleasure; desire is pleasure. We are not denying desire. It would be utterly stupid to say that we must live without desire, for that is impossible. Man has tried that. People have denied themselves every kind of pleasure, disciplined themselves, tortured themselves, and yet desire has persisted, creating conflict, and all the brutalizing effects of that conflict. We are not advocating desirelessness, but we must understand the whole phenomena of desire, pleasure, and pain, and if we can go beyond there is a bliss and ecstasy which is love. We are going to talk about that this morning, but not intellectually because that has no meaning. It has no meaning to theorize about desire, to theorize about love, to spin words verbally, intellectually, everlastingly about whether it is possible to live in this world without conflict.

A man, a human being, has no nationality, no religion. A human being is one who is in conflict, in misery, in fear, in anxiety, in great agony of existence over the loneliness, the boredom of life. To inquire into pleasure, you must first have clarity to examine. You cannot have clarity if you condemn pleasure or say, "I must have it," whether it is sensuous pleasure or the pleasure that you derive from various psychological reactions. When you condemn or demand pleasure, you cannot understand it. I do not mean by that word *understand* an intellectual, conceptual understanding, an understanding created by a word or an idea, the idea being organized word or thought. If you function or think in terms of a formula or a concept with regard to pleasure and pain, you won't understand it. You have to look at it; you have to go into it. You cannot understand it or go into it if you deny, accept, or insist that you must

have pleasure because all our social, moral, religious, and ethical values are based on pleasure.

I think it would be stupid to deny that our morality is based on pleasure. Our attitude toward life is based on sensuous delight or on inward, psychological delight. All our searching, groping, wanting, demanding is based on pleasure. Our gods are based on the delight of finding a different world, away from this torture, away from this fear. The thing that we are seeking is based on this demand for some deep, abiding pleasure. It would be neurotic to deny that.

If we would examine it objectively, sanely, with clarity, there must be neither condemning nor demanding it. If that is clear between the speaker and you who are listening—I am sorry that you have to listen, and I don't know why you do listen; we must both be clear that we do want to go into it, because otherwise there can be no revolution. It'll be the same field, but in a different corner, and therefore there will be no radical revolution in the psyche, in the mind itself. Our brain cells and the whole structure of the psyche, of our daily existence, are based on pleasure—pleasure through achievement, through success, through ambition, through competition, through ten different ways. Unless there is a radical revolution in that, we can talk endlessly about change, the need for a new kind of society, and so on, but it will have no meaning whatsoever. We are going to learn, which means that you are not going to be taught by the speaker, and having been taught, say, "I've got it," and from that try to function in a different way. We are going to learn about it. What we are concerned with is the active present of learning—not having learned or I will learn.

Then there is no accumulation of having learned, as an idea or a conclusion from which you are functioning, or from which you are acting. You are acting as you are learning. That is the total difference. Therefore it is not an idea or a symbol or a concept from which you are acting. If you can really understand this, totally, completely, then action has a quite different meaning. Then you are not acting from an idea, from a concept, but acting, and acting has no future.

I don't know if we see the beauty of this because we have always acted from the past. We have ideas about what action should be—good action, evil action, righteous action, action according to certain principles, according to certain formulas, concepts, ideas. We have established these philosophical ideas, or ideas derived from experience, which are concepts. From them we act, and the action is always trying to approximate itself to the idea. There is always conflict between the idea and the action, and we are everlastingly trying to bridge the gap between the two, trying to integrate the two, which is impossible. We are not learning an idea, or a new concept. What we are doing is learning, which is always the active present. If we see that, not intellectually, not sentimentally, not in a woolly way, but with tremendous clarity, then action has an extraordinary beauty and brings tremendous freedom in itself.

We are learning, or going to learn in the sense of the present, in the active present, what pleasure is and why it has become so tremendously important. We are not denying it; we are not becoming puritanical. What is pleasure? There are so many different kinds of pleasure, sensuous and psychological. They are both interrelated. We can't say that this is sensuous and this is psychological, so we are not separating them; we are looking at the whole process of pleasure, whether it be sensuous or psychological.

What is pleasure and how does it take such an important part in our lives? We are always thinking about what will be pleasurable. There is the image, whether it is sexual or of another kind, and there is thought, which breeds this pleasure. We must find out what pleasure is, and learning what pleasure is in itself is the discipline. The root of the word *discipline* means "to learn," not conforming to a pattern, to an order, and all the things that are often called discipline. The very act of learning is disciplining, and the word discipline itself means to learn—not having learned, not suppressing, not practicing something or conforming to a pattern. The very act of learning is the way of discipline, so there is no "I must" or "I must not" have pleasure. What is pleasure? Please, do not wait for me to answer it. We are learning. I may articulate it, put it into words, describe it, go into it in detail, but you have to learn. We are doing it together. Therefore you are listening not only to the speaker but you are also listening in yourselves, observing the question which is put to you.

Pleasure is related to desire. I have tasted a certain food, and I want more of it; it gives me delight. There is sex, the pleasure of a lovely evening, of a sunset, the light on the water as the river flows by, the beauty of a bird on the wing, the beauty of a face, a sentence that awakens a deep delight, a smile. Then there is the desire that says that I must have more of this, and the desire, whether sexual, psychological, or otherwise, which has tasted a certain pleasure and wants it repeated. The repetition comes the moment thought comes into being. Let us keep it very simple because it is a very complex issue. Yesterday evening, among the clouds and in the wind, suddenly there was a spot of sunlight shining on a green field. That light was an extraordinary light, full, rich, and the green had such aliveness. The eyes saw it; the mind recorded it and took great delight in that beauty, in that light and in that incomparable green color. I want a repetition of that delight, so today I look for that same light, that same beauty, that same feeling, which is thought. The act of seeing was one thing, and then thought came in and said, "I would like more of that; I must repeat that again tomorrow." The repetition of that is the beginning of pleasure. When I saw the light on that field there was no desire, no pleasure; there was a tremendous observation and delight. But thought came in and said, "By Jove, how nice it would be if I could have more of that tomorrow."

That is what we are doing all the time. It may be sexually; it may be when someone flatters you and says that he is your friend. Thought steps in and wants it repeated. The beginning of pleasure is the beginning of thought in conflict. It is thought that demands, that creates conflict. My problem is not the delight of seeing something beautiful, but commences when thought says that there must be a repetition. Then the delight becomes a pleasure, and I feel that I must have more of it. The idea of "more of it" is created by thought thinking about it. I see a nice face, a beautiful face with a clear smile, and I think about it. First I see it, and then I think about it. The thinking about it is the beginning of torture, of pain, of pleasure—how to have it, how to hold it, how to dominate it. When I have dominated it, it is destroyed, and I go to something else, and so on and on and on. Can I look at that green field with that extraordinary light and that tremendous rapture of beauty without thought interfering? That is the issue. The moment thought enters, it becomes a torture, a pleasure, a pain, a conflict, with all the results and side effects. Thought destroys that which was beautiful. My problem is not the avoidance or the welcoming of pleasure but the understanding of the whole thought process. I see a beautiful, powerful car. Thinking about it accentuates, strengthens the desire. The desire becomes a pleasure, and imagination and all the rest of it come into being. I must now inquire into thought, into

thinking, not whether I can stop thinking, because I can't, but whether it is possible to understand the machinery of thinking.

This is really a very serious subject. You must give a great deal of attention to it, and you can very easily get tired. You cannot attend for a whole hour with such tremendous energy. If you have really gone into it yourself up to now with all your energy, attention, capacity, with urgency, then your body, your mind, everything is tired out. If you say, "Please go on talking about it, and I will know what you mean then," it means that you want to listen and have me explain; that you are no longer vitally with it. Next time we will go into this again, this thought machinery. In order to understand it, you have to go into the question of time, time as memory, time as the past. It is a very complex problem, and you must come to it with a fresh mind, not a mind that is already tired, weary of life. To go into the machinery of thought, which is memory, you have to go into the unconscious as well as the conscious; you have to understand time—time by the watch and psychological time—and whether there is an end to time. All that is involved in the inquiry into what thinking is. That requires a very sharp mind, not a dull, weary mind that is just curious, that has exhausted itself in an office for forty years. It requires a clear, sharp mind, a mind that can think clearly, purposefully, that does not waver between this and that. It must have the energy to pursue to the very end.

When you have done it, you will know for yourselves what pleasure is, the endless pain of pleasure, and whether it is possible to live in this world—living with tremendous delight, bliss, and ecstasy, not being caught in pleasure and pain. To come to all this, a very earnest and serious mind is necessary, not a flippant mind, not a mind that is full of vanity and says, "I know." Most of us are such vain human beings. To understand all that we are talking about requires great humility, and humility means learning. You cannot learn if you are not simple.

Question: I want pleasure, of different kinds. I resist the pleasure because I know that it is going to bring pain, and I am afraid of pain. Yet my mind wants constant pleasure. How am I to be free, free of resisting pleasure, being afraid of pain, and yet wanting pleasure?

KRISHNAMURTI: It is like a man who wants to fulfill himself, through books, through literature, through painting, through music. He wants to be someone, but he knows that in that very desire to fulfill there is pain, agony, distress, and fear. Yet he wants to fulfill.

What am I to do? I must inquire, not how to be free of fear, of pain, but whether there is such a thing as fulfillment, whether there is such a thing as constant pleasure. The problem is not how to be free of pain, demanding pleasure, but whether in pleasure itself there is not pain. I want to fulfill because it is a tremendous pleasure. I want to be known, to be famous, as a musician, as a writer, as what you will, because in that fulfillment there is great pleasure because I shall be known, my name will be in the papers, and all that silly rot. It gives me tremendous pleasure, and I don't call it "silly rot." I try to fulfill, but there is always someone better than I am, someone better known, a greater writer, a better musician. In that, there is competition, there is pain; I have to play up to people; I have to be a hypocrite; I have to do all kinds of ugly things. All that brings pain. I want to fulfill, and in that fulfillment there is pleasure. At the same time I want to avoid pain. What I have to inquire into is what I am fulfilling, what I am doing.

The whole world worships success. If I have money, position, prestige, fame; if I am someone and am known to a lot of newspaper readers, it is very pleasurable; it gives me a nice feeling, but what is it all about? Is there such a thing as fulfillment; what am I fulfilling, and why do I want to fulfill? I want to fulfill, become famous, because inwardly I am nothing; I am empty; I am lonely; I am a miserable creature, and I put on all the feathers of fame because I have a little technique, with a violin, or a piano, or a pen. I am escaping in fulfillment from that emptiness, from that loneliness, from that everlasting self-activity and boredom, because I have a little technique. That fulfillment is an escape from the fact of what I am. Can I resolve what I am, this ugliness, this emptiness, this self-centered activity with all its neurotic disease and demands? When I can resolve that, I do not care whether I am famous or not, fulfilling or not fulfilling; I am beyond all that stupid stuff. Then pleasure, thought, and pain have a totally different meaning; I am beyond them.

Question: Will you please go into learning while acting?

KRISHNAMURTI: They have found in certain factories that if a man keeps on repeating work in the same way, doing the same thing, he produces less because he gets bored with doing the same repetitive thing, but if he is allowed to learn as he is doing, he produces more. That is what they are discovering, so they let the worker learn as he is doing.

Look at it the other way. Most of us have ideas. To us ideas, formulas, concepts are tremendously important. Nationality is an idea. The Negro, the Hindu, the white are ideas. Though those ideas have produced certain terrible activities, for us ideas, ideologies, formulas are tremendously important, but action is not important. We act according to those concepts, those ideas; we approximate action to the idea. There is always a division between the idea and the act, and therefore there is always a conflict. A man who would understand and end conflict has to understand whether he can act without idea; he must be learning as he is acting.

Let us take love. It is not a simple thing; it is quite complex. We do not know what love means. We have ideas about it—that we must be jealous to love, that love is divided into divine and human. We have many ideas. To find out what it means, the depth of it, the beauty of it, whether there is such a thing as love—which has nothing to do with good works, with sympathy, with tolerance, with gentleness, although all those may be included in it—if I really want to find out, I must throw away all my ideas about it, and in the throwing away of all my concepts about love I am learning about it. That is all.

July 17, 1966

Fifth Talk in Saanen

I often wonder why you listen and I talk. Are we exchanging ideas, concepts, or are we taking a journey together, exploring, examining what we discover, so that it is not a case of speaker and listener? Is it that you want to be taught, either what to think or how to think, or do you want to gather information and data which you can add to what you have already collected during your lives? Perhaps it might help somewhat to overcome our various problems—and I am sure it would be rather interesting—if each one of us could find out why we listen to this particular speaker, what it is that we are groping after, what it is that we are seeking, and why we seek at all. If each one of us could discover for ourselves in the privacy of our own minds and hearts what it is that we are after,

then perhaps the journey that we are taking together would have some significance. There must be in ourselves and therefore in society a radical mutation, a revolution in our whole way of thinking, living, acting. If that is not clear, then our journey together will have no meaning whatsoever.

We see how immature the political, the religious, the economic activity is that is going on all about us. There is only one political problem, the unity of mankind, and no one seems to bother about that. There is a great deal of talk about it, but to bring it to fruition there must be not only an economic change, a psychological change in the social structure, but also in the whole structure of the psyche, of the mind. That is what we are going to talk about this morning. We are going to inquire into what thinking is, what the mind is, what the whole of consciousness is. First of all let us be very clear that we are not dividing consciousness into various departments, fragments, as the conscious, the unconscious, and all the various interpretations of that. There is only one state, what we are, the whole of ourselves, of which we know so little, which we have not penetrated deeply— the whole of our psychological structure, our reactions, our limitations, our conditionings, our longings, our brutalities, our violence, and so-called love. Unless there is a great revolution in the whole structure of our being, our lives will always be immature; there will always be sorrow of some kind or other; there will always be conflict, misery, and confusion. Merely listening to some description, some explanation, some theory will in no way alter the fact of what we are.

Again, how is it possible to bring about a mutation in what we are? That is our whole concern. I am like you, like everyone else in the world. We are the products of environment, of the society in which we are born, of the religions, which have made such propaganda, brainwashed us to believe and not to believe.

We are the result of all that, and to bring about a change within the limitation of that is no change at all. Change surely implies transcending, or going beyond this limitation. How is that possible? What are we to do? Learning is neither suffering nor pleasure. When you are learning there is no division as something which you like or don't like, which you resist or which you hold on to. You just learn, and it seems to me that one of our difficulties is that we don't see the importance of learning, discovering, finding out for ourselves. That is not possible when we are thinking in terms of pleasure and pain, resistance or repression. Learning is only possible if we can look at ourselves as we are, not according to some philosophy, or to some speculative, theological concept, but see what actually is. If we can put away all that, then we can examine what we actually are; and in that examination we are learning. There is no learning if we are merely accumulating. If we learn a language, accumulation is necessary as knowledge or as skill. But when we are learning about ourselves, the totality of ourselves, our reactions, the way we think and why we think that way, our motives, the various influences that we are prone to, the fears, the anxieties, the guilt, the sense of oppression—all that we are—if we cannot look at ourselves clearly, it is not possible to bring about a radical change at the very root of ourselves. As we said the other day, it is very important how we look at ourselves.

Have you ever tried to look at yourself? The 'yourself' is never constant; it is always in a flux, in a movement. If you look at it with a concept, with a fixed idea, then you are merely interpreting it according to pleasure and pain. But if you can forget, put away, slough off this concept of what you should be or ought to be and have not been, if there is no censor, then you can look at yourself. Then you can follow the movement

of every thought, every feeling. This morning we are going to consider the nature of thinking. As a means of bringing about a change in ourselves, we have used thought: thought as desire, thought as will, thought pursuing an idea according to which we must conform, thought as time. Thought says, "I am this, or I have been this and I will be that." Thought itself has become the instrument which hopes to bring about a revolution within—thought being the response of memory, which is the accumulation of centuries of experience of humanity, and of the particular individual.

We are that background—it is us—and to any challenge, to any questioning, to anything new, we respond according to that background, according to our conditioning. Can thought as will, as desire, as gaining, as losing bring about a revolution in us? If thought will not, then what will? We know what is meant by thought bringing about a revolution, a change. I say to myself, "I am this," whatever it is—afraid, envious, greedy, pursuing my own personal satisfaction, functioning in a self-centered activity. I see that, and I say to myself, "I must change because it is too painful; it is too silly; it is too immature; there is pain." I exercise will, suppression, control, discipline, which is the functioning of thought, and I see that I don't change at all. I move in another part of the same field. Perhaps I am less irritable, a little more this and a little less that, but thought has not revolutionized my psyche, my whole being. You must have noticed that, too. Thought only breeds more conflict, more pain, more pleasure, more struggle. So what will bring about a change, a revolution within this field?

When you ask that question of yourself, what is the answer? How do you answer it? You have struggled all your life. If you have enough money, you go to an analyst. If you haven't, you go to a priest. Or if you do neither, you watch yourself, control yourself, discipline yourself—you will do this, you will do that, ten different things. Yet out of that struggle there is no flowering; there is no beauty; there is no freedom; there is no peace. You end up in a dead end. You all know this if you have gone through this inquiry. Then what will bring a change? How will you answer that question? It would be very much worthwhile if each one would answer that question for himself, answer it and not wait for someone else to tell him. If you are waiting for someone else to tell you, you are not learning. As I said, we are taking a journey together. There is neither a teacher nor a follower; there is no authority; there is only the privacy, the solitude of your own inquiry and discovery. If you discover for yourself, then out of that discovery a new energy is born, a new resurgence. But if you are merely waiting for someone to tell you, then you are back again in the old rut that has very little meaning.

How do you answer this question? You are taking a road, going to some place, to your home. You ask someone and he tells you that you have taken the wrong road. You have walked a long, weary way, and you discover that the path or road doesn't lead to where you want to go. You make several inquiries, and you find for yourself that the road doesn't lead anywhere. Then what do you do? You stop, turn around, and take the other road, but first you stop. First you empty your mind, or rather the mind empties itself, of all the patterns, of all the formulas. It empties itself of all the strongholds of memory, and the very emptying of the whole being is the process of revolution. But no one can empty a mind that is so committed that is always occupied, that is never empty. A mind is empty that has listened, watched, observed all its movement, the total movement, which can be done in a flash. When you have observed it and have seen the futility of this everlasting thought as an instrument which can bring about a revolution, then naturally when you see all that, you turn your back on the old road. This can only take place when the mind, the whole psyche is completely empty. That emptiness is maturity, and out of it there is a totally different dimension of activity and living.

You have listened for about half an hour to what has been said, and where are you? Is there an idea, an idea being rationalized thought? Is there a coming to a conclusion and trying to agree or disagree with that conclusion, or to develop it? If you are doing that, it is still within the field of self-centered activity as thought, but if it is an actual learning, a thing that we are learning together—not accumulating and then according to that accumulation acting, but learning as you are going along—then you will see for yourself this act of maturity, which has nothing to do with physical age. This act of maturity is the mind which is not occupied at all, and therefore there is no problem.

The mind becomes the soil for a problem. The problem then takes root. After it has taken root we wonder how we are going to resolve the problem. If we meet the problem and resolve it instantly—not a mechanical problem, not a technological problem, not a problem of skill, but the human problem, the problem of our anxieties, despair, the ten different problems that we have—if we meet it instantly and not give an interval between the fact and what we should do about the fact, there is no soil in which any problem can take its root. Our minds, our hearts, our whole beings are full of unsolved problems because we never come into contact with any of them directly. We are frightened. To come into contact with anything, with nature, with the extraordinary beauty of a mountain, we must come very close to it. If we are at a distance or at a great height, all mountains look alike, flat, with one or two peaks sticking out, but when we come very close, then we begin to see that there are valleys, that there are waterfalls. We see the rock, with its shape, and the beauty of a line. When we are very near, we are very closely in contact with what we see. Unfortunately we never allow ourselves to come into close contact because we have isolated ourselves, repressed ourselves, and so ten different defenses exist that we have built up.

All these defenses, repressions, fears drop away on the instant—and we are using that word on purpose—immediately, when you come into contact with them directly. You can come into contact with them only when thought has been understood, when you have seen a certain importance of it in certain fields, when there is this emptiness of observation. You can only look when you are empty, when you are not occupied, when you are not committed. You cannot look at nature, at a tree or a flower, a mountain, a river, the sky, when your mind is full of thought, preoccupied, concerned; when the mind is tortured by its own pettiness, its own disease and anxiety.

What can you do actually about self-centered activity? One of the most difficult things to realize is that there is nothing you can do to bring about a change. When you are confronted with a problem, and you look at it completely silently, without any commitment, then you are immediately in contact with it, not as the observer and the observed, but with the fact of *what is*. Then you will see for yourselves that there is a tremendous change which is not brought about by thought, by pleasure, or by the avoidance of pain.

Question: *Thought goes on and on and on, all the time, endlessly. How is it possible to put a stop to it?*

KRISHNAMURTI: If I say, "I don't know," what will you do? I really do not know. Sir, listen carefully to what is being said. So many ways have been tried—going to a monastery;

identifying ourselves with some image, theory, or concept; through discipline, meditation, forcing, suppressing, trying to put an end to thought. Man has tried everything that is possible, tortured himself in a thousand different ways because he realizes that to think is to be full of sorrow. How is it to be done? There are several things involved. The moment you make an effort to stop it, then it becomes a problem. There is a contradiction. You want to stop it, and it keeps on and on and on. That very contradiction breeds conflict; all contradictions breed conflict. So, what have you done? You have not ended thought but you have introduced a new problem, which is conflict. Any effort to stop thinking only feeds, gives more energy to, thinking. You know very well you have to think. You have to exercise every energy that you have to think clearly, spotlessly, to think sanely, rationally, logically. Yet you know that sane, rational, logical thinking does not stop thought. It goes on and on.

What are you to do? You know that any form of repression, any form of discipline, suppression, resistance, or conformity to an idea that you must stop thinking is a waste. You put all that aside. Have you? If you have, then what will you do? You will do absolutely nothing! First you think you must stop it. That is an idea and behind that there is a motive. You want to stop it because thought has not solved the problem. So can the mind—not just a part of it, a certain fragment of it, but the totality of the mind, in which is included the nerves, the brain, the feeling, everything—can the mind realize that it can do nothing about it; and then, will it go on? You will find it will not go on.

Comment: *I must have looked at the problem the wrong way.*

KRISHNAMURTI: Sir, you have a problem, a mathematical problem, a personal problem; you have gone into it, investigated, searched out, talked it over, and you cannot find an answer. Then what happens? You just leave it, don't you? But it is very important to find out how you leave it. If you leave it out of despair, out of fear, out of some motive, then your mind is still occupied with the problem. But if you leave it alone because you have looked at it in every possible way, then you leave it completely alone, which means that your mind is no longer occupied with it, afraid of it, wanting to find an answer, wanting to escape from it. Then, if you leave it alone, out of nothingness the answer is there. Haven't you noticed this about trivial things? If you have a mathematical problem or a human problem with which you have wrestled without finding a solution, if you then say, "I cannot do anything more"; therefore, it matters very much how you say, "I can't do any more"—out of that you will find that suddenly thought comes to an end.

That introduces quite a different issue. Thought must be used. We all agree to that. Thought has its value, its importance, its place. Can a human being live in a state of mind which is so tremendously active that it is empty? A highly tuned drum is always empty inside and when you strike it, it gives the right tone. Is it possible for the mind to be so totally empty? I hope you understand what I am talking about. It is not just some vague, dreamy, mystical thing. It is only out of emptiness that you can see the beauty of life, the beauty of a tree. You cannot see if you are not empty—with no commitments, always learning, not accumulating, observing, awake, being aware without any choice, therefore giving tremendous attention. Have you ever noticed that when you are completely attentive, with your nerves, your mind, your heart, your ears, you understand? In that intense attention there is no thinking. It is only when you are inattentive that the whole circus begins.

Question: What is the difference between the process of thinking and thought?

KRISHNAMURTI: Surely there is not much difference. Do not divide everything into such divisions. The process of thinking is that I ask you a question with which you are familiar, and if you are very familiar with the answer, your response is immediate; if you are not familiar with it there is a time interval, a lag between the question and the answer; memory is in operation; you are asking, looking, waiting. The whole of that process produces a thought, an answer. When you come to the point where you say that you really do not know how to stop thinking—you are not waiting for someone to tell you; you really do not know—then you have stopped thinking, haven't you? When you say, "I really do not know the answer to this question; for the first time I listen to it," out of that innocency of not knowing, thought—which is not innocent—comes to an end.

Question: When you are talking, are you thinking?

KRISHNAMURTI: Not very much, I'm afraid. Of course, as we are talking in English there is the memory of the language and the use of that language to communicate as clearly as possible; there is that thought, but the questioner wants to know, "Are you thinking in any way different from that; are you thinking when you are talking?" If you are thinking as you are talking, then you become repetitive. If you are not thinking but speaking out of that emptiness, then the words may be repetitive, but the context, the thing that is being said is fresh, is something new; it has a totally different vitality.

Question: There are wars. There is hatred. The newspapers are full of the filth of brutality, political chicanery, and so on and on and on. Should we keep an open, empty mind and look at all that without judgment?

KRISHNAMURTI: First of all, is that possible? There is a war going on in Vietnam. People on both sides are getting hurt and being killed. You are, let us say, an American or a Vietnamese. You have your reactions. You are a pacifist and you don't want to kill a thing, or you are a communist and you want your side to win. We are always taking sides, aren't we?

Comment: We should cut out taking sides.

KRISHNAMURTI: No, no, no! Don't cut out anything. Don't say, "I must not take sides; I must be this and I must not be that," but see what actually one is. One is nationalistic, one is committed to a certain pattern of life, as the American way of life or the Hindu way of life and goodness knows what else. One is committed as a communist, a socialist, a laborite, and with that background, with that conditioning one is bound to react. What is one to do? If the reaction is very strong, then one begins to hate the Vietnamese or the Americans, or one becomes a pacifist, or this or that. None of that is going to stop wars. Emphasis on Americanism or Tibetanism or whatever it is, is not going to stop wars. What will stop wars? That is the fundamental question. What will stop this hatred, this violence that is going on in America between the Negro and the white, in many places between the communist and the bourgeois? What will stop all this? It is recorded in history that man has had fifteen thousand wars in the last five thousand five hundred years. That means two and a half wars every year. Human beings are committed to a life of violence, ambition, greed, competition, the search for fame, the prestige of the nation. All that is violence. How can one, a human

being—not an American, a Vietnamese, a communist, not the label, but as a human being, which is you and me, whether one lives here or there—how can one put an end to violence?

That is the question, not to take sides, this or that, but how can we end violence? It cannot be ended through an idea of nonviolence. This is rather difficult. Let us go into it. I am violent, as a human being. I am ambitious, greedy, envious, competitive, self-centered, by the very nature of my being. My very brain cells are the result of centuries of animalism, and I am violent. After reading history, after suffering, I say, "I must not be violent; violence does not lead anywhere." I want to be free of violence, and I think that by having an ideal of nonviolence, I can use that ideal as a lever to get rid of my violence. It never takes place.

What will free us is not the ideal of nonviolence but the fact of violence, knowing the fact of *what is,* not the idea of what it should be, which has been tried many times. They have preached endlessly about nonviolence, in India and everywhere else; every religion has talked about nonviolence, saying, "Be kind; be gentle; don't hurt; love one another." Religions have not produced peace; on the contrary, there have been religious wars. What can bring about an end to violence is looking at it, facing *what is,* which means no nationality.

Comment: War is the process of history.

KRISHNAMURTI: Yes, madame. I know all this. India was overrun by the Chinese, and when we talked on this subject in India, they said, "What are you talking about? We are being attacked; therefore we must defend. An army is necessary." We are back again. The movement of hate, of war, will go on unless all of us see that hate cannot possibly end through hate, through defense. If we went and talked to the Vietnamese about not hating, they would throw us in the river or shoot us because they would think we were pacifists. That is what we mean when we say that there must be a total revolution in the mind so that we are no longer Christians, Buddhists, Catholics, communists, Americans, Hindus, Germans, and Italians—we are human beings. The unity of man is what matters, not one country against another country.

July 19, 1966

Sixth Talk in Saanen

I think this morning we should consider the question of action. We should go into it rather deeply and see if we can find and learn an action which is not contradictory, a life in which there is no conflict of the opposites, no contradiction. Most of us live a private and a public life. A public life is broken up into fragments; we live in public with different masks, different attitudes, different poses. We have so many masks; we put them on very easily and take them off only in the privacy of our own minds and hearts. In private life, if one is at all serious or if one is aware, there are also various masks. With friends we put on one mask; in the intimacy of the family we have another mask, and if we are ever alone, we have a totally different mask. Each mask is in contradiction to the others, both the public and the private. Most of us are not even aware of these masks. We just drift, adjusting ourselves to various influences and pressures, acting and reacting according to what these masks dictate. We live a life of contradiction and conflict until we die. None of these states seems to be permanent; each one has its own life, its own activity; and we become aware of them only when there is a great conflict, a crisis. Then we try to find out what to do, how to act, and strangely, each

phase, each mask dictates its own discipline, its own activity, its own way of life.

If we are at all serious, we become aware of that, and we try to integrate all these different contradictions. The more we try to bring these together into some kind of unity, the greater the conflict, the greater the contradiction. I think most of us know this; most of us know the various pretensions, the vanities, the assumptions that we each have, both public and private. If we take away these masks, what is left? If we are serious and earnest about the matter, we should find out not only what these pretenses are, with their vanities, their hypocrisies, their contradictions, their activities, each in opposition to the others. We should also find out for ourselves if we can strip all these away and see *what is*.

When there is no pretense, when there is no mask, when there is no assumption of what should be and what should not be, when we have put away all influences, social, political, economic, climate, food, and all the others, then we should find out not only what is left but if we can live with what is left. It is important to go into this matter. If we lead a noncontradictory life, a life in which there is no effort, and therefore no contradiction whatsoever at any level, then only is there freedom. It is only in that freedom that there is peace and a flowering of something totally new, a new joy, an ecstasy, a bliss that is not of desire and pleasure.

We only take off the masks when we are absolutely alone in the deep privacy of our minds and hearts, but if we could, this morning, uncover for ourselves the pretenses, the masks that we put on when we meet strangers and when we meet intimate friends, perhaps we would find out for ourselves what real action is. Perhaps we would also find out whether it is possible to live in this world, go to the office, run a house, be related to a husband or a wife, carry on all our social activities, and at the same time live a life which is whole, total, so complete that there is not a breath of contradiction or conflict. In the learning of that there is great beauty. In that beauty there is great joy, but to understand it we not only have to go into this question of desire, which is pleasure, but also we must forget totally this fashionable and commonplace assertion of the unconscious.

It has become the fashion to talk a great deal about the unconscious, to go into it, interpret the various motives, pressures, hidden demands, and hints. In setting aside what is called the unconscious, we should also be totally free of all dreams, except the physical dreams that take place when we have overeaten, or something of that kind. We have a great deal of work to do together this morning if we would go into this question of a life, of an action, in which there is no contradiction whatsoever. If we can find that out, if we can learn about it, then we can go beyond pleasure, beyond desire, and come upon something which is joyous, which is great bliss. We cannot come upon it without understanding these contradictory states of our existence, with all their various subtle forms, masks, pretensions. This morning, if we may, we are going to go together, explore and learn. It is not a matter of being told what we should discover, what we should not discover, what the masks are, what the pretensions are, but of becoming aware of it. If we discover for ourselves, that very discovery releases great energy for further discovery.

Let's begin. At first we are going to learn together. We are going to learn by exposing ourselves to ourselves because this is not a mass meeting or gathering, with someone who is analyzing the whole thing, and you just listening. I don't feel at all like that; it is too ugly, too silly. If we are neurotic, unbalanced, perhaps it might be useful to go into a little analysis, and perhaps most of us are a little unbalanced, but the discovery of

the cause and the analysis do not bring about a freedom from the fact. In discovering the fact, and giving full attention to the fact of what discovery is, there is no analysis, there is no time interval to examine, to discover what the cause is. When we give total, complete attention and find for ourselves or learn for ourselves *what is,* we undergo a tremendous revolution, and that's what we are going to do together this morning. In attention there is no thought; there is no time; there is no observer and the observed. If we give complete attention to something, it doesn't matter what or where it is—in the kitchen, when we are listening to something, when we are reading, or when we are looking at the beauty of a sky in the evening—if we give complete attention, with our hearts, with our minds, with our nerves, with our ears, with everything that we have, then in that we will see that there is no observer; there is no observed; there is no time interval in which to examine. In that attention there is nothing; even the fact disappears.

That's what we are going to learn, not only to uncover the various masks, the pretensions, the defenses, that we have so carefully and cunningly developed, but to see and learn whether it is at all possible, living in this world—which is an ugly, confusing, miserable world of destruction and brutality—whether it is possible to live without a mask, without resistance, and therefore act totally, without contradiction. I hope it is clear that the unconscious, as it is called, has no meaning whatsoever. There is only an awarenes as you enter this tent, an awareness of all the colors, the faces, the people, an awareness in which there is no choice. If we are just aware, as we are when we look at a flower, or when we listen to the noise of that airplane overhead, if we just listen to it totally, neither resisting it nor getting irritated with it, just listening completely, there is no unconscious. It becomes such a trivial affair.

We have laid the ground for the examination of the mask, of the pretense. Can I, can you be aware without condemning, judging, justifying; just be aware of our masks, of our pretensions? Unless we really are aware of this, to go further into it becomes impossible. As we uncover these various masks and pretensions, we will come to a point where we are absolutely nothing. That is frightening because most of us don't know what it means. We only know it verbally. We have looked at it from a distance, with a little apprehension, or we are fed up with our lives, with our relationships, and we want to isolate ourselves, put away everything and be alone, which is only a reaction. If we actually, factually are aware of each mask, or if we see instantly the whole fabrication of making masks, we are free of them instantly. There are two things involved. Either we uncover each mask, each pretension bit by bit, day after day, or we uncover the whole process of it instantly. If we uncover little by little, gradually, that obviously takes time. A gradual process involves time, and in that interval between the little bit that we uncover today and what we uncover tomorrow, a new mask has come into being.

It is very difficult for most of us to see that there is no such thing as gradual understanding, gradual seeing, gradually acquiring deep meaning. We are conditioned to accept a gradual evolutionary process. Most of us are nationalists, English, German, French, Italian, Indian, Chinese, and we say that we will gradually become internationalists, European or American. After becoming international we will become supernational, and then ultimately there will be unity of man—when we are all dead, when we have all murdered each other, when every country with its politicians has wrecked the world. We say that ultimately there will be some unity, but it never takes place.

If you see the nature of nationalism, the whole content of it, not merely the verbal, not just the flag-waving, or the pacifist, but the whole process of it, if you comprehend it totally, it is finished. You no longer belong to any country, any group, any race; but to do that you must give attention. That means that you must no longer be lazy, indolent, and be caught in this gradual stuff. Either you see the whole process, the whole fabrication of this mask-making, of these pretensions, immediately, or you don't see it at all. Don't say, "I will gradually understand it; like peeling an onion, I will gradually undo peel after peel, take off skin after skin." Don't say to yourself that you will do it gradually. Either you see it instantly or you don't. If you don't, leave it alone. Don't say, "I must see it; I must force myself to see it; I want a different kind of life." You won't get it. It doesn't happen that way. It is like a person who is rich but pretends that he is poor. It is a mask; he takes comfort in the mask. If you are rich, don't pretend. Then it is finished. What is important is not to have conflict.

You have to find out or learn for yourself whether you see the whole structure, the machinery of pretension, whether you see it totally, immediately, or whether you don't. If you don't, find out why you don't. Perhaps you are frightened. Perhaps you say, "I don't know where it is all going to lead me to. I have built so many resistances, so many defenses behind which I take shelter, and you are asking me to break through all that. Where will it lead me to? Guarantee me that I will find something which is far beyond all this." Then you are willing to break through, if you have any faith at all left, and most of us fortunately have no faith in anything.

Discover for yourself and learn for yourself why you live behind masks, pretensions. That is not very difficult to discover. It is because you want to be thought, oh, so many things that you are not. You want it to be thought that you are a great man, a great writer, a great this or that. You don't want to have what you are discovered. There is the fear of losing something that you already have in your hand, in your heart. Please, don't just merely listen casually to what is being said because that has no value whatsoever. You can come to these meetings year after year, and casually in a holiday mood consider what is said. When you go back home to your various places, you will begin again this whole life of confusion, misery, and conflict. But if you listen, and to listen implies learning, then you are riding on a river which is fathomless, which has tremendous weight behind it, which is moving, carrying you along. If you so listen, then find out why you have these pretensions, and don't spend a single second on examining the cause of it, analyzing it, dissecting it, fighting it, postponing it. When you analyze it and search for the cause, you are merely avoiding. You know very well why you have these masks, these pretensions, these defenses. You don't have to be told by anyone. You know it. What is important is to be aware of this resistance, these defenses, these pretensions.

When you are aware, break them. If you don't want to break them, remain behind them; remain as you are. Don't introduce another problem—because all of us have so many problems as it is, which these masks, these defenses have created. If you say that it is inevitable, that it is natural, that you can't help it, that it is the way of life, then remain with it. Don't introduce another problem—that you must break the masks, break down the defenses. Don't make that into a problem. If you don't make it into a problem, an issue, then you can come upon it in an easy, friendly spirit. It is only when you care to understand it that it begins to break down. If you say, "I must understand it; I must break through," you will never do it. If you have

broken down these pretentious masks, defenses, then you never ask the question, "What is there?" Then there is an action which is never contradictory, an action which is always fresh, always new.

What we know of action is repetition. It is like a man going to an office for forty years until he retires and dies, and the widow has the money. His activity is repetition, doing the same thing over and over again, perhaps a little more cleverly than the other fellow, and therefore he gets a little more money, but it is the same pattern repeated day after day. This repetition of activity gives us great comfort. We are secure in it. There is never a doubt about it; there is never a questioning of it. It is like being carried along on a wave of something which society has established, as in a war. In a war everyone is terribly united together; we have no responsibility; everything is told us, and we just carry on. For us action generally means repetition, and therefore there is nothing new; there is nothing fresh; there is nothing that will give us new energy. But when there are no defenses, no pretensions, no masks, then there is a totally different kind of action, an action which is not based on previously accumulated experience and knowledge, which is necessary at a certain level of skill. There is a mind which is always fresh, young, and innocent. Innocency has no mask, no defense. It is totally vulnerable, and out of that innocency and vulnerability there is an action which is really an extraordinary thing, in which there is no sorrow, no pain, no pleasure, but an extraordinary sense of joy.

Before you begin to ask questions, before we begin to go into details, live with what has been said for a few minutes, a few seconds. Don't jump immediately and say, "I want to ask a question." What we have talked about is quite a serious affair, and it requires tremendous inquiry, consideration. It is really a meditation, not the silly thing called meditation. If I may suggest it most respectfully, don't immediately say, "I want to ask you something."

Remain with it. Let it simmer inside you. Also, when you leave the tent, don't immediately start chattering about whatever you do chatter about.

It is like planting a seed in the earth. We plant it very carefully. We dig a hole, nourish the soil and plant it. We must give it water, rain, and sunshine, but if we are all the time pulling it out to see if it is growing, we kill it. That is what we are always doing. We hear something—which may be true or false, that is not the point—but we hear something, and then we react to it immediately, brush it aside or accept it, deny it or do something about it. We don't take care to see that the thing is given an opportunity to flower.

This does not mean that we are preventing you from asking questions. To ask a question is very important, but what is still more important is to ask the right question, and to ask the right question we need tremendous penetration into that question. We should ask questions about everything, about nationality, kings, queens, about the ways of government, about religions, about everything of human concern. It is necessary to have a great deal of skepticism. It is necessary never to say yes but always to say no and inquire. Most of us are yes-sayers because we have been so trained from childhood. The father, the mother, the priest, the government, everything around us is so conditioned, is so much influencing us that we just accept everything. Therefore we never ask, and when we do ask, we ask the most silly questions.

To ask a very serious question, and a right question, is very important because when you ask the right question, you get a right answer.

Question: How can I be innocent and vulnerable and live in the world?

KRISHNAMURTI: I am afraid the question has been wrongly put, if I may say so. "How can you live in this world and yet be innocent?" First, be innocent, and then you will live in this world, not the other way round. Be vulnerable, be tremendously vulnerable. You do not even understand what it means to be innocent! If you are innocent, you can live in this world, in another world, in any world. But if you are not innocent you try to compromise with this world, and then all hell is let loose. But learn about this sense of innocency. Don't try to get it. It is not the word. It is that state when you have no pretensions, no masks, no conflict. Be in that state and then you can live in this world. Then you can go to the office; you can do anything. If you know what love is, you can do what you will. There is no conflict, no sin, no pain. When the questioner says, "How can I come upon this innocency, this vulnerability, this sense of having no defense, no pretensions, no masks?" that is the right question, not how to live it. Then you will live in this world totally differently.

Question: How can I, who have been tortured, my brain, my mind twisted, beaten, conditioned, almost broken, how can I learn, come upon this state in which there is no defense?

KRISHNAMURTI: I have explained it, but explanation is not the real thing. You can listen to a dozen explanations, but the real thing is not the word. The word is never the thing; the symbol is never the reality. The questioner says, "I, who live in this world, have to make money, live a married life, or not, with all its complications. How can I break through these pretensions?" I do not think that you can. Please listen. You can't do a thing. If you do, it is still self-centered activity. If you say, "I must get that; I must break through," it is still the 'me' that has first defended itself and now seeks a different form of defense. But if you realize the fact, the actual state, that you live a life of pretense—I mean by "pretense" the private life and the public life, a secret life, deep down, covering it up—when you realize that, you do not have to do a thing; then it itself will act. You do it, sir, and you will see.

Comment: To be aware is to suffer.

KRISHNAMURTI: I am aware of the microphone; I am aware of the people here, with their dresses of different colors; I am aware of the trees, the mountains, and the river. I am also aware of myself. It is only when I begin to condemn myself, saying, "This is right," and "This is wrong," that in becoming so-called aware—which is not aware—I begin to suffer. I suffer because I do not like what I am. I want to break through it, to change it. Then there is conflict; there is pain. But if you are aware as I am aware of this microphone, without any choice, if you just watch it, look at it, in that there is no suffering. It is only when you like it or don't like it that you introduce the whole problem of conflict.

Comment: You said something I did not understand.

KRISHNAMURTI: Delighted! (Laughter)

Comment: You said, "If you can't see and be free of mask-making on the very instant, find out why you can't." You also said that the desire to find out is a self-centered activity, and therefore one will never break through the making of the mask. I am confused on that point.

KRISHNAMURTI: Why do we make masks? We know why—for defense, fear, uncertainty, not knowing what is going to happen, clinging to the known and being frightened of the unknown. The desire to be secure is the making of the mask, publicly and privately. When you say, "I must break through it," then it is a self-centered activity, which will only create another mask. I see that any activity from a center, any activity with a motive, is self-centered activity, and therefore the desire to break through the mask is only the creation of another mask. I see that clearly. What do I do? I say, "I cannot do anything about it because whatever I do only breeds another form of pretension, another mask, another defense." The very seeing of that stops all activity from the center. I stop all activity. There is a complete negation of all activity. That, I can understand immediately. That does not take time. I have understood instantly that any action on my part breeds further mischief. Therefore there is no action; there is complete negation; there is no defense. It is the positive action of the egocentric movement which creates the defense, which creates the mask. When the mind has understood that process, and there is an immediate stopping of it, then the total activity of the egocentric process comes to an end. Then there is a state of complete negation. That negation becomes the positive, which is the state of innocency, vulnerability. I haven't done anything! It is not that I have become innocent; that is too silly.

Question: Why are we concerned with what the right question is and what the wrong question is? Is not the right question in itself the right answer?

KRISHNAMURTI: I have only qualified the question as "silly" or the "wrong" question, but that is what we are always doing. We are saying, "How can we stop wars?" I feel that is a wrong question. As long as human beings remain as they are, there will always be wars. The right question is, "How can the human being change totally, immediately?" That, it seems to me, is the right question, and in that very question is the answer. If we put it with all the passion, intensity that is involved, that itself brings the answer.

Comment: The new man you speak of would be unable to remain a new man and be a political leader or run any of the businesses as they are. This man would have such an influence that it would turn upside down the whole political organization.

KRISHNAMURTI: The only political question is, as we said the other day, the unity of man. No politician at the present time is interested. We cannot look to politics to produce the unity of man, nor can we look to the religious people; they are not interested in this. If you and I, as human beings, are not concerned with nationalism, with separate religions, and all the rest of it, then you and I, perhaps, can bring about a totally different state of mind.

July 21, 1966

Seventh Talk in Saanen

We have been saying during all these talks that human nature, what we actually are, has changed very little during all these centuries. There is a great deal of the animal in us, aggression, acquisitiveness, seeking power, position, and prestige. We have actually changed very little. Though technologically, medically, scientifically there have been vast changes, tremendous so-called progression, human beings throughout the world remain almost as they were five or seven thousand years ago. We still are in conflict within ourselves; we are still at war with others; we have divided ourselves into religions with various dogmas, into nationalities, into

economic spheres, but basically we remain almost as we were when history began.

Seeing all the human misery, not only physically, but psychologically, inwardly as well as outwardly, it seems so absolutely necessary to change radically, to bring about a total revolution in the mind. Most of us lead very superficial lives. We are technologically greatly skilled. Outwardly we have progressed. We have a great deal of knowledge which we have accumulated through centuries, in every direction, and we have almost conquered nature, but inwardly we are very superficial. If we are at all serious—and it is only the very serious who have life, who do live—we ask ourselves whether it is possible go to beyond this superficiality. We have tried to go beyond the mere surface of existence, through religions, through various forms of ritual, through beliefs, through taking drugs, the very latest form of stimulation. All these bring about a series of experiences, but human beings remain as they were, with all their misery, with all their conflicts and their extraordinarily superficial lives.

The more intellectual we are or the more emotional one is, the more we read books, acquire knowledge and become very clever, very argumentative. We build a defense behind which we protect ourselves. If we are emotional, we become very sentimental, doing good work, getting lost in social reform, interfering with others, trying to guide, help, and change society. All that is extraordinarily superficial. How has it come about that human beings, though they have had so many experiences of wars, of constant battles within and without, with all their misery and suffering, both physical and psychological, still live on the surface?

The more we live on the surface, the more we get caught in the net of new theories, new theologies, new philosophies, changing religions, changing groups. With all this we are familiar. How are we to break through the crust of superficiality? When we ask how, we invariably look to a system to help us, a method, a formula, an idea, which we can use to penetrate and go beyond this superficial outward existence. I think that very question "How?" is a detriment because we fall in the trap of asking someone, a teacher, a professor, someone who knows much more than we do—at least we think he does. When we say "how," we are always looking for a pattern, a system, which we can imitate, follow, practice. We don't see that the very practice, the very imitation, the very following—it doesn't matter who it is, including the speaker—the moment we imitate, follow, set up an authority, we have already become superficial.

It is one of the curses of humanity that, psychologically speaking, we have established the pattern of following, accepting authority as a guide, inwardly, to help us go beyond the superficiality. I hope those who are listening, who are actually serious, who have not come for the first time just out of curiosity, who are really quite earnest about this kind of thing, are listening to find out if they themselves are following an idea, a pattern, a formula, and if they are, to see that the very acceptance, admittance, and following make the mind superficial, petty, and narrow. It is like the people who are great nationalists—they are the poison of the world; they prevent the unity of human beings; they bring about wars; they divide human beings as this and that. In the same way, when we are imitating, following, we have already set a limit, a boundary to our thoughts, to our feelings. That very boundary, that very limitation brings about a life which is very superficial. We think that through possessing knowledge which we have acquired from the books of others, through experience, through tradition, we are already beyond, deeper than the ordinary, superficial life.

Does knowledge, psychological knowledge, not the knowledge of skills, of technology, of science, of mathematics, of medicine, but the knowledge that we have stored up about the psyche, about ourselves—does that knowledge make for a life that is not merely on the surface? I question whether such knowledge does bring about a depth to our lives. Obviously it does not.

Do the various religions bring about depth to life? Again, obviously not. You may withdraw to a monastery, become a hermit, isolate yourself, enclosed within a dogma, within a belief, within an idea. Surely that does not lead to a deep, profound life inwardly, nor does science. Religions, dogmas, knowledge, imitation and following, the setting up of authority of any kind, psychologically, do not bring a rich, full life that is beyond the transient, beyond the surface life in which there is the constant battle, the constant competition, the constant travail of human anxiety. What does? What makes a human being into an individual? We ought to be able to distinguish between the individual and the human being. The individual is the localized entity, the Englishman, the Frenchman, the nationalist who has the boundary of a certain culture or tradition, but the human being is part of the world. There are worldly problems, problems of war, problems of hate, conflict, competition, ambition, greed, envy, anxiety, guilt—these are human problems, which are our problems. The world is becoming more and more superficial, though there is more and more comfort, social security, the avoidance of more and more wars, and greater amusement—whether the amusement lies in going to church and getting excited about some ritual, or the amusement of football, cricket, or tennis. All this is making us extraordinarily content outwardly, superficially, while inwardly, deep down in our hearts, in the secret privacy of our own minds, there is such dearth, such emptiness.

How is one to go beyond all this? One can't follow anyone anymore. The teachers, the priests, the concepts, the theologians are all too absurd, too immature; one has put that aside long ago, if one is aware of all these problems. One is no longer committed to an idea as a communist, or as a socialist, because the political problem is the unity of man, not according to the communist, labor, or this or the other idea. The moment one divides the world into patterns, there is again disunity.

One must put aside all this, actually, not theoretically, not problematically. One has no faith anymore in religions, in priests, in communism, in socialism. None of these are going to solve one's problems. One has put this question, knowing that one is superficial, outwardly leading a life that has very little meaning because there is always death, there is always conflict, there is always something mysterious which one knows nothing about. One is always seeking, seeking, seeking, and therefore leading a more and more superficial life, because a man who seeks may think himself very serious, but he is not. What is he seeking? He is seeking ultimately some gratification, some kind of enduring pleasure. He may call it by different names, give it a holy connotation, but it is actually the continuation of his own pleasure, a projection of what he desires. Being serious, one discards all this in the psychological realm, as one must if one is at all intelligent, skeptical, revolutionary, not obeying any authority. In the field of technology there must be authority; there must be someone to tell one because there is knowledge which is necessary. But psychologically if one has wiped away all this, one is no longer nationalistic, no longer committed to any country, any religion, any group, any form of ideology. Then one asks oneself if it is possible to go beyond this utterly vain, lonely existence.

I think most of us do ask this question. We may ask it very seriously, or merely out of curiosity. If we ask it seriously, and not out of curiosity, then whom do we expect to answer the question? The moment we expect another to answer it, we are already in the field of superficiality. Then we are looking to someone; the someone becomes the authority, and we are willing to follow that authority because we want to go beyond this meaningless, utterly stupid and valueless life. When we do ask that question, how will we find the answer, knowing no one is going to tell us? We don't want anyone to tell us. If they do, they can only tell us in terms of the positive—do this; follow that; don't do that; don't do this. Then they become our authority, and then we are completely lost.

Will time solve this question?—time being tomorrow, or ten years from now. Or do we believe in some kind of future life, or in resurrection? Will time solve this? We are not talking about time by the watch, chronological time, but time which is a gradual process, a gradual change, mutation, a gradual revolution. Revolution is never gradual, and revolution is never according to a pattern. The moment it is according to a pattern, to an idea, it is no longer revolution. Only a serious mind can answer this question, and we must be serious because life demands it; the world demands it; all the incidents and crises of every moment of our lives demand that we be serious, not serious in some belief, not serious in following something, which is infantile, but with the spirit of seriousness, with a mind which says, "I really must find out"; and to find out we must go to the very end of it, whatever it demands.

A mind that is serious is not a mind that pursues some line, that practices some belief, some dogma. A man who is violent and practices nonviolence may think he is dreadfully serious, but it is an actual avoidance of violence, an escape from the fact of violence. Such a man is not a serious man at all. One has tried various ways to go beyond this ordinary, monotonous, routine-burdened life, taking LSD or other drugs; oh, so many ways! At the end of it all, man is still shallow, empty, bound by his own visions, thoughts, and self-centered activity.

Will psychological time solve this problem, since it is a gradual process? Obviously not. If you say that someday in some future life, or in five years time I'll be happy, I'll have food when I am hungry, it is of little value now. I am not satisfied by the promise of a future meal. I want food now. One of our unfortunate deceptions is that we can use time as a means to something, as a means of change, revolution, mutation. It is not possible. No amount of time, no authority in any form, no following, no asking someone else to tell me what to do, no looking to a religion, to a pope is going to make a complete revolution in the mind. I deny all those totally, knowing that they are absolutely empty, a circus. Then what has taken place in a mind that is serious, that has denied time as a means of bringing about a mutation within oneself—time being today or tomorrow, the extension of today?

I deny all that. I deny authority—which means no following, not looking to another, not depending on anyone, no guru, no teacher—intelligently, not as a reaction, not as a revolt, but because I see the truth of it, because I see the intelligence of it. When I have put aside all that, what has taken place in the mind? In the past I have believed; I have had faith in someone to tell me what to do; I have followed the scriptures, or Marx or Engel or the latest theologian; or perhaps I don't believe in anything and have merely become cynical, hopeless, which is another reaction, and therefore I do not have a serious mind at all. If I, seeing all this, understanding all this, if I am not in revolt but

understand it and see the worthlessness of it, if I have put it all away, then what has taken place in my mind? Through negation of what has been accepted as the norm, as the pattern, as the way to something, to this or that, through the denial of all that, the mind has become astonishingly sensitive and therefore extraordinarily alive and intelligent, and through what is called the positive, it has become negative. It is only when the mind has completely denied all that we have called the positive way of existence that there is a state of negation. That very state of negation is the depth of life because it is only in total negation that there is something new, something which is not the result of seeking, wanting, groping after. It has nothing whatsoever to do with any system or philosophy. Then the mind, being rid of every conditioning, every influence, all the encrustations of centuries, seeing the whole significance of it, not in reaction but seeing what it is all worth and putting it totally aside, then the mind becomes astonishingly alive, sensitive, and intelligent. It is only when the mind is completely empty of the old that there is the new. Then there is no longer the question of whether one is leading a superficial life, because then one lives, and the very living is a movement which is not the movement of the old pattern, the old life. It is a totally different way of living in which there is not the animal at all. That is really the revolution because it is like love. Love must be always new; love is not memory; love is not desire. The moment desire comes into it there is pleasure and the memory of the continuation of that pleasure, and therefore it ceases to be love. A mind which has understood all this, which has understood time and authority, is free. Only a mind that is totally free knows the beauty of life. That mind is not bound by any boundary, and the life is one of extraordinary peace and beauty.

Perhaps we can discuss what we have talked about. We can ask questions, discuss, go into it more in detail. But, as we said the other day, a right question brings the right answer; a wrong question will have no meaning. If the right question is asked, the right answer is in the question. This does not mean that we are trying to choke off questions. We must ask all these questions, doubt, have tremendous passion. To find out we must ask questions, and in asking questions we will find out for ourselves whether we are asking the right question or the wrong question. In questioning we are exposing ourselves to ourselves, not to the public. Who cares what someone else thinks?

Question: How is it possible to go beyond physical pain and its irritation?

KRISHNAMURTI: "One may want to go deeply and be terribly serious and earnest, but if one has physical pain constantly and the irritation of it, the boredom of it, the agony of it, how can one go beyond?" I am afraid it is very difficult. If one has constant pain one finds a very good doctor, a first-class doctor who is not just a drug merchant, and he may help one. Even if one does have constant pain one can learn to dissociate oneself from the pain. Life is a resistance, a defense; one fights everything, building a wall around oneself; but if one accepts it one goes with the pain. Everyone has physical pain—a great deal, a great many days, or pain for an hour or so. That is an unfortunate occurrence in human life, but one can begin to be dissociated from it. One can look at it, not resist it. To bring in a simile, an example, of a night one can be awakened by a dog that is barking, a machine that is making a noise all the time, a radio overhead that is blaring out some absurd stuff. The instinct is to resist it, to get angry about it, to get irritated with it, but if one listens without resistance,

just listens, goes with it, moves with it, then one will see that this noise is no longer affecting one. In the same way one can look at one's pain, one's toothache, the incessant and constant pain; one can observe it objectively and then one can, perhaps, go beyond it.

Comment: As I listen to you it seems to me that in a certain way I understand perfectly, but the other thing does not take place. I see it very clearly, but the real thing does not happen.

KRISHNAMURTI: The question is, have I really seen it, or do I just think that I have seen it, which is entirely different. Have I seen it merely intellectually, verbally, theoretically? If I see it intellectually, verbally, theoretically, it has no value whatsoever, but if I see it non-theoretically, nonverbally, nonintellectually, then it is bound to take place. Therefore I must examine what I mean by seeing. Do I see it verbally, or do I see it nonverbally? Do I see it intellectually or nonintellectually?

I cannot answer for you. I cannot tell you how you look, but you can find out for yourself how you look, how you listen, how you see, how you observe, how you understand, whether it means something to you. How do you look? How do you listen? How do you observe? How do you understand? Does it mean anything to you? We are using the word *see* to imply all that. What do you mean when you say, "I see"? Do you mean that you hear the word, and because that word has a reference you understand it; or, do you hear the word and translate that word according to your memory? Please follow all this carefully, sir. When you say, "I see," you generally mean that you heard the word. You have understood because I am speaking English, and that word has a meaning to you. You are looking through that word at the thing, and therefore you are not looking. The word is interfering. The word, the symbol, the idea, the memory—all those are interfering with your observing, seeing. Can you look, can you listen, without interpretation, without the word, without the memory? There is a river flowing by. Can you listen to that noise, listen and not react? There is a train going by. Please listen to it. Are you listening without the word, without thought, without memory, without recognition, or are you saying, "It is a train and I am irritated because I want to listen"? When you listen like that, in that state you have affection, you have tenderness, you have love, but if you say, "That train! It is interfering with my listening; it is a nuisance and I get irritated with it," you are not in a state of listening, observing. To observe, to listen, demands great affection, great care; we do not care, we do not have affection. All that we know is irritation, resistance, suppression, or recognition. All those destroy care, affection, listening.

Comment: We are a lot of monkeys, going up and down a chain, making an awful noise. We are never silent for a single minute, and therefore we do not listen. It is this noise which is the intellectual, the everlasting thinking, worrying, going over and over again. The other is the intuitive.

KRISHNAMURTI: The word *intuitive* is a most dangerous word, like *nationalism*. I can have an intuition because it is what I want. I want something deeply; I feel that it is right, and I call that intuition. We must distrust every word because every word, unfortunately, is loaded. We know only one thing, that our minds are like monkeys, restless, chattering, up and down, everlastingly moving, moving, moving, thinking, worrying. How can such a mind look? Obviously it cannot. Then we say, "How am I to train it to be quiet?" We spend years in training it to be quiet, and then it becomes another kind of monkey. (Laughter)

This is not a joke. Please do not laugh. People have spent their whole lives going from one monkey world to just another monkey world. To realize what silence is demands tremendous inquiry. It is not just a matter of a moment. It is only the completely silent mind that can observe, that can listen, that can learn—learning in the sense of what we are talking about, not accumulating knowledge and taking notes. Learning has nothing to do with acquisition because learning is a movement, and this movement can only come into being when there is silence. Unfortunately it is not possible to go into this question of silence now. Perhaps we can discuss it next time, because we have to go into it very, very deeply. A mind that is silent is an extraordinary mind. It is a free mind. We cannot make the mind silent by force, by discipline, by control, because then it becomes sterile, dead, but to understand what silence means we have to see, we have to look. Look at a flower completely, without all kinds of memories and thoughts in operation; just look. When we love someone with all our being, not just with memory, desire, sex, and all the rest of it, we love out of that tremendous silence. Then we have communication without words, without idea, without recognition.

July 24, 1966

Eighth Talk in Saanen

This morning I want to go into something rather intricate. It may appear difficult, but it is really quite simple. The importance of it lies not in doing something, asking oneself what can be done about something, or searching out a way to achieve something, but in the act of listening. All communication, even at the verbal level, lies in just listening, not in trying to find out what the speaker is saying, not in making a tremendous effort to understand, to grapple with the problem of what is being said. Listening is an art, and if one can listen with effortless attention, without any decision to listen, without any purposive attention, but as one would listen to that river passing by, then the very act of listening is a total action in itself. One's mind is so complex, one's intentions, one's motives are so contradictory and hidden that one loses all simplicity. It requires a very simple mind, not a mind that is unbalanced, but a very clear mind, like a pool, like a lake that is so clear and the water so limpid that there is not a ripple, and one can see the very bottom of the lake, with all the pebbles, the fish, the weeds, and the living things that live under the water.

If one can so observe and listen, one has to do nothing else. One does not have to exercise intellectual arguments; one needs no conviction, no faith, nor any endeavor to be serious, but one needs merely to see the totality of existence as a whole, to see the whole sky, not through any window, not through a specialized mind that looks at the sky and knows all its composition, the nature of its being. A specialized mind cannot see the total, cannot perceive the whole of life— love, death, hate, wars, acquisitiveness, the constant battle within oneself and outside, the ambition, the power—as a total emptiness, a total movement. If one could so see, listen to the whole movement of life, all problems would cease, all relationships would have a totally different meaning, existence would have a quite different depth.

Why is it that you look at life in fragments? I am asking not for you to answer, or to try to find out. The speaker is going to do all that, in as much detail as possible. All that you have to do this morning, if I may suggest, is just to listen. Listen for forty or forty-five minutes, if you have that interest, that seriousness, that intention, that vitality, and that energy. Listen, and afterwards perhaps you will be good enough to ask questions and then

we can go into it more, but I suggest that you listen very easily, happily. It is a lovely morning. The mountains are very clear and the meadow is sparkling; every tree, every living thing is full of life and beauty.

To see all this there must be no fragmentary, specialized outlook. Why is it that we look at life in fragments? Why is it that we have broken up life, this vast stream of existence into compartments, into classified series of fragments? Why have we broken up this marvelous world, physical world into nationalities, into dogmas, into political, religious, social, and economic worlds? Our relationships are broken up. The husband, the wife, the son, the family, the group, the community, the nations are all working separately. Why do we have the division of love and jealousy, of God and the devil, of the good and the bad? Everything is broken up, and our own minds, our own hearts are divided, fragmented, and through this fragmentation we never see the whole, although we try in every way to integrate these fragments into a whole. Nothing can be integrated. You cannot integrate white and black, hate and love, or goodness and jealousy. As they cannot ever be integrated, we need a quite different approach to the whole problem. To understand or to observe life as a whole, not divided into fragments, there must be no center, no 'me' who is looking out, no experiencer. The observer, the nationalist, the man who believes or doesn't believe, the communist—each one has a center in varying degrees and depths, clever or not, dull and stupid or highly intellectual, very learned or very ignorant. As long as this center exists there must be fragmentation, as life and death, love and hate, and all the rest. Please just listen and not ask how to get rid of the center. You can't get rid of it. How can you get rid of the whole of life? You can't! The more you make an effort to get rid of it, the stronger that center gets.

We see this fragmentation taking place, and we also know, through observation, through clear thinking, why we do this. We are conditioned from childhood to think in a certain way. A man who is a mathematician, a scientist, has taken a particular line, and everything else is secondary. He has broken life up, made life into fragments. Life is a contradiction until we can see for ourselves the whole of life, the whole of human beings, the whole of the world, like these mountains, streams, and valleys. As long as the mind is fragmented, broken up, specialized, as long as a man says, "This is my line and I'm going to follow it," or "This is the way for me to fulfill, to become, and I'm going to pursue it," there is misery and more suffering. Each one of us has this center from which we look, from which we judge, evaluate, and strive with tremendous effort. Life is broken up and this breaking up of life, which is caused by the center, is time. If we look at the whole of existence without the center, there is no time. That is a most mysterious thing.

Time is one of the most complex things to understand. It is fairly simple to understand it intellectually, but to see the meaning of it, to understand the nature of time, the significance of time, the depth of time, we must not only understand chronological time by the watch in our pocket or on our wrist, but also we must understand and observe the psychological thing which creates time as yesterday, today, and tomorrow. Time is a movement, a total thing, and if we break it up into yesterday, today, and tomorrow we are caught in the bondage of time. Then we develop theories of gradualism, or of immediacy, the "now." There is the gradual theory, that gradually human beings will become more benevolent, more kind, more this and more that. We see the utter hopelessness of dependence upon a future life—the future being the tomorrow—upon the gain that will

take place in a few months, years, or centuries. That again is a fragmentation of time. In all that we are caught, and therefore we do not understand the extraordinary movement of time without fragmentation. There is actually only time by the watch and no other time. That train goes by precisely at this time every day, and if you would catch it you must be at the station at the time it leaves. Otherwise you will miss it. Chronological time has to be observed exactly. The observation of time by the watch is not a contradiction, is not a fragmentation of that other time.

Time which is not of the watch is invented by memory, by experience, or by the center that says, "I will be something." There is the question of death and its postponement by avoiding it, pushing it away. Thought makes for the fragmentation of time which, except chronological time, does not actually exist. We do not understand that extraordinary movement of time in which there is no fragmentation because we are always thinking of what I was, what I am, and what I will be. All that is the fragmentation of psychological time, and you cannot do anything about it, except listen. You cannot say, "I will get rid of time and live in the present because it is only the present that matters." Actually, what does "the present" mean? The present is only the result of the past, but there is an actual present if there is no fragmentation of time. I hope you see the beauty of this.

Time for us becomes of enormous importance, not chronological time, not going to the office every day, taking the train, the bus, keeping an appointment. All that is very trivial. We have to do it, but what is important is psychological time, which we break up into yesterday, today, and tomorrow. We are always living in the past. "Now" is the past because the "now" is the continuation of memory, the recognition of what has been, which cannot be altered, and what is going on at the present time. Either we live in the memory of youth, in the remembrance of things that have been, or we live in the image of tomorrow. We live lives of gradual decay, of gradual withering. With the coming on of senility the brain cells become weaker and weaker, lose all their energy, vitality, and force. Therein lies the great sorrow. As we grow older, memory disappears and we become senile, which is the repetition of what has been. That is how we are living. Though we are very active, we are senile. In the present, in the moment of action we are always living in the past, with its influence, its pressures, its strain, its vitality. All the knowledge which we have acquired and stored up through enormous struggle, through time, is knowledge of the past. Knowledge can never be of the present. From that past knowledge we act, and that action is what we call "the present." That action is always engendering decay.

We are acting in the image, in the symbol, in the idea of the past; and that is the fragmentation of life. We invent philosophies, theories of the present; we live only in the present and make the best of it. Nothing else matters. Such living in the present is a despair because time which has been divided into the past, the present, and the future only brings about despair. Knowing despair, we say, "It doesn't matter; let's try and live in the now, in the present, because everything is meaningless. All action, all life, all existence, all relationship, everything must end in the division of time and therefore in despair, in decay, in trouble." Please do listen, because we can't do anything about it. That is the beauty of what will take place if we do nothing but listen. This doesn't mean that we are going to accept what is being said; there is neither acceptance nor denial. It is stupid for anyone to say, "I am living in the present." It doesn't mean a thing. It is equally stupid to say, "I deny the past." We can deny the

past, but we are the result of the past. Our whole functioning is from the past. Our beliefs, our dogmas, our symbols, the particular line we are trying to follow, whatever it is, is still the result of the past, which is time. We have broken up time into the past, the present, and the future. This naturally breeds fear, fear of life which is not of time, and the movement of time which is not broken up into yesterday, today, and tomorrow. That movement of time can be perceived totally only when there is no fragmentation, when there is no center from which we look at life.

Beauty is not of time, but what does have time is the expression of a particularization of what we feel in terms of time. Beauty, like love, cannot be divided into yesterday, today, and tomorrow. When we divide it, there are all the problems that are involved in the relationship which we call love—jealousy, envy, domination, the feeling of possessiveness. When beauty is not the result of fragmentation of time, painting, music, and all the modern gimmicks and tricks have no meaning whatsoever. Anything that is the expression of time, of the period, of this modern revolt, denies beauty. Beauty cannot be translated in terms of time. It can only be understood, lived, known when there is total silence. We cannot see the beauty of the mountain and the clear blue sky when the mind is chattering endlessly, when the mind is occupied with problems. We can see that beauty only in total silence, and that silence cannot be achieved through time, through saying, "I will be silent tomorrow; I will practice certain methods," and all that childish rubbish. Silence comes about in all its totality, depth, beauty, and vigor only when the fragmentation of life ceases right from the beginning.

A silent mind is a timeless mind, and from that silence one can act. It is a silent mind because it has no time. It is always in the present, always in the now. As one cannot act positively through will to break down the bondage of time, one cannot do anything. If one does anything, one is caught in time. One must really understand that one cannot do a thing. This does not mean that one becomes lazy, slack, that one leads a life of stupidity, a meaningless existence. One sees the totality of life, the extraordinary complexity of existence, and realizes that one can't do anything. What can one do about that noise? One can either resist it or listen to it and move with the noise.

If one realizes that one cannot positively or in any way do anything about the fragmented life that one leads, the fragmented life of contradiction which is the lot of human beings; if one actually sees the reality of it, not intellectually, argumentatively, or verbally; if one realizes totally that one can do nothing about one's life, with its sorrows, pleasures, joys, miseries, conflicts, ambitions, competition, with the search for power and position, with all the fragments of one's existence—then time as yesterday, with all its memories, experience, and knowledge comes totally to an end. Out of that ending of time there is beauty, not what you see, not the mountain, not the picture, not the brook—those are all fragmentations—but the beauty which is born unsought, without premeditation. That beauty comes only when there is no time, or when time is not broken up. Out of that beauty comes silence. A mind that is not silent and a heart that is not quiet are always in conflict and misery. Do what one will, it will always bring misery upon oneself and upon others. If one has listened easily, quietly, not being mesmerized by the speaker, then one comes upon it darkly, unknowingly, and there it is. It may last a single second, a minute, a day, or a century; that doesn't matter. When one wants to grasp it, when one says, "I must have it the whole of my life," then one is fragmented; then one begins again the fragmentation, the contradic-

tion, the anger, the jealousy, and all the rest. To see the totality of existence, time as past, present, and future must come to an end.

Can we talk it over together? Can we discuss, not how to achieve this enormous quality of beauty, but how to see, to observe the way our life is fragmented and broken up? If we see the fragments and see that we cannot do a thing, that we cannot integrate them, since all action is fragmentary as long as there is a center, and the center is the result of the fragmentation of time—if we can observe it, expose ourselves to it, then perhaps we shall come upon something that is not made by time, time as yesterday, today, and tomorrow. Then time has a stop. Time as fragments comes to an end. If we can this morning really see our lives, how we have broken them up, then perhaps something can come about—not out of the unconscious, for there is no such thing. There is only consciousness, which we have divided into the unconscious and the conscious. From that division all the fragmentation and the misery of fragmentation begin.

Question: Do you see all things as beauty?

KRISHNAMURTI: I wonder what the questioner means. Can you see as beauty someone being killed, war, burning, suffering, dirt on the road, the squalor of poverty? Why do you ask that question? Is it because you want to see everything as beauty—the wife and the husband that nag and quarrel, anger, jealousy? Do you want to see all that as beauty and have a lovely image, a sense of mystical nonsense? Sir, you must see things as they are, see facts as facts, and not have the opinions about the facts. You must see factually, with no pretense, the ugliness, the brutality, the horror, the tremendous things that are going on in this world. All the churches, with their dogmas, crosses, and signs are unreal. They are symbols and the symbol is never the real. When I recognize that the symbol is not the real, then the symbol has no meaning. Have I not answered your question, sir?

Comment: Yes, with some qualification.

KRISHNAMURTI: Qualification of what? Look, sir, have you understood what I said? A mind that is no longer thinking in terms of yesterday, today, or tomorrow, a mind that is not fragmented, broken up, will know what beauty is. Then you won't ask me, "Do you think all life is beauty?" First find out for yourself why your mind is broken up, why your life is specialized as the husband and all that business. In finding out, ask questions. Begin to find out, and out of that beginning ask tremendous questions.

Comment: The trouble with all of us is that words are so shallow. The words we use have no meaning. If we talk about certain things, we use certain expressions; the words just come.

KRISHNAMURTI: Is that true? "My wife" or "my husband" are words, but they mean a tremendous lot, don't they? People are willing to kill for the words "my God" or "I am a communist." An idea is just a rationalized word, an organized word, and for that we are willing to kill, to brutalize, to destroy ourselves. Don't say, sir, that words have very little meaning. If we realize that the word, the symbol, the expression is not the fact, as the word *tree* is not the tree, then we are not caught in words. Our thinking, our minds are full of words, conditioned by words, such as "I am an Englishman, a Frenchman." For us words have extraordinary importance. We may call it shallow, but a word, an expression, a symbol has great

meaning. But when we know that the word, the symbol, the expression has no real meaning, that only the fact has meaning, then we use words or expressions which no longer catch our mind. Sir, there was an effort to investigate the whole question of propaganda. A commission was formed and began its work. Do you know who stopped it? The church, the military, and the businessmen!

Question: In a little village there is a poisonous snake, and there is a woman, crying her heart out because the snake has bitten her baby and the baby is dead. I can kill the snake or I can leave it alone. What am I to do?

KRISHNAMURTI: What do you do? Do you wait until you come to this tent to be told what to do? Or do you do something there? You act! If you are callous, indifferent, you don't do anything; if you are moved, you actually, immediately, do something. Sir, all our activity is based on the idea that we must help, that we must be good, that this is right, and that is wrong. All action is conditioned by an idea, by our country, by our culture, by the food we eat. All that conditions our actions because they are based on an idea. When we see that action is approximating itself to an idea and therefore it is not an action, then we will put away all idea and know what action is. It is very interesting to observe how we have broken up action: righteous, immoral, right, true, noble, ignoble, national action, action according to the church. If we understand the worthlessness of such action, then we act. We do not ask how to act, what to do; we act and that act is the most beautiful act at that moment.

July 26, 1966

Ninth Talk in Saanen

All of us must have asked ourselves whether it is possible to become totally new, to become young again, not in body obviously, but in the mind, in our hearts. Is it possible to be totally reborn, not to begin life all over again as a young man or a young girl, but to see life, with all its vast complexities, its pains and suffering, its anxieties and fears as though we were looking at it all for the first time, and then resolve it, not carry on the burden year after year until we die? Is it at all possible to renew the mind and the heart so that they look at life entirely differently? I would like to talk over that problem this morning and try to find out whether it is possible to do something about it, to have a fresh mind, a mind that is clear, unconfused, never touched by worry, by problems, and all the travail that we are used to, and to have a heart that knows no jealousy, which is full of affection and love—so that we are reborn totally each day.

Is there any method, any decisive action, positive or negative, that can bring about this new state? Most of us must have asked this question, if not deliberately then perhaps rather vaguely or, if we are inclined to peculiar sentimentality, mystically. Having asked that question of ourselves, either we do not have the full energy, the force, and the vitality to go beyond the question and find out actually for ourselves, or we ask it rather casually, indifferently, out of curiosity. Obviously there must be a change outwardly, economically, and socially in order to bring about the unity of man, whether the individual is brown, black, white, Russian, communist, socialist, or whatever he may be. It is necessary that we participate actively in order to get rid of this present ugly state of affairs, to get rid of these differences that exist racially, communally, politically, nationally. We must also get rid of that absurd invention of great business called ''religion,''

which is a great corporation controlled by the priests and the hierarchy, like any other business. It divides man into Protestant, Catholic, Hindu, Buddhist, Muslim, and so on. Any intelligent, clearsighted, serious man puts that aside completely and is not touched by all that silly nonsense. He is concerned with ending poverty throughout the world, not in one particular corner of the world, not in America, nor in the so-called united Europe, the Common Market, but with ending the enormous poverty, degradation, and all the things that poverty brings, in Asia. The scientists assure us that it can be done, and it must be done, to end wars, to put an end to this constant physical insecurity. All of that any intelligent, sane, rational man fully intends to do. We are not talking of the do-gooder, nor of the reformer, because neither the man who wants to do good nor the reformer can bring about a total physical revolution. Yet that revolution must take place.

Leaving that aside as a necessity and an urgency of alteration that must be done by any intelligent man who is aware of the world and its crises and its terrible misery, that must be carried out by each one of us, there is a much deeper question involved. In a mind and in a heart that has been conditioned for centuries, caught up in the psychological structure of society, hedged about by the innumerable influences that man is forced to accept, in such a mind and heart is it possible to have a rebirth, not in some distant future, not in some other life as the whole of the Orient believes—and that same belief in a different form exists in this Western world—is it at all possible to have a rebirth, now, in this present moment? We are not limiting ourselves to time, but a rebirth, a renewal, is needed that is not dependent on time at all. That is the question we are going to find out about.

We can only ask that question when we have seen the absurdity of the average life that we lead, the life of the middle class, the bourgeois, the communist, the life of ever-lastingly repeating a pattern. We are always copying, imitating, continuing a past that does not bring a new perception, a new vitality, a new existence. When we ask that question, not only must we be very clear in our intention, but we must also realize fully that no one can answer that question. No authority can tell us if the mind, which is the result of time, or the brain, which has been trained, civilized, and polished but yet remains the animal, can live in that state—not realize for just one single minute, not continue in that state, but live it.

The moment we ask whether it is possible to have a continuity of that state, we are no longer living. A man who is living fully, clearly, is not concerned with the tomorrow. There is no concern at all; he is living and is not looking to a future continuity. Any form of continuity, except knowledge of a skill, is totally destructive to the new. What con-tinues is habit, memory, the repetition of a pattern of pleasure and pain, of desire. The repetition of any habit, of any pattern cannot bring about this state of mind that is totally new, young, decisive, alive, and not burdened by the past. That is the first thing to realize if we are going to inquire into this question of whether the mind can renew itself, be new each day, be fresh, uncontaminated. Any form of continuity except knowledge and skill is totally detrimental, is a block to a fresh mind, to being reborn. What has con-tinuity is the self-centered activity in which most of us are caught—ambition, greed, envy, the pursuit of pleasure, the avoidance of pain, imitation, following, and all the other things that the center does. That center is the result of this continuity, and we cannot say, "I will end that continuity by will, by determination, by desire"; but when we see, comprehend, understand the whole implica-tion of what is involved in this continuity,

then, by itself, it comes to an end. We can realize it, not intellectually, not emotionally, but actually, as something factual, only when we are inquiring into this question of the birth of a new mind, of a fresh heart, of in-nocency, because dying is the cessation of this continuity.

For most of us death is the ending of something we have known, something which we have experienced or acquired, and we are afraid of the final ending of something of the past. We are not so much afraid of physical dying because we know the body is undergoing changes every year. Those changes the mind cannot control. Physically we decay, through disease, through accident, through various wrong ways of living. We are afraid, not of the unknown which lies beyond death, but rather of losing what we have, of not being able to continue with the known. We cannot say, "I will deliberately end the past in order to have a rebirth, a new mind, a fresh heart." We cannot achieve it; we cannot deliberately practice some system. The very practice of a system is in itself the continuity of the past, and therefore there is nothing new.

If one listens, not only to the speaker, but to every intimation, to all the world in agony, to the world in pleasure, the world at war, then the very act of listening is the greatest miracle, the greatest mystery. If one can listen and not translate what one listens to, or interpret what one hears, or condemn, or judge, or carry on all the rest of that interference of thought, which is self-centered activity—if one can actually listen, then one will find for oneself that though one can do certain things like altering the political situation, bringing about economic unity, wiping out poverty, all of which one can and should do, one cannot do a thing about the other. Analyzing, dis-secting, exposing oneself, examining all one's states of being only lead to more confusion, more misery, more strife; but if one listens, as one would listen to that stream running by, quietly, without any sense of acquiring, retaining, or rejecting, then one will see that that very listening ends self-centered activity.

I am not asking you to do anything but just to listen. I am not indulging in ideas, in theories, in fantasies, in anything mystical or conceptual. I am just pointing out what actually is. If you listen with an open heart and mind, a mind which is not committed to anything but just listening, then that very listening becomes an action, and it is the only action, the only operation to end this so-called continuity, this repetitive, imitative process of demands and pursuits. You can see for yourself very clearly that what has continuity can never perceive or understand something new. It is only when there is a death to something that there is anything new. To die to ourselves, the "ourselves" which form the very center of this continuity, to die to the known, to be free of the known, that is the renewal of the mind; that brings a freshness. Then you see the mountain, the river, the tree, the woman, the man, the child, humanity as something totally different, as something new.

That is what most of us are asking, demanding, because the more intellectual one is, the more one is aware, the more one is informed about the world, of all of history which is constantly repeating itself—the more one asks whether man can be reborn, born afresh, so that he can live a different kind of life, a different way of acting, have a different perception of existence. That is all we are seeking, every day. We are becoming older every day; even the young people are getting older, and if each one of us is aware of all of these things, then the only question that is worth asking is: Is it possible to be reborn, so that the mind and the heart are renewed, fresh, so that they can renew themselves all the time, so that they are all the time fresh, all the time young, alive, new?" That demands a great deal of energy, not the energy manufactured by conflict, by

violence, by intention, by effort. All that has its own energy, but we are seeing for ourselves that to renew every day, to be reborn every day, to die every day to everything known so that there is the fresh, the new, and to live in that, not to maintain it, but to be in that state demands an astonishing energy which is not the energy of conflict.

We must inquire what this energy is. If we are healthy, strong, vital, we have a great deal of physical energy, which is used for aggression, for violence, trying to get somewhere or do something. There is a great deal of energy engendered through conflict, and most of our relationships are conflict. We need energy to go to the office every day; we need energy to learn, to do, to act. The energy which is brought about, put together, engendered, bred by the mind in pursuit of pleasure, gain, and fame never will bring a fresh mind, a young heart. We have to inquire what the energy is which will bring about the death every day of everything that the mind has conceived, seen, observed, and stored up. It requires energy to die to something that we have acquired, that we have stored up, to the things that we have known, remembered, accumulated. The death of the mind that has experience every day, the death of the brain that reacts to every movement of life, the ending of the animal in all of us—because a great deal of the human is still the animal, and to die to that all that requires energy. It is not an intellectual thing. The intellect can never create the necessary energy. It creates energy in action, in doing something, in following an idea, in formulating something and carrying that formulation into action, but that is not the energy of which we are talking. We are talking of an energy, a vitality, a force that is necessary in order to die every day so that the mind and the heart are fresh, new.

Together we are going to find out what that energy is. It is not for the speaker to tell you. We are going together to share in our inquiry. We are going to participate in that extraordinary energy which we must have. We are asking ourselves what that force is that keeps the mind young. I don't know how you answer it, what your answer is, if you have an answer. It is very important for each one of us to find out if we are waiting to be told, if we are expecting someone to answer. There is no one to answer it, not your gods, not your priests, certainly not the communist. He is not interested in it. How do you respond to this question of dying every day to everything known, experienced? In the very dying there is the new.

There must be a simple approach to any complex problem. A human problem with all its complexity especially must be answered very simply. The word *simple* is loaded. There are various concepts of what simplicity is. If you are brought up in the East, simplicity is one meal a day and a loincloth, and that obviously is not simplicity. Here that word has a different connotation. We are using the word simple in the sense of not being complicated, not being weighted down by ideas, by concepts. It is a very difficult thing just to be simple. To find out about that energy which is always renewing itself without any motive, we have to become extraordinarily simple. What is that energy? We can put the answer in one word, but that word is so loaded, so burdened by centuries of repetition that it has lost its real beauty. That word is *love*. Just listen to it, not to the fragmentations of what is called love. We know love only as sexual love, physical love; love that is surrounded by jealousy, by anxiety, by fear; the love of God, the love of man. That is what we call love. We also use that word when we are tremendously intimate with another, sexually, or merely in physical contact. We use it when a relationship exists between two human beings, in which there is no conflict, no domination, no attachment. We use that word for the moment when we

have that extraordinary feeling, but the feeling has gone the next moment. Thought interferes and there is the demand for continuity, for repetition of the pleasure. All the machinery begins to operate.

We are talking of a word, which is not the fact. The word or the symbol is never the fact. We are talking of a word in which there is no fragmentation, in which there is no sense of "the other," in which the observer has totally ceased, and therefore the observed is no longer there. This we must understand very deeply; otherwise, that word has very little meaning except the common bourgeois meaning. That love, which is not the word, that energy makes the mind and heart reborn so that they are always fresh. Only that energy keeps the mind fresh, not in time. Whatever the experience, whatever the impression, whatever the knowledge that has been acquired, it dies the moment it has come. It comes, is experienced, and ends, all in one movement. You cannot acquire that thing that lies beyond the word. You cannot practice it. This word *practice* is a terrible thing. Doing something day after day in order to acquire is a most ugly, bourgeois, cruel thing.

Have you noticed the extraordinary change that takes place, without effort, when you are very quiet, in your room, in a bus, or when you are by yourself in a forest. The mind is so full and so rich that it is not thinking, not looking, not observing. It is so total because it is neither the observer nor the observed. Only that state is love, not the ordinary thing which we have talked about. Only that love can end continuity. Then life has a meaning because death is an ending to continuity.

Question: Is it not necessary to have continuity of normal physical habits in order to listen in to other lives around us?

KRISHNAMURTI: Does continuity ever listen to anything? We said that one must have a physical continuity; one cannot just go and jump in the lake, but does it help to listen to someone else? What lies behind the question? You listened to a Catholic and got something from that listening. You listened to a Buddhist and got something from that. You listened to the communists and collected. This collection has been gathered by listening to various lives. You have collected them, and that collection has a continuity. We are saying that there must be the very ending of all collection. What you collect is a museum, but a museum never creates a picture. A picture is only brought into being by a man who is no longer concerned with the museum, with the gallery, or the owner of the gallery. He is concerned with the feeling of painting. If he has a certain capacity then he paints, but painting, expression, has so little value. It has value only for the collector who makes money out of it. If a painter or a musician is concerned with money and collecting it, then he ceases to be a painter or a musician.

Comment: I feel that my daily life is unimportant, that I should be doing something else.

KRISHNAMURTI: When you are eating, eat. When you are going for a walk, walk. Don't say, "I must be doing something else." When you are reading, give your attention completely to that, whether it is a detective novel, a magazine, the Bible, or what you will. The complete attention is a complete action, and therefore there is no "I must be doing something else." It is only when we are inattentive that we have the feeling of "By Jove, I must be doing something better." If we give complete attention when we are eating, that is action. What is important is not what we are doing but whether we can give total attention. I mean by that word not something we learn through concentration in a school or in business but to attend, with our bodies, our nerves, our eyes, our ears, our minds, our hearts—completely. If we do that there is a tremendous crisis in our lives. Then something demands our whole energy, vitality, attention. Life demands that attention every minute, but we are so trained to inattention that we are always trying to escape from inattention to attention. We say, "How am I to attend? I am lazy." Be lazy, but be totally attentive to the laziness. Be totally attentive to inattention. Know that you are completely inattentive. Then when you know that you are totally attentive to inattention, you are attentive.

July 28, 1966

Tenth Talk in Saanen

During the last nine talks, we have more or less covered the various problems with which we as human beings have been burdened for many centuries. We have never been able to resolve either the wars or the sufferings that we go through physically and psychologically, nor have we resolved the many complex issues that confront each of us daily. We live on the surface, hoping that somehow, sometime, these problems will be solved. Unfortunately problems cannot be solved unless we face them, unless we know how to come to grips with them, unless we see what they actually are. We have been trained through many, many centuries as human beings to avoid all problems, to escape from them, to suppress them, to run away from them, or to defend ourselves against them; but unfortunately, though we try to escape, to run away, to build a defense against them, they still exist. We have very cunningly built a network of escapes. Apparently we cannot look directly at anything. Our minds have opinions which prevent us from looking at things as they are, from facing what actually is. Our minds and our hearts are never empty to observe, to look.

We either have problems which we cannot resolve or we have committed ourselves to various activities—political, social, religious, and so on—or we have our own particular neurotic problems with all their complexities, and so our minds and hearts are never empty. A mind that is committed must always be confused, and we are confused, though we do not acknowledge it directly to ourselves. We are confused about politics, about religion, about what we should do, what we should think, what right thinking and wrong thinking are, what right behavior is. We are so completely confused, and the more clever we are, the more incapable we are of acknowledging to ourselves that we are totally confused, not partially. We think we are partially confused and that there are moments when we are not confused. The moments we spend when we are not confused have their own action, and there is another type of action when we are confused. The action born of nonconfusion is always in conflict with the action born of confusion. Each reacts upon the other, and we never realize in ourselves that we actually are completely confused. If we acknowledge this, we can then proceed to find out how to be free from that confusion, but we can never find out if we have formulations, ideologies, commitments, psychological assertions. We usually go on through life confused, miserable, not accounting to ourselves, in a miserable, confused, weary state until we die. That is our lot. We have built a network of escapes. We have constantly invented various traps into which we fall. One of the greatest traps is the idea that we must seek and find. We do not actually know what we are seeking. We say we are seeking truth, love, God—all the many, many things that each person, according to his temperament, is

seeking. We never question why it is that we seek at all, what it is that we are seeking, and if there is such a thing as that which we seek through asking and questioning.

If we do not search we will find that the most important thing in life is not to search at all because then we are confronted with life, then we are faced with what we actually have to do. It is extremely difficult for most of us not to try to find, not to seek something. Most of us are here because we are seeking something. Generally we seek because we are utterly confused. A clear mind, a mind that is alive, vital, full of energy, that sees life at every instant as new, is never seeking. The idea of "seek and you will find" is, to me, utterly absurd. How can a confused, petty, self-centered, little mind ever find anything beyond its own projections? A wise man, a man who is aware, never seeks. When you do not seek at all, you do not invite experience. Then you are beginning to clear your confusion. Most of us want more new experiences, a greater variety of experiences, more thrills, more visions, more clarity, but a mind that is demanding the 'more' is avoiding what actually is. Having cultivated these escapes, we inevitably and most naturally run away into them; but if a man is serious, earnest in his intentions, not intellectually and verbally, but actually, then his main concern is to dissipate all confusion and all escapes. There is no seeking, asking, or inviting more and more experiences.

Why do we seek the 'more'; why do we seek something new? It is because our minds and lives are small, shallow, empty, dull, boring, and we want to escape from all that at any price. That is our chief concern. We have our gods, or we say we are seeking a new direction, or that all religions lead to the same something-or-other. We are collecting from various leaders, so-called spiritual beings. All this indicates a petty, narrow, limited mind. Such a mind has no space within itself, and there is more and more confusion, not less. We say, "This is the right path, and I'm going to follow it." Only the neurotic, the unbalanced now assert that. All the organized business affairs called "religions" have utterly failed; they have no meaning any more. If we do not seek, and no longer have any faith in any of the infantile organizations, then we are confronted with what actually is, with ourselves. If we are not able to resolve that center, that little corner of the vast field of life, we are everlastingly in battle with life.

After one has given up all the psychological, religious, spiritual organizations, the so-called "paths leading to truth," the problem arises of freeing this little entity, this little corner which one has cultivated, looked after, struggled with, and with which one has fought against the vast movement of life. How can one free it so that there is not this silly little thing called the 'me', the 'mine'? Can one resolve it? We are not talking about whether one should go to the office, whether one should do this or that, whether one should have more money or less money, more clothes or less clothes, and all that kind of stuff. That will all be answered very clearly, without any contradiction, without any confusion, when the psychological state has been cleared, when the little corner of this vast, complex existence, which is the individual, which is the family, which is the 'me' and the 'mine', which recognizes and identifies itself with nationality, with a particular group, with a particular idea—all will be answered when that little corner, with all its beauty, its glory, and its extreme delicacy has come to an end.

It is only possible to resolve, to understand that center when there is no escape whatsoever, when we are capable of looking at ourselves very clearly, without condemnation, justification, or denial. To look very clearly we must have space. To look at a tree very, very clearly, to look at our wives, our husbands, our neighbors, or to look clearly at the stars of an evening, or the mountains, there must be space, but what we call "space" is the space which we have created; the space we know is between the observer and the observed. There is not only a space as time but also a space as distance. We maintain this space in all our existence, in all our activity. The observer is always keeping at a distance from the observed. In this little space we are experiencing, judging, evaluating, condemning, seeking.

Please do not merely listen and hear words. If you are merely hearing words and intellectually saying, "It is obvious," then you are not actually facing facts. The intellect is a most deceptive thing. Intellect is absolutely necessary in order to reason sanely, rationally, healthily, but the whole of life is not intellect, any more than it is emotion or sentiment. If you are actually listening to what is being said by the speaker, you will not only see the actual fact, the actual reality of the space, but, if you push it further, you will also see that as long as this space exists, there must be conflict. This space is contradictory, and where there is contradiction there must be conflict. It is like the man who is empty, lonely, insufficient, for whom life has no meaning. He projects a future through which he will fulfill, through literature, through painting, through music, through some kind of experience or relationship. The fulfillment is the object, and the fulfiller is the observer. The observer and the observed always have a space between them, and therefore there is always that sense of conflict.

If one realizes that, not intellectually but actually, what is one to do? Space is necessary. Without space there is no freedom. We are talking psychologically. Freedom is not a reaction against society, becoming a beatnik or a Beatle, or growing long hair—all that is not freedom. Freedom is something entirely different, and that freedom can only come about when there is immense space, not the space which one knows exists between the observer and the observed. That is only a very small space, and when there is only that small space, there is no contact. It is only when one is in contact, when there is no space between the observer and the observed that one is in total relationship—with a tree for instance. One is not identified with the tree, the flower, a woman, a man, or whatever it is, but when there is this complete absence of space as the observer and the observed, then there is vast space. In that space there is no conflict; in that space there is freedom.

Freedom is not a reaction. You cannot say, "Well, I am free." The moment you say you are free, you are not free because you are conscious of yourself as being free from something, and therefore you have the same situation as an observer who is asserting he is free. He has created a space, and in that space he breeds conflict. To understand this requires not intellectual agreement or disagreement, or saying, "I don't understand," but rather it requires coming directly into contact with *what is*. It means seeing that all your actions, every moment of action is of the observer and the observed, and within that space there is pleasure, pain, and suffering, the desire to fulfill, to become famous. Within that space there is no contact with anything. Contact, relationship, has a quite different meaning when the observer is no longer apart from the observed. There is this extraordinary space, and there is freedom.

To understand this space is meditation. To understand it deeply, to feel it, to be of it, to live and let it function as a part of us, to be in that space is quite a different thing. We begin to understand when, how, and what to do. We only know space because of an object. There is space created by this tent—the space inside the tent and the space outside the tent, the space between us and the moun-

tain. The space we know is that between the observer and the star which he sees of an evening, the distance, the miles, the time it will take to go there. We accept that space, live in that space, have all our relationships in that space, and we never ask ourselves if there is a different dimension of space. We are not talking about the space of the astronauts, of the people who walk in a weightless state. That is not at all the space we are talking about; that is still of time, of the observer and the observed. We are talking of a space in which there is not the object as the observed. It is very important to find out about it, not through words because they would be symbols. The word and the symbol are not the reality. The word *space* is not the actual space. We must find out, uncover that extraordinary space and therefore freedom in it.

Meditation is of importance—not how you meditate, not the practice of meditation, not the way you maintain certain visions, not that childish, infantile business which unfortunately has been brought to the West from the East. You must have a great deal of skepticism, and I hope you have plenty of it when you are listening to what is being said, here or at any other place, for then you will find out for yourselves. It is a rather childish business if you come to these gatherings to experience some new fantastic, mystical state. That you can easily achieve through some drug. If you have a serious intention to find out for yourself—not to seek but to see something totally new, to find out about a new flower, a blade of grass which you have never seen before although you may have walked along the path where it grows hundreds and thousands of times—you see something totally new. You discover something which is a rebirth, which is not related to the past; your mind is made young, fresh, innocent. Meditation is important because it is only the meditative mind, the mind that is looking, hearing, listening, observing, being aware of all its reactions, its subtleties, never condemning, never justifying, never trying to become famous, but just watching—it is only such a mind that has significance. There is no one to answer your question for you. If you ask a right question, in that right question itself is the answer, but if you ask another person and accept what that other person says, you become a foolish person. Then you live on faith and hope, and you are inviting despair, anxiety, and fear. But if you observe as you are walking, moving, acting, you discover for yourself the whole meaning of existence. It can be discovered only when there is this state of observing, listening. That means never resisting, never suppressing, never defending. When the mind is vulnerable, when the brain is no longer functioning as the animal with its greed, envy, ambition, aggressiveness, violence, then it is capable of listening totally, and therefore it is discovering, seeing for itself.

What you discover is not what you want to discover. Throughout the centuries, for thousands upon thousands of years, before Sumeria, before Egypt, before India, before Greece and Rome, human beings have always been groping after this extraordinary state. Man has given it many different names according to his fancy, his culture: God, creation, Brahma. Man has always hungered after it because he has realized that life itself is so short. His life, not life itself, but his particular little corner, which has very little meaning but to which he clings, is so short. Knowing that there is death, he is hoping to find something far beyond time, space, and knowledge. There is such a thing only when the mind and the heart are free from the known, and therefore there is vast space. Only in that space can there be peace and freedom, and only in that state can man realize and listen to a dimension which he cannot otherwise find, no matter what he does. He can only come to it naturally, darkly, without the

"wanting." He may find it, and when he comes upon it, that is enough. It may last a lifetime or a second, but that second is of the vast, timeless space.

What is important to realize, not intellectually or verbally, but actually, is that one is totally confused, which is an obvious fact. Reading any newspaper, any magazine, going to any church, listening to any political talk, one is really quite in despair to see how terribly confused one is. If one realizes that one can never escape from that actual fact, one will begin to discover how one looks at the fact of what one actually is, not what one thinks one should be. That again is an escape. Then one will discover for oneself that one is looking at it as the observer and the observed, creating space and inviting in that space infinite conflict and contradiction. When one realizes all that, one's mind is in a state of meditation. The individual mind is the local mind, the Gstaad mind, the Swiss mind, the English mind, the Russian mind, and so on, but the human mind is not the individual mind. The individual mind has its place: one must go to the office; one must have one's bank account; one has his own little family; but the individual mind can never become the human mind. The human mind is an immense entity which has lived ten thousand years and more, and it is that human mind in its travail which can understand a dimension which is totally new, untouched by the known.

Comment: I would like to understand the significance of a space in which the observer and the observed are not.

KRISHNAMURTI: We only know one space, the space as the observer and the observed. I look at this microphone as an observer, and there is the object which is the microphone. There is a space between the observer and the observed. This space is distance—distance being time. There is the observer and the distance between him and a star, between him and a mountain. To cover that distance we need time. The faster we go, the quicker we cover that space, but it is still the observer traveling towards the observed.

You are asking what the other space is which is not this. I can't tell you. I can only tell you that as long as this space as the observer and the observed exists, the other is not. The speaker has also stated that there is a way of freeing the observer who is always creating the space as the observer and the observed. However much you may extend that little space, it will always exist. There is an airplane overhead. You, as an observer, as a listener, are listening to that sound. You are the listener and the sound is there. There is a gap. The gap is a time interval. It is getting further and further and further away, expanding into the universe. You are always the observer, and there is always the observed: you—your wife; you—your house; you—the river; you—your country; you—the government; me as a communist or a Muslim or whatever it is—and the noncommunist, the atheist, the barbarian. As long as this space exists, as long as there is contradiction, there must be conflict. To free the mind of the observer, no escape is possible. Don't escape; don't seek. Face the fact of what you are; don't translate in terms of what you think you are, of what you should be, which is again an escape. When you face the fact of what you actually are, without escaping, without naming it, without the word, then the fact becomes totally different. When you do that with every reaction, with every movement of thought, then there is a freedom from the observer; then there is a totally different dimension of space.

Question: How can one experience this different dimension of space?

KRISHNAMURTI: You are standing there; I am sitting here; that's all. All you know is the space between you, standing there, and me; between you and the mountain, you and your wife, you and a tree, you and your country. When you know that space, you know you are never in contact with anything. You are in isolation. Therefore, with you as the observer, and me as the observed, there is no contact. That's all.

Question: Do you believe that freedom comes when you are mature?

KRISHNAMURTI: First of all, I don't believe in anything. (Laughter) Don't laugh, please, what I am saying is very serious. Why should one believe in anything, even in flying saucers? Why should one believe there is God or no-God? Either there is or there is not. Why should one believe? If one has seen that, one acquires an extraordinary mind. Does freedom come at the right moment? Freedom comes for anyone who is really in earnest to find out. There is no time, no maturity; it is not a question of ripening through old age, achieving it through righteous action. Maturity does not come through age, through the body growing. It comes when one is really serious and has understood that one cannot possibly escape. When one sees life as it is, when one sees oneself as one is, from there one can move.

July 31, 1966

Saanen, Switzerland, 1966

✳

First Dialogue in Saanen

I think all of us should be very clear as to what we mean by these discussions. First of all, it is not an entertainment. It isn't something we go to because we have an hour or two to spare, like going to a concert. It isn't mental gymnastics, showing off our cleverness or erudition. What we are trying to do is to discuss so that we can expose ourselves, not to the speaker, but to ourselves, to find out what we think, what we feel, what our reactions actually are. That demands a great deal of serious intelligence, not just a verbal quibble or an intellectual exchange of ideas. Whatever we discuss, we should go to the end of, logically, reasonably, sanely, without any personal emotion or personal point of view, trying to discover for ourselves the truth of what actually is. To make these discussions worthwhile requires a great deal of intelligence, a certain amount of attention, and a certain quality of intention which pursues to the very end, whatever the difficulties, whatever the hindrances we may find ourselves caught in. Let us go into each subject, each problem that we have, so completely that when we leave this tent, we are free of it, not ideologically but actually. In the same way that a person drops, puts away, smoking, drinking, let us be completely rid of any problem that we discuss. We have a vast number of problems. We may not be aware of them, but there they are. We may conceal them behind a mask, unwilling to face the reality of what our problems are; but I feel that these discussions should break down the defenses which we have deeply cultivated so that at the end of each discussion, whatever the problem may be, it is not my problem or your problem but the problem of man. If we could go into it hesitantly and gently, take the journey together, partaking of all the implications in it, then perhaps these discussions will be worthwhile.

What shall we discuss?

Question: We all have some kind of belief, and we come here in the hope of attaining what we believe. Madame Curie had a belief and worked enthusiastically until she found what she wanted. Is not some kind of belief necessary to have enthusiasm?

KRISHNAMURTI: This is a discussion. It is not a question-and-answer meeting. It isn't that you ask a question, and I reply to it. In that way, after putting the question you have no further responsibility. It should be quite the contrary. Because you have put the question, you have tremendous responsibility, responsibility in the sense that you are vitally interested in it. After putting the question, you don't lean back in your seat and say, "Well, I'll wait for him to reply." Whoever puts a question, please let us realize that both of us are going into the problem. You and I are both eager to find the truth of the matter, whatever it is. You are not merely asking a question, hoping to find an answer.

Does belief give enthusiasm? That's one point. Can enthusiasm sustain itself without a belief, and is enthusiasm at all necessary, or is a different kind of energy needed, a different kind of vitality, drive? Most of us have enthusiasm for something or other. We are very keen, very enthusiastic about concerts, about physical exercise, or going to a picnic. Unless it is nourished all the time by something or other, it fades away and we have a new enthusiasm for other things. Is there a self-sustaining force, energy, which doesn't depend on a belief?

The other question is: Do we need a belief of any kind, and if we do, why is it necessary? That's one of the problems involved. We don't need a belief that there is sunshine, the mountains, the rivers. We don't need a belief that we and our wives quarrel. We don't have to have a belief that life is a terrible misery with its anguish, conflict, and constant ambition; it is a fact. But we demand a belief when we want to escape from a fact into an unreality.

For example, I know there is death. It is a fact. I can't avoid it. I may like to avoid it; I may pretend; I may push it away from me, not think about it, nor talk about it; but there it is, a fact. Being afraid, I must have a belief that will give me comfort in facing this terrible reality. Apparently for most of us belief of some kind is necessary, belief in brotherhood, in the end of war, in the end of sorrow, in pacifism, in leading a good life. Why should we have any beliefs?

Comment: Because we don't know.

KRISHNAMURTI: Then don't; and don't have a belief.

Question: How can I be interested in discussing it if I don't?

KRISHNAMURTI: Does belief in ending sorrow give an interest in sorrow? Do please find out. I have sorrow of various kinds; I'm miserable, unhappy, unfulfilled. Someone tells me that sorrow can end. I say that I want to find out. I don't have to believe what he says. I want to find out if it can actually end. To find out, I have to see what is implied in it. My interest is not in the belief that it can end, but rather whether I can go into it so that I have no sorrow. Having a belief that sorrow can end is a waste of energy, and I need all my energy to investigate.

Question: Mustn't one have physical health, a good healthy body, so that doctors are not necessary?

KRISHNAMURTI: That's not what we are discussing at the moment. May we go into this to the very end of it, not just leave it and take up something else? We are asking ourselves why we need beliefs, ideals, examples, heroes, leaders, teachers, Masters. Why?

Comment: We are too lazy.

KRISHNAMURTI: Then be lazy! Why have a belief?

Comment: Because I'm afraid to be alone.

Comment: Because we need comfort.

KRISHNAMURTI: You're not answering the question. One says, "I am lazy." Others say, "I am afraid to be alone; I need comfort; therefore, I must have a belief." That doesn't solve the issue.

Comment: We don't know why we live, and therefore we believe.

KRISHNAMURTI: Life is a terrible bore, with loneliness and anguish. We believe there is something else. We avoid the issue. We know why we invent beliefs.

Comment: It is not a question of belief but of having a purpose.

KRISHNAMURTI: My life is drifting, useless, and if I have a purpose, an ideal, if I have something to aim at, I pursue it. Why?

Comment: If you have no purpose, then you have no intelligence and no energy.

KRISHNAMURTI: Do you have energy and intelligence if you have a purpose? You know people who have purposes, who have ideals, who have beliefs. Are they intelligent? Is a man who has a belief intelligent?

Question: What belief?

KRISHNAMURTI: Any belief. It doesn't matter what the belief is. Any belief conditions your way of thinking, and therefore your mind functions according to the belief or purpose which you have projected. Let us go into it slowly. Let us approach the problem quietly, with patience. Let us not add more words. First of all, the fact is that we are unhappy, we are miserable, we are in conflict, we are confused. That is an obvious daily fact. If we can clear that up, why do we want a belief? Because we don't know how to clear up our confusion, we say, "I must have a purpose; otherwise, I'll just dissipate my life."

Why do we need a belief? Is it not an escape? Please don't accept what I am saying, but actually observe it. The people who have preached nonviolence for a number of years are violent in their hearts, in their beings. They have forced themselves to discipline; they have tortured themselves according to some idea; they are peculiarly brutal in their relationships, but they have this marvelous ideal of nonviolence. What's the point of it? What is the point of having an ideal of nonviolence when we are violent? Why do we have to believe in nonviolence? The fact is that we are violent. We want to know if it is possible to be free of it; we don't want a belief. We don't want examples of people who have preached nonviolence, for they have tortured themselves, suppressed their sex, and many other things. Why do we need a belief when there is the fact of *what is?*

If I am confused, will having a belief in clarity give me enthusiasm to get rid of my confusion? It only creates contradictions. I dissipate my energy in this contradiction, in this effort. Do I say to myself, "I am going to throw away all my purposes, all my beliefs, because I first want to be rid of confusion"? Realizing that I am confused gives me energy. There is a waste of energy when I don't realize that I'm confused, or knowing that I'm confused, I believe in ideals.

The speaker has talked for the last forty years about throwing away all beliefs, all ideals, all heroes, all ideations, all teachers. Have you done it? No, of course not; you are conditioned to a life of concepts, not actuality. Why not find out for yourselves if you need an idea, a belief, a purpose, a human being who knows more than you do, a Master, a teacher, a guru? If you find that you need any of these, find out why you need it. If you say, "I need it because I'm lazy," will having an ideal of being very alert make you any less lazy? But if you say, "Why am I lazy?" perhaps you will find that it is because you don't go to bed early, because you are wasting your energy sexually, in games, in a dozen ways, or perhaps your glands don't function properly. Perhaps you are lazy because it is your habit. Your wife gives you tea and goodness knows what else. You live a lazy life; you like it; you want it. If you like it, be lazy, but don't have a conflict about laziness. Be completely lazy and see what happens.

In the same way, if you are confused, and someone says there is a state of mind in which there is clarity like sunshine on a lovely day, without any mist, without any fog, in which you can see everything clearly, in which every line is clear, why do you believe in that person? The fact is that you are confused. To be free of confusion you don't need a belief. You want to know whether it is possible to be free of the confusion. You don't have to believe me because I say that you can be free.

Question: I am aware that between you and myself there is space. Is there any way that I can make myself free in this space?

KRISHNAMURTI: The speaker said the other day that there is space of different kinds, that there is space between you and me, which is an observable, actual fact. There is space between you and your most intimate person—wife, husband, whoever it may be. Why do you want an ideal of a contact in which there is no space? The fact is that there is that space, and in that space there is all our misery, conflict, and the problems of relationship.

Is it possible for me to have no space between you and me? I don't have to believe in it. That would be stupid. There is a belief in life after death. If I am going to die, I want to know what it means. I want to know what life means. Why should I have a purpose? I know what life means as it is—the misery, the everyday conflict, going to the office,

being kicked around by the boss, being insulted, all the humility and all the ugliness of forty years spent in a beastly little office—coming home, quarreling with my wife, patching up, sex, the whole circus of life. Why do I have to have any belief at all?

Comment: Having a belief is like putting a penny in the slot, hoping a bar of chocolate will come out.

KRISHNAMURTI: That's the same thing in different words, only you have a slot in which you can put the penny. (Laughter) If you can, when you go out, leave behind in the tent all your ideals, and see what happens. First of all, you don't really believe in your ideals. That's a fact. If people really believed in reincarnation, what they do in this life would be tremendously important because next life they are going to pay for it if they don't behave properly now. They don't believe it because they don't believe in leading the real life. It is an escape.

Can each one of us face his escape—from confusion, from quarrels with wife or husband, from the meaningless existence, the boredom of life, with the things that he wants to do and can't, from the complete frustration, the feeling of guilt, the agony of it, this agony that we human beings go through? Can we look at it all, face our escapes from it all without an ideal? Ideals have no meaning when we have to face reality.

The French Revolution, the communist revolution, and all other revolutions have been brought about because of ideas, utopias. Millions and millions of people have been killed because those in power think that they have the right, that they know. After passing through many years of experiment, torture, liquidation, killing, exile, they come back to the same point, that of leading a bourgeois life.

Question: Don't you need dialogue to face any problem?

KRISHNAMURTI: With whom are you having a dialogue? When I am facing a problem, with whom am I discussing the problem? If it is myself, who is the entity that is talking to the other? Why should I discuss with myself, have a dialogue, saying that this is right, that is wrong, this I should do, that I should not do, this is moral, that is immoral, asking what society would say? You are having a dialogue with yourself in a state of confusion. If there were no confusion, I wouldn't have a dialogue with myself. Or am I having a dialogue, a speech, an interview with my higher self? The higher self is invented by me. It all becomes too absurd. Either I see clearly, or I don't.

Comment: You have pictured to us a state, a space in which there is no sorrow; there is understanding, compassion. We are looking at that, and we still have distance between what is and that.

KRISHNAMURTI: I am in sorrow, and I have listened to someone who describes a state in which there is no sorrow, who says that sorrow can end. With sorrow there is always cunning, deception, hypocrisy; but with the ending of sorrow there is wisdom, there is intelligence. He says, "Don't make that into an ideal, into a concept, but see if you can be free from your sorrow." He has gone into it step by step. We are now asking ourselves why there is this monstrous structure of ideals, concepts, formulas, when they are just words without any reality. The reality is that we are confused; we have problems; we are miserable. We don't ask how we can end all of that. We always ask, "Can I move from this to that?"

Comment: If I do not believe in God, in religious leaders, and all the rest of it, it is almost like saying, "Whatever happens, I know that I can cope with it."

KRISHNAMURTI: That would be a most dangerous assertion because I am not capable. To be capable, to have the necessary vitality, energy, it should not be dissipated in ideals, in beliefs. How can you face facts if you have a divided mind, if there is an ideal, and the fact? You must have a mind that can say, "I can look at the facts." You cannot if you have ideals, if you have a divided mind, an idealistic mind and a nonidealistic mind.

Question: How can you bring up children without ideals, without beliefs? You will isolate them in the world.

KRISHNAMURTI: Do you think that if you bring them up without beliefs, you isolate them, choke them, cut them off from a lot of other people who believe, so that they have no relationships? There are two things involved. First, you yourself have to be free of ideals, beliefs. In the process of helping the child not to have beliefs, you yourself are getting rid of beliefs. You can't say, "I'll wait until I get rid of all my beliefs, and then I will teach them." By then the child is dead, or gone to some other person. If I understand the futility of beliefs, I can help the child to face the world, which is drowned in beliefs; that child will have intelligence enough not to be isolated.

Let us stick to what we were talking about. Can I, being confused, afraid, guilty, little-minded, petty, anxious, fearful, greedy, and acquisitive, being all that, can I face it without any ideal? I realize that having an ideal is an escape; it has no meaning. When I am unhealthy, if I say to myself, "I must be healthy; I must be healthy," that doesn't make me healthy. What makes me healthy is to eat the right food, and find out what the disease is. That means that I have to face the fact that I'm ill.

If you have no beliefs, it's a great relief. You put off a heavy burden. Then you walk lighter; then you can look into problems more freely. Can you do it? Can each of you actually, not theoretically, leave all beliefs, purposes, ideals, ideations, concepts? If you can't, then let's find out why you can't.

Comment: When you are ill, you realize that your health has gone, but then you believe that there is a state of good health.

KRISHNAMURTI: When you are ill, do you really believe in a state of good health? You say, "I have a toothache; let me go to the dentist." You do something. You don't believe in some perpetual good health.

Question: Isn't belief a psychological state?

KRISHNAMURTI: It is a very complex psychological state; it demands that I have beliefs, a purpose, an ideal. It is not a physical state; it is a psychological demand. Psychologically I can't face death, confusion, misery. I can't face what I am—my ugliness, my pettiness, my loneliness. I must have some kind of entertainment. Psychologically I need it; it feeds me; it sustains me; and I live like that. Psychologically I am no one, a poor, withered entity. I need a perfume; I need a richness; I need concerts; I need to come and listen to these talks, or be entertained by a church. I need it. Or, psychologically, I'm so denuded, insufficient, that I commit myself to some action; I become a communist, a socialist, a liberal, or whatever it is. There is only one fact—the fact that I am confused, miserable, and psychologically I

can't face it; therefore, I have to invent beliefs, purposes, gods, and ideals. Why can't I face it, not tomorrow, not at some future date, but now?

Comment: If you have no belief, you can become very violent.

KRISHNAMURTI: In spite of the Christian beliefs of peace and meekness, Christians have created many wars. Don't make the thing so absurd. You are defending beliefs. You have never said, "Why do I have beliefs?"

Comment: If you have a belief, it arises from an area that is not clear. As soon as you look into that area, you start to think about it, and that's dialogue.

KRISHNAMURTI: You have an area which is not clear, which is confused, and you have another area, which you think is clear. You have a dialogue between these two. That's called thinking, investigating, searching, asking. The area that is confused and the area that is not confused are both the same. There is a conflict between them, which indicates a state of confusion. It's not clarity.

Question: Can I look at confusion? And what is the state that looks at confusion?

KRISHNAMURTI: I'm confused about politics, about religion, about my wife, about what to do. I look at myself. Who is the entity that is looking? He's part of my confusion. Why don't I stop and look at myself? When I am confused in a jungle, I don't go around like a squirrel or a monkey all over the place. I stop to take stock of where I am, but I stop.

Question: Does that not bring up the question of psychological fear? We are suddenly faced with the fact that we have been trapped by the mind for years.

KRISHNAMURTI: We are frightened. Therefore the problem is not the ideal but whether it is possible to be free of fear.

Comment: Once you have faced it, you can no longer have an ideal.

KRISHNAMURTI: Of course. A man says he believes in brotherhood. When everyone is butchering each other, both inwardly and outwardly, why have an ideal of brotherhood? It is tommyrot.

Psychologically we are afraid; we are confused; and being incapable of resolving the confusion, not knowing what to do with the fear, we invent the idea. We must drop the idea, the ideal, the purpose. We must be sure that it is dropped completely so that it doesn't interfere, doesn't come back in some other subtle way. That is what I mean by stopping.

Out of my confusion I have chosen a leader, a teacher, an ideal, a guru—out of confusion. If I were clear, I wouldn't choose. It wouldn't even occur to me to choose. But, I have chosen him, and I realize, by Jove, what I have done. What *have* I done? Out of my confusion, I've chosen a leader—Hitler, whoever it is. Hm? Now first let me drop that—drop the leader, drop it. Not, what to do next? Don't put that question, "What am I to do?" When you put that question, "What am I to do?" you're already inventing an idea.

Comment: I have an area that's confused. And I look at that area of confusion. And you say that's confused, and the mind that looks at it is a division of the mind. It's all the same thing. So, stop.

KRISHNAMURTI: No one understood what I meant by "Stop." That's what I'm explaining, sir.

My mind, my psyche, my psychological state has invented the idea. Right? And that ideal is preventing me from looking at the fact. So, the first thing I have to do to look at the fact is to drop the idea. Right? Have I dropped it?

Question: Dropped the idea?

KRISHNAMURTI: The ideal, the idea, what should be, what should not be, the noble, do you follow? The concept. Have I dropped it? It's only when I drop it that I can look at this.

Let's go over this again step by step. Psychologically I am confused; I am afraid. I know this. I am also aware that out of this fear, out of this uncertainty, I invent a concept. To understand the psychological state completely, I must drop the concept. If I come back to the problem of how to face the fear, I haven't dropped it. Isn't fear an idea? I have already moved so that I am investigating the fear; I haven't stopped. When I have dropped the belief, the purpose, the idea, the ideal, I must stop and take a breath. Then my mind is no longer burdened with ideas, with concepts. Then I can look; then I can find out how to look. That's all.

We are talking together so that we see things clearly. We have to be rid of the psychological structure of defense, and that is one of the most difficult things to do. Is it possible to have the energy, the vitality to look at the fact, or must we lose that vitality in psychological defense? I'm afraid I can't answer whether we can or cannot. We either do it or we don't. It is an obvious fact that we have these defenses, and we can live and die with them, with constant misery, confusion, and conflict. To be open, to look, to investigate, to find out, we must stop; we must have the feeling that we have completely dropped all defense.

Does each one of us, when we leave this tent, feel that we have unburdened ourselves, thrown away our ideals, so that we can look at ourselves as we are? Then we can proceed; we can find out; we can discuss what to do. We can discuss whether the fact can be changed, or if mere confrontation with the fact brings about a mutation. That can only take place if we have dropped the other. Tomorrow morning we will talk over together the only problem: how to face the fact, not how to get rid of ideals.

If you haven't got rid of them after nearly an hour and a half, good luck; carry them to your homes; but I hope you have dropped them and have stopped. Do you know what it means to stop? Not jump to the next conclusion. It is like a man who smokes, who says, "I will stop," and actually stops smoking. If he says, "I must choose something; I must do something in order to be occupied so that I am not thinking about smoking," he is still smoking. But if you can drop your ideals, then you will find for yourselves that there is not only a new energy, but there is also a new perfume, which is of passion, and without that perfume you can't look.

August 3, 1966

Second Dialogue in Saanen

We were discussing yesterday morning whether it is at all possible to free the mind of all beliefs, ideas, concepts, formulas, ideals, and all purposive, directive action. Unless we understand very clearly why it is important for a mind to be psychologically free of beliefs, we will never be able to face facts, to come directly in contact with *what is*. We are going to discuss this morning whether a mind, without having a belief, an idea, a concept, can face what it actually is. We will also go into the question of whether

the mind can face fear without any escape, such as belief. We will go to the very end of this problem of fear and what to do about it. To discuss it fully, we first have to inquire whether action, any kind of activity, is possible without a formula, without an idea— idea being organized thought.

Question: Is it possible to face myself? Between myself and the fact is all the psychological structure of memory, tradition, the culture in which I have been brought up.

KRISHNAMURTI: Let us be very clear what we are discussing.

Comment: We must live without any conflict at all.

KRISHNAMURTI: Don't let us indulge in theories. We are not using intellectual gymnastics, nor are we opposing one theory to another. We are trying to face facts, which is one of the most difficult things to do. As we said yesterday, we have built around ourselves so many defenses made up of beliefs, ideas, words, and symbols, through which we try to face *what is*. This, obviously, is not possible.

Can I really be free of belief—of what I should be, what I am, what I was? I may not be expressing your particular sentiment, your particular question, but it involves the whole thing. Is it possible for me to act, to do something, without a formula? That is really an extraordinarily important question because, so far, we have always functioned, acted, according to an idea, according to a belief, according to what someone has said— it doesn't matter whether it's Marx or Christ. Our action has approximated itself to a belief, to an idea. We are now saying something so totally different—to act without an idea—that it may sound completely crazy, a neurotic statement. It may be true or it may be false. We have to go into it very, very deeply, step by step, to find out for ourselves if we can act so that every moment is new. Ideas are never new; beliefs are never new. All action, whatever it is—sexual, going to the office, any activity—is based on a memory, a concept, an ideal, a tradition, a thought which has a remembrance. Is it possible to be free of it? Don't tell me it is, or it is not. Don't take sides, or say, "If we do this, it will happen." Those are all theories, excellent in their own way, but they have no meaning to a man who really wants to find out if it is possible to live in this world without any idea—brotherhood, the unity of man, the love of God, and dozens and dozens of others.

Question: You pointed out that the mind is totally unclear, and that no sensible action can be taken as long as the mind is in that state. If part of the mind is not clear, the whole thing is unclear; so how can we even look at your question as long as our mind is so unclear?

KRISHNAMURTI: What will you do? You state that your mind is totally confused. You don't know whether there is a God, or there is no God; whether there is reincarnation, or no reincarnation; whether you must love your country, when many people say we have gone beyond all that. Some say that you must have a king or a queen, but the republicans say, "Oh, that's old stuff; put it all out." You are brought up in this confusion; you are this confusion. Realizing that whatever you think, whatever you do, whatever your aspirations may be, noble or otherwise, they are all the outcome of this confusion and are therefore still confused, what will you do?

Question: Shouldn't I just do nothing, and look completely at my confusion?

KRISHNAMURTI: It is not, "You should look," or "You should not look." You are coming to me and saying, "Please tell me what to do."

Comment: Well, that's what I've done; I've looked at my confusion.

Comment: We can do a simple action without thinking.

Comment: We must pay attention to the results of scientific research; otherwise, we throw away all scientific knowledge.

KRISHNAMURTI: We need scientific knowledge, and all the implications involved in it. That is entirely different from the psychological demand of the human being who says, "I must have beliefs." There is the Christian belief, the Hindu belief, the communist belief, the socialist belief, each dividing man more and more. We are asking whether it is possible to have no beliefs, and if it is possible to act without an idea.

This requires a great deal of attention, not just saying, "Yes, I agree with you," or "I don't agree with you." It is a tremendous problem. I must ask myself why I try to escape from the fact of what I am, whatever I am. I don't like something in myself; I want to run away from it and either go to a church, to a concert, take a drink, go somewhere, or come to a meeting like this. If I say, "I'm frightened; therefore, I escape," that's not the reason at all.

Comment: I do all these things because I'm lonely.

KRISHNAMURTI: Why do you try to escape from your loneliness? Why don't you face it? Do please ask yourself why you have built a structure, a network of escapes around yourself.

Comment: Deep down in us there is great fear; therefore, we run away.

KRISHNAMURTI: I am deeply afraid; therefore, I run away. Is that a fact?

Comment: We have been taught to be afraid.

KRISHNAMURTI: I don't know if you have noticed what is implied in this question. For instance, young children don't mind being friends with Negroes, with brown people, with anyone, but older people come and tell them, "Don't play with those people." The adults put fear into the children. I am asking quite a different question. The questioner said, "I am deeply frightened; I have great fear; therefore, I run away." Whether you are taught to run away or not, is it true that fear makes you run away?

Comment: You run away because you are annoyed.

KRISHNAMURTI: Whether it is annoyance or fear or something else, why do you run? You generally say that you can't face yourselves, that you are afraid, lonely, this and that; and therefore you run away. You are not answering my question. Why are you running away?

Comment: Because I can think about being afraid.

Comment: All the time inside of us there is some sort of ideal of how we should be, and this is in conflict with what we really are.

KRISHNAMURTI: I have great fear, anxiety; I am lonely; I am unhappy; I am miserable; I am frustrated; I become envious, jealous, bitter, cynical, and go to do something to make myself more happy. I move away from *what is* to what is not. Why do I do this? The questioner says, "I am dissatisfied with what I am." Then why do I run?

Comment: I don't like it.

Comment: I can't stand still. That's why I run.

Comment: I run away to save myself.

Comment: By running away it may be easier.

KRISHNAMURTI: It's a supposition again, "If I did this, this wouldn't happen." One can talk like this endlessly. We are trying to go into the issue involved. Please have patience with me and listen to me for two minutes. I want to know why I run away. My question is not running away from something to something, but the action of running. I am frightened, lonely, anxious, miserable. That's a fact; I don't like it and make a movement away to something. I take a drink, go to a nightclub, to a meeting, or whatever it is. I'm not talking of *what is* and 'what should be', but of the interval between them, the act of running. If I can find out about that, perhaps I won't run. If I can find out why this movement takes place, I may be able to solve the problem. I may, although I may not, but I want to know why this action takes place. The response has been, "Because I don't like this, I want to change it; I want to move to something better." I know these games which man has played through centuries upon centuries, but have I ever questioned what this movement is, and what it involves?

Comment: Everything is moving in the world.

KRISHNAMURTI: Everything is moving; that river is extraordinarily full this morning; I hope it won't come in here. It's moving. Of course we all know that. You have not understood what I said. How difficult it is to make one understand a simple fact!

Question: I don't like something, so I just run away to something I like. Is your question why I adopt that particular technique of finding something that pleases me, and why I run away from what I don't like?

KRISHNAMURTI: No. I am asking you something entirely different. Why does this movement take place?

Question: Why do you ask the question?

KRISHNAMURTI: Because, this is what we are always doing, running from this to that. I am asking what this means, the movement itself.

Comment: If you ask that question there must be an answer.

KRISHNAMURTI: We are going to find out. I say there is an answer. I would like to show it to you, but you don't stop.

Comment: It isn't from this to that. Probably there is no movement at all.

KRISHNAMURTI: I think I have moved; I think I have run away; and there may be no movement at all. What we think is a running away is no running away at all. I don't like this; I move away from this to that. I consider the moving away from this an escape, but the thing I have escaped to is the same as this. Therefore I haven't moved. It is a most extraordinary thing if you can discover this for yourself.

I don't like what I am and I say to myself, "I must change what I am and move to what I should be." The "should be" is an idea, a concept, a formula which I have invented; and I think I shall achieve that by moving away from this; but that is the same as this because that will become the new center; from there I go to somewhere else, and that new thing will become another center. I am not really running away at all; I am merely changing from one center to another center, which is still the 'me', which I don't like. When I think I am running away, I am really static. Though I think I am moving, I am really static, which is the most terrible thing to discover. So from one state of dullness I think I shall move to another state which is not static, but the movement itself becomes static. The problem arises: how to break down something which is static, and not create more statics.

Comment: There is only one way, which is to examine what I am, what society is.

KRISHNAMURTI: We must understand that when we think we are changing, we are really not changing at all. It isn't like putting on a new coat and discarding the old one because the entity that puts on the new coat is always the same entity. This doesn't mean that I must get rid of the self, which is the philosophy of the Orient.

Comment: You were speaking in your last talk about space, and if I understood, there is only one space.

KRISHNAMURTI: To go from here to the place where I live there is time, there is space, and there is definitely a movement. I walk, take a car, go by a cycle or by train. There is definitely a movement from the tent to where I'm going. I apply the same thing to myself. I say, "I am this; I am unhappy." If I'm young, I want more sex; if I'm middle-aged, I want to live more happily, and so on. I want to move away from *what is* to something else. Physically I move away from the tent to my home. There is a movement, and I apply that same thing to myself. I say that I am angry, that I am violent; I will move away to nonviolence. I never stop and look; I never ask myself if I am really moving. I think I am moving; I think I am gaining what I want, but am I actually, or am I only putting on a new coat, while the same violence still continues?

Comment: Fear still remains.

KRISHNAMURTI: I am not talking of fear; I am not talking of what I am. I am only talking of this movement from *what is* to what I think should be. I am saying to myself, "Is it a movement?"

Question: If there is no movement at all, why do we think there is?

KRISHNAMURTI: Find out. Up to now all religions, all philosophies have stated that you should change, move from this to that. If someone comes along and says that it may

not be like that at all, you don't even examine it.

Question: Isn't that movement a shift of concentration?

KRISHNAMURTI: When you are concentrated, you are exclusive, and in that exclusiveness there is no movement at all. You are concentrated on this, and later on you are concentrated on that. If you are totally attentive, why do you want to move from this to that?

One asks oneself, "Is there a change at all?" If the movement from this to that is static because this is essentially the same as that, although called by a different name, put in a different cloak, then one asks if there is a change at all.

Question: Is there a movement at all?

KRISHNAMURTI: If there is no movement at all, if there is no such thing as evolution, then there is only decay. That is all we know, and that is what we are running away from. The movement leading you to there is the same as this. You are caught in a vicious circle. You think you are changing, changing, changing, and this change is called evolution. May there not be a totally different way of looking, living?

Question: During my whole life, haven't I changed at all?

KRISHNAMURTI: Whether you have not changed at all or I have changed is not the question. You are eager to apply everything to yourselves. You want to do something. You don't see first what is implied. Do you know what would happen to you if you really discovered this fact, if it meant something to you? You would be in a state of horror if you discovered that the movement from this to that is the same as this. What you think you're changing to is what has been. If you realize this, you ask, "What have I done for forty years of my life?" Don't add this new torture; you have enough torture as it is.

Let us begin to understand slowly step by step. We started out by asking ourselves if we need any belief at all. Apparently belief, psychological belief, is a means of defense, a means of protecting ourselves. These beliefs are utopias, examples, ideals of 'what should be'. We are making a movement from *what is* to 'what should be'. This movement we call change, from antithesis to synthesis, and from this synthesis to another antithesis, and so on and on, spirally climbing.

Do we realize, as human beings, that for two million years or more man has said, "I mustn't kill, because I'll be killed." Yet he keeps on killing, and keeps on talking about peace. What has he learned, except to protect himself more and more, in a different, more subtle manner? This protection is called movement, evolution. I see that it has no meaning at all. It is like putting up an umbrella against the rain. If I don't have the umbrella, if I just think I have it, I am soaked through all my life. I realize that any movement from *what is* to 'what should be' is the movement of *what is*. Therefore it is not a change at all.

If you realize it, which is a tremendous thing, you are faced with a problem of complete despair. If you don't invent philosophies, you are in despair because you realize that the movement of change is no change at all. You say, "I am what I am; how terrible!" That is an agony. Most of you live with this agony. If you say you must break it up, you must find a different way of living so that life isn't just an agony, what action can be taken? The only action you know is the movement from this to that. When you realize that it is a sterile action,

that it has no meaning, you ask whether there is an action which is not based on an idea or which does not approximate itself to an idea. Until you find that out, you are bound to be in despair; from that despair you run away. The running away to something is the same as the despair, but you have called it by a different name. See what your mind has done? Are you to live forever with your despair? Running away from despair to something which is not despair is still despair. Are you to live all your next forty years in despair?

That's what most people do. They say, "I am living; I have an ideal, a belief; there are these wonderful people to whom I'm going." All this is born out of despair, and therefore is still despair. What is to be done is to find an action which is not based on a belief, an idea, a concept, a formula, or which is not approximating itself to something?

Comment: There is an action when you act without a center.

KRISHNAMURTI: That is a supposition. It is like saying to a man who is hungry, "I'll give you a book which is full of recipes telling how to cook a marvelous meal."

Comment: Actually when the difference between the experiencer and the experience is understood and finally abolished, then. . . .

KRISHNAMURTI: Forgive me for saying so, but you are just repeating what I have said. Don't repeat something that is not actual to you. If you don't repeat, you are learning. That is a most marvelous thing for you to discover for yourself.

Comment: Once the experience has come and gone, it doesn't really matter whose words you use.

KRISHNAMURTI: I quite agree. If it is lost, it has gone down the river.

Comment: Yes.

KRISHNAMURTI: When you go out of this tent, do not act according to an idea, to a memory.

Comment: When you are in conflict, there is fear of a loss of identity if that difference between the experiencer and the experience is abolished.

KRISHNAMURTI: What are you identified with?

Comment: At the moment when it happens, nothing, but there is a reflex which brings one back.

Question: Why must I know despair?

KRISHNAMURTI: I am not saying you should know it! If you have no despair, you are living perfectly happily. Don't let me introduce the problem of despair to you, for goodness' sake! The Vietnamese and the Americans who are dying in Vietnam—their mothers, their sisters, and their wives are in despair.

Question: Is there an 'I' to know this despair; is there something running away from despair to know this despair with?

KRISHNAMURTI: You will find out only when there is no movement of escape, when you realize that, do what you will—discipline, control, you know the tortures you go through—do what you will, it is still what has been.

Question: How does one overcome the very real moment of terror?

KRISHNAMURTI: You want a quick answer, and there is no quick answer. You can take a pill, a drug, but that's no answer. You'll be back again in the same state tomorrow. But if we take the voyage together step by step, not impatiently, not rushing, hesitantly, with care, with affection, you will find it for yourself.

Question: What are the causes of war?

KRISHNAMURTI: We all know through centuries what the causes of war are: nationalism, my country and your country, my love of my country and your love of your country, economic separation, different kinds of societies, my prejudice against your prejudice, my leader against your leader, and so on and so on. We have known this for two million years and more, but we are still at it. Human beings know the danger of nationalism, and they still wave the flag. There is something abnormal about the human mind.

I'll put it differently. Our life functions in routine, in patterns. I repeat what has been, hoping it will change, and this hope is the movement which prevents me from facing my despair. Without hope, I'm lost. I hold on to it. It doesn't matter whether it is real or unreal, false and mythical. The hope is what has been. I don't realize that at first, but when I do realize it, not intellectually, not emotionally, but actually, I say, "I have lived, struggled, brought other human beings into the world, and I go on, for what?" I become more and more in despair, more and more depressed. I end up in an asylum, or I take a drug; I go to the latest cinema or the latest entertainment.

What am I to do? To find out, I have to inquire into this question of functioning with an idea. If I don't function with an idea, with a belief, with a doctrine, what is action?—action with regard to the actual fact, action with regard to despair, not with regard to some future state. If my action is based on a hope, or something or other, it is no answer. I have to find out how the mind always refuses to move away from what it has known, how it refuses to function differently.

If you will go into it with the speaker, you will find out for yourself, but if you say, "I had that experience yesterday. When it happened I was so happy; please tell me how to get it back," it's all silly. Throw it down the river; it means nothing. There is only one question facing us now, whether there is an action in which there is no approximation of an idea. To find that out, don't say that there is or there is not; you don't know. Don't say, "You have been talking about spontaneity." There is no such thing as spontaneity. That's just an invention, because you are always acting with memory. Don't translate it, but try to find out for yourselves whether there is any action without idea. When you have discovered it, then you can proceed to see what you can do with regard to despair. If you can't find it, we will discuss it very carefully, step by step, tomorrow. But don't pretend that you've found it. Don't say, "Yes, I have had moments of clarity." It's like that noise of the train; it goes away. To inquire, you not only need freedom but also great care, and care means affection, love.

August 4, 1966

Third Dialogue in Saanen

We will continue with what we were discussing yesterday, unless you have some other question you want to discuss.

Question: Why don't we face the fact? What prevents us?

KRISHNAMURTI: We cannot come to that issue until we have completely understood why we escape, and what this movement of escape is. In order not to face what actually is, we have cultivated many escapes. Without understanding why we escape, what the movement of that escape is, and what is involved in the whole structure of that movement, we cannot possibly face the fact. We also must understand what action is. My action in moving away from the fact to something, as was pointed out yesterday, is a static movement, though we may think that it is an actual, positive movement. Until we understand this very, very clearly, we cannot possibly face the fact. There is no question of jumping, avoiding, or skipping over something. Unless we go into this very slowly, step by step, we cannot possibly come to the realization of facing a fact.

Before we go into this question, I would like to ask whether meeting every day like this, and discussing, is a bit too much. Are you sure? We have to work very hard. To share anything there must be not only the giver, but also the receiver; and when one receives, there is no giver; it is complementary, a movement together. We have to walk together; we must have energy, vitality, interest, drive. Can we go on like this for seven days and not get tired of it? You say nothing, so we'll continue.

We said yesterday that we have cultivated innumerable beliefs, dogmas, ideas, formulas, repetitive activity, as a psychological means of self-defense. It is impossible to understand *what is,* if we have beliefs because these beliefs will prevent us from looking at the fact. All of us have these beliefs, dogmas, ideas, or ideals. We always want to become better, do something nobler, understand more. It is a running away, an action of escape from *what is.* We asked what this movement away from *what is* means, the movement itself. We think we are moving, acting, and we saw yesterday that the movement is static. It has no vitality because the thing that one is going to is the projection of *what is,* a continuity of what has been. It is not something new. The movement that we make away from *what is* is not a movement at all; it is just a change to something else which is not actual.

I have to act with regard to the fact, with regard to *what is,* with regard to what I find. There must be action, and I have to investigate and understand what is meant by action. If I don't understand that fully, if I am concerned with changing the fact, with doing something about it, I can't face the fact. I must understand what action is, and 99.9 percent of our actions are an approximation of a belief, an idea, a concept, an image. Our action is always trying to copy, to conform to an idea. I have an idea that I should be brotherly; I have an idea as a communist; or I have the idea that I am a Catholic; according to the idea I act. I have certain memories of pleasure or of pain, certain remembrances of some deep fear, an image of that fear; and according to those memories I act, avoiding some particular issues, and acting for profit, for a deeper happiness. All of this is ideation, and according to that ideation, I act. When there is an idea and action, there is conflict between the two. The idea is the observer, and the act of what I am going to do is the object.

I see that I am afraid. I have an idea about fear, what I should do, how I should avoid it. I have an opinion. The 'I' is the idea, the opinion, the memory, the formula, the observer, the censor; and the fear is the object about which I am going to act according to the idea. There is a conflict between the observer and the observed; that is one of the most difficult things to understand, to come over or to go beyond, and if I don't understand it, if I don't see the deep significance

or the meaning of it, I can't deal with the object which is called fear.

Why is there an interval of time, of space between the observer, who is the idea, and the object? You are looking from your balcony and see that mountain and the waterfall. There is an interval between you and the mountain with its waterfall; there is a space, a time lag which makes for distance. When there is this interval of space, of time, then the observer is different from the thing that he has observed. Please don't agree; this is a most complex thing. You're following the explanation verbally, but the explanation is not the fact. The word *mountain* is not the mountain; it's just a symbol to indicate the mountain. The fact is not the word. Explanation is not understanding. Please don't agree and say, "Yes, get on with it; tell me more."

If you realize that the observer has a space between himself and the observed, and in that space there is conflict, then you want to do something. The more intense the conflict, the more demand there is for action. The observer says, "What am I to do? How am I to act? How am I to get over it?"

In the same way that there is a distance from you who are looking out of the window to the mountain and its waterfall, there is distance between the observer and the thing he calls fear. He wants to do something. He wants to break, go, get beyond it, destroy it. With regard to that waterfall, you can go to it; you can walk there, if you have the energy. That's no problem. You can turn your back on it and forget it, but with fear you can't. It is always there. Unless you really understand action which is not based on an idea, in which there is no observer and the observed, you can't meet the fact.

I am jealous, which is a common lot of our lives, which all of us know. I feel jealous for various reasons. Perhaps I accept it as inevitable, as a natural part of what is supposed to be love, and I say, "That is part of my daily existence." But when that jealousy turns into anxiety, hatred—and all jealousy inevitably has in it hatred—when the pressure, the strain of jealousy becomes very strong, then I am forced to do something. Then action takes place, action according to the observer, with regard to the object. Then I say, "I must get over it. What am I to do?" Anxiety comes out of it.

What then is action? (Silence) Is the tent too hot? Or are we talking about hot subjects? (Laughter) Must action always breed conflict? Apparently it does. Whatever we do breeds friction in our relationship. In whatever we do there is conflict, there is misery, there is confusion. Why must action engender this anxiety, this fear, this strain, this conflict? Unless we answer that question very deeply, unless we realize it, we cannot possibly face the fact. Life is action; action isn't something we do apart from living. So we ask if there is an action which has no conflict in it at all.

Comment: As long as. . . .

KRISHNAMURTI: Please, not "as long as." That is a supposition.

Comment: When action is based on idea, there is always the observer and the observed.

KRISHNAMURTI: Don't state in your own words the same thing which has been said. It is a fact that there is me and the object, the space; in that there is conflict. What will you do?

Comment: If I am aware of the conflict. . . .

KRISHNAMURTI: Please, not "if." I am not being impatient; I am not avoiding the question, but these statements commencing with "if," "when," "should," "as long as," all these conditional clauses prevent you from actually looking at the fact.

Question: Who is the entity that is looking?

KRISHNAMURTI: We haven't reached that point yet. Let's approach the problem differently. We see life as a struggle, a conflict; it's a breeding ground of hopeless despair, loneliness, anger, the desire to dominate, and the feeling that we are suppressed. That's our life. That's what we call existence, living; and in that field we act. Every action, however much interrelated with each other, creates more conflict, more battle, more confusion. At the end we ask if there is a life, an activity, an action which in no way brings confusion, conflict.

Comment: There is a desire to fulfill and deep frustration because we do not.

KRISHNAMURTI: Again, you are restating the same fact.

Comment: I don't know about that yet.

KRISHNAMURTI: Then, sir, if you don't know, say, "I don't know," and keep quiet.

Question: Will the answer come then?

KRISHNAMURTI: To be quiet needs tremendous intelligence. A cow is quiet, ruminating. I'm not comparing; I'm just stating it. A man who is napping is very quiet, but to be really quiet, without seeking, without wanting, needs tremendous intelligence; and then perhaps the answer comes, but we are not in that position, so we must have the patience to go step by step, which we apparently are not willing to do.

Comment: The process of living breeds conflict and strain.

KRISHNAMURTI: Yes, that's what we have stated. Then what? You see, you won't proceed further. As long as there is space, an interval, between the observer and the observed, there must be conflict.

Question: Why should the state of the observer and the observed create conflict?

Comment: If there is love, there is no conflict.

Comment: When I am really intelligent, there will be no fear.

KRISHNAMURTI: When I am heavenly, saintly, tremendously, deeply, supremely intelligent, everything will be over. But I'm not! So please have the goodness not to introduce the words "when," "if," and "should." You are avoiding the question.

Comment: There need not be conflict in action.

KRISHNAMURTI: But we know action is conflict. I battle with my wife or my husband, with my boss. That's a fact.

Question: If you get a baby, is that possible? (Laughter)

KRISHNAMURTI: I'm afraid if I got a baby it *would* be a conflict! (Laughter) I'm afraid this question can only be answered by the mothers here. (Laughter) You see, we are back again in something that has no meaning at all. I hope you are having a good laugh—not at her expense; we are not laughing at her, but at the whole idea.

Question: Since I do not thoroughly understand either myself as the observer, or the actions that I do, how can I talk about some new action?

KRISHNAMURTI: I am not talking about new action, or asking you to find a new action. First you have to realize that you never see the fact that there is the observer and the observed. Objectively you may; there is the mountain, and you. To get to the mountain, you take the train, go by car, or walk. There is an action. You never realize, psychologically, that there is an observer and the observed; that there is me, who is the observer, and the observed, anger. You say, "I'm angry." That's all you know. You must realize that you have never looked at this fact of the observer and the observed.

Comment: I am lacking real love.

KRISHNAMURTI: I am afraid we are not talking of real love, or false love. We are talking about an actual fact—that I lack love. Follow that; I lack that. That is the object; the 'I' is the observer. I lack love. We don't realize this separation. We say, "I lack love"; but when we realize the separation between what we generally call love and I who want it, or I who don't have it, then there is the observer and the observed. The first thing to understand, to realize, is that there is in me psychologically this fact, of which most of us are unaware—that I am separate from the thing which I observe. "I and God" is one of the ancient tricks we play; I must reach God. There is the object, and the observer. When I realize this, I either want to get hold of it, conquer it, dominate it, suppress it, run away from it, or I have opinions about it. The next fact I have to realize is that the observer is nothing but ideas, memories, formulas, opinions.

I am not saying that you should not have opinions; that's not the point. The observer, the censor, the entity that judges, condemns, approves, that dominates, that wants to fulfill is there. I want to be a great writer, or I have a particular line which I think is marvelous in writing. There is a separation: I and the thing. Action becomes a means to fulfill or to overcome the object, and there is conflict.

Question: What is the entity who observes and sees the thing, the object?

KRISHNAMURTI: The question is easy to ask, but to find the answer requires a great deal of penetration, insight.

I see a mountain. Of course, I and the mountain are not the same. I might like to identify myself with the beauty of the mountain, but I am not the mountain. That's a fact. However much I may pretend, or have mystical experiences about the mountain, the fact remains that I am different from the mountain. It becomes much more complex, much more difficult to understand and go into, when we realize, first, that 'I' and the object are two different states. When I realize that, I act; and that action breeds more conflicts, more trouble, more travail, more pain. What am I to do with regard to envy, with regard to the desire which I have to dominate someone? I know that what I do will breed more conflict, and I say, "How stupid of me; I don't want to breed more conflict; I don't want more strains." How am I to put an end to conflict in action?

Comment: Don't act.

KRISHNAMURTI: My life is action. Talking is action; breathing is action; to see something is an action; to get into a car, to go to my house is action. Everything I do is action. You tell me, "Don't act!" Does that mean just to stop where I am, not to think, not to feel, to be paralyzed, to be dead?

Comment: The idea, which is unreal, and reality can never go together.

KRISHNAMURTI: I realize that action is life. Unless I am totally paralyzed, dead, or insensitive, I must act. I see that every action breeds more pain, more conflict, more travail. I am going to find out if there is an action in which there is no conflict.

Question: How am I to find union between the observer and the observed?

Comment: By accepting conflict.

KRISHNAMURTI: For three million years we have accepted conflict. Our life is conflict. There is a war on between my wife and myself. I want to dominate; I want to become powerful; I want to be known. I live in a perpetual state of conflict with myself and with society, of which I am a part. I live in conflict, and I realize that whatever I do breeds more conflict, more confusion, more misery to myself. So I say, "What am I to do? How am I to act?" Don't tell me, "Love; be complete, be identified with peace, be unified with God"; none of those mean anything.

Comment: We must understand our actions.

KRISHNAMURTI: How am I to understand action? To understand something, I must look at it; I must examine it; I mustn't be prejudiced about it; I mustn't have a defense against it; I mustn't escape from it; I must become very familiar with it. To understand anything I must look with no barrier between myself and what I look at. But I have barriers; I want to suppress the beastly thing; I want to run away from it.

Comment: If one watches one's thoughts, one's feelings, one's activities, then one begins to understand.

KRISHNAMURTI: Who is the watcher that's looking at the thought, who says, "I understand it"? Is the entity that is observing different from the thought? Thought is the entity, which means that the observer is the observed.

I say to myself, "I must understand my feelings, my thoughts, my activities, my relationships. Whatever I do, I must look, observe, watch." I watch my thought. It goes all over the place, wandering, contradictory. I look at it and try to understand it, to control it, or to identify myself with it. I make an effort, and that effort is a conflict, but when I realize that the thinker, the observer, is the thought, is the observed, then conflict comes to an end.

Question: In the tale of Beauty and the Beast, *which we all know, Beauty liberates the Beast. Must we acknowledge evil reality as part of ourselves?*

KRISHNAMURTI: I'm not talking about reality, about beauty, about the animal. There is a simple fact. Don't translate it into terms of your own particular idiosyncrasy. I think,

and I say, "By Jove, I must watch my thinking." I watch it, and my thoughts are ugly, beautiful, noble, or something. I am different from the thought. As long as this difference exists between the thinker and the thought, there must be conflict because I'm always doing something about it—trying to understand it, to break it down, to examine it, to suppress it. But is the thought different from the thinker? Thought has invented the thinker, so there is nothing to understand about thought. You will see the beauty of it, if you go with it.

Comment: We acknowledge that the thought and the thinker are one.

KRISHNAMURTI: There is no acknowledging; there is no identifying; there is no bringing together.

Question: Why can't we go along quickly together?

KRISHNAMURTI: Because we are refusing to face a very simple fact. We want to make everything so complicated. We can't just listen to the noise of that airplane passing overhead. When we listen to the noise, not as a listener and the noise, but when we are completely paying attention to the noise, then there is only noise, not the listener and the noise.

Comment: We are conscious of the fact that there is the center, and the thought.

KRISHNAMURTI: The electronic brain replies to a question according to the information it has. We have stored up information through experience, through heredity, through culture, through impression, through influence, through climate. That electronic storing is the thinker, who separates himself from the thought, and then says, "I must do something about it." The actual fact is that the thinker is the thought, is the memory, is the experience, is the observer, is the experiencer and the experienced. If you realized this, if you really understood this very, very simple fact, life would change totally, absolutely—not tomorrow but now.

If you really realize that you are the result of your culture, your society, your economy, your religion—you are that; the two are not separate—if you actually realize that you are not different from it, if you realize it as you realize a pain, then you will see something entirely different take place.

We all crave experience. Do you understand what happens when you realize that the experiencer is the experience? Do you know what happens when you look at a flower without any kind of evaluation, without any kind of judgment, without the thinker thinking about the flower, just looking at it? Do you know what takes place? Have you ever tried it?

Comment: We disappear.

KRISHNAMURTI: Do you? (Laughter) I am asking in all seriousness; I didn't mean it cynically or humorously. When you look at the flower without thinking, what takes place?

Comment: There is only a state of seeing.

KRISHNAMURTI: What do you all say? Have you ever tried to look at a flower without going through all the process of analysis and knowledge, of thinking—just looking at it? What takes place?

Comment: Integration takes place.

Comment: The flower takes place.

KRISHNAMURTI: May I suggest something? If you have half an hour or so to spare this afternoon, look at a tree or a flower, at your wife or your husband. Just look, not as the husband, who has had innumerable insults, flatteries, hurts, pleasures, sex, and all the rest. Will you try it and see what happens?

Comment: Perhaps the observer disappears.

KRISHNAMURTI: Try it!

Comment: There is no conflict then.

KRISHNAMURTI: This is a most extraordinary business.

Comment: Sometimes we are saying within us, "I am yourself."

KRISHNAMURTI: I am talking about a flower, and watching the flower. Now, would you listen to the noise that airplane is making? Just listen to it. (Pause) Now, what has taken place? You listened. First find out what it means to listen.

Comment: You become one with the noise.

Comment: It fills you up; you are filled with it.

KRISHNAMURTI: Are you listening to the noise?

Comment: Yes.

KRISHNAMURTI: It matters enormously how you listen. An airplane went over just now, and you listened. You say, "Yes, I listened to that noise; it filled me"; or you say, "I didn't like that noise because I wanted to ask you a question"; or, "I want to listen to you." You have to find out, before you listen, what is listening. What is listening?

I have to find out what is listening; I have to find out how I listen. The noise is not important, but how I listen to the noise is important. How do you listen? Do you listen at all? These are not just trivial questions. You have to find out for yourself if you listen. Do you listen to your wife, to your husband, or do you have a setup pattern going all your life, and when the pattern operates you call that listening? One of the most difficult things to do is to find out what it is to listen, when you are listening. You can only listen out of silence. When that airplane went over, some of you were listening to the noise; some were not listening, or not understanding what listening is. If you listen, you can't have noise. You can't have your mind buzzing away. You can only listen when there is total silence.

Generally we realize that the thinker and the thought are two separate states, if we realize at all. Usually we are indifferent; we just think. But when we realize that the thinker is separate from the thought, what takes place? First, we have to listen to that fact, which we have discovered for ourselves, that the thinking and the thought are two separate states. From that listening we discover that thought is the thinker; the two are not separate. There is no identifying, the thinker identifying himself with the thought. Thought is the thinker.

You, the observer, look at that microphone. You say, "That is not me." Of course it's not you. Obviously you can't identify yourself with a dead thing, or with a living thing. There is the observer and the

observed. How do you look at it? The "how you look" is more important than the object. Do you look at it with a lot of noise, with thoughts that the microphone is or is not good; it is this; it is that? Or do you look at it with complete silence? When you look at it with complete silence, what takes place? Don't wait for me to answer. I'm not going to tell you because that would become another jargon to be repeated. To look at anything, to listen to anything, there must be complete silence. What is important is not the object but the silence, the quietness, the attention, whatever word you may give to it. Only when the mind is completely silent can you look, can you listen. Then listening, acting, and seeing are the same. Do you see the beauty of it?

August 5, 1966

Fourth Dialogue in Saanen

We started our discussions with the question of belief, the role it plays in man's life, and whether beliefs, dogmas, formulas, ideals are necessary, because they really prevent action. When a mind is anchored to a belief, to a dogma, to an ideal, action must inevitably not only breed conflict, but contradiction; therefore, action is never innocent, clear. Clear action is only possible when there is no contradiction and no confusion.

As human beings we are very confused, and few of us are aware of that fact. When we are aware, we try to run away from it. The more confused we are, the greater is the demand to find an anchorage, some place, some ideation, some experience, some knowledge which we hope will give us clarity. This confusion in action has been bred into us by society, of which we are a part. Society includes politics, religious dogmas of various kinds, nationalities with their contradictions, sovereign states with their vested interests in their armies, their navies and other military groups. Society, of which we are a part, is responsible for this contradiction, this confusion.

We are confused and we think that by clearing up the symptoms, or by investigating them, we will be free of confusion. We think that we can clear up some of the symptoms by not belonging to any religion. Nowadays a sane, intelligent man doesn't belong to any organized religion, does not hold to any particular dogma, or consider himself of any particular nationality. Only those who are committed to a certain pattern still cling to a belief, to a nationality. The more awake we are to what is taking place in the world, the more we abandon belonging to any particular religion, nationality, race, or color.

We are likely to blame the symptoms and seek their cause. Confusion is much deeper than that. We must discuss it, go into it together, to find out if action can be free from confusion so that action is fresh, innocent, clear; so that it doesn't breed more and more confusion and misery. We are confused, and there is no denying it. The more clever we are, the more we find anchorages, and we think from that state of relative stability that our actions are clear. They are not. On the contrary, the more we are secured to a belief, the greater is the confusion. This is obvious when we look at the world. The more we assert that we are Catholics, Hindus, Buddhists, communists or whatever, the more contradictory our lives are and the more it breeds war. It is like those scientists who invent the most dreadful means of destruction, and yet say that they love their children. The two can't go together. They are responsible for this confusion; each one of us is also responsible because we still hold on to our nationalities, to our particular religions, to our particular ideologies.

We must discuss this problem of confusion because it is going to help us to understand how to face fear. When the mind is not afraid, when it has no fear of any kind, then only can it function extraordinarily clearly. Then it will not create confusion for itself. If we realize that we are confused— first of all, why are we confused? When we ask why, we examine the symptoms and the causes.

As a human being, I am confused; and I say, "Why?" I see that I am a Hindu, with all my superstitions, with all my partial truths, my partial way, and all the rest, which are inventions of a mind which is afraid. I hold on to all that and create a contradiction between you, who are a Christian, and me, as a Hindu. You dislike my particular form of belief, and I dislike yours; so we dislike each other. Though we tolerate each other, though we talk about brotherhood and all that nonsense, actually, as long as I belong to my religion and you belong to yours, there is a contradiction between us. We may tolerate, but there is always this sense of antagonism, which inevitably must breed confusion.

I hope you are asking yourselves why you are confused. What is your response to this question? Do you examine the cause and the symptoms? Do you examine the causes that have produced this confusion—because you belong to a particular religion or nationality, or are committed to a particular course of action, as communists, socialists or what you will? Do you say, "I must be free of those in order to be clear, in order not to be confused"? That's the action you generally take, isn't it? Let us listen carefully to what is being said.

We are confused; being confused, we examine the causes through the symptoms, and we say, "We must get rid of those causes."

We want to get rid of them because we want to have a state of mind which is not confused.

I see I am confused because I belong to some stupid religion. All religions are stupid because they are inventions of very cunning minds which are afraid to face facts, life, fear. I say to myself, "I must get rid of this." Through the symptoms I try to find the cause, and then try to get rid of the cause. Will that produce a state of mind that is not confused? Please don't agree or disagree. Examine it carefully.

Comment: It's a new conflict.

KRISHNAMURTI: Yes, and my mind is conditioned by a particular propaganda. All religions, all new revolutions are propaganda. I want to get rid of it in order not to be confused. The getting rid, the pushing away is a conflict, and that breeds more confusion.

Comment: I don't think society is the only cause of our confusion.

KRISHNAMURTI: Of course not. Society, relationship. . . .

Comment: The whole of it. We are confused by our human nature.

KRISHNAMURTI: That's part of the psychological structure of society, which includes you.

Comment: It's not only that.

KRISHNAMURTI: All right; add one more.

Comment: I see a danger; I react; I seek protection instinctively; and I see confusion in myself on account of this danger.

KRISHNAMURTI: We want to protect ourselves physically or psychologically, so we invent beliefs, dogmas, gods, all of which are part of our culture, our heritage, our society.

They all create confusion. How will we be rid of that confusion? If we do not get rid of it, action will always be confused and will always breed conflict. We generally say, "I am confused; there is the cause; I want to get rid of the cause." We find the cause through the symptoms. We examine, examine, examine the symptoms, find the various causes, and then struggle to get rid of them. Does that free the mind from confusion?

I want to face the fact, which is fear; and facing that fact, I have to act. I can't just sit back and say, "Well, I'm afraid." I have to act, negatively or positively; and to act, the mind must be free of all confusion. If not, I'll create more fear, more confusion. What shall I do?

Comment: At one moment there was no confusion, and at other moments I am confused. I remember the moment of clarity in moments when there is no clarity, and I get depressed.

Comment: There is the higher self, and there are various sheaths of confusion. I must peel them off to get to the center.

KRISHNAMURTI: That is an invention of the Hindus, and the Christians have their own inventions. I'm asking, "What will you do?"

Comment: Look at the fact.

Comment: Examine fear.

KRISHNAMURTI: You say to examine fear; another says to look at the fact. Do you know what it means to examine, to look? It is so easy to say, "Examine," and so easy to say, "Look at the fact." Do you know what is involved in examination? To examine anything, there must be no confusion; there must be freedom. If the scientist goes to his laboratory full of worries about his family or whatever it is, he can't look. He must be free to examine. To look at a fact, I must also be free; I mustn't bring a confused mind. How will you meet this problem? As I said, it's like the army is preparing to kill and breed its own children. There's no relationship between the two. Do you understand? So, the army is part of us because we are national, so there is this contradiction. Therefore, there is confusion.

Comment: Any form of commitment to any impulse, to any influence, to any propaganda, whether it is done through a religion or by a businessman, whether it is the propaganda of my wife, or me to my wife, is the breeding ground of confusion.

KRISHNAMURTI: Then I have a problem. I am committed to so many things: I believe, and I don't believe; I am ambitious, seeking success, position, prestige, power; I am haughty, and parts of me are timid—they have a sense of humility, a withdrawal, a desire to be kind. There is this immense contradiction in me, and in the very denying of one, I am creating a conflict which breeds its own confusion. I see all this. What am I to do?

Comment: When I see all this, the only question I can put to myself is whether analysis is necessary at all.

KRISHNAMURTI: I wish that some of you who have been through all this would discuss it. Is analysis necessary? If it is not necessary, then how will we find the cause, and having discovered the cause, not through analysis but by some direct perception, how will we get rid of it?

Comment: I think that as long as I have the wish. . . .

KRISHNAMURTI: The moment you say "as long as," or "when there are no wishes," you are just postponing the problem.

Comment: You don't have to accept confusion as beautiful, enjoyable, and a necessary part of life.

KRISHNAMURTI: I don't. Confusion is terrible! It's destroying the world. The politician, the priest, the scientist are all confused. I am confused in my relationships. Everything that we are caught in is confusion. I don't have to accept it; it is a fact. What am I to do?

Here is a fact: we are confused. Not that it is beautiful; it's a part of life that we must put up with. Any intelligent man doesn't want to put up with it. He wants to kick it out; he wants to throw it away; and in the very act of getting rid of it, there is confusion also. What are you going to do?

Comment: If possible, we should make our mind silent.

KRISHNAMURTI: Sir, you must have been hungry, and wanted food immediately.

Comment: Yes, but I waited.

KRISHNAMURTI: You waited, but you got it. Now you say, "I'll wait and see if I can cultivate silence." During that interval of waiting and cultivating silence, you are breeding more and more confusion. Please don't say, "if," "when," "sometime," "somehow." Those have no meaning.

We are confused, and we know very well the cause of this confusion—the newspapers, the radio, the priests, the politicians, our own desires—there is this turmoil going on all the time. How will we be free of the turmoil?

Comment: Confusion comes when there's a split. If you admit the split, you are no longer in confusion; you are no longer divided.

KRISHNAMURTI: That's "when" and "if" again. I want to find food, and you have given me ashes—"when," "if," "should," "must," "believed," "don't believe in all that; believe in this."

All the things you are suggesting—"do this, don't do that; think this, and don't think that; you should, you should not"—all have no meaning.

Question: Why is action necessary?

KRISHNAMURTI: Living is action. To go from this tent to have my food, I have to act. If I'm somewhat insane, I can end up saying, "There is no action; I can't act," and just wait for someone to feed me. There are people like that.

We are confused and we know the causes. It doesn't take a great deal of intellect or a great deal of intelligence to find out the causes—ourselves in relation to society, religion, politics, the army, the navy, the king, the queen, the division of nationalities, the prejudices, the bombings, the scientists who invent monstrous means of destruction, breeding children whom they say they love. You know you must act. You can't just say, "I'll sit and wait for someone to tell me what to do." What will you do?

Comment: If I see that I am distorted, it doesn't seem to matter whether the distortion is there or not while I am looking at it. The trouble seems to appear when I cease look-

ing at the distortion and try to do something about it.

KRISHNAMURTI: That is the problem.

Comment: The answer can't be just to cease looking at the distortion.

KRISHNAMURTI: We are going to find out.

Question: Don't you see any harmony in the world? We have here a very beautiful structure, where every girder is working against the others. That is not confusion; that is an example of harmony.

KRISHNAMURTI: Is there harmony in the world, actually, not theoretically? In heaven everything is harmonious. Actually, in this world is there harmony, between me and my wife, between me and my parents, between me and whatever it is?

Comment: The more we know of this world and the more we understand it, the more we find amazing harmony.

KRISHNAMURTI: You say that the more we know, the more harmony there will be. We know a great deal. We have lived for two million years. There have been fifteen thousand wars in the last few thousand years, yet we know we mustn't kill each other. We know how ridiculous it is to divide ourselves into French, German, English, whatever it is. We also know how to invent new gadgets and go to the moon. We know so much, and yet we are not harmonious.

Look at your problem. You are confused. Don't invent that there is harmony, that angels hover over you to protect you. You know, the circus. If you cut out all that, as you must, you're faced with the fact that the scientist creates disharmony; the politician, you in your office, the businessman, the army, the navy, the flier—everyone is adding, adding, adding to it, each contradicting the other, each saying that you must do this and you must not do that. There have been Mussolinis, Hitlers, Churchills, all telling us what to do. You know all this. What will you do? Will you invent some more beliefs, join some more organizations, follow a new leader? If you are aware, what will you do?

Comment: I will throw the whole lot overboard and get on with my own life.

KRISHNAMURTI: Your own life is related to every other life; you can't just throw them all overboard.

I see clearly the futility of analysis. I see that it is absurd to try to discover the cause. I know what the causes are: my fear, my demand for protection, the beliefs which I have—my country is bigger, nobler than your country, my leader is more perfect than your leader, there is only one savior, and there is only one God—fighting, fighting, fighting. I'm part of it all. My right hand does something which my left hand doesn't know, and my left hand does something which my right hand doesn't know, like the scientists, like the politicians, like the priests, because they all have beliefs. They start from a conclusion. I see all of this, of which I am a part; and I also see it is a waste of time to analyze through the symptoms. Therefore I say to myself, "What am I to do?"

I have been through all this rigmarole. Personally I haven't, but I have seen people go from one church to another, from politics to no-politics, to communism and then get rid of communism—through one mess after another, through life for forty years. Is there a different way of approach? Is there a different way of looking at all this, a way which is total, not fragmentary? All thinking is fragmentary: my country, my God opposed to

your God. Thinking in any form must be fragmentary. I have looked at everything in fragments: God in heaven, hell on earth; businessmen making money, concerned with new buildings, and destroying Vietnam; organized religions seeking power, position, converting more people to make the religions more popular; people starving, and people dividing themselves into countries, into races. All that is fragmentary. I say to myself, "That is not the way to understand confusion—through fragments." Thought cannot resolve the confusion because thought has bred confusion.

Comment: My thoughts are the opposite of my feelings.

KRISHNAMURTI: Don't say that thoughts are the opposite of feelings; feelings are a part of your thoughts. We can't separate them. We seem unable to look at anything totally. We look at things fragmentarily; we consider things through thought; and thought in essence breeds confusion. The real function of any politician or any human being is to bring about the unity of mankind, not English mankind or French or German, but the whole of mankind; not the East and the West and the South and the North. These are the inventions of a mind which is fragmentary, and this fragmentation is the result of thinking. Thinking in itself is fragmentary and will not solve this problem. When it tries to resolve the problem, thought will only create more fragments which will create more confusion.

Can you look at this whole problem: the church and the religions talking about goodness, God; the businessman, the scientist breeding children and then sending them to war, destroying their own flesh and blood? Can you throw all that overboard, all of it, not through thinking, not because someone tells you to do it? You see that thinking has produced the contradictions, the divisions, the confusion, and so you say, "Out! I don't belong to anything. I do not commit myself to anything." Are you in that position? Can you honestly say that you are not committed to anything, to any formula, to any religion, to any priest, the priests not only in Rome, in Canterbury, or in Banaras, but in Moscow or in the Labor Party? (Laughter) They're all priests. You are committed to your family, to your country, to a particular form of belief, to a particular pleasure. Even though pleasure breeds pain, you still go on. You don't say, "This problem cannot be solved through fragmentary thinking at all." Since all thinking is fragmentary, what thought has created as the country, the religion, the god, the priest, the king, the queen must all go out! That's the greatest revolution. Can you put away all that completely, without effort, because you see that it produces conflict; it's poison and you don't touch it?

Comment: When a priest comes along and starts talking to me, I find myself getting confused again.

KRISHNAMURTI: Avoid the priests! Don't go near them! Whether it is a politician, a priest, a propagandist, or a book, don't go near it.

Question: What if you are in relationship with them?

KRISHNAMURTI: I don't want relationships which breed conflict, which breed confusion. This means that I am willing to stand completely alone, completely innocent. I don't mind if you don't feed me; I don't mind if you don't come here every morning. I'm not committed to you.

Comment: Once we are no longer attached, we can be completely open to anyone, and they can no longer get at us, but we are not blocking them.

KRISHNAMURTI: Therefore you have no resistance to them; they can say what they like.

Comment: When you throw away all that, you have to throw away yourself because you are part of all that; and when you throw it away, you have already got rid of your confusion.

KRISHNAMURTI: You have done it! There is no 'me' to be thrown away. I am the result of all this which I have created out of my fear, my ambition, my greed, my envy. Can I, living in this world, be alone, be innocent? When I have put away all that, whatever the analysts, the psychologists, the doctors, the scientists, the modern priests, the whole lot of them say or don't say, I am no longer confused; but it is not the result of thinking, which only creates resistances. It is not through analysis, not through examination, not through desiring not to be confused, but through seeing totally. I cannot see totally if there is thinking. Now I am prepared to face fear. Now I am prepared to see what fear is, because my fear has created all this—the country, the politician, the gods, the whole works. I have also said, "Thought breeds fragmentation," so I must be really alert to watch the fear, and not let thought interfere.

Can I, as a human being, not as an Englishman, not as a Catholic, not as a Hindu—all that is finished, given up as being too infantile, too immature—can I now look at fear, and do I know what it means to look, to listen? If I am listening with thought, then I am listening through fragmentation, as liking or not liking the noise of that airplane.

If I don't know what it means to look, to listen, don't let me pretend by saying, "I should, should not; it must be, must not be." If I don't know what it means to look or listen, that's a simple fact. Then I can proceed. Most of us are so vain and pretentious; we have not a spark of humility; and it needs humility in the right sense, not in the priestly sense, to examine, to look.

Question: I look at fear, but I want to get rid of it. This is the natural response of most healthy people. When I want to get rid of it, what is taking place?

KRISHNAMURTI: Why do I want to get rid of it? Because it is agonizing; it is destructive; because I want to hold the pleasure which I have known. Behind the urge to get rid of it is the energy of pleasure. Without understanding pleasure I can't face fear. If I am looking at fear through pleasure, it is a fragmentary observation. My concern is to sustain pleasure, to continue pleasure, and fear interferes with it. Fear is the result of wanting pleasure continued, so I say, "I must get rid of it." Thought, which has bred fear, which demands the continuance of pleasure, denies or resists fear. I must again go into the very complex question of pleasure; I have to understand it. If I say, "Am I to get rid of the pleasure I derive from sex, from smoking, from enjoying the mountain?" my mind is already functioning fragmentarily. I must understand the whole structure of pleasure and see totally. Then pleasure has an entirely different meaning.

To face fear requires enormous passion, which is not pleasure. All that I know as passion is derived from pleasure. I remember the lovely, happy evening that I spent yesterday, the pleasure of sex, the memory of it, the image I have built up. I must understand the drive to be ambitious and the urge to fulfill, in both of which there is immense pleasure.

To understand fear, and go beyond it, I must understand all these things—pleasure, thought, how thought breeds fragmentation, and the fact that fragmentation brings about such confusion that I'm incapable of any action which doesn't breed further confusion.

There's a different way altogether. You can see the whole thing immediately, see the whole structure instantly, not in terms of time. To do this there must be the highest form of sensitivity, both physical and mental. There must be tremendous sensitivity. Then you'll see it instantly, and you're out of it.

August 6, 1966

Fifth Dialogue in Saanen

Human beings are most gullible. We will believe in anything. Given sufficient pressure, propaganda, we will do all the rest. We so easily accept a new leader, a new idea, a new diet, a new doctor. People take advantage of us, people exploit us because we are always seeking pleasure, wanting more health, more intelligence, more spirituality, whatever that word may mean; we are always seeking someone who will give us more stimulation, following, looking up to someone, putting all our faith in one basket. We should be very careful, during all these discussions and talks, to put aside all gullibility, to have a great deal of skepticism, to question, to demand, to never become yes-sayers but rather to be no-sayers. We are very vulnerable to wrong things as well as to right things, and apparently the wrong things have greater control, hold greater sway over us. I'm just asking that we should be very careful in this tent to examine everything that is said for ourselves—everything. Because here there is no leader, no teacher. You are not a follower. And that's one of the greatest curses—to follow anybody. And we do all these things being gullible, following, looking up to somebody, putting all our faith in one basket, seeking somebody who will give us more stimulation and so on.

Behind all this lies this extraordinary demand for pleasure, for gratification; and that's what we are all seeking. Whenever that pleasure is thwarted, there is conflict, pain, bitterness, frustration. We are all in this category. If we would face fear, be totally free of it and go beyond it, we not only have to go, as we did yesterday, into the question of belief in its various forms—why we defend ourselves, why these beliefs cause confusion, and what the nature of confusion is, the structure of confusion—but we must go into the complex problem of pleasure. We know that a great part of our brain is still the animal, and the animal is always seeking pleasure. If we have observed pets, we know how delighted they are when we pet them, when we give them something. Not only is it self-satisfying to be adored by a dog, but also the dog, the animal, loves to please us. We struggle to have pleasure through ambition, through power, by doing good, by becoming a leader, a politician. Political parties control through promises, offering great utopias, subjugating a whole nation through promises. We must understand this structure of pleasure. We are going to discuss it this morning. Do not accept what I say, but question, ask, investigate, examine, listen very carefully to what is being said so that you will find the right answer for yourselves, so that you won't deceive yourselves.

It is very important for us to find out for ourselves how we create beliefs, are caught in them, and thereby bring about greater confusion, greater conflict, division, and fragmentations of the mind. To go into this question of pleasure, we mustn't take sides; we mustn't become Puritans and say that we must not have pleasure, or say, "I must have pleasure." Isn't it a pleasure when you look at a mountain, a river, sparkling meadows,

when you see a woman with a beautiful face? Isn't it a pleasure to hold someone's hand? Very few say, "No; pleasure is a dreadful thing," and become terribly puritanical, terribly austere. Austerity is an extraordinary thing. It doesn't come through suppression of pleasure; it doesn't come about through discipline, through conformity, through denial, through holding oneself back, trying to conform to an idea. Austerity of that kind is harsh, bitter, and has no meaning. It only leads to the grave, to something that has no value at all. But there is an austerity that comes when one begins to understand the nature of pleasure. It comes without any effort, without any suppression, control, discipline, and all the rest of those harsh methods, which all the saints throughout the ages have employed.

When the mind has understood belief, defense, self-defense, the resistance which breeds confusion; when we have gone into the nature and the meaning of pleasure, then we will perhaps be able to come upon fear and be totally free of it. What is pleasure? Is there such a thing? We want pleasure; we seek pleasure; we know there is this constant urge to avoid pain and pursue pleasure, but most of us have never asked what pleasure is. I know we want it. After all, the ultimate pleasure is so-called God. We have never inquired into that feeling, into that demand. We have never pursued it to the very end to find out what it is—not to deny it, not to suppress it, not to say, "Instead of having pleasure I will have something else"—but to find out what it means and whether there is such a thing, actually, as pleasure.

Please don't wait for me. This is a discussion.

Comment: Pleasure is a sense of being more than you were before.

KRISHNAMURTI: Are you giving me explanations for what pleasure is, telling me that it is more than what you had before, that you have become more beautiful, more intelligent; that you have had tremendous sex? Are you giving me explanations, or are you trying to find out what pleasure is?

Comment: I think pleasure is. . . .

KRISHNAMURTI: Madame, I can give dozens of explanations myself. I'm rather good at it. (Laughter) Not that I'm vain, but I can give explanations. I will, if you want me to. More and more money, experience, fulfillment, ambition to reach something, to attain a state which no one has attained because then I become very important. We desire to fulfill, to be known. We know all the explanations, the reactions, the interrelations between all the reactions, and the pains involved in it. Please don't give me explanations. When you give explanations, you are blocking yourself.

Comment: I do not quite understand what you are driving at.

KRISHNAMURTI: What I'm driving at is very simple: don't give me explanations of what pleasure is. Every man knows in different ways what pleasure is. When you begin to explain to me, or to someone else what pleasure is, aren't you blocking, stopping investigation and examination?

What is pleasure? It is a very complex thing. Don't just brush it off. At the moment of pleasure, do you know you're having pleasure, or do you know when the thing is over; do you remember it and say, "By Jove, what a lovely state that was"? Please go into this very slowly for yourself.

I'm asking myself, and you ask yourselves what pleasure is. Is it always something that has gone, that has passed, a thing that I have remembered, or the pleasure that I'm going to have? Is it either in the past or in the future?

Question: Isn't pleasure only an illusion?

KRISHNAMURTI: When you smoke, when you take coffee, when you have your particular dish that you like, when you sleep with a man or a woman, don't tell me it's all an illusion! (Laughter) Come off it! You cannot face facts, and you want to face fear! I am asking myself, and you, if you and I know what pleasure is, not pleasure as a dead thing, but such a pleasure as the sunset of yesterday. I don't know if you saw the two rainbows. It was really quite an extraordinary sight, a great pleasure to watch and see the colors. At such a moment you don't say, "How pleasurable it is!" A second later you have the memory of it. Then you say, "How nice; I wish I could have some more of it." You project the thing that gives you pleasure into tomorrow, into the future. I am asking if you know what pleasure is, and if there is such a thing as pleasure.

Comment: You can't speak about it.

KRISHNAMURTI: But that's what we're all seeking, sir. You may not speak about it, but that's all we want.

Comment: Somehow it seems to me that there are only those sensations which have been only partly lived.

KRISHNAMURTI: In the past?

Comment: They have been partly lived in the past, which it is possible to recall as pain or pleasure. *The things which we have totally lived are already part of us.*

KRISHNAMURTI: So you have a reaction in the present in relation to the past, or in relation to the future.

Comment: I personally have never experienced it from the future.

KRISHNAMURTI: I am not talking about what I experience. This is a human question. I want to know what pleasure is; therefore, I'm seeking.

Comment: We can only re-evoke an experience which has been partly lived, even if there was at the time a conscious sensation of pleasure.

KRISHNAMURTI: As an example, there was a rainbow, there was a feeling, there was a sex act, there were dozens of experiences yesterday, from which I derived tremendous pleasure.

Comment: Unless you wrote it down in your mind as pleasure while looking at the rainbow, or directly after, it is almost impossible to re-evoke the sensation.

KRISHNAMURTI: You have stored up, and the recollection of that you call pleasure, whether it is a physical sensation, a psychological sensation, or an intellectual sensation. And you call that pleasure. Something is already past, already dead, and you revive it. The revival of the dead, or the invitation to a repetition in the future, you call pleasure. But I'm asking if I know what pleasure is. I know the pleasure that I derive out of something that has passed, or that I hope to experience in the future, but do I know at the moment of ex-

periencing what pleasure is? Am I always living in the past or projecting myself into the future?

Comment: It cannot be denied that pleasure is a continuing thing; so if it is there, it must be in the present, too.

KRISHNAMURTI: Wait; if you go with it, you will see it in a minute for yourself. What we want is the continuance of a pleasure that is gone, or a pleasure that we are going to have. The continuity of pleasure is what we are seeking, either in the past or in the future. We want a continuity from the past to the future through the present. That's what we call pleasure, and I ask if that is pleasure. We have loaded pleasure with so many meanings, like love, death, God, communism, and so on. I want to understand pleasure. I know that I want a thing which has given me pleasure yesterday to continue. What continues is the memory of yesterday's pleasure, or the pleasure that I'm hoping to have tomorrow. I want a continuity of something that's over, or something that's going to happen. I want something dead, which I call pleasure, to continue through the present to the future, and is that pleasure? Please don't accept it or deny it; just look at the extraordinary beauty of it.

Comment: Pleasure is there in the present, in the instant.

KRISHNAMURTI: You say that. Is it so? I don't deny it; I don't know; I'm not doubting it; I'm not saying that it's right or wrong; I'm questioning it. I say, "Is there?"

Comment: Sir, the present has some quality, because when we remember it, we remember it either as pain or as pleasure.

KRISHNAMURTI: Do you know you're enjoying yourself, or having pleasure, at the moment? Let us say that you are eating something that is very tasteful. There is a reaction, and that reaction you call pleasure, naturally. At the moment of eating, tasting, is there pleasure, or does it come a second later? I'm just asking; I'm not saying you're right or wrong. Probably you are right.

Comment: If you live in the present, you have pleasure.

KRISHNAMURTI: Ah, not "if," "when," "should," "must"!

Question: Is experiencing pleasure?

KRISHNAMURTI: Are you aware at the instant of pleasure?

Comment: No.

KRISHNAMURTI: At the moment of tasting a fruit, do you call it pleasure? Pleasure is something entirely different from the fruit, from the physical responses. Please don't tell me "memory." You are not watching yourself.

Comment: I don't see why you say that we want the memory, because what we want is the thing which we experienced at the moment. That's a different condition.

KRISHNAMURTI: You want to have in the present the thing which you have had in the past. That moment has gone, and you want it to be repeated.

Comment: Yes.

KRISHNAMURTI: That's all we're saying.

Comment: It's the thing we want, not the memory.

KRISHNAMURTI: Have you watched yourself when you have had great emotional, physical "enjoyment"? What do you do? You want more of it, don't you?

Comment: Yes.

Comment: Sometimes, not always.

KRISHNAMURTI: I am trying to find out what pleasure is. Is it something purely physical, a reaction, or is it a psychological demand for the continuance of a physical response?

Comment: Either the physical or the psychological reactions may be better.

KRISHNAMURTI: I am not trying to deny it. I am not saying, "This is pleasure; that is not pleasure." We are investigating; we are examining. Let us drop the word *pleasure* for the moment and take a different word.

Question: Why take a different word?

KRISHNAMURTI: Perhaps we will come at it differently, that's all.

Comment: There is a difference between joy and pleasure.

KRISHNAMURTI: Is there a difference?

Question: We are talking about pleasure which comes as a result of our conditioning. Is there any unconditioning?

KRISHNAMURTI: We are going to find out, sir, only unfortunately we don't seem to proceed. We get stuck with words and explanations.

Comment: Pleasure exists, and as soon as we name it, it ceases to exist; we're getting all bogged down under this verbal misunderstanding.

KRISHNAMURTI: Semanticism is necessary.

Comment: Sometimes I can experience pleasure directly, but as soon as I experience it, the directness has gone; so I have only a concept.

KRISHNAMURTI: I eat something which gives me great pleasure. I want the reaction, which I call pleasure, to continue. I like to be flattered; it gives me great pleasure. I want you to go on, feed me with it all the time. I am asking myself, what is pleasure?

Comment: At the same time we must ask ourselves what desire is.

KRISHNAMURTI: We know what desire is, and how it arises. I see something beautiful, and I want it. Desire doesn't exist by itself. There is perception, sensation, desire. We've been all through that, sir. Let's go on. Is there a pleasure without thought? Don't answer me, sir, please! Do give me two minutes for inquiry. When you answer so quickly, I'm already lost. You may have the answer; you may be perfectly right, but give me a chance! (Laughter)

If there is no thinking, will there be pleasure? Pleasure is not only the instant pleasure, the instant desire, but also the demand for the continuity of a psychological pleasure which I have had. In all that is included thinking; in all that there is the process of recognition. In all that there is the word. The word, the recognition, the demand for a continuity, designing, communicating, and expressing—all that is what we call thinking. There is the instant pleasure of eating a fruit, and a second later I want more. The 'more' of anything is not the actual moment. The 'more' is already the past, and I want more of it. There is a recognition of something which has given me pleasure, which I want to continue. That is what we're all seeking.

What is the role of thought in this? If it has no role at all, then is there pleasure? The fruit, the pleasure of the sexual act, the pleasure of looking at a mountain, the pleasure of ambition, the desire to be a great man and having that desire carried out—in all of these there is great pleasure, and I want them to continue. When that desire is frustrated, there is pain. Is not all that related to thought?

Comment: At the actual instant, there is neither pleasure nor pain. It only comes a second later.

Question: When you talk of pleasure without thought, without desire for further pleasure, is that meditation?

KRISHNAMURTI: No, I don't call it meditation. Meditation is what we are doing now. We are exposing ourselves to find out, and to do this, we must be free from all entanglements, from all prejudice, from all preconceptions. Otherwise we cannot examine; and this whole process is meditation.

I am asking myself, if there were no thinking about the fruit, about the sex act, about the beautiful river, about the flattery, the insult, about wanting to fulfill myself, about fame, ambition, and all the rest, would there be what we call pleasure? This is really a good question, if we listen quietly to it, because we will go into it very deeply if we follow it through. I see a door opening; I want to go through it.

Thought may be a block to pleasure, or thought may create pleasure. If thought creates pleasure, then it is fragmentary, and being fragmentary, it is contradictory. Being contradictory, it breeds conflict and then pain. Thought, as we know it, is thinking about something. I see a lovely smile on a child's face; I see the face of a beautiful woman or of a man with really an extraordinary glow. I think about it all because of desire, because at the moment it has given me pleasure, and I want that pleasure to continue.

Comment: Thinking about anything must always be fragmentary.

KRISHNAMURTI: We said yesterday that thought is always fragmentary. Thought must always bring about a fragmentation of the total. I want to see the totality of that marvelous thing called a mountain, not just the shape, the lines, and what name it has. If I begin to think about it, thought gives it a fragmentary significance. I see that wherever thought functions, with regard to pleasure, with regard to anything, it must be fragmentary. Being fragmentary, thought says, "I must have it, and I will resist everything else—pain, any intrusion, any interference." I say to myself, "Is there pleasure which includes all that we have said?" Pleasure must be total; otherwise, it is fragmentary, and if it is fragmentary, it breeds conflict. I'm asking myself if pleasure is a fragmentary affair of thought, or if there is a pleasure which is so total that there is no fragmentation, no contradiction, no conflict. If there is no total pleasure, it is not pleasure.

My thought about food, sex, the mountain, ambition, the desire to fulfill must always be fragmentary. If I listen to that airplane with thought, then it is a fragmentary noise because I don't like the noise. If there is no thinking, I can listen totally; there is neither like nor dislike; it's a noise. Pleasure breeds pain because it is the result of thought. Don't agree; look at it yourselves. Pleasure, which is brought into being by thought, memory, experience, knowledge, and response to that, must always be contradictory. Thought always breeds fragmentation, and that's what we are seeking—fragmentary pleasures. The scientist in his laboratory doesn't care if his children, when they grow up, become soldiers and get killed. Is there a pleasure which is not the result of thought, which is nonfragmentary and is not a contradiction to anything? Discover it. Don't accept what I am saying. I may be saying the most foolish things. Don't be gullible and say, "Yes, I would like to have that pleasure; how am I to get it?" If you go through what we have discussed and understand the nature of thinking, then inevitably you will realize for yourself that pleasure created by thought is always fragmentary, and that a thing which is in fragments must always breed conflict.

Comment: Surely there must be a state where there is pleasure and no thought.

KRISHNAMURTI: I don't know. It may be true. It is a lovely idea.

Comment: When you look at the skies, you have no reaction.

KRISHNAMURTI: You're not listening when you are asking this question. You're merely supposing when you say "should be," "when," "if." You haven't seen the beauty of this structure—not whether you like it or you don't like it.

Such pleasures as sex, food, ambition, or wanting to fulfill are obviously all fragmentary.

Is there something which is not contradictory, which is not the result of thought, and therefore perhaps a pleasure which I never know? I can't say that it is pleasure. The moment that I say it is, thought has entered, the word, the recognition, and demand to express it, to communicate it—all that. Therefore the mind has to come upon it, upon something which is not the result of words or thought, something which has nothing to do with mysticism. I must understand thought, the nature of thinking, its structure, its meaning, not explanations about it. Its action in any field must be fragmentary and therefore must breed contradiction, conflict, and all the misery of man. It's like marvelous violinists, pianists, or singers. That's all they have. Follow? They are fragmentary human beings with a tremendous name. Is there a field, a dimension, which is not touched by thought, and therefore a pleasure, an ecstasy of which thought can never possibly conceive?

You must understand the fragmentation which is pleasure and pain, the contradiction and confusion which come from avoiding the one and wanting the other, and the confusion which comes through a defense of beliefs. You must understand what thinking is, and the whole structure of recognition. Until all this is very clear, you cannot be free of fear. But you can eradicate fear totally, instantly, without going through all this process; you will eradicate it instantly if you understand the whole thing.

I hope you are not getting tired of being talked at, of exposing yourselves; all this is tremendous work.

Question: Will you please go into the problem of violence. Perhaps that will give us a clue to thinking.

August 7, 1966

Sixth Dialogue in Saanen

This morning we were going to discuss why thought brings about fragmentation of action, and in relation to that we were going to talk about violence, because that was the last question that was asked before we ended the previous meeting. Perhaps in talking over together this question of violence, we may discover for ourselves the nature of thinking, which must of necessity be fragmentary.

What do we mean by violence? Is violence something opposed to nonviolence, as hate is opposed to love? Violence includes, surely, not only the physical act of deliberately hurting another when we are very angry and strike someone or say a harsh word, or killing another, as happens during a war, but also there is psychological violence, as hate, envy, ambition, competition, forcing ourselves to conform to a pattern, defending ourselves, suppressing. Surely all those are acts of violence, psychologically. So when we talk about violence, what do we mean? The mere physical act of saying an angry word, or hitting somebody, of killing an animal for sport—so-called sport—or deliberately, because it's harmful. Even though the ardent follower of nonviolence has an ideal, he's extremely violent. His violence consists of suppressing his desires, his passions, and making others conform. The pacifist, the conscientious objector, the man who says, "I will not kill another human being," may not kill in a particular war, but they have their favorite wars, wars of defense. Whatever that may mean. There is no war of defense at all, but that doesn't matter.

One fragment says, "I must love," and there is the other fragment, hate. In suppressing hate, we are already violent because every form of suppression, distortion, torture, mental and physical, is obviously violence. Contempt, distrust, suspicion, resistance, pride, haughtiness, the sense of superiority, the urge to fulfill, are all ways and expressions of violence. Should we take one fragment of violence and examine that, or should we take the whole, total expression of violence?

Where do you draw the line between violence and nonviolence, or is there no line at all? When the dictator liquidates millions for the future race, for personal ambition, or for the sake of a certain ideal, human beings accept it. We find excuses for all that.

When you talk about violence, what do you mean by it? It is really quite an interesting question, if you go into it deeply, to inquire whether a human being, living in this world, can totally cease to be violent. Societies, religious communities, have tried not to kill animals. Some have even said, "If you don't want to kill animals, what about the vegetables?" You can carry it to such an extent that you would cease to exist. Where do you draw the line? Is there an arbitrary line according to your ideal, to your fancy, to your norm, to your temperament, to your conditioning, and you say, "I'll go up to there but not beyond"? Is there a difference between individual anger, with violent action on the part of the individual, and the organized hatred of a society which breeds and builds up an army to destroy another society? Where, at what level, and what fragment of violence are you discussing, or do you want to discuss whether man can be free of total violence, not a particular fragment which he calls violence?

Question: Can we be totally nonviolent?

KRISHNAMURTI: Can we, sir?

Comment: Violence has its origin in our feelings.

KRISHNAMURTI: I agree. However, we can discuss endlessly about the violence of human beings, but is it possible to totally end violence?

Comment: It would be possible to live without violence if each one were nonviolent.

Comment: When I myself am totally nonviolent, when I end all violence in my own life, then perhaps I can live in a society which is entirely based on violence.

Question: Should I as a human being in relationship with other human beings—and I must always be related, because I cannot possibly exist in isolation—should I end total violence in myself, and is it possible to do so? Or shall I wait for the whole society to be totally nonviolent?

KRISHNAMURTI: It isn't as simple as that. Are we discussing the cause of violence? Do we see the symptoms and know the cause of violence, in ourselves, in society—the policeman, the law, the murderer, the entity who is so conditioned by poverty in a slum, in a ghetto, that he's violent because he's choked in that particular corner of life, as is going on in every big town?

Comment: In any action, or inaction, brought about by an effort of will, there is self-violence, as opposed to a type of choiceless, necessary action.

KRISHNAMURTI: We know what violence is without expressing it in words, in phrases, in action. As a human being in whom the animal is still very strong, in spite of centuries of so-called civilization, where shall I begin? Shall I begin at the periphery, which is society, or at the center, which is myself?

You tell me not to be violent because it is ugly. You explain to me all the reasons, and I see that violence is a terrible thing in human beings, outwardly and inwardly. Is it possible to end this violence?

Question: Can we act without will or choice, which are the very essence of violence?

Comment: The essence of violence is egoism, and if we could be nonegoists. . . .

KRISHNAMURTI: Quite right, sir, if we could be. (Laughter) If we could all be marvelous human beings, it would be lovely. We are not, unfortunately. Please, sir, just look at the problem. Don't find an answer. Don't define it. The saints who outwardly are extraordinarily kind are inwardly tortured human beings. I ask myself, "What is violence, and is it possible to end it?" Who is asking the question, and who is going to say it is, or it is not possible? Who is the entity that is going to find the answer? Don't say, "The observer and the observed must be together, and then, everything will be all right." Don't let's repeat all that stuff which we have talked about. Let's forget what we said yesterday. If you don't forget it, you can't learn. If you repeat what you have learned, or what you have heard, then you are no longer learning.

Question: What is the basic material in me which, when provoked, when attacked, when insulted, when pushed, turns to violence?

Comment: Thought.

KRISHNAMURTI: Please do go slowly, because if you reduce everything to thought, you can't explore; you have blocked yourself.

Comment: As long as we are too much aware of ourselves, there must be violence.

KRISHNAMURTI: What is the material, what is the matrix, what is the substance in us that so quickly turns to love or hate, that so quickly says good and bad, and acts in that division?

Comment: It is self-protection.

KRISHNAMURTI: Go behind it. What is that 'me', the material, the entity that says, "I must protect"?

Comment: In the conditions of life, some persons are unafraid, and in the same conditions others are very much afraid. The first become violent.

KRISHNAMURTI: We have said all that. Please push the question a little further. What is the substance, what is the material, what is the thing that reacts this way?

Comment: Fear that my possessions, my pleasure will be taken from me.

KRISHNAMURTI: Take a little time. What is behind all this?

Comment: The center.

KRISHNAMURTI: Take a little time before you plunge into an answer. What is it? Probably most of us have not even thought about it; and if you respond very quickly, it is merely a verbal statement, a description, but if you want to find out, you must be a little silent, a little quiet.

You say that it is the center, it is the ego; it is the property which, when attacked, responds. This is not *what is*. You are merely describing the symptoms, and the questioner wants to know what is beyond all these words, if there is anything.

Comment: We don't know, because the problem is endless.

KRISHNAMURTI: All right, it's endless. But you haven't listened to his question. He says, "What is the material, what is behind all this which, the moment it is touched, explodes?"

Comment: When a person has lived in the slums all his life, and he sees rich people going about, he must explode.

KRISHNAMURTI: That also we have said.

Comment: He may not; some accept.

KRISHNAMURTI: Some explode. Some say, "Well, this is my karma, my past life." But you are not answering that gentleman's question!

Comment: It has to do with a lack of integration in human beings.

KRISHNAMURTI: Integrate between what? Between love and hate? Between violence and nonviolence?

Comment: No, I don't mean that. The moment a human being finds himself with two possibilities and the necessity of a choice, there is violence already.

KRISHNAMURTI: That's what we said earlier. As long as there is choice and will, there is violence.

Comment: If the human being is fully. . . .

KRISHNAMURTI: Not "if"! You're all supposing. Stop.

Comment: I can see it but I can't communicate it.

KRISHNAMURTI: I understand. That questioner said, "I don't know." If you don't know, why don't you simply say, "I really don't know"? Don't say that the center must protect itself, possessions must be defended when thieves attack, I should protect my sister when she is attacked by another man— all those everlasting questions. The question is: What is the stuff, the material, the essence that, when touched, explodes or accepts or submits? If you ask someone else he'll give you an opinion, according to his conditioning. Can you say, "Really, as a matter of fact, beyond all these conditionings, I don't know. I won't invent," or have you so carefully built walls of defense that you never can say, "I really don't know"? Do you know?

Comment: Everyone has an idea.

KRISHNAMURTI: Idea is not the thing.

Comment: We think about what is, *but others are not accepting what we think. That's why it appears that we don't know.*

KRISHNAMURTI: How are you to find out if you don't know?

Comment: We can find out if we desire it.

KRISHNAMURTI: That has nothing to do with what we are talking about. When we don't know, why can't we be simple about it? If I don't know, what am I going to do? Am I going to ask someone?

Question: What is the state of not-knowing?

KRISHNAMURTI: I really don't know. When the questioner asked what the material was, I wanted to get in touch with the material, and not say that it is this or that. To discover anything, I have to have a very free mind, which says, "Please, I really don't know." I haven't found out for myself, as I find out for myself what hunger is, so I totally reject your definition. I want to find out, so I say that I really do not know. I really don't know, and I'm not waiting for someone to tell me. What shall I do?

Comment: Do nothing!

KRISHNAMURTI: But I have to answer that gentleman's question.

Question: Is it a valid question?

KRISHNAMURTI: It is a valid question.

Question: Can a human being live in this society, not becoming a hermit, not withdrawing into some mountain or into a little cave?

KRISHNAMURTI: We now have two questions. First: "Living in this society, which is entirely based on violence, can violence end?" We also ask another question: "Why is thought fragmentary; why does thought bring about fragmentation in life?" As to the first question, I really don't know whether violence can end totally, not little bits here, little bits there. If I don't know and I'm not waiting for someone to tell me, what am I to do?

Comment: Be aware of the violence.

KRISHNAMURTI: Please, we have gone beyond all that. That gentleman asked a question which each of us had to answer, which is: "What is the material that always responds, violently or nonviolently?" What is that stuff? You can say it's my conditioning; it's my culture; it's my temperament; but the temperament, the culture, the conditioning is not the material. The material, like mud, like a plastic thing, can be shaped to any shape, any size, but what is that material?

Comment: My feeling, my sense of separateness.

KRISHNAMURTI: Yes, sir; we know all that.

Question: Is it the sense of freedom?

KRISHNAMURTI: You're still describing the periphery, but not the material. The conditioning, the temperament, the society, the culture, the place I live in, the food I eat—all that has shaped the material, that mind, that mud, that pliable thing. I want to find out what that soft thing is, which is shaped into a particular society, a particular culture.

Suppose you really don't know; you're just having guesswork. One says this, and someone else says that, and a very clever man comes along and says, "Oh, no, it is neither of those; it is something else." There you are. You are caught. But suppose you say, "My friend, I really don't know. I would like to find out." Then you begin to ask, "Does it exist?"

Comment: It is part of you.

KRISHNAMURTI: Is the part of me my memory, my temperament, my culture, my society, my relationship with another?

Question: Is it possible that I can have a sensation of this material, this energy?

KRISHNAMURTI: There is this energy, which is being shaped by the society in which I live, by its culture. There is energy which has been encased, put into a particular shape, and it reacts, violently or nonviolently. Can that energy never be conditioned so that it will never react violently, whether I'm in the slums, whether I'm the Pope, whether I'm a rich man or a poor man? It is all energy, right?

Comment: That energy is not conscious.

KRISHNAMURTI: Then what is conscious, if that energy is not conscious?

Comment: The moment that energy acts, there is consciousness.

KRISHNAMURTI: It is too bad that you're asking so many things at once. If you could go slowly, you would find out for yourselves.

It does not matter whether there is a material or no material. The state of mind that is inquiring is much more important than what it discovers. Unless you understand it, what is discovered is not important, but in order to discover you must have that state of mind, that energy, love, or whatever it is.

What is that state of mind that is capable of learning? As we go along inquiring, we are learning. This learning becomes consciousness. For a mind to learn it must begin by saying, "I really don't know." I don't know Russian; I can't pretend that I know Russian. So I don't know.

Question: Sir, can we stop a moment?

KRISHNAMURTI: Delighted. I'll stop even longer.

Comment: If I don't know, then I can begin to learn.

KRISHNAMURTI: You can walk through life in a state of always learning, therefore always being fair to life.

Question: Does the state of learning never reply?

KRISHNAMURTI: It will reply presently. None of you have really said, "I don't know; I'm going to find out."

We began with a question. We know violence at every level of our being, both physical and psychological. As a human being living in this world, can I end violence, not fragmentarily, but totally? It can only end totally if thought, which creates fragments, doesn't function. So I have to go into why thought always functions in fragments. Do you know for yourself that thought, as a businessman, thought as a scientist, thought as a family man, thought as a laborer, all function in fragmentation? This fragmentation is bred, brought about by thought, which has created the social structure, which has made me incapable of being a scientist. I'm a laborer because I can't pass the examinations, I can't enter the special schools; therefore, I am shoved aside.

Does thought necessarily bring about fragmentation?

Comment: Again we don't know.

KRISHNAMURTI: You will know presently. You will see it. Why do you say, "I don't know"? There is the scientist in his laboratory who through his knowledge, through his experience, is creating the bomb which is going to kill his son. Both are the result of thought.

Comment: The physical eye can only see very clearly one part of this tent.

KRISHNAMURTI: But that one part is not the whole of the tent. Because I look at one part of the tent and then at another part, I have a perception of the whole of the tent—its shape, its nature, its construction. Do the additions of various parts make the tent?

Comment: Of course.

KRISHNAMURTI: Physically, yes, but you're missing the point, sir. A wheel has many spokes. Do the spokes make the wheel? Do the parts make the whole, or if I understand the whole, can the parts then be fitted in?

Comment: Yes.

KRISHNAMURTI: That's all we're saying. Must thought inevitably create fragments? Thought has created the unit as "my family," "my community," "my society," "my country," "my God," "my queen," and another thought has created the other country, and so on. All are but fragments.

Question: What kinds of thought are you talking about?

KRISHNAMURTI: I am talking about all thought, including memory, including going to the office where thought functions, including the thought of "my family," "my desires," "my appetites," and my thought of becoming famous.

Question: Has thought created my ideas of what I should do?

KRISHNAMURTI: It has. At the office I have to function as a businessman, but when I come home I'm not a businessman. There I may cheat; here I won't cheat.

Question: Do you mean also the thinking we are doing at this moment?

KRISHNAMURTI: All thinking—in this moment, or when you're outside the tent. I'm asking: Is not all thought, all thinking necessarily fragmentary?

Comment: Thought must be fragmentary because thought is the response of memory, knowledge, experience, tradition, the storehouse from which it reacts, either from the past or out of the future which it has created.

KRISHNAMURTI: Have you found out if thought is fragmentary? If you haven't found out yet, what are you going to do? How will you find out?

Question: Isn't thinking itself a fragment of the mind, a part of the mind?

KRISHNAMURTI: Yes. Therefore it must necessarily be functioning in part. What are you going to do? Are you going to put all the fragments together—hate, love, everything—put them all together, mix them up and say, "This is the real stuff; this is the whole; this is integrated"?

Comment: The moment we have used a word, a phrase, a symbol, it has already become a fragment.

KRISHNAMURTI: But we live in fragments: "my country," "my wife," "my husband,"

and I say to myself, "Is it possible to function nonfragmentarily?"

Comment: I think that can happen, in a sense.

KRISHNAMURTI: Not you think it can happen.

Comment: It can happen.

KRISHNAMURTI: I don't know. It may or it may not happen. I want to know; I want to find out; I'm passionate about it.

Comment: When I don't know and want to know, I discover that thinking is fragmentary.

KRISHNAMURTI: May I have two minutes to go into this? I'm violent. Violence is a fragment of my nature—only a fragment, because I'm also kind. I'm occasionally generous, and at times I am proud, haughty, which is another fragment; occasionally I play with humility, and so on. That's my life. I live in fragments, and each fragment is in contradiction to the others. I say to myself, "Is this an everlasting process? Can it end?"

This is not an intellectual, verbal, theoretical question, because I am torn between all these fragments; I am confused; I don't know what to do. I know very well that they can't be integrated; all the parts can't be put together so that I can say, "This is the whole." Then I see that fragments exist as long as thinking is. Then the next question arises: Can I stop thinking? I can't stop thinking because I must know where I am going; I must know my house, my wife, my children, my office. Thought is necessary at one level, but may not be at all necessary at another level. It may be necessary when I write a letter, when I'm communicating something to someone, when I am designing, when I have to remember something. I owe somebody something, which I must pay back; therefore, I must have thought, memory. But I see that it may not be necessary at another level altogether, and this may not be contradictory. I must find out where thought is necessary, knowing that it is fragmentary, knowing that the fragments are destructive, that they create confusion, conflict. I realize that I must not let fragmentation take place psychologically. If there is no psychological fragmentation, then probably there'll be no fragmentation in the daily activities.

So my concern then is: Can fragmentation cease psychologically? If it can end, then this nonpsychological fragmentation can function completely wherever it is. For most of us, this question is theoretical, and you may say, "Please, it's too complicated; I really don't know; just tell me." It would be more intelligent and it is necessary for you to say, "I don't know; I'm going to find out for myself whether psychologically thought can cease to function fragmentarily." When you say, "It is my country, my God, my belief," when thought says and acts, it must function fragmentarily. I see that thought is memory, experience, tradition—the storehouse. I must have that storehouse to talk, to write, to go to my house, to go to the office, but why should I have a psychological storehouse which breeds fragmentation? Can I live without a storehouse, except the storehouse of knowing how to do things?

When you are waiting, expecting, you really are in a state of not knowing. I'm not talking about your wanting someone, or some book, or some teacher to tell you what it is. Let's keep to this simple thing, which is really most complex. Can there be no psychological storehouse at all? Don't translate it as no-self, the higher self—that's Eastern philosophy, that's Western philosophy, and you escape from that. As long as I have one, I am violent, because I'm against you.

You have your psychological storehouse, your memories, your experiences, your dogmas, your country, your gods, your beliefs, your doctrines. If I also have a storehouse, we're always in battle; every storehouse breeds conflict and therefore violence.

Can that psychological storehouse be broken up, finished? If you say, "Please tell me how to break it up in order for me to have a good relationship with my wife," it has no meaning. If you are a pacifist because you want to live at peace with the world, you have a motive, and that very motive is fragmentation. Do you see how complex it is? It isn't just a child's morning discussion; you have to go very, very deeply into this.

Can thought, which breeds fragmentation, end? People have said it can, and they have a method to end it. Look what they have done! You have your method, and I have my method; you have your motive for ending it, and I have my motive for ending it. The motive has already bred the fragment. I want to end thought, so I invent a meditation; I say, "Do this; don't do that." The very thing which I want to eliminate is being strengthened.

Comment: Sometimes people who are nonviolent are those who struggle over it.

KRISHNAMURTI: I quite agree that persons who are nonviolent are neurotic, because they are violent in different ways.

Comment: Sometimes, yes; sometimes not.

KRISHNAMURTI: Like the curate's egg. Do you know what the curate's egg is? Part of it is bad, part of it is good, and they give it to the curate. (Laughter) That's an old English expression, and probably the modern generation doesn't know it.

Comment: Life is full of choice, and therefore life is full of violence. We have to choose.

KRISHNAMURTI: I don't see the necessity of choice at all. It is only a mind that is confused that chooses. Don't you see it? When it's clear, you don't choose. When it's clear, there is no necessity for choice. You don't choose between this and that and then act, if your mind is very clear. You act. Why is the mind not clear? It is confused because people have said and the books have said that you must choose, and you accept it. But if you begin to question choice, then you inevitably come to this point: a confused mind is always at the mercy of choice, and therefore there is a conflict. A clear mind never chooses; what is there to choose? It sees things very clearly. It doesn't say, "Should I be a Catholic, or a Protestant, or should I become a Hindu?" If you see the absurdity of it, you're none of those. But if you say, "Protestants have a little bit of truth, Catholicism has a little bit of truth, Hinduism has a little bit of truth, and so have the Muslims," then you will collect all the truths together and carry on.

Comment: Making decisions is very close to choosing, but I guess it is necessary. The only danger is the time interval and the change which can take place in it.

KRISHNAMURTI: One of the most difficult things in this mad world is to have a clear mind. Everyone is telling me what to do— my husband or wife, society, the newspapers, the politicians, the priests, the archpriest who is the dictator, the elder brother. I refuse to be told what to do; I refuse to be influenced.

Comment: You are advocating a paradoxical type of mind that has no reality in human nature.

KRISHNAMURTI: Human nature being what it is, is in itself very paradoxical. I'm not advocating anything—God forbid! I'm not advocating a new philosophy, a new theory, nothing at all. I'm just pointing out what actually is. It is the animal, and it is being civilized. The animal is in conflict with 'what should be', and that's our life. I am taking human life as it is, not as it should be. 'What should be' is nonexistent. Therefore it becomes paradoxical. If you take *what is,* it is misery; it is confusion.

We have talked of very serious things this morning; we have not been making verbal statements. We started inquiring into violence. There is no paradox, no contradiction; we are violent; all of us. The man who wants to be the highest religious priest, or the saint, is violent. Ambition breeds violence, as in the politician, as in the general. Can I live in this world totally without violence, amidst its monstrous contradictions, its violence and hate—not for one moment, not occasionally, but totally? It is possible when the mind, when thought is no longer creating fragments.

To go into the whole process of thinking, you have to watch it, learn, observe how you act, how you think, how you feel, what your reactions are when you meet a person with a dark skin. You must know all this.

Question: Is a person violent all the time?

KRISHNAMURTI: You are violent one moment, and nonviolent another; kind and brutal—kind to your family at home, yet you go out with a gun and shoot someone. This is what is taking place. To understand all this you have to understand the nature of thinking.

August 8, 1966

Seventh Dialogue in Saanen

As this is the last discussion, what shall we talk over together?

Question: How is the energy that one has through intense awareness to be maintained?

KRISHNAMURTI: I don't know, either. (Laughter) We all have problems of different kinds: financial, economic, emotional, psychological, physical—what to do and what not to do. There are despairs, there is anxiety, there is every form of psychological disturbance. We shan't meet again until next year and one of our major issues is: How am I going to live during this whole year? What is the significance, the meaning, of my life, my work, the whole of my existence? We have had a holiday here; we have rested; we have discussed; we have gone into various problems—jealousy, energy, this and that—looked at them from every angle, from every point of view, and what have we left at the end? Where are we? If we take stock of ourselves, what is the effect of all this month? Are we going back to the same old routine, the same old confusion, the same old misery, or have we planted something in this confusion which we think is clarity, understanding? Have we broken away from all this confusion, trying to do something about it, trying to reach something? Is there a totally different way of living? I think we ought to ask that question of ourselves, not merely ask, "Do I mean this; do I mean that?" which has no significance when we are vitally concerned with our own lives and with the life of the society in which we live.

There are so many contradictions. They are sending a man to the moon, spending millions and millions and millions—and there is starvation all over the world, especially in the East. The thing is too appalling. It is not only a human problem, but a problem of the world, and we have to act. We can't just go on everlastingly theorizing about various things. It seems to me that it would be worthwhile if we could discuss this morning, not intellectually, not theoretically, not what the speaker means, not what you mean, not what someone else means, cutting out all that kind of thinking and facing, coming to grips with the central issue of our existence—going into it quietly, seeing how we can renew the total mind and not go back to gossip, not take up smoking or give up smoking, not have sex or no-sex, not be concerned with those trivial human things that we are caught in.

The most important thing, if I may suggest, is to consider whether it is possible to bring about a revolution in the mind—which has been so heavily conditioned, which has so many varieties of contradictions within itself—and make it totally new, young, fresh, innocent, full of energy and decision. A young mind, in the real sense of that word, not in terms of years, is a very decisive mind. It doesn't choose; it sees clearly and does something directly without ideas, whether the family accepts it or doesn't accept it. Because it is so young, vital, vigorous, its decision is immediate. It may be wrong, but it is decisive. If it is wrong, it discovers it and moves on. The more the brain and the totality of the mind become old, the more sluggish, the more indecisive, the more unclear they get, searching to find out what to do.

Can we, this morning, see, talk over together whether it is possible for the mind to make itself totally new, fresh—which is obviously not dependent on age, on how many years we have lived? Can we discuss that?

Comment: If we use our energy, and do not use it as thought, it will not be fragmentary.

KRISHNAMURTI: We can go on everlastingly asking questions—serious, worthwhile questions that have significance and meaning, or questions that can be very easily asked and very easily answered. But can we, this morning, put away all these questions and give our whole attention to discover, to actually be fresh? We are getting old, not only in years, but the brain is wearing itself out. It is not so young and fresh and active, not so vigorous as it was. As we advance in age, there is naturally a dulling process going on. The wave of deterioration is catching up with us all the time. Whether we are very young or very old, this enormous weight of destruction is going on.

Don't you want to find out whether you can totally renew your mind—not what I think, what you think, what the latest theologian thinks or what the priests think? All that has become so utterly trivial.

Comment: One is still afraid.

KRISHNAMURTI: Is that what keeps us from having a mind that is always fresh, not in theory or intellectually, but actually and factually? Is that what prevents our looking at life, at the mountains, at the trees, at the neighbor, whether the neighbor is immediately next to us or in Vietnam? Is this the problem?

We have spent a month in this tent talking over together the various problems of our hearts and minds, physical, psychological, and so on. As this is the last day, doesn't this inquiry burn you? Aren't you really passionate to find out? It seems to me that is the only problem we have. We know our actions are contradictory; we are confused; there is utter despair, loneliness, misery, confusion, worry, problems, and this terrible ambition with all its complications. They all don't seem to end; they go on and on and on. After a month in this lovely valley, don't we demand that there be a total change of heart and mind? If there isn't, what shall we do?

Question: How can one empty the storehouse which the mind and the brain have collected through these thousands upon thousands of years? How can it empty itself and be young?

KRISHNAMURTI: I am asking the same question. Because if it can be answered, then I will solve all my daily problems: my rudeness to people, my roughness with people, talking sharply, shouting at people—not that I must wait until the storehouse is empty! We are in such a state of confusion. We can't peel off this confusion layer after layer after layer. Trying to do that leads to such disgusting despair. Is it possible for the mind to empty itself and be fresh, young again, uncontaminated, so that when I see the blue sky after yesterday's rain, it is something that I have never seen before? It isn't the same sky; it isn't the same face; it isn't the same problem; there is something new; a revolution has taken place. Don't you want to know what to do, so that this may happen?

Comment: If I ask myself something which I haven't known before, if I drop all my preconceptions, and step forward without any reservations, I find that the mind has then emptied itself, and I can discover.

KRISHNAMURTI: Are you telling me a method, the way to do it?

Comment: I am trying to describe my own experience.

KRISHNAMURTI: You're telling your own method, the way you have done it.

Comment: I'm trying to describe what I have done.

KRISHNAMURTI: Look, sir. No one can tell us; no one can say, "I have got it; you should do this." You never listen to the question. First, listen to the question. It is a tremendous question; it is a most complex question, and everyone gives an answer, "Do this, don't do that; this is what I feel; this is my experience; this is what I have done." Let us first realize the simple fact that it is an enormously complex problem. Man has tried in different ways through centuries to solve it. The teachers have said to meditate; they have said to give up this stupid life, become a monk or a nun and lead a different kind of life. Man has tried everything possible: new theories, new ideas, new ways of overcoming contradictions.

That's what you're all doing. You don't say, "This is a tremendously complex question; I really don't understand it; it is too complex for me because my mind is so petty, so small. From that pettiness I'm answering, with lots of reactions." Stop answering; invariably the answer is from the little, shallow mind that we have struggled with to improve, to add to, to suppress, to put away, but it is still petty. Can you stop replying—not to me, not to the speaker, but to yourself?

When you are confronted with an enormous problem, any answer that you give to the problem, whether you are a scientist or a most erudite, a most experienced person is from a small mind, a fragmentary mind. Why don't you try saying, "I won't answer; I can't answer," and see what happens? When you say, "I can't answer," really mean it; don't just wait for someone to answer it. This doesn't mean to go to sleep, to go into some mystical silence, which very few know anything about. When you are confronted with a most complex mathematical problem, don't you first stop and look? You look; you see what is implied. The more complex it is, the more subtle it is, the quieter the mind becomes. It isn't that the speaker is trying to prevent your asking questions; first find out whether your heart and mind are capable, when confronted with this enormous issue, of not reacting, jumping to conclusions, formulating ideas, wanting to express them, wanting to communicate. Stop all that.

If you have done so, then you can begin to ask seriously whether it is possible for the mind to free itself from this burden of the ages. You don't know. First, is it possible? What is involved in this? You must have an extraordinarily sensitive brain, which doesn't all the time react in the animalistic way, and is not caught in a habit, in repetition, in imitation. Is that possible? The physical brain itself, every corner of it, not just a particular fragment, must be so alive, so alert that it is not caught in any theory, in any opinion, in any argument, in any tradition. For the brain to come upon it, to discover it, there must be meditation—not the stupid meditation of repetition of words, prayers, and all that kind of silly nonsense, but meditation to find out whether the brain can be quiet, free of all the normal so-called animalistic reactions.

We have discussed the various forms of these reactions: you hit me, and I hit you back, or I suppress it. Can the brain itself be extraordinarily quiet, and yet very vigorous, capable of reasoning, healthy? Obviously a neurotic brain, a mind that is tortured, a brain that has broken down through constant submission to some relationship, to some idea, to some conditioning can't do this. Since the brain cells themselves have been so heavily conditioned, so heavily brutalized by repetition of pleasure, pain, love, hate, going through that circle, the first thing to find out

is whether the brain can remain without that reaction of the animal. That's part of meditation. To proceed further, the next movement of meditation is to see whether the totality of the mind—which is the brain, the physical being, the nervous responses, the emotions, the anxieties—can free itself.

We don't do any of these things; we're full of ideas of what we should do, what we should not do, what the speaker said, what he didn't say—didn't he mean this, didn't he mean that—we can carry on endlessly. We must spend time—chronological time, not psychological time—to see how we react. I heard the other day of a man who has been listening to the speaker for forty years. He got terribly excited about nothing at a committee meeting. We're all like that. If you touch our sore spot, we flare up. Can we be aware of our simple reactions of hate, jealousy of someone who has a little more power than we have—the simple things, not the most complex things—and from there move, like a river that passes the dirty towns and villages. It keeps on moving, moving, moving. This movement of renewal is only possible if we begin at the most simple level; for that you don't have to read books, attend meetings—except perhaps this one! (Laughter) You don't have to join societies or organizations. Begin at the first rung and never climb the ladder. We always want to climb, climb, climb, go higher and higher, out of vanity. Let the first rung, the first step, be the last one. There is nowhere to climb, nothing to achieve. The ladder with so many rungs, steps, doesn't lead anywhere. There is only one step, the first step; and if we know how to meet that first step, if we know all about it, then the whole circus is over. Then there is humility, real humility, because we are not climbing, climbing, climbing. Where there is humility, there is learning—not accumulating, not climbing the ladder. Learning means that there is no climbing, no storing up of knowledge, no prejudices such as "my country"—such silly nonsense it all is!

Where there is learning, there is no storehouse; there are no steps to climb to reach God, utopia, or the final glorious ideal. There is only one step; there are no other steps. That's where the clever ones, the people who have gone into it a little bit, are in despair, because they see that there is only one step, and they can't go beyond it. They write books, invent new philosophies, and catch man with phrases, such as twentieth century humanitarianism, existentialism, or some other word. When we see that there is only one step, and we don't know how to meet it, there is unending despair because we want to climb the ladder. There is no despair if we really see that there is only one step. There is no reaching, no gaining, no searching, no achievement, no saying, "I am better than someone else." Leave all that muck to the theologians, to the priests, to the politicians, to the writers. Then you will see what beauty is. It is not in the mountain, in the river, in the sky; it is not in a painting, in a book or in any object that man has created. Where beauty is, there is love. There is beauty when there is only one action, which is every minute, and no other action. If we have action which must be done in order to get something, if we have a motive in action, it only leads to more complexity.

We begin to see that in this one step, all life *is*. Then we will see that to die to this first step is the beginning of a totally new existence, a totally different quality of mind, because then there is no movement, no experience, no change; therefore, the mind is always renewing itself because it's never

climbing, never comparing. Where there is no step, there is love, but there is no love for the man who is climbing the ladder. The ladder and the rungs on the ladder are the invention of the mind, of thought; and thought has created God on the last rung, on the top rung of the ladder. God is not up there at all. That's just an invention of the mind. But there is a totally different dimension which is not put together by thought, when man is no longer moving, climbing, seeking. When man is no longer escaping, he listens to everything. It is that movement, that listening—not acquiring, not adding—that brings about a fresh mind, naturally, sanely, with great health, capacity, and vigor.

One returns to something that is very beautiful: to a mountain, to a river, to a lovely flower. One wants to go back and look at it again. It is natural, healthy; but if that mountain, that river, that flower acts as a stimulant, then it ceases to be beautiful. Then it's merely a drug, and you're lost. Though I said, "Don't attend meetings," I hope we shall meet next year, not as something in the nature of a drug or a stimulant, not for you to listen to words, to ideas, and translate them into concepts and formulas, but that coming together, meeting together, talking things over together, we shall see something extraordinarily beautiful; and without beauty, and therefore without love, our minds and hearts become dull, cynical, bitter, harsh, brutal.

I hope that you will have a pleasant journey.

August 9, 1966

Index for Questions

Rome Dialogues, 1966

London, 1966

Paris, 1966

Saanen, 1966

Saanen Dialogues, 1966

Index

Acceptance: of conflict, 85; defining, 142; and deterioration, 60. *See also* Conformity

Accumulation: and fear of death, 31; and inertia, 27–28; versus learning, 220; and time, 200. *See also* Knowledge

Acting: and learning, 215–16, 218. *See also* Action

Action, 72–77, 173–75, 225, 228, 230; and the absence of pretension, 228; and attention, 246; and beauty, 301; and belief, 260; and clarity, 31; and conditioning, 241; and conflict, 56, 225; and confusion, 247, 278; without contradiction, 228; and despair, 265; and facing fear, 276; and the field of the known, 180; fragmentation of, 241; and freedom from confusion, 275, 276; and freedom from identification, 151; and hope, 267; without ideas, 260–61, 267; as inaction, 122; versus intellect, 8; and learning, 20; and listening, 245; meaning of, 151; not of time, 58, 59; and observation, 152; and physical danger, 155; questioning, 72; repetition of, 228; and saying no, 60; and seeing, 2, 170–71; and silence, 32, 71; and thought, 134

Action and ideas: and conflict, 38–39, 216, 218–19; and the sense of danger, 184; and the time interval, 152. *See also* Action; Ideas

Action and inaction: and sorrow, 57. *See also* Action; Inaction

Action of will: and time, 21–22. *See also* Action; Will

Activity: and inertia, 28. *See also* Action

Adjustment: as hindrance to change, 55. *See also* Conflict; Conformity; Discipline

Affection: achieving, 65; defining, 6; and relationships, 34; and seeing the totality of life, 5, 6. *See also* Love

Aging: and destruction, 298. *See also* Old age

Aloneness: beauty of, 149; and commitment, 280; versus loneliness, 38; meaning of, 38; need for, 118; and the removal of masks, 225; and sensitivity, 99. *See also* Emptiness; Sorrow

Ambition: and the absence of love, 52; and conflict, 81–82; and energy, 164–65; and thought, 170; and violence, 297. *See also* Conflict; Contradiction; Society

America. *See* Authority; Conditioning; Nationalism; Society; War; Words; World problems

Amusement: and belief, 258; and emptiness, 232. *See also* Escape

Analysis: and ending fear, 210, 212–13; futility of, 279; need for, 277; and thought, 108; and the unconscious, 188; uselessness of, 154–55. *See also* Authority

Anglican. *See* Authority; Belief; Conditioning; Divisions; Religion; Words

Animal brain: and pleasure, 282. *See also* Animals; Brain

Animal instincts: and pleasure and pain, 147. *See also* Animals

Animals: and conflict, 297; and human behavior, 43; and human beings, 16; and human culture, 49. *See also* Brain

Answers: absence of, 118. *See also* Examination; Problems; Questioning

Antithesis to synthesis: spiral of, 265

Anxiety: freedom from, 183; separation from, 161. *See also* Conflict; Sorrow

Arts: and escape, 100–101, 182; and fragmentation, 239, 288

Asia. *See* Authority; Conditioning; Nationalism; Society; War; Words; World problems

Atma: and pleasure, 37

Attention: and the absence of effort, 63–64; as the action, 246; and awareness, 185; versus the awareness of inattention, 190; and communication, 41–42, 161; difficulty of, 26; and discussion, 253; effortless, 142–43; and the ending of thought, 223; and examining, 33; and the field of the known, 174; and the hindrance of the gradual, 227; and the hindrance of verbalization, 50; and inattention, 152; and learning, 53, 73; and listening, 140, 144, 237; and looking, 130; and meditation, 68; and mutation, 6; and seeing, 2; and seeing the fact, 57; and silence, 51; and sorrow, 144; state of, 226; as a total activity, 161; and understanding, 128

Austerity: defining, 282

Authority: acceptance of, 181; and belief, 255; and change, 174; and confusion, 2, 259, 280; danger of, 281–82; denial of, 184, 234; dependence on, 196; and dependence on the past, 47; and following patterns, 232; futility of, 233; as hindrance to communion, 161; as hindrance to inquiry, 221; as hindrance to the new, 214; and the law, 17; and love, 64; nonreliance on, 38; as a path to darkness,

154; defining, 54; function of, 10; and imitation, 13, 16–17, 19; and inertia, 28–29; inquiry into, 219; and learning, 293; and the observer and the observed, 202–3; and the past, 205; radical revolution in, 154; and revolution, 126; and thinking, 37; and transformation, 174; and yesterday, today, and tomorrow, 188–89. *See also* Mind

Contact: and cessation of fear, 106, 108; with death, 176; and desire, 36, 61; and fear, 155, 175, 176; and the hindrance of fear, 178–79; versus isolation, 221–22; with loneliness, 182, 183; and the observed, 111; and relationships, 33–34, 43, 106; and space, 249; and total relationship, 249. *See also* Facts

Continuity: and desire, 36, 87–88, 91; ending, 245; and fear of death, 63; function of, 245–46; as hindrance to renewal, 243; as hindrance to the new, 70; and pleasure, 61–62, 117, 146, 284, 286–87. *See also* Religion

Contradiction: and belief, 274; and clarity, 131; and conflict, 85; and confusion, 277; ending, 121; and ending thought, 222; and human beings, 128; and human problems, 297–98; and the idea versus the fact, 9; in life, 136; life without, 153; living with, 94; need to eliminate, 132; between the observer and the observed, 23; and pleasure, 287–88; and private and public masks, 225; and religious revolution, 80; versus seeing the whole, 238

Cooperation: need for, 126

Copy. *See* Imitation; Repetition

Creation: achieving, 123; meaning of, 122–23; and the new, 148. *See also* Mutation; New; New mind; Truth

Creative: versus conflict, 80; and the new, 192. *See also* Creation

Crisis: and awareness of masks, 225

Culture: and conformity of action, 74; and experience, 66; and response to the word, 104–5. *See also* Background; Conditioning; Society

Cybernetics. *See* Computers; Electronic brain; Technology

Daily existence: and meditation, 148. *See also* Daily life

Daily life: examining, 125; importance of, 135; as reality, 125; seeking beyond, 280–81; and thought, 167. *See also* Life; Living; Sorrow

Danger: and ending habit, 98–99; and the immediate, 184; insensitivity to, 98–99; physical and psychological, 155; response to, 104; seeing, 171. *See also* Fear

Death, 30–32; as the cessation of continuity, 243; fear of, 62–63, 103, 104–7, 155–56, 175–76, 178; and the new, 244; and the search for beyond time, 250; understanding, 178; and understanding living, 63, 64. *See also* Religion

Dependence, 118–21; on challenge, 209; and fear, 104; freedom from, 38; reasons for, 119–20

Desire, 35–39, 85–89; and conflict, 85, 215; and the observer, 154; and pleasure, 93–94, 146–48, 215, 216, 217, 286; and thought, 112; and understanding pleasure, 61–62; understanding the nature of, 86–88. *See also* Contradiction; Perception

Despair: and the creation of philosophy, 265; ending, 301; escape from, 266; and living in the present, 239; philosophy of, 93; and the search for truth, 47. *See also* Sorrow

Determination: as hindrance, 96–97. *See also* Effort

Dialogue: defining, 257, 258. *See also* Communication

Dimension: not created by thought, 301; and space, 251; without time, 206. *See also* New; Truth; Unknown

Discipline: and conformity, 17–18; defining, 136–37; and listening, 70, 101–2; meaning of, 193; and pleasure, 216; and society, 110; understanding the structure of, 150; and understanding through examination, 37; and violence, 203. *See also* Conflict; Suppression

Discovery: and energy, 221; meaning of, 142; and the origin of thought, 164; understanding, 293. *See also* Questioning

Discussion: conditions for, 80; and self-exposure, 253. *See also* Communication; Listening

Disorder: and time, 184. *See also* Order

Distance: and space, 251. *See also* Time

Distortion: and conflict, 93

Distraction: approach to, 26–27; and awareness, 185. *See also* Concentration

Divisions: between action and ideas, 218–19; causes of, 68; and change, 203; in the conscious and unconscious, 54; of consciousness, 240; and disunity, 233; between the fact and the observer, 107; as hindrance to attention, 143; as hindrance to peace, 126; as hindrance to understanding, 6; and not seeing the whole, 237; between the observer and the observed, 23–25, 134, 202–3, 270–72; of the past, 200; in private and public life, 225; and relationships, 44–45; and religion, 242; seeing the danger in, 98–99; between the thinker and the thought, 161; and thought, 145, 163, 168–69; and time, 23–25, 142–143, 239. *See also* Fragmentation; Nationalism; War

Dogma: and war, 4. *See also* Belief; Methods

Doing: and learning, 51–52. *See also* Action

Domination: ending, 107. *See also* Authority; Power; Relationships

Doubt: need for, 123. *See also* Examination; Questioning; Skepticism

Drink: and habit, 98

Dropping ideals, 259–60. *See also* Ideals; Ideas; Images

Drugs: and the attempt to escape thought, 201–2; and the search for meaning, 144; and shallowness, 234

Duality: defining, 67–68; and the observer and the observed, 68–69; and psychological contradiction, 85. *See also* Contradiction; Divisions

Dull mind: and love, 64. *See also* Mind; New mind; Petty mind

Dying: to the past, 31–32; and renewal, 244. *See also* Death

Dying and living: understanding, 176, 178. *See also* Dying; Living

Dying daily: and awareness, 156; and ending fear, 106, 108; and energy, 244–45. *See also* Dying and living; Mutation; New

CPSIA information can be obtained
at www.ICGtesting.com
Printed in the USA
LVHW102255270921
698873LV00002B/41

9 781934 989494